THIS GRAND & MAGNIFICENT PLACE

Revisiting New England: The New Regionalism

SERIES EDITORS

Siobhan Senier, University of New Hampshire
Darren Ranco, Dartmouth College
Adam Sweeting, Boston University
David H. Watters, University of New Hampshire

This series presents fresh discussions of the distinctiveness of New England culture. The editors seek manuscripts examining the history of New England regionalism; the way its culture came to represent American national culture; the interaction between that "official" New England culture and the people who lived in the region; and local, subregional, or even biographical subjects as microcosms that explicitly open up and consider larger issues. The series welcomes new theoretical and historical perspectives and is designed to cross disciplinary boundaries and appeal to a wide audience.

Christopher Johnson, *This Grand and Magnificent Place: The Wilderness Heritage of the White Mountains*
Denis R. Caron, *A Century in Captivity: The Life and Trials of Prince Mortimer, a Connecticut Slave*
Paul M. Searls, *Two Vermonts: Geography and Identity, 1865–1910*
Judith Bookbinder, *Boston Modern: Figurative Expressionism as Alternative Modernism*
Donna M. Cassidy, *Marsden Hartley: Race, Region, and Nation*
Joseph A. Conforti, editor, *Creating Portland: History and Place in Northern New England*
Maureen Elgersman Lee, *Black Bangor: African Americans in a Maine Community, 1880–1950*
T. A. Milford, *The Gardiners of Massachusetts: Provincial Ambition and British-American Career*
David L. Richards, *Poland Spring: A Tale of the Gilded Age, 1860–1900*
Donald W. Linebaugh, *The Man Who Found Thoreau: Roland W. Robbins and the Rise of Historical Archaeology in America*
Pauleena MacDougall, *The Penobscot Dance of Resistance: Tradition in the History of a People*
Jennifer C. Post, *Music in Rural New England Family and Community Life, 1870–1940*
Mark J. Sammons and Valerie Cunningham, *Black Portsmouth: Three Centuries of African-American Heritage*
Christopher J. Lenney, *Sightseeking: Clues to the Landscape History of New England*
Priscilla Paton, *Abandoned New England: Landscape in the Works of Homer, Frost, Hopper, Wyeth, and Bishop*
Adam Sweeting, *Beneath the Second Sun: A Cultural History of Indian Summer*
James C. O'Connell, *Becoming Cape Cod: Creating a Seaside Resort*
Richard Archer, *Fissures in the Rock: New England in the Seventeenth Century*
Sidney V. James, *The Colonial Metamorphoses in Rhode Island: A Study of Institutions in Change*
Diana Muir, *Reflections in Bulloughs Pond: Economy and Ecosystem in New England*
Nancy L. Gallagher, *Breeding Better Vermonters: The Eugenics Project in Vermont*

For a complete list of books in this series, please visit www.upne.com and
www.upne.com/series/RVNE.html

1
Mt Washington
6.213 ft.

2
Mt Adams
5.653 ft.

3
Mt Jefferson
5.116

Moosehillock
5
N. Peak 4.636
S. Peak 4.530

Mt Pleasant
4.713

Limit of Forest
Trees Wht Mt
4.443

7
Monadnock
3.450

8
Kearsarge
2.461

10
Road from D.
Col. to Boston.
Highest part
1.393

11
Moose Mountain
1.000

12
D. College 4.56
Cont River at
Hanover 306

Portsmouth
Level of the Sea

J. F. Dana del.   A Bowen Sc

COMPARATIVE VIEW

Of the Heights of Mountains &c. in N. Hampshire.

THIS GRAND & MAGNIFICENT PLACE

The Wilderness Heritage of the White Mountains

Christopher Johnson

University of New Hampshire Press
Durham, New Hampshire

PUBLISHED BY UNIVERSITY PRESS OF NEW ENGLAND
HANOVER AND LONDON

University of New Hampshire Press
Published by University Press of New England,
One Court Street, Lebanon, NH 03766
www.upne.com
© 2006 by Christopher Johnson
Printed in the United States of America
5 4 3 2 1

Library of Congress Cataloging-in-Publication Data

Johnson, Christopher, 1947 Sept. 13–
This grand and magnificent place : the wilderness heritage of the White Mountains /
Christopher Johnson—1st ed.
    p.   cm.—(Revisiting New England : the new regionalism)
Includes bibliographical references and index.
ISBN-13: 978–1–58465–461–2 (cloth : alk. paper)
ISBN-10: 1–58465–461–9 (cloth : alk. paper)
1. White Mountains (N.H. and Me.)—History. 2. Wilderness areas—New Hampshire
—History. 3. Wilderness areas—Maine—History. 4. White Mountains (N.H. and Me.)
—Description and travel. 5. White Mountains (N.H. and Me.)—Environmental condi-
tions. I. Title. II. Title: This grand and magnificent place.
F41.3.J64 2006
974.2′2—dc22   2006020193

Frontispiece: *Comparative View of the Heights of Mountains &c. in N. Hampshire.* From
John Farmer and Jacob Moore's *Gazetteer of the State of New Hampshire.* Courtesy of
Dartmouth College Library.

The passage on page 10 is from BOWMAN'S STORE: A JOURNEY TO MYSELF by Joseph
Bruchac, copyright © 1997 by Joseph Bruchac. Used by permission of Dial Books for Young
Readers, A Division of Penguin Young Readers Group, A Member of Penguin Group
(USA) Inc., 345 Hudson Street, New York, NY 10014. All rights reserved.
Portions of Chapters 1, 4, 6, and 9, in slightly different form, were originally published in
Appalachia.

University Press of New England is a member of the Green
Press Initiative. The paper used in this book meets their
minimum requirement for recycled paper.

Contents

Acknowledgments

This book exists because of a large community of people who share a love of the White Mountains and were willing to impart their knowledge and insights to me in the writing of this book. I am indebted to Gerald A. Danzer, Cheever Griffin, Ron McAdow, Rita Sullivan, and Nancy Woloch for reading the original proposal and providing insightful suggestions. Their advice was invaluable.

In researching and writing the material on the Abenaki people in chapter 1, I owe a great debt of gratitude to my wife, Barbara, whose knowledge and understanding of Native Americans were indispensable. Peter Newell, chief of the New Hampshire Intertribal Native American Council, and his parents, Don and Beverly Newell, were generous in opening up the doors of the council to our presence and in providing contacts. One of the contacts that Peter suggested was David Stewart-Smith, who shared important information about the Pennacooks and their history in New Hampshire. Alice Nash, of the University of Massachusetts at Amherst, provided insightful comments on the manuscript for chapter 1 and suggested several sources on the Joseph Laurent camp in Intervale.

In 2004, I was fortunate enough to attend a symposium titled "Nature and Culture in the Northern Forest," sponsored by the Association for the Study of Literature and Environment and held at the Appalachian Mountain Club's Highland Center in Crawford Notch. The conference, organized by Pavel Cenkl of the Northern Forest Studies Association, was both stimulating and comprehensive. There I met Melanie L. Simo and Brian Muchow, whose suggestions for sources on wilderness were extremely valuable and whose hospitality on my research trips to New Hampshire was much appreciated.

David Govatski, formerly of the U.S. Forest Service and now offering ecological and historical tours of the White Mountains, generously shared his extensive knowledge of the mountains' natural history and human history. Others who were willing to give me the benefit of their knowledge were Larry Anderson, the author of *Benton MacKaye: Conservationist, Planner, and Creator of the Appalachian Trail*; Paul Bofinger, former president/forester of the Society for the Protection of New Hampshire Forests; Charlie Niebling, of the SPNHF; Karl Roenke, of the U.S. Forest Service; Rebecca Orestes, also of the Forest Service; Carleton Schaller, of the Friends of the Wild River; Ned Therrien, formerly of the U.S. Forest Service; Julie Wormser, of the Appalachian Mountain Club; Dan Yetter, of the Friends of the Wild River; and George Zink, of the Friends of the Sandwich Range and the Wonalancet Out Door

Club. In addition, Karl Roenke made available to me several key documents at the White Mountain National Forest office in Laconia, New Hampshire.

A number of libraries and historical societies helped immeasurably by providing access to White Mountain sources. The staff at Rauner Special Collections Library at Dartmouth College was unfailingly helpful, and a special thanks goes to Jay Satterfield, Sarah Hartwell, and Patricia Cope. At the New Hampshire Historical Society, David Smolen and Bill Copeley guided me to sources that I would not have otherwise found. Northwestern University has a superb White Mountain collection, and Russell Maylone and the staff of the Special Collections Library helped me wend my way through their materials. Jewell Friedman of the Franconia Heritage Museum and John Gardiner of the Twin Mountain Historical Society both helped me gain access to the wonderful photographs and engravings from their collections that appear in this book.

The White Mountains have been the subject of countless paintings, photographs, and maps, and Carmine Fantasia helped greatly in identifying the best of the images and clearing permission to reproduce them. Likewise, Joseph Mehling, Dartmouth College's photographer, lent his experience and professionalism in photographing several of the maps and artifacts that appear in the book. In preparing the final manuscript, Nanci Shirrell lent her common sense and good humor.

For reviewing and commenting on parts of the manuscript, I want to thank Larry Anderson, Iris Baird, Paul Bofinger, David Govatski, Brian Muchow, Alice Nash, Karl Roenke, Martha Saxton, Melanie L. Simo, David Stewart-Smith, Dan Yetter, and George Zink.

I also want to acknowledge Lucille Daniel Stott, the former editor of *Appalachia*, published by the Appalachian Mountain Club, for her guiding hand on articles on the White Mountains that were published in the journal. Her responses helped me realize that there was a place for a new book that explored the White Mountains as a wilderness.

Finally, I owe a huge debt of gratitude to the staff at University Press of New England. Ellen Wicklum showed immediate enthusiasm for the project, and her support and suggestions were truly sustaining forces throughout the writing. I also want to thank Will Hively for his fine copyediting of the manuscript.

THIS GRAND & MAGNIFICENT PLACE

INTRODUCTION

O N THE SOUTH EDGE OF THE WHITE MOUNTAINS of New Hampshire, not far from the small town of Wonalancet, is the Ferncroft Kiosk, which displays a large, colorful map of the Sandwich Range Wilderness and several posters showing animals to be found in the region. From the kiosk, a network of trails spreads north toward several mountains, including Mount Passaconaway, Mount Paugus, and, farther to the east, Mount Chocorua. But the goal for the hiker on this crystalline day in September is the more modest Mount Wonalancet, which is 2,780 feet high.

From the kiosk, the hiker heads north on the Old Mast Trail, but after walking only a tenth of a mile, he turns left onto the Wonalancet Range Trail, which parallels Spring Brook for a short distance, veers left, and follows an old logging road through a hardwood forest. The trunks of two fallen trees, both behemoths, lie across the path, forcing him to crawl underneath. A little more than half a mile from the kiosk, he comes to a sign that announces that he is entering the Sandwich Range Wilderness—meaning that logging is prohibited and no vehicles or human-made structures are permitted. From this point on, nature predominates. The trail grows rougher and steeper, ascending through dense forest and passing boulders encased in moss. After one and a half miles, the trail climbs even more sharply, and the hiker throws aside his walking stick and uses his hands to scramble over boulders. Finally the trail levels off, and he reaches the flat summit of the mountain.

The trail continues on to Hibbard Mountain and joins other trails that penetrate deep into the heart of the Sandwich Range and eventually spill out onto the Kancamagus Highway to the north. But the hiker has gone far enough for one day, and he sheds his backpack and sits cross-legged on the ground and listens. And what is most remarkable to him is the solitude, the all-encompassing, infinitely deep solitude. He drinks from his canteen, listens to the occasional call of a bird, and soaks in this rare feeling of complete and utter aloneness, and without regret he feels as if civilization has slipped away.

Besides the feeling of solitude it engenders, what is most distinctive about the trail is its replication of the history of the White Mountains. It connects to trails leading to mountains named after three of the most prominent leaders of the Native Americans who inhabited this region before the arrival of white men: Passaconaway, Paugus, and Wonalancet. The Old Mast Trail that enters the forest from the Ferncroft Kiosk is a reminder of the mast trade in New Hampshire, of a time when agents of England's Royal Navy traveled through the colonial forests and marked the tallest and straightest white pines to be cut as masts for His Majesty's ships. The old logging road along Spring Brook is a testament to the importance of logging to New Hampshire and the White Mountains. But most of all, the existence of the Sandwich Range Wilderness is a tribute to the history that wilderness has had in the White Mountains in the four hundred years since explorers first viewed "the Crystal hills" from the Atlantic Ocean.

Today the White Mountain National Forest contains four protected wildernesses in addition to the Sandwich Range: the Great Gulf, the Presidential Range–Dry River, the Pemigewasset, and the Caribou–Speckled Mountain; together these five wildernesses encompass 112,000 acres. In addition, in 2005 the U.S. Forest Service, which manages the White Mountain National Forest, recommended an expansion of the Sandwich Range Wilderness and the creation of a new wilderness in the region of the Wild River; this will add 34,500 acres to the amount of protected wilderness in the Whites. These areas enjoy statutory protection as wilderness. Logging and road building are banned, as are motorized equipment and bicycles. In all these wildernesses, you can strap on a backpack, disappear into the forest, face the challenges of survival, and experience the delights of solitude.

How these wildernesses came to be protected is a complex story that has unfolded over the four centuries since English colonists first arrived on the shores of New Hampshire and gazed upon the distant mountains. In many ways, the White Mountains make a fascinating case study for tracing how Americans' perceptions of and policies toward wilderness have evolved through those four hundred years. The Whites were the setting of some of the first wilderness exploration in America, as well as early scientific studies of the ecology of wilderness areas. They inspired a cultural heritage of painting and literature that helped to transform Americans' attitudes toward wild nature in the mid-1800s. The mountain vistas attracted scores of artists, whose canvases brought nature's beauty into thousands of parlors throughout the United States. Some of the nation's most noted authors, including Nathaniel Hawthorne and John Greenleaf Whittier, sang paeans to the Whites in stories and poems that reached wide circulation.

Early notions of tourism developed in the Whites as well, and in this development, the Crawford family played a key role. Early in the nineteenth century, Abel Crawford and Ethan Allen Crawford built the first hiking trails in America, and they guided scores of visitors to the summits of the mountains and into the depths of the forests. They never lost their wonder at the beauty of the landscape, and in the 1840s, *Lucy Crawford's History of the White Mountains* recorded for posterity Ethan's love of the wild landscape as he surveyed it from the summit of Mount Washington:

> The day was fine, and our feelings seemed to correspond with the beauties of the day, and after some hours had swiftly passed away in this manner, we concluded to leave this grand and magnificent place and return to a lower situation on earth.[1]

After the Civil War, people began flocking to the mountains in search of relief from the hectic pressures of an increasingly urban society. The image of the rugged outdoorsman took hold, and activities such as fishing, hunting, hiking, and camping drew thousands. White Mountain tourist attractions, notably the Old Man of the Mountain and the Flume, became national symbols of the wonders of natural beauty. From the 1850s on, innkeepers and railroad companies created an infrastructure that eased access to vacations in the mountains. Grand resort hotels proliferated throughout the region and offered luxurious accommodations to their guests. But in the last two decades of the nineteenth century, a minority of adventurers began to seek purer experiences of the outdoors and placed a premium on the experience of wild nature. In many ways, they heeded and were guided by the words of Henry David Thoreau in his famous essay "Walking":

> [I]n Wildness is the preservation of the World. Every tree sends its fibres forth in search of the Wild. The cities import it at any price. Men plough and sail for it. From the forest and wilderness come the tonics and barks which brace mankind. . . . I believe in the forest, and in the meadow, and in the night in which the corn grows. . . . Life consists with wildness. The most alive is the wildest. . . . Hope and the future for me are not in lawns and cultivated fields, not in towns and cities, but in the impervious and quaking swamps. . . . When I would recreate myself, I seek the darkest wood, the thickest and most interminable and, to the citizen, most dismal swamp. I enter a swamp as a sacred place,—a *sanctum sanctorum*. There is the strength, the marrow of Nature.[2]

Even as outdoor enthusiasts were beginning to embrace wilderness experiences in the White Mountains, though, the region faced perhaps its greatest crisis ever, as logging and paper companies commenced a furious effort to cut timber. The resulting environmental damage attracted national attention, energizing a broad coalition of conservation groups that pushed for passage of landmark legislation—the Weeks Act of 1911. In addition to leading to the creation of the White Mountain National Forest, the law established the means

Intro.1. Henry David Thoreau (ca. 1856). In American letters, Thoreau was the first to celebrate wilderness. In his essay "Walking," published in the *Atlantic Monthly* in 1862, he stated unequivocally, "[I]n wildness is the preservation of the World."

Daguerreotype from the collections of the Thoreau Society at the Thoreau Institute at Walden Woods.

by which the federal government purchased millions of acres of privately held lands in order to preserve and manage them for the public's benefit.

But after the passage of the Weeks Act, economic trends ensured continuing battles over the preservation of the region's wilderness characteristics. By the 1940s and 1950s, renewed timber cutting and the explosion of ski resorts, hotels, second homes, golf courses, and outlet stores placed new kinds of environmental pressures on the mountain landscape. At the same time, environmental activists, deeply influenced by Benton MacKaye, Bob Marshall, Arthur Carhart, and Aldo Leopold and their ideas about wilderness and environmental stewardship, sought innovative ways to protect the Whites.

As the cultural, social, ecological, and economic history of the Whites unfolds in the pages that follow, two competing visions of wilderness vie for prominence—a dichotomy suggested by Max Oelschlaeger, professor of philosophy and religious studies at the University of North Texas, in his book *The Idea of Wilderness*. In one vision, which is instrumental, colonial settlers, Puritan adventurers, entrepreneurs, investors, and consumers gaze upon the wilderness and see a cornucopia of economic opportunities that can be exploited to materially improve people's lives, build the nation's economy, and bring wealth to entrepreneurs.

In the competing vision, the wilderness possesses intrinsic value for the aesthetic pleasures that its beauty inspires, the scientific understanding that it engenders, the personal growth that it stimulates, the national pride that it stirs, and the spiritual truths that it points to.[3] The vision of wilderness as inherently valuable first emerged through the Romantic art and literature of the early nineteenth century and has gained strength ever since through the eloquence of Thoreau, John Muir, John Burroughs, Mary Austin, Rachel Carson, Terry Tempest Williams, Edward Abbey, and others too numerous to name.

These two visions have clashed in the White Mountains, making the region a battleground between the forces that championed one vision or the other of wilderness. By tracing the evolution of the White Mountain wilderness, we can learn what constitutes wise stewardship of all wilderness areas, from the Alaska Wilderness Refuge to the Grand Staircase-Escalante in Utah. And even if we live in or near our nation's populous cities, we can learn lessons that will help us to achieve a wiser balance between instrumental uses of the land for economic development and preservation of nature's landscapes for their intrinsic value.

Before we embark on a journey through the history of the White Mountains, it is helpful to take a brief look at the mountains today. The White Mountain National Forest encompasses almost 800,000 acres of land in New Hampshire and western Maine and boasts forty-eight mountains that are more than 4,000 feet high. Within the national forest are nine officially designated Scenic Areas: Gibbs Brook, Nancy Brook, Greeley Ponds, Pinkham Notch, Lafayette Brook, Rocky Gorge, Lincoln Woods, Sawyer Pond, and Snyder Brook.

The fact that the White Mountains are a national forest and not a national park is critically important. National parks exist for the purpose of recreation and preservation. National forests, on the other hand, are managed by the U.S. Forest Service for multiple uses, which include recreational activities, economic development, logging operations, watershed protection, and wildlife protection. Recreation is supposed to take precedence, but finding the right balance among recreational use, environmental protection, and economic development has been a source of ongoing conflict.

Different types of forests cover the region's mountains. Below 3,000 feet, northern hardwood forests of birch, beech, and maple predominate, interspersed with oaks and white pines. In autumn, these are the trees that explode into the brilliant reds, oranges, and yellows that are justifiably world famous. At elevations higher than 3,000 feet is the boreal forest of conifers, including spruce and fir. And as hikers climb past the timberline, they find krummholz, stunted trees that have been twisted and gnarled by the perpetual winds and the snow and ice. Krummholz is testament to the harsh weather conditions found at the upper elevations of the mountains.[4]

One of the most extraordinary aspects of the Whites is their network of 1,200 miles of hiking trails. These trails attract millions of hikers a year and encompass an incredible range of difficulty, ranging from half-hour walks to multiday journeys through the protected wildernesses. The trails, some of which date back more than 150 years, have opened up wilderness to millions of Americans. Making the backcountry accessible has had costs, though, such as the trampling of precious plants by careless hikers. Unquestionably, finding a balance between making nature accessible and protecting the environment is one of the ongoing challenges facing the Whites, as well as other natural areas in the United States.

But the greatest challenge has been finding an appropriate balance between economic development and the preservation of wild nature. The region exists so close to the major population centers of the East Coast, and its resources, particularly trees, are so abundant and accessible that the temptation has been to exploit those resources with little regard for ecological impact. Yet, as we shall see, the White Mountains have also been a place where Americans gradually set aside the suspicions of wild nature that were a legacy of the colonial area and learned the aesthetic, scientific, recreational, and spiritual value of wilderness. The means by which attitudes toward wilderness evolved and affected policy is a remarkable part of American environmental history. We begin with the first people of the mountain region, the Abenaki, whose relationship with the mountains, forests, rivers, and other parts of the environment becomes a baseline against which we can better understand the attitudes toward wilderness of the explorers and settlers who later migrated into the White Mountains—the beautiful, stirring, multifaceted White Mountains.

PART I

Exploring and Settling the White Mountain Wilderness, 1600–1820

For centuries, the Abenaki people have inhabited northern New England, where they have developed lifeways that are well adapted to the dense forests and mountainous terrain. When European colonists arrive in the early 1600s, they view this land as a "wilderness"—a region that is virtually uninhabited and uncivilized—and they set out to tame it. A number of explorers venture into the mountains and begin to learn their geography; they draw maps, survey the land, and appropriate it from the indigenous people. But when two ministers, the Reverend Jeremy Belknap and the Reverend Manasseh Cutler, explore the White Mountains in 1784 and climb Mount Washington, they immediately admire the land's magnificent beauty and recognize its unique flora, fauna, and landforms. In the late 1700s and early 1800s, settlers migrate into the region and establish farms, found towns, build roads, create dams, and cut trees—initiating major changes in the landscape of the White Mountains.

Chapter 1

ABENAKI HOMELAND, EUROPEAN WILDERNESS, AND EARLY EXPLORATION

IN 1524, THE ITALIAN EXPLORER Giovanni Verrazzano sailed along the coast of New England and entered the harbor of today's Portsmouth, New Hampshire. "We departed from thence," he later wrote in a letter to the King of France, "keeping our course Northeast along the coast, which we found more pleasant champion and without woods, with high mountains within the land."[1] Verrazzano's account was the first written reference by a European to what we now call the White Mountains. It was the beginning of a complex relationship that Americans would have with those mountains— a blend of awe at their beauty, fear of their power, superstition born of the unknown, and a quickening of opportunism toward the presumed mineral wealth of the region.

Eventually, in the nineteenth century, the White Mountains would take center stage in transforming American attitudes toward wilderness. To understand how American society reached that turning point, it is essential to understand the attitudes of three groups of people that helped to shape the early history of the White Mountains: the Abenaki people who had inhabited the mountains for centuries, the English colonists who began settling New Hampshire in the early 1600s, and the explorers who ventured into the mountains from the 1640s to the late 1700s.

To the Abenaki, the White Mountains were part of a larger homeland, which they had adapted to by using its resources for food, clothing, shelter, and recreation. They saw in the mountains the presence of what Europeans called "the spiritual." According to historian Neal Salisbury, "The fruit of the Indian experience was an ethos in which relationships in the social, natural, and supernatural worlds were defined in terms of reciprocity rather than domination and submission."[2] Examining how the Abenaki people lived in their White Mountain "home" provides a stark contrast to the ways in which white settlers later perceived and interacted with the White Mountain "wilderness." Those settlers viewed the immense North American wilderness with a blend of fear toward the dangers it posed and hope about the economic opportunities promised by furs, fish, game, timber, minerals, and other natural resources. Their attitudes formed a powerful ideology that led them to carve a European-American civilization out of that wilderness. Yet, as later chapters will make clear, a passion to conserve the beauty and ecological integrity of the White Mountains gradually tempered the drive to tame the wilderness—a process of enormous significance in the environmental history of the United States.

When Europeans arrived in northern New England in the early 1600s, the entire region was populated by the Abenaki people, who spoke a dialect of the Algonquian language family and who called their home *wôbanaki*—the Dawnland—where the sun first shone forth to greet each new day. They believed that they were the creation of Ktsi Nwaskw, the force known as the Great Spirit.[3] Joseph Bruchac, a renowned storyteller and a descendant of the Abenaki, tells his people's story of creation with simple eloquence:

> Ktsi Nwaskw, the Great Mystery, decided to make human beings. So Ktsi Nwaskw fashioned giant people out of stone. Life was breathed into these stone beings and they stood and began to walk around. But, although they were able to breathe and walk, to hunt and eat, there were things that those first people could not do. They could not bend down to the earth and they could not feel sympathy or love, for their hearts were also made of stone. They killed more than they needed to eat, and they crushed things under their heavy feet.
>
> Ktsi Nwaskw saw that these stone people were not good for the earth. So they were turned back into stone. That is why there are so many stones here in the Northeast. Sometimes when you turn over a stone you may see that it has a face on it, and you are supposed to remember what happened to those people who treated everything else in creation with contempt.
>
> Now Ktsi Nwaskw looked for something else that could be used to make people. There were the ash trees. They danced in the wind and bent close to the earth. Ktsi Nwaskw fashioned new people from those trees. Those new people were rooted to the earth and were in balance with the life around them. They were our ancestors, the first Abenaki. We are the children of the trees.[4]

This story captures how the Abenaki viewed the world in which they lived. The stones and the trees were living beings, for the construct "person" included not only humans but also other-than-human beings that had in common a similar structure: an enduring vital part (which Westerners call the spirit or soul) and an outward appearance that could be transformed under certain conditions. For this reason, the Abenaki shared the earth with and maintained social relations with all other beings.[5]

In the late 1500s, approximately 150,000 indigenous people inhabited New England, though these numbers are, at best, approximations.[6] Historians have traditionally divided the Abenaki people into two groups: the eastern Abenaki, who spoke one dialect and inhabited the region that is now Maine, and the western Abenaki, who spoke another dialect and occupied today's New Hampshire and Vermont. However, historian David Stewart-Smith has proposed that the tribes who lived west of the Kennebec River and east of the Connecticut River—the area that encompasses the White Mountains—be referred to as the central Abenaki because they developed lifeways that were distinct from those of the eastern Abenaki and the western Abenaki.[7]

The two tribes that lived in the White Mountain region and about which we know the most were the Pigwacket, centered in today's Conway, New Hampshire, and Fryeburg, Maine; and the Pemigewasset, who inhabited the valley of the Pemigewasset River. The Pigwacket inhabited the region until 1725, when colonists defeated them in a war that drove many to the village of St. Francis in Quebec, Canada. Descendants of those Abenaki continue to live in the village, which has been called Odanak since 1917.[8] Other Abenaki bands in northern New England included the Micmac, Maliseet, Penobscot, Passamaquoddy, Cowasuck, Pocumtuck, Nipmuck, Kennebec, Sokoki, Missisquoi, and Arosaguntacook.[9] A tribe that played a pivotal role in the history of the indigenous people of the region was the Pennacook, whose main village overlooked the Merrimack River in today's Concord.[10]

A tragic difficulty in reconstructing the history of the Abenaki people is the devastation caused by disease in the early 1600s, radically disrupting the continuity of their culture. From 1616 to 1618, an epidemic, possibly a strain of plague brought to New England by European traders, swept through the region, killing as much as 90 percent of the population.[11] Because of the resulting cultural discontinuity, we cannot always trace specific cultural practices or religious beliefs to a particular tribe or location in the White Mountains. In spite of these complications, though, historians in the past thirty years have been able to paint what they think is an accurate portrait of Abenaki lifeways by examining history, folklore, and the testimony of descendants of the Abenaki.

For the Abenaki south of the mountains, the growing season was long enough and the soil fertile enough that the people developed productive farming techniques. The people planted crops in May, when the women, who were primarily responsible for crop production, sowed maize, beans, and squash for eating and tobacco for ceremonies.[12] Setting fire to the woods was an important technique for clearing fields, chasing game from forests, facilitating travel, destroying insects, and stimulating the growth of grasses and berries. Using fire to clear cropland, a practice known as "swidden," benefited the forest ecosystem by stimulating a diversity of flora, returning rich nutrients to the soil, and burning dead underbrush to encourage the growth of new vegetation.[13]

In the White Mountain region, the Pemigewasset and the Pigwacket developed different lifeways because of the cold climate and the rugged terrain. Because of the short growing season and the rocky soil, they relied on hunting, fishing, and gathering for food. The most common game animals were moose, deer, bears, wolves, wildcats, raccoons, otters, and beavers. They used fire less frequently than the people to the south to clear fields and drive out game and instead developed a high level of skill at stalking game through the forests.[14] The density of the forest also affected their transportation, as they wore paths through the woods and, in winter, traversed the trails on snowshoes or glided along the frozen rivers.[15]

In using natural resources, the Indians displayed attitudes toward the land that were far different from those of the English colonists. William Wood, an Englishman who lived in the Massachusetts Bay Colony from 1629 to 1633 and later provided an account of his observations in the book *New England's Prospect,* noted that the indigenous people had a storehouse of knowledge about "the craggy mountains and the pleasant vales, the stately woods and swampy groves, the spacious ponds and swift-running rivers," which they bestowed with names.[16] When the people harvested maize from the earth and took fish from the rivers, they regarded them as gifts supplied by the beings with whom they shared the earth.

In the Algonquian people's view of the world of nature, the concept of manitou was central; it was the expression of the power of spirit, the vital part, which quickened the souls of people, animals, rocks, and trees and tied them together as equal parts in creation. The creatures of the forest were pivotal in the Abenaki people's lives as other-than-human beings with as much importance as human beings to the interdependence of life. For help in interpreting the signs of nature, the Abenaki turned to the m'teowlin, or "deep-seeing one," a tribal member who could provide guidance and protection. The m'teowlin had extraordinary knowledge of ways to use nature for the benefit of the people; they knew how to tame the wild rivers for people's benefit and how to cure the sick by using herbs.[17]

Nature affected the Abenaki in yet another way—by shaping the kind of political structure they developed. The rough terrain and dense forests made communication among different bands difficult, so villages functioned as quasi-independent units, although individual bands came together to cooperate for fishing and other economic activities. The leader of each village was a sagamore. The sagamores of various bands and the tribal chiefs had occasionally come together to discuss issues of defense and territory, but in the

1.1. Passaconaway. Passaconaway led the Pennacook people from the early 1600s until his death in 1655. Realizing that the American Indian tribes of northern New England had to unite to augment their ability to negotiate with the white population, he led the creation of the Pennacook Confederacy. New Hampshire Historical Society.

early seventeenth century, they began to make formal alliances. Central to this process was Passaconaway, a Pennacook sagamore who was probably born between 1555 and 1573, rose to leadership in the early 1600s, and guided his people until his death in 1665.[18] In 1629, Passaconaway led the creation of the Pennacook Confederacy, allying more than twelve tribes in New Hampshire, Maine, and Massachusetts to defend against the Mohawks and Micmacs and to develop a strategy for coexisting with the European colonists.

Passaconaway possessed the powers of a m'teowlin, and William Wood noted the widespread belief in Passaconaway's mastery of nature. "[I]f we may believe the Indians," Wood wrote, "who report of one Passaconaway that he can make the water burn, the rocks move, the trees dance, metamorphose himself into a flaming man. . . . This I write but on the report of the Indians, who constantly affirm stranger things."[19] Such stories reveal a deep complexity in the attitudes of the Abenaki people toward nature. Certainly they employed the land for practical ends, but even as they were using natural resources, their worldview ensured that they would recognize the inherent value of nature, as expressed through other-than-human beings that inhabited the rocks, the trees, the rivers, and the mountains.

When English settlers began to arrive in New Hampshire in the early 1600s, they carried very different attitudes toward nature and wilderness. Two groups had a major impact on the early history of New Hampshire and the White Mountains. One was the Puritans, who settled first in Massachusetts and then established colonies in southern New Hampshire; their descendants eventually moved north into the White Mountains. The other group consisted of Anglican planters, or settlers, who crossed the Atlantic to establish plantations in northern New England. While the Puritans sought to cleanse the Church of England, the Anglicans remained loyal to it. In spite of their religious differences, though, both groups had powerful economic motives for colonizing North America. They looked upon the earth and its riches as inexhaustible resources and had no concept of Aldo Leopold's land ethic or the idea of conservation.[20] The resulting attitudes of both groups toward nature stood in clear contrast to those of the Abenaki people.

In addition, the Puritans carried an extra layer of negative attitudes toward wilderness that had its origins in their interpretation of their mission on earth. When the Puritans arrived in Massachusetts Bay in 1620, they dedicated themselves to the project of founding a saintly kingdom—a New Canaan—on earth to counteract the corruptions of the Roman Catholic Church and the Church of England. According to the Puritan minister John Cotton, their "maine meane" was "of peopling the world, and . . . of propagating the Gospell."[21] In the eyes of John Winthrop, the first elected governor of the Massachusetts Bay Colony, America was to be "the good Land" in which the Puritans would create a Christian civilization.[22] In 1630, as Winthrop crossed the Atlantic on the *Arbella* with his small band of Puritan settlers, he announced this mission in words that have rung through American history:

> [F]or we must Consider that we shall be as a City upon a Hill, the eyes of all people are upon us; so that if we shall deal falsely with our God in this work we have undertaken, and so cause Him to withdraw His present help from us, . . . we shall open the mouths of enemies to speak evil of the ways of God, and . . . we shall shame the faces of many of God's worthy servants, and cause their prayers to be turned into Curses upon us.[23]

As Roderick Nash pointed out in his landmark study of American attitudes toward wilderness, *Wilderness and the American Mind*, "It was, after all, a *city* on a hill that John Winthrop called upon his colleagues to erect."[24] But when the Puritans reached New England, they were not prepared for a countryside that was, according to an early history of Plymouth Colony titled

Mourt's Relation, "wild and overgrown with woods."[25] The winters were harsh, the soil was rocky, and innumerable wild beasts roamed through the forests. Faced with these daunting conditions, the Puritans emphasized the need to tame the wilderness and bring it under their control—an attitude toward nature that their descendants would later carry into the White Mountains.

Besides physical dangers, the wilderness also posed moral dangers. In the absence of established churches in the wild countryside, Satan was free to roam. The inhabitants of the land, the Indians, lived in "the snare of the Divell," and the Puritans considered them to be "bond-slaves of Satan."[26] And within the vast spaces of the forest, sinners could engage in licentious behavior. In *Of Plymouth Plantation,* William Bradford, who served as the governor of Plymouth from 1627 to 1656, roundly criticized the frontier settlement of Mount Wollaston (in today's Quincy, Massachusetts), where, removed from the tight cohesion of the Boston-based theocracy, Thomas Morton used "strong drink and other junkets" to seduce the innocents of the small village into the paths of sin. In Morton's own words, "They also set up a maypole, drinking and dancing about it many days together, inviting the Indian women for their consorts, dancing and frisking together like so many fairies, or furies, rather; and worst practices."[27] The appalling behavior in the remote settlement came to an abrupt end when Miles Standish of Plymouth Colony arrested Morton and the Pilgrim fathers transported him back to England. Such behavior reinforced negative Puritan perceptions of the wilderness.

Given the harrowing physical and moral dangers of the wilderness, the Puritans viewed the mastery of nature as essential to the stability of their society. In sermons they beseeched the members of the community to transform the wilderness into a garden, a term that referred metaphorically to the Garden of Eden and physically to the productive fields that would feed the Christian civilization. Captain Edward Johnson's history of the early years of New England, *Wonder-Working Providence of Sion's Savior in New England,* vividly captured this drive to cultivate a garden out of the wilderness. A staunchly orthodox Puritan, Johnson wrote *Wonder-Working Providence* to justify the divine mission of peopling North America, which he referred to throughout his book as a "desert Wilderness." As he embarked from Southampton, England, friends pleaded with him to consider seriously what he and his family were sacrificing—their houses and all the other advantages of civilization—to go into "that Rocky Wilderness, . . . to run the hazard of your life."[28]

When he arrived in New England, he narrated the wonders that the Puritans had worked by creating gardens of civilization from the dismal wilderness. In Roxbury, Massachusetts, for instance, "very laborious people" had transformed "dismal Swamps and tearing Bushes" into "goodly Fruit-trees, fruitfull Fields and Gardens."[29] In Haverhill, "the people are wholly bent to

1.2. Sir Ferdinando Gorges, detail from *Some Who Have Made Bristol Famous* (1930), Ernest Board. In Board's painting of luminaries from Bristol, England, Sir Ferdinando Gorges is prominently featured. Gorges, who was the commander of the fort at Plymouth, England, became fascinated by the economic potential of New England when he heard descriptions of the land from three Native Americans. © Bristol's Museums, Galleries & Archives.

improve their labour in tilling the earth, and keeping of cattle. . . . The constant penetrating farther into this Wilderness, hath caused the wild and uncouth woods to be filled with frequented ways, and the large rivers to be overlaid with Bridges."[30]

Even as Puritans like Edward Johnson were creating a theocracy in Massachusetts, a group of English investors was establishing colonies in the area that today we call New Hampshire and Maine. Their motives were primarily economic, and they set in motion a series of events in northern New England that would eventually lead to the exploration and settlement of the White Mountains. One of the prominent investors of the early 1600s was Sir Ferdinando Gorges, the commander of the naval post in Plymouth, England. Although Gorges never journeyed to New England himself, he secured financial backing for the establishment of Maine and New Hampshire. In addition, he explicitly spelled out the economic reasons for colonizing New Hampshire, revealing colonial assumptions about the best uses of land. To Sir Ferdinando and other English adventurers, the purpose of colonization was the exploitation of the immense riches of the wilderness, by harvesting fish in the teeming waters off the coast of Maine, capturing the seemingly infinite supply of fur, or mining the earth for the mineral riches that they were sure lay buried in its depths. Sir Ferdinando's words reveal three assumptions about land use that would have an enormous impact on the White Mountains:

- The wilderness was empty, which reflected a European disregard for the indigenous culture that flourished in North America.

- The land was useful only if settlers exploited it economically—for instance, by trapping furs or establishing farms. The assumption would lead, in the 1700s, to the creation of farms and villages in the valleys of the White Mountains.

- The resources of the land were inexhaustible. The assumption of inexhaustibility would lead to the near destruction of the White Mountain forests at the end of the 1800s.

Gorges had been the commander of the Plymouth fort for ten years when a friend of his, Captain George Waymouth, returned to England from North America in 1605 with five captive Indians, three of whom lived in Gorges's household.[31] After learning English, they regaled him with tales of the beauties and riches of their homeland, and as they spun their descriptions, Gorges immediately grasped the immense potential of the land they were describing— that it would be "proper for our uses, especially when I found what goodly Rivers, stately Islands, and safe harbours those parts abounded with."[32]

In 1620, the royal government formed the Council for New England and granted it a charter, called the New England charter, to sell land and govern colonies located between 40 degrees and 48 degrees north latitude. This claim stretched from Philadelphia all the way north to the tip of Newfoundland and impinged on a number of other claims, particularly those of the French along the St. Lawrence River.[33] Investors purchased the patents with the expectation of earning healthy profits, and they, in turn, recruited planters to establish plantations in the newly claimed lands. Gorges was elected a leader of the council and eventually assumed its presidency.

Between 1620 and 1623, the council moved aggressively to issue patents for colonies. The first grant in the region that eventually became New Hampshire was to David Thomson, a purveyor of fish in the London markets and an acquaintance of Gorges's. The council granted Thomson six thousand acres of land at the mouth of the Piscataqua River, and he called the settlement Pannaway.[34] Thomson established a trading company, but it never made a profit, and he ended up abandoning the settlement after only a few years, moving on to Massachusetts.

Meanwhile, in 1621, Gorges formed a partnership with Captain John Mason, and together they agreed to pursue the foundation of colonies that, they hoped, would prove more profitable than Pannaway. Mason, like Gorges, was an energetic and ambitious man who had risen to prominence in the military—in his case, as a naval officer. In 1615, in recognition of his military service, the royal government appointed him governor of the English colony at Newfoundland.[35] The two men quickly discovered that they shared a grand vision—the colonization of New England.

Settlement of the province proceeded slowly, though, and when Parliament began to show impatience with the lack of progress in establishing colonies, Sir Ferdinando penned a key pamphlet that the Council for New England published in 1622. Titled *A Brief Relation of the Discovery and Plantation of New England*, it extolled the richness of New England's land and publicized the vast possibilities for economic profit. New England was, in Sir Ferdinando's words, "a most ample discovery of the most commodious Country for the benefit of our Nation, that ever hath been found." In this wonderful land, the air was healthy, the soil had "fertility fit for corn, and feeding of cattle wherewith to sustain them."[36]

Gorges sang the praises of the fecundity of the soil, which would yield "wonderful increase, . . . with infinite variety of nourishing roots, and other herbs, and fruits."[37] The land teemed with wildlife: "The Country aboundeth with diversity of wild fowl, as Turkeys, Partridges, Swans, Cranes, wild Geese of two sorts, [and] wilde Ducks of three sort."[38] Other plentiful raw materials included "Hemp, Flax, . . . several veins of Ironstone, commodities to make Pitch, Rosen, Tar" for the spars and masts of the powerful royal navy.[39] Sir Ferdinando's glowing account was remarkably effective, and later that year, the council granted Mason and him a patent for the province of Maine.

After receiving the grant for Maine, Gorges and Mason could not establish colonies immediately, because they were drawn into an English war with Spain. Meanwhile, a second plantation, following on Pannaway, was establishing itself in the Piscataqua region. In the mid-1620s, Edward Hilton, who, like

David Thomson, was involved in the fish trade in London, arrived at Pann-away. Hilton's brother, William, soon joined him there, but when Thomson abandoned Pannaway for Massachusetts, the two Hilton brothers migrated in the opposite direction, moving seven miles inland to the point where the Oyster and the Newichawannock rivers feed into the Piscataqua. There they established a new plantation, Hilton's Point.[40]

In 1629, the war with Spain and France ended, and Gorges and Mason turned their attention once again to North America. On November 7 of that year, they agreed to divide their original Maine patent. Gorges retained the territory north of the Piscataqua River, which he called the province of Maine. Mason gained the rights to the land between the Piscataqua and the Merri-mack rivers and called it New Hampshire, after his native home of Hamp-shire.[41] Ten days later, on November 17, 1629, Mason and Gorges received yet another patent from the Council for New England for an enormous area that reached all the way to Canada.[42] This grant, called Laconia because of the ter-ritory's numerous lakes, encompassed an immense wilderness, including the White Mountains. In this wilderness, the colonists knew, were white-peaked mountains to the north, which explorer Christopher Levett had referred to as "the Christall hill, being as they say 100 miles in the Country."[43]

To establish colonies and explore the northern lands, Gorges and Mason founded the Laconia Company and hired a military officer, Captain Walter Neale, to lead an expedition. While Neale's primary mission was to establish colonies, he was also charged with exploring the enormous interior of Laco-nia. In addition, the Laconia directors expected him to establish trade routes with the Indians as far away as the "Lake of the Iroquois," which might have referred to Lake Winnipesaukee or Lake Champlain.[44] Neale arrived in the spring of 1630, accompanied by Ambrose Gibbons. Gibbons was to be the factor of the colony—the official responsible for establishing trading posts, bringing goods to the Laconia interior, and trading them for furs, which he would then process and export to England.[45]

Gibbons quickly set up a trading post at a falls on the Newichawannock River, about fifteen miles upriver from Pannaway. While Gibbons was estab-lishing his small trading post, a patent was granted in 1631 for a third colony in New Hampshire, which was to be located on the Piscataqua River. Thomas Warnerton, one of the partners, led the establishment of this new colony, which was called Strawberry Bank in recognition of the strawberry bushes that grew there in abundance. This colony, destined to become the most popu-lous in the region, was the nucleus of Portsmouth.[46]

As these colonies were establishing themselves, the Laconia Company wanted Walter Neale to open up the fur trade to Lake Champlain as quickly as pos-sible, and to do so, he was expected to lead exploratory expeditions into the

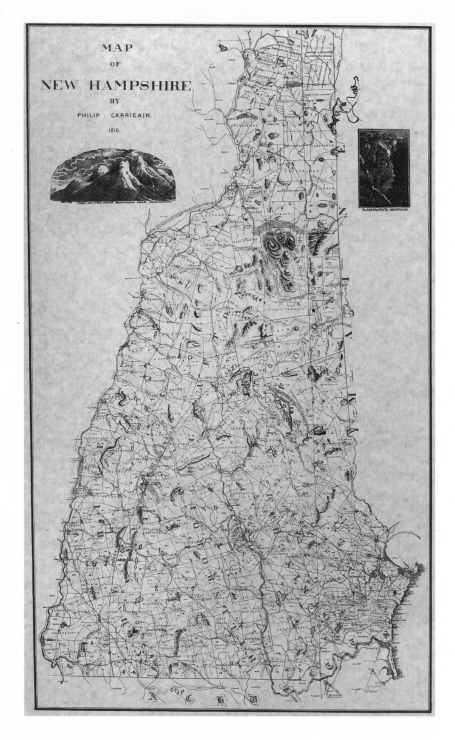

Laconia interior. For unknown reasons, he made no attempt at exploration during his first year. In subsequent years, though, he did try to explore the New Hampshire wilderness, but how far he reached is shrouded in uncertainty. One historian who thought that Neale explored Laconia extensively and reached the White Mountains was the Reverend Jeremy Belknap, whose *History of New Hampshire,* published in three volumes from 1784 to 1792, was the first authoritative history of New Hampshire. Belknap even claimed that Neale was the first white man to climb Mount Washington, but, in fact, Neale probably never got as far as Lake Winnipesaukee, let alone the White Mountains.[47] In the end, the Laconia Company directors grew disillusioned with Neale's lack of progress in exploration and, in 1633, called him back to England.[48] During this period, the Laconia Company itself went bankrupt and ceased operations.[49]

After the dissolution of the Laconia Company, Sir Ferdinando and Captain Mason divided their claims, with Gorges concentrating on the development of the province of Maine and Mason focusing his efforts on New Hampshire, where he hired Henry Josselyn to manage the settlement on Newichawannok. Gorges and Mason remained friends until Mason's sudden death in 1635. Upon Mason's demise, Josselyn continued to manage the captain's plantations for a short time, but soon after, he relocated to Maine.

In 1637, the two strains of colonial culture—the economic and the religious— came together in New Hampshire when John Wheelwright, a Puritan minister who was banned from the Massachusetts Bay Colony for his allegedly heretical beliefs, traveled north to scout the best location for a new settlement and decided on a site near the Squamscott River. There he established a colony that came to be known as Exeter. Several members of Wheelwright's congregation followed him, and together they built a thriving plantation. The leaders of Massachusetts, though, grew concerned about the existence of an independent Puritan settlement so close by. To counterbalance Wheelwright's influence, the General Court of Massachusetts in 1638 dispatched a group of Puritans to establish a settlement at Winnacunnet. The leader was a minister named Stephen Batchellor, who named the settlement after his native Hampton in England.[50]

By the 1640s, then, the Piscataqua River region had four plantations: the two new Puritan settlements at Exeter and Hampton and the two older ones at Hilton's Point and Strawberry Bank. From these settlements, the colonists

1.3. *Map of New Hampshire* (1816), Philip Carrigain. Philip Carrigain created this map in 1816—the earliest detailed map of New Hampshire. It shows the pattern of settlement in New Hampshire, with a heavy concentration of towns along the coast and a vast wilderness in the interior. The most prominent geographic feature is the White Mountains. Courtesy of Dartmouth College Library.

began to explore the mountains to the north. The early exploration of the Whites began with Darby Field, who, according to John Winthrop, was the first white man to climb Mount Washington, in 1642:

> One Darby Field, an Irishman, living about Pascataquack, being accompanied with two Indians, went to the top of the white hill. He made his journey in 18 days. His relation at his return was, that it was about one hundred miles from Saco, that after 40 miles travel he did, for the most part, ascend, and within 12 miles of the top was neither tree nor grass but low savins, which they went upon the top of sometimes, but a continual ascent upon rocks, on a ridge between two valleys filled with snow.[51]

Field embarked on his journey in the fall, accompanied by two Native Americans. After slowly pushing their way north, they reached the foot of the Great Mountain, where they found an Abenaki village of two hundred people. Some of the Abenaki agreed to accompany Field and the two other Indians in climbing the mountain, but when the party came within a few miles of the top, the Abenaki would go no farther, for they attached religious significance to the mountain. The other two Indians, though, accompanied Field the rest of the way to the summit, presumably because they were not native to the region and did not attach the same religious significance to the region's highest mountain.

During the same period that Field was climbing Mount Washington, a brother of Henry Josselyn's, John, visited New England twice, in 1638 and in 1663. During his second visit, he lived on his brother Henry's plantation at Black Point, Maine, which he used as a base from which to explore northern New England, observing the flora and fauna of the region. Upon returning to England, he published his observations in two volumes: *New-Englands Rarities Discovered* (1672) and *Two Voyages to New-England* (1673). Both books stirred keen interest about northern New England.

Josselyn's vivid descriptions might have set off a wave of exploration of the White Mountain wilderness, except that for nearly a century, wars between colonial troops and indigenous people roiled New England. They included King Philip's War, from 1675 to 1678; Lovewell's War, from 1723 to 1725; and the French and Indian War, from 1754 to 1763. One of the bloodiest battles in the north country occurred in the Abenaki village of Pequawket, near what is now Fryeburg, Maine, during Lovewell's War. In 1725, in retaliation for Indian attacks against white settlements, Captain John Lovewell led his troops up the frozen Merrimack River, and on May 8, they attacked Pequawket warriors at Saco Pond, now known as Lovewell's Pond. During the battle, the Pequawket warriors killed Lovewell and fifteen of his men, but their leader, Paugus, also perished.[52] Hearing of Lovewell's fate, Colonel Eleazer Tyng mustered another force to

1.4. Carrigain map: *View of the White Mountains from Shelburne.* For Philip Carrigain's map, J. Kidder of Concord drew illustrations, from which Abel Bowen of Boston made woodcuts. The White Mountains are depicted in a highly stylized manner, reflecting the lack of knowledge of their geography. Courtesy of Dartmouth College Library.

avenge the defeat, but at Pequawket he found only the corpses of Lovewell's fallen soldiers, whose names they carved into a tree at the site of the battle.

The ideology driving these colonial forays into the northern forest was one of conquest, in which the ultimate goal was to tame the wilderness and prepare it for settlement and economic exploitation. The ideology drove military officers to continue exploring the north country. Three months after Lovewell's Fight, in the fall of 1725, Captain Samuel Willard of Lancaster, Massachusetts, led a military expedition that scouted for Native Americans throughout the southern and middle sections of the White Mountains. Willard kept a journal of his troops' movements through the mountains, making it one of the earliest firsthand accounts of the mountains. He estimated that his party traveled 503 miles through the wilderness, but even though he certainly overestimated the distance, he and his men did travel hundreds of miles through the Whites—an extraordinary achievement for the time.[53]

After Lovewell's War, hostilities ceased for a time in the north country, and colonial officials began the gradual process of organizing land in and around the White Mountains for future settlement. Three developments took place that would eventually have a major impact on the White Mountain landscape: surveying the region, harvesting pine trees for ship masts and spars, and building roads to connect the wilderness interior to the settled regions along the New Hampshire coast. All three developments started to domesticate the landscape of the White Mountains, and the first step in that process was to survey the land. In 1741, the New Hampshire Assembly commissioned surveyors to mark a definite boundary between New Hampshire and Maine. Walter Bryent led a party that began to survey the region north of the Salmon Falls River, but a group of Native Americans, mistaking them for a military expedition, prevented them from traveling as far north as they wanted to.[54] Several years passed before Bryent was able to resume the surveying mission, but he did so in 1746, leading a party into the White Mountains. Six years later, in 1752, a party of colonists traveled north on the Connecticut River to the Coos region, where they intended to survey the land as a first step toward settling the area. As they traveled north, though, scouts from the Indian village of St. Francis observed them and suspected that the surveying operation was the first step toward establishing settlements. They made their displeasure known, and colonial officials temporarily suspended the survey and settlement efforts.

Another stage in beginning to settle the northern wilderness was harvesting New Hampshire's majestic white pines to make masts and spars for England's Royal Navy. White pines were perfect for masts, as the most mature trees grew straight and tall, reaching diameters of five or six feet and heights of more than 250 feet.[55] The northern forests of New Hampshire contained vast quantities of white pine, and in 1688, King William I laid claim to them, issuing a decree that all pines greater than twenty-four inches in diameter were to be reserved for the Royal Navy. Representatives of the Crown traveled through the forests and branded suitable trees with the royal mark, a broad arrow. A local logging industry developed rapidly to meet the Royal Navy's demand for the enormous pines. Entrepreneurs signed contracts to cut and transport the logs to Portsmouth, where they were loaded onto special mast ships and sent to England. The contractors, in turn, hired axe men to cut the enormous trees. The mast trade proved highly profitable, yielding anywhere from £95 to £115 in payment per log.[56]

However, a complicating factor in the development of the mast trade was the resumption of hostilities between the indigenous people and the white colonists during the French and Indian War (1754 to 1763), forcing the Crown's mast-trade contractors and axe men to be wary of attacks by Native Americans.[57] One incident during the French and Indian War clearly showed the colonists' ferocious determination to clear the north country of its indigenous inhabitants: the attack by Major Robert Rogers and his rangers on the Native American village of St. Francis in October of 1759. With two hundred of his rangers, Rogers made his way through the northern forest and arrived at the outskirts of St. Francis. On the evening of October 3, he and two of his officers dressed as Indians and crept undetected into the village. After reconnoitering, they returned to their hiding place and planned a surprise attack, which they launched at dawn, overwhelming the village and killing Indians in their sleep. However, several indigenous people awakened during the attack and fled into the surrounding forest, leaving the rangers free to ransack the village. In addition to two hundred guineas, they carried off a silver crucifix, a church plate, and candlesticks from the tribe's church. (The tribe had previously converted to Christianity.)

The retreat of Rogers's men from St. Francis inspired a number of legends that were told and retold in numerous White Mountain guidebooks of the nineteenth century. In one story, the party carrying the crucifix and candlesticks became hopelessly lost but happened upon an Algonquian who offered to guide them through the Great Pass (Crawford Notch) to the coastal settlements. They did not realize that the guide was a St. Francis Indian who was determined to avenge the attack on his people's village. The guide led the rangers along the Connecticut River and then eastward along a stream to the northern passageway through the mountains. As they wandered deeper into the forest, the guide stopped at one point and would go no farther, professing fear of the Great Spirit, who inhabited the mountains. Then he handed a rough map made of birch bark to the ranger who had been carrying the plunder from the St. Francis church. As the guide handed the map to the ranger, he appeared to slip accidentally and scratched the back of the ranger's hand with it. The guide departed, and a few minutes later, the ranger noticed that his scratched hand was swelling, and soon his entire body was trembling with pain. The ranger realized that their guide had poisoned the map, probably with the venom of a rattlesnake. Panicking, the poisoned ranger ran to the top of a nearby cliff and flung himself to his death. The men, desperate to escape the fate of the Indian elder's curse, buried the plunder along with their companion.[58] The tale expressed the anxiety that the colonists had about the wilderness, but it served also to rationalize the removal of the Abenaki people from the region.

In 1763, the French and Indian War ended with the signing of the Treaty of Paris, which eased tensions in the backwoods so that exploration and settlement of the mountains could proceed. A major discovery in the region came soon after in 1771, when a hunter named Timothy Nash was tracking a moose in the mountains and lost sight of it. Climbing a tree on Cherry Mountain to see if he could locate the animal, he suddenly saw a mountain wall to the south that plunged into a valley.[59] Scurrying back down, he made his way to the valley and stumbled into the Notch of the Mountains—what we now call Crawford Notch.

The discovery of the notch was an early turning point in White Mountain history because it opened up a direct trade route between the upper valley of the Connecticut River and the New Hampshire seacoast. Settlers built a rudimentary road through the notch—a road so rough and steep that teamsters had to use ropes to haul horses and wagons through. But as rough as the road was, it successfully opened up trade between the interior of New Hampshire and the coast. With improved transportation, settlements could begin to take root in the upper Connecticut Valley. Gradually but inexorably, the first settlers of these towns cut trees, built permanent structures, and cultivated the land, initiating the gradual process of establishing European-American civilization.

Before long, towns dotted the edges of the mountains: Suncook, Pennacook, and Boscawen to the south; and Lyme, Orford, Haverhill, Lancaster, and Northumberland in the Coos intervales on the upper Connecticut River.[60] One of the biggest problems these newborn towns faced was their isolation, and to connect them to the more settled regions to the south, enterprising pioneers began to build roads through the dense forests. The process of road building radically changed the landscape of the White Mountain wilderness. The wilderness would never disappear, but forever after, it would be crisscrossed by roads and divided into parcels, resulting in a fragmentation of the landscape that would have a major impact on the forest ecosystem.

Even as civilization was beginning to transform the valleys of the White Mountain in the 1760s and 1770s, though, the mountains remained forbiddingly wild. Almost as soon as the American Revolution ended, the Reverend Jeremy Belknap and the Reverend Manasseh Cutler led the first scientific expedition into the mountains in 1784 for the purpose of studying their geology, botany, zoology, and climate. These two ministers' extended journey was another turning point in the early history of the White Mountains because it began the long process of creating an awareness of the scientific value of wilderness.

The expedition commenced in Ipswich, Massachusetts, on Monday, July 19, 1784, when five men with a keen interest in collecting scientific data about the young nation gathered at the home of Reverend Cutler, the minister of the local Congregational Church. Cutler was joined by Dr. Joshua Fisher, a highly respected scientist and doctor from nearby Beverly who was the president of the Massachusetts Medical Society. Rounding out the party were a Mr. Heard, a Mr. Hubbard, and a Mr. Bartlett. These five rode horseback to Dover, New Hampshire, where, on July 20, they joined the other members of the expedition, including the Reverend Daniel Little, a minister from Kennebunk, Maine; and Dr. Belknap, the minister of the First Congregational Church in Dover. The magisterial Reverend Belknap was a minister, a biographer, and the author of *The History of New Hampshire*. Dr. Belknap, who was driven by a wide-ranging scientific curiosity, had planned the expedition with Cutler.

After leaving Dover on the morning of July 21, the party reached the town of Rochester, where they were joined by a Mr. Wingate and hired a guide named

1.5. Rev. Jeremy Belknap. In his *History of New Hampshire,* published in three volumes from 1784 to 1792, Belknap penned vivid descriptions of the White Mountains. Rev. Manasseh Cutler and he led an expedition into the Whites in 1784 that initiated scientific exploration of the region. New Hampshire Historical Society.

Mr. Place to lead them into the mountains.[61] They continued northward, reaching Conway, where they met up with Colonel Joseph Whipple, who owned a sizable farm in Dartmouth (now Jefferson). Also joining the party as a guide was Captain John Evans, who had managed the construction of a rudimentary road through Pinkham Notch in 1774 and had climbed Mount Washington twice. At 8:15 on the morning of July 23, the party set out on the final stage of their journey. As they traveled, Mr. Whipple drew a map of their route, which Reverend Belknap would later copy and include in the *Journal of a Tour to the White Mountains in July 1784,* his account of the expedition.

Finally they arrived at a meadow near the head of the Ellis River, where the Appalachian Mountain Club's Pinkham Notch Visitor Center is found today. From this site, they looked admiringly upon "two very high peaks and several ridges, one of which was bare"—the Presidential Range.[62] The members of the party arose early on Saturday morning, July 24, and set out at 6:15 to climb the Great Mountain (which would not officially be named Mount Washington until 1792). As they ascended, Reverend Cutler observed closely and wrote detailed descriptions of the landscape. They climbed first through a woods that consisted, in Cutler's words, of "spruce, hemlock, pine, beech, etc., I suppose more than 100 feet." They came to a mountain stream, where, the reverend noted, "The stones in this river were curious, containing talc, starry appearances, and many very light, but we have not time to examine them critically."[63]

1.6. Rev. Manasseh Cutler. Cutler was originally from Killingly, Conn., where he developed an interest in botany. He kept a detailed journal of the 1784 expedition into the White Mountains, including the earliest descriptions we have of flora and of geological formations on Mt. Washington. New Hampshire Historical Society.

They found the climbing to be arduous, and halfway through the morning, two of the men turned back. Dr. Fisher, "finding a pain in his side, which disabled him, returned to the camp, where Mr. Whipple's negro man attended to take care of the horses and baggage."[64] A little later, Dr. Belknap began to labor because of his weight and the effects of an accident he had suffered the day before; he also returned to the camp. Eventually the remaining members of the party reached the timberline, where Reverend Cutler wrote the first recorded observations of alpine plant life on Mount Washington, noting, "The mountain above the shrubs has the appearance of a close-fed pasture, with many detached rocks rising above the surface. As we advanced we found it to be a mere mass of rocks, covered with a mat of long moss, their crevices and between them filled up with various kinds of vegetables."[65]

Reverend Cutler was the professor on this tour, leading his scholars in studying the plants closely, feeling their textures, even tasting them. He noted the effects that the severe mountain weather had had on the vegetation at the high elevation and described what is now called krummholz:

Among the rocks were spruces about three or four inches high, which had been perhaps growing several thousand years to obtain this height; the winds and snows have kept their tops even with the surface of the rocks, which made them appear as through they had been mowed; and they were sufficiently firm to support us as we walked upon them.[66]

When they had climbed to the upper reaches of the mountain, they came to a plain, where the degree of ascent eased, and there they experienced the extreme instability of the weather on Mountain Washington. Clouds rolled in, which Dr. Cutler described vividly: "Large columns rise . . . until they reach a colder and rarer region of the air, when they spread horizontally and descend to the regions below."[67] The group continued, and at 11:32 that morning, they gained the summit. From there, they climbed to what Cutler called "the pinnace of the Sugar-loaf."[68] According to Laura and Guy Waterman, the first "summit" was probably either Boott Spur or Lion's Head, while the "Sugar-loaf" was the actual dome-shaped summit of the mountain.[69] The sun emerged from the clouds, and a thrill coursed through Reverend Cutler as he observed the astonishing vista and noted the variety of landforms visible: "At the summit we had an extensive view N.E., N., and N.W. In these directions the plain was not so level, several mountains towered [above] . . . and seemed to vie with those we were ascending, but still were far below them, and our field of view exceedingly extensive."[70]

Clouds quickly reenveloped them, so the party ate dinner and hoped that the weather would clear so that they could take measurements with the sextant and other instruments. By now it was midafternoon. The clouds had not dissipated, the temperature was plummeting, and they decided to start their descent immediately. Much to their chagrin, though, the guides informed them that they could not locate the route down the mountain. Moreover, the clouds made it impossible to see more than a few feet ahead. The guides argued among themselves about which direction to take until finally the expedition's leaders insisted that they settle on a route. For an hour they descended, but the route led to "a very steep precipice"—probably the head of Tuckerman Ravine.[71]

Captain Evans, alarmed that the party would not be able to reach the bottom of the precipice safely, told the group to stay in place while he crept ahead to reconnoiter. In a matter of moments, though, he was swallowed up completely by the cloud bank, and after a considerable amount of time, he still had not returned. Fearing the worst, one of the party called out to Evans as loudly as he could, but there was no answer. By now the clouds had cleared enough that they could see far below them, and the sight filled Cutler with terror: "As far as I could see below was a most horrid precipice, and it now appeared to me that no person could go any further without great hazard of his life."[72] Mr. Whipple then lowered himself a short distance below the group

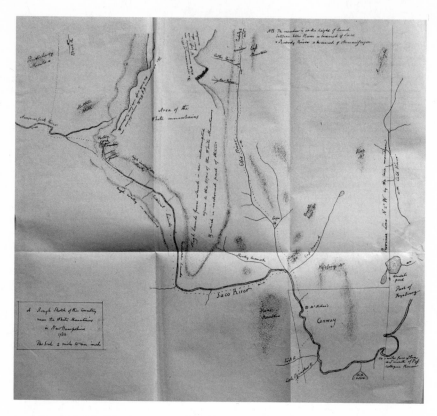

1.7. *A Rough Sketch of the Country near the White Mountains in New Hampshire, 1784*. Rev. Jeremy Belknap drew this detailed sketch of the route that the Belknap-Cutler expedition followed in 1784. The map shows how sparsely settled the region was. Courtesy of Dartmouth College Library.

and shouted "very loud several times"—and finally Evans answered.[73] He yelled that he had fallen and slid down on his back for several hundred feet but had finally caught hold of the rocks with his axe and stopped himself. By some miracle, he had escaped injury. Evans let them know that he would descend one more precipice and enter the woods below. But he warned them not to follow him, for the precipice was far too hazardous.

At this point, Reverend Cutler's journal breaks off, but, fortunately, Jeremy Belknap narrates the rest of the episode in his *History*. The party climbed back up to the plain, and from there, they slowly wound their way down the eastern side of the mountain, reached the upper borders of the woods, and rejoined Evans. Relieved yet exhausted, they set up camp for the night.[74] When they awoke, it was Sunday, July 25, six days into their journey. That day, they finally reached the bottom of the mountain and reunited with Dr. Belknap and Dr. Fisher at the base camp. Shaken by their ordeal, the party set off the next morning for Mr. Whipple's farm in Dartmouth, where they rested. Finally, on Wednesday, July 28, after nine exhausting days in the wilderness, the members of the expedition parted ways. Belknap and Cutler headed south toward the Notch of the Mountains, while Dr. Fisher stayed behind to gather bird, animal, and plant specimens.

When Dr. Belknap reached the notch, he knew immediately that he had entered a region of unparalleled beauty, and he responded with awe and reverence: "At the Notch [is] a meadow," he enthused, "through which a brook runs into Saco River. This meadow, surrounded on all sides with mountains, some of them perpendicular, is a singularly romantic and picturesque scene."[75] As they descended through the notch, he observed that the Saco River was "surrounded by rocks, which on one side, are perpendicular, and on the other, rise in an angle of forty-five degrees—a strikingly picturesque scene!"[76] They continued south through the notch for eight to ten miles and lodged that evening in Bartlett, bringing to an end their historic expedition into the White Mountains. Writing later about his passage through the notch, Belknap celebrated the sheer gorgeousness of the landscape. "Almost everything in nature," he wrote, "which can be supposed capable of inspiring ideas of the sublime and beautiful, is here realized. Aged mountains, stupendous elevations, rolling clouds, impending rocks, verdant woods, chrystal streams, the gentle rill, and the roaring torrent, all conspire to amaze, to soothe, and to enrapture."[77]

With their close observations and passionate response to the beauty of the vistas, the Belknap-Cutler expedition began to establish the idea that the White Mountains had intrinsic value for scientific and aesthetic reasons. Reverend Cutler was the first traveler into the Whites to describe the alpine environment, noting the diminishing heights of the spruce and hemlock, the appearance of the short shrubs that we call krummholz, and the lichen. In his meteorological observations, he provided an accurate accounting of the instability of the weather conditions and vivid descriptions of the cloud formations. At the same time, Dr. Belknap's vivid descriptions of the mountains conveyed intense feelings about their beauty. During this expedition, its two leaders reflected a confluence of scientific interest and aesthetic response that would come to full fruition in the next century, when the White Mountains would achieve national significance as a unique wilderness ecosystem and as symbols of America's wondrous natural beauties.

Chapter 2

FIRST SETTLERS AND THE
TAMING OF THE WILDERNESS

I N ROYALSTON, MASSACHUSETTS, in the early spring of 1794, Lot Woodbury and his wife and young children were saying their final farewells to
friends and family, for they were about to embark on the long journey to
establish a home in Lloyd's Hill, a new town in the northern wilderness of the
White Mountains that would eventually change its name to Bethlehem. Lot
had piled all their prized possessions onto a sled, which his team of oxen would
pull through the snow. Slowly the young family, which included the two-
year-old twins, Zariah and Oliver, and the newborn baby, Asa, made their way
north through the well-established towns of Massachusetts and southern
New Hampshire.

As they traveled north, the towns grew sparser, and the stretches of forest
grew lengthier. Lot undoubtedly pondered the dangers posed by the wilderness that he and his family were entering—predators on the prowl for livestock, extremes of temperature, the threat of starvation in their first or second year in the north country. Finally the oxen entered a shallow valley and
then strained to haul the laden sled up the hill toward the settlement, which
could not yet be called a town. The family arrived at the cabin of Jonas Warren, who had generously offered to allow the Woodburys to live with his family until Lot could construct a log cabin of his own. Jonas was one of only a
few who had settled so far at Lloyd's Hill; the others were Benjamin Brown
and James Turner.[1]

After the French and Indian War ended in 1763, hundreds of settlers like
Lot Woodbury were attracted by the availability of cheap land and began mi-
grating north to the White Mountains to carve out a living from an often inhospitable environment. These first settlers were determined to fulfill the
extraordinary promise of the New Hampshire interior that Sir Ferdinando
Gorges had first promoted 150 years before. In the years since, explorers had
established a basic geographic understanding of the region, surveyors had measured and apportioned the land, axe men had begun to build roads and other
infrastructure, a logging industry had been established on the basis of the
mast trade, and the colonial military had forced most of the Abenaki from

their lands, though some native people continued to inhabit the region. Now, first settlers like Lot Woodbury were poised to take advantage of the land's potential and to bring European-American civilization to the wilderness. Propelled by an instrumental view of the land and dreams of economic self-sufficiency, they began to transform the White Mountain environment by clearing land, planting crops, building homes and barns, constructing dams and bridges, and building roads. Examining how the first settlers went about creating this civilization and analyzing the patterns of settlement that emerged are critical to understanding the evolution of the White Mountain wilderness over the next two hundred years.

As these early settlers established their foothold in the northern forest, two patterns emerged in how they interacted with the mountain environment. First, they used economic practices that were based on a perception of unlimited abundance of natural resources, particularly of land, timber, water, and wildlife. Their perception of plenitude was understandable, for they could gaze upon mile after mile of unbroken forest and walk along streams of ample, pure water. Yet the assumption of abundance would eventually have negative long-term effects on the mountain ecosystem when it led to environmentally harmful practices, including deforestation and the pollution of rivers.

Second, the first settlers created what environmental historian William Cronon has called, in his book *Changes in the Land,* "a patchwork quilt" that transformed the appearance of the White Mountain landscape, particularly its valleys.[2] There, the settlers created a pastoral countryside that slowly but inexorably encroached upon the mountain wilderness. By building roads and canals, cultivating crops, and putting up houses and barns, they domesticated significant parts of the region, so that what remained of the mountain wilderness existed in an uneasy relationship with the towns and farms.

While the motivation for settlers to migrate to the White Mountains was primarily economic, they were attracted also by the beauty of the land. For example, to the early settlers of Tamworth, the area looked, in the words of a town historian, "formidable but promising"—a region of thick forests, rivers and streams, ponds, lakes, and "here and there a savannah of grass meadow."[3] In *The Early History of the Town of Bethlehem, New Hampshire,* published in 1883, the Reverend Simeon Bolles wrote that the town's first settlers admired the "beautiful scenes of forests and flowers, its rippling streams and natural water power, productive soil and purity of never-failing springs."[4]

In spite of the settlers' awareness of the region's beauty, though, their concerns remained overwhelmingly practical—how to build shelter for their families, how to plant crops to produce a significant yield before the first winter, how to cut enough wood to warm themselves, how to treat the inevitable illnesses that would run through the family, how to kill wild animals and pre-

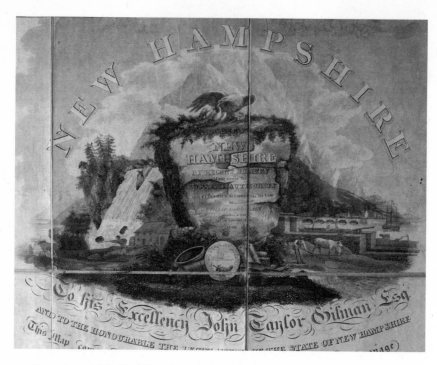

2.1. Carrigain map: title. The title treatment of Philip Carrigain's 1816 map of New Hampshire highlights settlement in the region, including scenes of farming and hunting. Nature, though, is very much present, as reflected in the images of the waterfall and the looming mountains.
Courtesy of Dartmouth College Library.

serve meat for the long winter. Underlying these practical concerns, though, was a heartfelt commitment to bring civilization to the wilderness. A straight line of continuity runs from the planters and Puritans of the early 1600s to these first settlers of the late 1700s—an ideology that assumed the necessity to master nature. Dr. Timothy Dwight, the president of Yale College, journeyed throughout New Hampshire in 1797 and 1803 and, in his classic *Travels in New-England and New-York,* urged a rapid carving of civilization from the wilds of the state's forests and mountains. "In so vast an expansion," he wrote, "the eye perceives a prevalence of forest . . . and instinctively demands a wider extent of smiling scenes, and a more general establishment of the cheerful haunts of men."[5] He eagerly anticipated the day when "at a little distance, the hills, and plains, and valleys around me will be stripped of the forests, which now majestically, and even gloomily, overshadow them; and be measured out into farms, enlivened with all the beauties of cultivation."[6]

As if to heed Reverend Dwight's exhortations, the first settlers quickly set about establishing institutions of civilization. They founded town govern-

2.2. Dr. Timothy Dwight. Dr. Timothy Dwight, the president of Yale College, traveled throughout New Hampshire in 1797 and 1803 and wrote *Travels in New-England and New-York*, in which he described the impact that cutting trees was having on the landscape of New Hampshire. The Granger Collection, New York.

ments, established churches, and set up schools. The early town records of Bethlehem show that all the early settlers played key roles in the town's government, serving as the town's selectmen, tax collectors, and highway surveyors. At a town meeting on March 4, 1800, Lot Woodbury was elected as the town's fence viewer, an important office because he ensured that the village's citizens kept their fences repaired so that livestock could not escape and trample neighbors' fields and gardens.[7] At the next town meeting, Lot was the moderator, and the town's citizens appropriated money for building roads and bridges.[8] The settlers were directly involved in building and shaping their young town, continuing the tradition of town meeting government that thrives to this day in New England.

In addition to establishing local government, the first settlers apportioned the land, creating Cronon's "patchwork quilt." Land in the valleys was divided into a rectangular mosaic of specialized uses: cultivated fields; grazing pastures; lots for residences; roads; bridges; and towns with main streets for churches, schools, and businesses.[9] These farming communities resembled orderly English villages. Cronon explained, "[T]he English believed in and required permanent settlements. Once a village was established, its improvements—cleared fields, pastures, buildings, fences, and so on—were regarded as more or less fixed features of the landscape."[10] This pattern was exactly the one followed by founders of towns in the White Mountain region. The towns they established and the infrastructure they created, such as roads, canals, and bridges, were intended to be durable fixtures of the landscape.

The goal of permanence had been evident even in the way the British Crown had granted charters for settlement in northern New Hampshire. After the English defeated the French in 1763, King George III wanted the northern part of the province of New Hampshire to be permanently settled so that its forests and rich soil would become productive and generate taxes for the royal treasury. One obvious resource was the region's numerous white pines; because agents of the Crown had already cut the easily transportable white pines in southern New Hampshire, the agents moved north to cut pines in the White Mountains and float them down the Saco River to Portsmouth, where they were loaded onto ships specially equipped to transport the enormous logs to England.

To tap this and other resources, Governor Benning Wentworth and his son and successor, John Wentworth, made a rapid succession of grants for the White Mountain region: Fryeburg (1762), Lancaster (1763), Plymouth (1763), Warren (1763), Lisbon (1763 and again in 1768), Franconia (1764), Littleton (1764), Conway (1765), Dartmouth (later Jefferson, 1765), Berlin (1771), Bretton Woods (later Carroll, 1772), Durand (later Randolph, 1772), Jackson (1778), Bartlett (1790), Bethlehem (1799), and Whitefield (1804). Every charter required the grantees, or proprietors, to fulfill certain conditions or risk forfeiting the charter, and all the conditions were meant to ensure that the settlements would be permanent.

The grant for the town of Durand, which later became Randolph, was typical. The settlers had to build a road three rods wide so that carriages could pass; six families had to settle there by January 1774; six years after that, at least sixty families were required to have settled. The town's citizens were supposed to reserve for the Royal Navy all the pine trees that were suitable for masts. The settlers had to reserve a tract of land near the center of the township for four-acre lots, of which each grantee received one.[11] Because granting residential lots was central to successful settlement, surveying the land became critical. Early deeds referred to topographical features to demarcate property, but later on, professional surveyors measured more precise property boundaries.[12] The final two provisions of the grant entailed payments by the grantees. They were required to pay one ear of Indian corn in rent to the King by January 1776, and by January 1, 1782, each settler had to pay to the King's representative one shilling for each one hundred acres owned. During this time, of course, the American Revolution intervened, rendering moot the provisions of the grant.[13]

When settlers like Lot Woodbury decided to brave the harsh conditions, they were doing so primarily in the hope of improving their standard of living, which depended on eventually developing goods that they could trade for a profit. They needed to learn about the soil conditions, the climate, the sources of water, and the predators that might threaten their crops. Yet even as they were gaining knowledge about the land, they were beginning to modify it into a pastoral landscape. The first thing they did, for instance, was to build a log cabin by cutting down the trees in part of the tract, stripping the limbs and branches and notching the ends so that the logs would fit together snugly. Then they "rolled up" each log over the previous one and drove in wooden pins to keep them in place.[14] They constructed the roof with poles and bark from the trees, leaving an open hole for smoke to escape. These makeshift roofs were sometimes less than totally effective, as shown by the experience of Samuel Knight of Warren. After Samuel married Mary Merrill in March of 1784, the newlyweds moved into his cabin, where they could lie in bed at night and study the stars through the gaps in the roof.[15]

The interior of the cabin was plainness itself—a single room without a floor, a window without any kind of decorations, and a door built of small poplar or maple logs that were hewn flat.[16] Later, once the settlers became more established, they built a chimney of stones and short logs. But even when the cabin was finished, it was completely isolated, and the family found itself surrounded by wilderness. In writing the history of Warren, William Little described the utter isolation of the typical homestead; it was surrounded by "one unbroken forest, in which roamed free the stately moose and nimble deer, and was heard the cry of the gaunt wolf—the sullen growls of the bear—the low and heavy sound of the partridge."[17]

Once the settlers had built a rudimentary cabin, they turned to the backbreaking work of clearing trees and stones so that they could plow and sow seeds for their first crops. They burned the tree roots or used oxen to pull the trunks from the ground; oxen were also indispensable in hauling away boulders, which the farmers used to build walls, further compartmentalizing the land. However, not all settlers owned animals to perform the heavy work; some did it themselves. Jon Remick, who settled in Bretton Woods, was reputed to have cut and corded one hundred cords of wood in twenty-five days—even though he weighed only a hundred pounds.[18]

When planting, the settlers learned to identify the qualities of soil that were associated with different trees. Hickory, maple, ash, and beech had moist soil beneath them, indicating the presence of black humus, which was ideal for planting. Oaks and chestnuts were more spread out from one another, allowing more sunlight to reach the ground and causing the soil to be drier and thinner, which required the settlers to invest more labor to prepare the land for crops. Conifers grew in sandy, acidic soil, which was poor for farming.[19]

After clearing the land, the settlers usually planted corn, which they sowed in late March, April, or May.[20] Other important crops were wheat, oats, barley, rye, and vegetables. Settlers who arrived in the spring sometimes cut trees, burned the stumps, and then, around the stumps, planted rye, turnip seeds, and pumpkins.[21] For clothing, they grew flax, which they spun into linen. All these crops, though, required a year or two to become firmly established, and families would often have to turn to fishing and hunting for protein to get them through the first winter. Even then, provisions might run out in late winter, at which point they would turn for help to neighbors or to Abenaki people who remained in the area.

As time passed, more farmers began to raise livestock because both meat and milk were profitable commodities.[22] Sheep were also profitable, as families could use wool for their own clothing or for sale or trade, giving it value as a commodity. However, in the early nineteenth century, the rising numbers of livestock caused significant changes in the mountain ecosystem. Livestock required two to ten times as much land as the cultivation of crops to produce equivalent amounts of nutrition, so the creation of pasturage led settlers to fell more trees in the surrounding forests.[23] In pastures used for grazing, grass, clover, buttercups, and weeds replaced trees and native grasses.[24] Grazing animals also prevented new trees from taking root because the beasts ate the shoots of young trees and trampled the soil, making it more difficult for the seeds of trees to germinate.[25] Thus, the establishment of farms initiated a reduction in the region's forests that would accelerate as the population of the region grew and as forest products such as lumber and firewood became more valuable as marketable commodities.

Raising livestock had another ecological consequence, as William Cronon explained: "Plowing destroyed all native plant species to create an entirely new habitat populated mainly by domesticated species, and so in some sense represented the most complete ecological transformation of a New England landscape."[26] Cronon explained that when farmers plowed the earth and sowed crops, soils that had been embedded in the earth came to the surface and were exposed to water and air, causing the organic components of the soil to lose nutrients.[27] In addition, plowed fields and tamped-down pasturelands did not hold water nearly as well as did forest soils, which were springy and absorbent beneath the forest canopy. As a result, cultivated lands experienced greater water runoff during rainstorms, causing soil erosion. Moreover, raising corn to the exclusion of other crops exhausted the soil until farmers learned to rotate crops and plant other types of crops, particularly legumes, which restored nutrients to the soil.[28] The impact of all of these changes— cutting timber, plowing, raising livestock, planting domesticated species—was not evident at first, but by the 1840s and 1850s, observers in the White Mountains noted the increased frequency of flooding, soil erosion, and the buildup of sediment in streams and rivers.

Raising livestock also transformed the mountain landscape in another highly visible way—through the building of fences. In the early years, settlers often did not have the time or resources to build fences, and livestock were allowed to graze throughout the countryside. The farmers marked their animals to indicate ownership. For instance, in the town of Warren, Obadiah Clement marked his sheep with one half crop on the upper side of the right ear and another half crop on the underside of the left ear; Joshua Merrill gave his animals a crop on each ear; and Stevens Merrill marked his animals with a fork like a swallow's tail on the bottom of the left ear.[29]

Before the building of fences became common, animals sometimes wandered off and became lost. The solution to such problems clearly was to erect fences, which soon began to crisscross the countryside. Fences organized the valleys into clearly defined parcels, a far cry from the original wilderness with its continuous forests interspersed with occasional savannas. Moreover, the network of fences reinforced the fact that the society was organized around the individual family, with each farm a self-sufficient unit that included its own house, barn, garden, cultivated field, and pasture.[30] The fences became ubiquitous symbols that the settlers had successfully wrested their turf from the wilderness and organized it for maximum productivity and order.

Fences were far from the only human-built infrastructure that was transforming the White Mountain wilderness into a pastoral countryside. Settlers were putting up sawmills and gristmills, plotting and constructing roads, digging canals, and expanding their villages into towns. The first piece of sophisticated technology that almost every town acquired was a sawmill, which was essential to a town's economy because it allowed the local residents to transform the wilderness's most plentiful resource, trees, into a tradable commodity, lumber. In Franconia, for example, Luke Brooks built an "up and down" sawmill on Coppermine Brook, on the eastern side of the Franconia Range. During the winter, Brooks cut down trees and slid them over the snow to his mill, where he stored them to await cutting. Sawmills became so important to local economies that towns sometimes offered a bounty to anyone who would build and operate one. The proprietors of Warren, for example, offered Joshua Copp a bounty of thirty pounds to build a sawmill, which he did on Black Brook.[31]

In the late 1700s and early 1800s, the lumber economy of northern New England expanded quickly. Although the Revolution had brought an end to the mast trade with England, American shipbuilders still demanded white pines, as well as white oaks for planking and black oaks for hulls. House builders used cedar for shingles, clapboard, and fence posts because the wood resisted termites and other insects.[32] Families could reap tidy profits by cutting trees they did not need and selling them to local sawmills. Doing so had

2.3. Artist's conception of sawmill, Carroll. A key piece of technology in the economic development of the northern forest was the water-powered sawmill. Some towns offered bounties to attract entrepreneurs to build sawmills. Twin Mountain Bretton Woods Historical Society.

the added economic advantage of opening up more land for cultivation and pasturage.[33] A spin-off product from trees was potash, which was an essential ingredient in making soap and gunpowder. As early as 1717, a farmer could clear the trees from four acres of land, burn the wood to make eight tons of potash, and sell the potash for anywhere from forty to sixty pounds—a nice profit, since the trees had cost the farmer only the price that he had paid for the land.[34]

The supply of trees seemed nearly infinite to the settlers, but as early as 1803, Timothy Dwight observed that tree harvesting in New Hampshire's forests might go too far. As he rode toward Lebanon in September of that year, he observed, "After ascending the brow of the hill, we found another plain, extending several miles to the north, of an irregular surface, and beautifully covered with white pines. Unhappily a great part of them have been since cut down. There is reason to fear, that this noblest of all vegetable productions will be unknown, in its proper size and splendor, to the future inhabitants of New-England."[35]

Even as early as 1820, the reduction of the forests was beginning to affect the climate of the region. Before settlement, the forest canopy had been nearly continuous, and winds had been moderate because there had been few open fields in which they could gather force. But as settlers logged tracts of land, the winds had open spaces in which to gain momentum, making their bite more bitter during the long winters. In addition, the thick canopy of virgin forests had kept the soils moist, but as trees were cut, the canopy thinned out, allowing more sunlight to reach the ground and dry out the soil, which absorbed more heat. As a result, the land was hotter during the summer but was also colder during the winter. In the early 1800s, such effects were minimal in the White Mountains because large stretches of the forest canopy remained, but as the century unfolded, as farms grew more numerous, as towns expanded, the forest canopy shrank, causing the region's temperatures to fluctuate more widely.[36]

Another technology that helped to transform the White Mountain landscape was gristmills, which made the growing of grains increasingly important to the local economy. Towns sometimes offered bounties to attract entrepreneurs who would build gristmills. In Warren, for instance, Captain William Butler built a gristmill on the Baker River after town leaders offered him a bounty. The settlers brought their grains there and waited as the waterwheels turned the huge millstones and ground the grain into meal and flour.[37] Families then used the meal and the flour for their own cooking needs, but they also sold it to merchants at a profit.

Although agriculture and the lumber industry were the two most important economic activities in the White Mountains, several other industries developed that left their imprint on the mountain environment. The early settlers of Franconia discovered iron ore in the 1790s, providing the impetus for early industrial growth in the western ranges of the White Mountains.[38] One iron foundry was built about a mile from the town's center and came to be known as the Upper Works. In 1805, the New Hampshire Iron Foundry Company built another foundry, called the Lower Works, near the Sugar Hill Bridge.[39] The company's blacksmith shop manufactured a dizzying array of products that were much in demand—box stoves, axes, kettles, stoves, frying pans, nails, horseshoes, and drills.[40] After fire destroyed the Upper Works in 1827, though, its owners declined to rebuild, because the cost of extracting the ore and shipping finished goods was prohibitive.[41] The Franconia area also had copper mines, and silver and lead were found on Cannon Mountain but were never mined, again because of the expense of transportation.[42]

As the economy of northern New England diversified, roads became more and more essential to trade and transportation. They gave shape to the classic New England town, connecting the sawmill and gristmill, which were the economic lifeblood of the town, to the merchants and residences in the town center and to the farms on the outskirts. Wentworth, at the junction of the Baker River and Pond Brook, followed this organizational pattern. We know

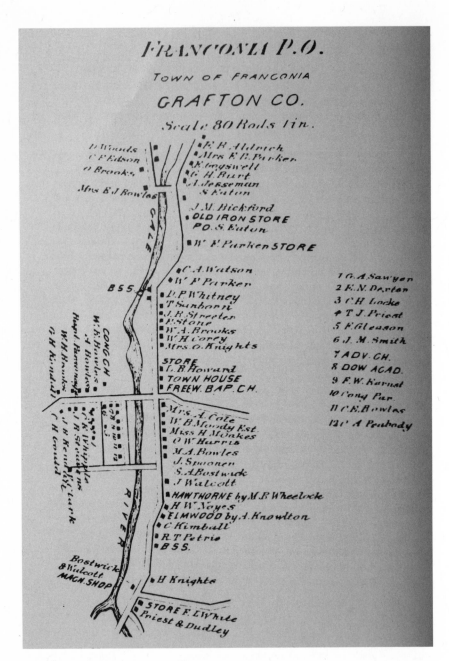

2.4. Franconia Village, ca. 1860. This early map of Franconia shows how the development of towns in the White Mountains was affected by geography. The town stretched along the Gale River, with residences, stores, the Free Baptist Church, and the Town House located along the river. The Old Iron Store reflected the fact that Franconia had nearby iron ore deposits and iron foundries. To the west, across the river, were the Congregational Church and more residences.

Franconia Heritage Museum.

a great deal about Wentworth because Peter L. Hoyt, a local doctor, wrote a town history that he updated regularly until his death in 1871. He was fortunate enough to talk to several of Wentworth's first settlers before they passed away, and from them he created a portrait of the town's early development. According to Dr. Hoyt, "From 1815 to 1820 several houses were erected around the Common, the place began to assume quite a Village-like appearance, and was usually spoke [*sic*] of throughout the town as '*the City*'; 'going to the city'; 'What is the news at the city.'"[43] Gradually Wentworth gained more businesses and services. A lawyer established a practice in the town in 1814, and between 1812 and 1816, two tradesmen built stores in different parts of the village.[44] These developments created complex economic and social interactions and a solid sense that a durable civilization had been established in the shadows of the mountains, which remained heavily forested.

Roads connected the mountain towns to one another to form a transportation web that promoted commerce. In 1803, the town of Warren decided to construct a road to Haverhill Corner, located along the Connecticut River. The town contracted with different individuals to build short sections, and even though construction took several years and cost the considerable sum of $15,074, this road eventually connected Warren to the river. Such avenues of transportation were critical to opening up the White Mountains to population growth and the shipping of commodities to points south. They also made it much easier for outsiders to travel into the mountains.

Even as the first settlers were constructing roads and the other infrastructures of civilization, they were confronting the most fearsome threat of the wilderness—such wild beasts as wolves, lynx, and bears. Numerous stories from the period underscore the hatred that first settlers felt toward predators. In the 1780s, for example, Samuel Knight of the town of Warren was chopping wood alone in the forest when a powerful thunderstorm came up. Drenched and cold, he began to make his way home, but after wading across a swollen brook, he suddenly heard a deep growl behind him. Turning around, he watched with horror as a bear rushed him, rose onto its rear paws, and clawed him with its forepaws. Knight desperately freed his right arm, pulled out his knife, pried it open with his teeth, and stabbed the bear in the side, piercing the bear's heart and causing the animal to fall to the ground "in a mad frenzy" and die.[45] Even though Knight had been clawed badly, he was able to stagger home. Next morning, he returned with neighbors to the location of the bear attack and realized that the bear had been nursing cubs. There is no evidence, however, that he felt any remorse over the orphaning of the offspring.[46]

Knight's encounters with bears were far from over. He had planted a field of corn that bears kept invading and eating. Fearing that he would lose his entire crop, he and a neighbor set off at dusk with their guns to kill the offending predators. As they waited behind the root of an upturned tree, two or three bears approached in the dark. Knight fired and wounded one of the bears, and the others fled, but the animal that Knight had shot now attacked him, and Knight used the butt of his gun to fend it off. As he struggled with the animal, he hollered for the neighbor to hurry up and shoot, but the man turned and fired wildly, hitting only the ground. Knight kept struggling with the bear until finally it succumbed from Knight's initial shot. When he angrily asked the neighbor why he had not fired, the man answered, "I ain't used to these running fires."[47] Apparently, not all pioneers were equipped with the quick wits and steady shot required to fend off wild beasts and to establish humanity's hegemony over wild nature.

Towns went to supreme lengths to rid the surrounding forests of wolves, paying bounties to hunters who set traps or shot wolves and brought in their heads as evidence of success.[48] If a pack of wolves harassed a town, citizens formed a posse to hunt them down. In 1830, Tamworth organized a "Siege of Wolves," in which six hundred men from the town and surrounding communities came together to drive wolves into an area that had been roped off, where the men planned to destroy them all. The townspeople managed to kill a number of wolves, but a greater number raced through the ropes and escaped into the mountains, leading a local historian who recorded the episode to note wryly, "There is no record as to the number of casualties that the confusion wrought among the hunters."[49]

Sometimes even the power of Christian faith was reputed to fend off wolves. In the town of Randolph, John Morse—"a man of energy and sterling character"—owned a sawmill and a gristmill on Cold Brook. When an itinerant preacher led local religious revivals in 1817 and 1818, Morse was overwhelmed by the call to spread the word of God. He was ordained as a minister but continued to work at his mill, where he would plan out his sermons as he cut lumber. One night, after preaching in East Jefferson, he was walking home along the Cherry Mountain road when a wolf ambled out of the forest, sat down in front of him, and, according to the story, "smiled at the traveler." Elder Morse returned the smile and then stared steadily and fearlessly into the blazing yellow eyes of the wolf. A minute passed, then another, until finally the wolf "slunk away among the trees." Faith had defeated the wild forces of the forest.[50]

Such stories about controlling predatory animals became part of the lore of settling the White Mountains. In the histories of early settlement, one is struck by the frequency and violence of human encounters with wild beasts. The narratives that tell of these encounters reflect a fascination with the physical details of battles, heightening the dangers that the first settlers faced. Perhaps even more important, such narratives dramatize the power that humanity established over wild nature and celebrate the heroism of the early settlers, conferring mythic status on them by enhancing their exploits and memorializing the courage that paved the way for the establishment of civilization.

Whether the settlers were facing down predators or hunting game for food, the impact was to reduce dramatically the population of predators and large fauna in the White Mountain region. Take moose as a prime example, which settlers aggressively hunted for food. In the spring of 1803, Joseph Patch and Stephen Flanders, Jr., of Warren were hunting moose along the Baker River. They spied the tracks of several moose and tracked them through the forest until they caught up with them and shot them. According to local historian William Little, these turned out to be the last moose in the area, and Little concluded wistfully, "Thus perished the last of that race of animals, . . . so many of which at one time roamed in the valleys around Moosehillock mountain."[51] The shooting of those moose occurred early in the 1800s, showing how quickly settlers had established hegemony over the White Mountain wilderness.

Impelled by the same instrumentalist perspective toward the land that had guided the first explorers and colonizers, the settlers of the White Mountains had taken practical steps to meet their economic needs by establishing towns and farms in the region's valleys, and they had done so with remarkable speed and efficiency. They set up beachheads in the wilderness with simple log cabins and small cultivated fields and then pressed their advantage by organizing towns, erecting houses and barns and sheds, putting up fences, and building roads and bridges. In 1803, Timothy Dwight had written hopefully of the time when "the hills, and plains, and valleys around me will be stripped of the forests" and would "be measured out into farms, enlivened with all the beauties of cultivation."[52] By 1820, his hopes had been largely realized. Certainly much of the region was still blanketed by forests, and the mountains themselves remained wild and largely unexplored. Yet, in close proximity to those peaks of wild nature, towns and farms had taken root along the rivers and in the valleys. Gradually, the infrastructures of European-American civilization—roads, fences, houses, barns, cultivated fields, grazing pastures—were beginning to compartmentalize the White Mountain landscape and to create a pastoral landscape in which humanity had bent nature to its uses. The Puritan dream of transforming wild nature into a productive garden was coming to fruition.

Yet even as early as 1820, there were signs of potential trouble beneath the apparently serene landscape of the valleys. The creation of farms and pastureland had set in motion ecological changes that were affecting the region's soil conditions, wildlife, and climate. Settlers, small-scale sawmill operators, and outside entrepreneurs had cut swaths of forest under the assumption that the trees of the northern forest were endlessly abundant. In the mid-1800s, the economic development of the region would accelerate, and the ecological strains would become more evident. But even as these changes were occurring, a very different view of the value of wilderness was about to emerge—a view that would begin to transform how Americans interacted with the White Mountain wilderness. In this emerging paradigm, the Whites would grow into one of the most beloved landscapes in America not because of their economic resources but because of their infinitely varied beauty, the diversity of their flora and fauna, and their ability to inspire personal renewal and spiritual regeneration.

PART II

Transforming Attitudes toward Wilderness, 1820–1900

The drive toward economic development of the White Mountains competes with growing admiration for the mountains' aesthetic, scientific, recreational, and spiritual value. The Crawford family and other early settlers begin to make wild nature accessible to a growing number of travelers who look to nature for relief from the growing stresses of American society. Artists celebrate the wildest aspects of the White Mountain landscape in paintings of unsurpassed beauty, and writers create literature that glorifies the magnificence of the region's attractions. After the Civil War, grand resort hotels offer luxurious accommodations to thousands of vacationers every year. But at the same time, wilderness enthusiasts journey to the mountains in search of authentic experiences of wild nature. They found hiking clubs, build trails into the remote areas of the White Mountains, explore the farthest corners of the mountain region—and inspire a wilderness renaissance.

Chapter 3

ETHAN ALLEN CRAWFORD AND
THE WILDERNESS EXPERIENCE

E VEN AS THE FIRST SETTLERS were building towns and civilizing the
valleys of the White Mountains, a family was moving into the mountains who would have an impact on the region that was equally great
but very different in nature. That family was the Crawfords, who would forge
a relationship with the wilderness that contrasted with that of the settlers in
towns. The Crawford family migrated to the region because of its wildness, and
they began to make the wilderness experience accessible to Americans by building the first hiking trails in America, guiding visitors into the backcountry,
teaching them the ways of the woods, and establishing simple yet comfortable inns. They opened up the exhilarating experience of mountains and
wilderness—exposure that had an enormous impact by nurturing a love of
the outdoors and stimulating scientific exploration of the White Mountains.

The saga of the Crawford family in America began when James Crawford
of Ulster, Ireland, sailed to Boston in 1726 and eventually settled in Union,
Connecticut. James's third son, John, married Mary Rosebrook in 1757, and
they had eleven children, several of whom migrated north along the Connecticut River to Guildhall, Vermont. One of their sons was Abel Crawford,
born in Guildhall in 1766. Meanwhile, Eleazer Rosebrook of Grafton, Massachusetts, who was Mary Rosebrook's brother, had met Hannah Hanes of Brim-
field, Massachusetts, and in March of 1772, they were wed. Rosebrook was a
restless, self-sufficient man who was always on the search for new opportunities, and soon after the marriage, he convinced Hannah to move to the still-
wild upper Coos (Connecticut River) Valley. There, he found an attractive
spot along the river near the present-day town of Colebrook and built a log
cabin, thirty miles from the nearest neighbor.[1]

During the Revolution, Rosebrook served in the Continental Army, and
while he was away, his family relocated for reasons of safety to Northumberland and then to Guildhall, Vermont, where they stayed until the end of the
war. When Rosebrook rejoined them in Guildhall, he established a farm that
flourished because of the fertility of the land, and the family grew to four sons
and two daughters, one of whom was named Hannah, after her mother.[2] In

3.1. Abel Crawford. The patriarch of the Crawford clan, Abel Crawford, migrated to the White Mountains in the early 1790s. When Eleazar Rosebrook purchased Crawford's land at Giant's Grave, Abel moved into the Notch of the Mountains (Crawford Notch) so that he would not "be crowded by neighbors." Twin Mountain Bretton Woods Historical Society.

Guildhall, Abel Crawford and Hannah Rosebrook, who were cousins, began to court and were eventually married. Hannah Crawford soon gave birth to two sons, Erastus and Ethan Allen, who was born in 1792 in Guildhall.[3]

During this period, Abel decided to venture forth from Guildhall and search for land on which he could establish himself and his family. He came to Bretton Woods and settled at Nash and Sawyer's Location, land that the state had granted to Nash and Benjamin Sawyer for discovering the Notch of the Mountains. Soon after Nash and Sawyer had received the grant, though, they lost title to it. According to Timothy Dwight, "They were both hunters; and, with the usual thoughtlessness of men devoted to that employment, squandered the property."[4] The locale in which Abel decided to put down roots was perfect; it was nestled in the Ammonoosuc River Valley with extraordinary views of the surrounding mountains.[5]

Meanwhile, Eleazer Rosebrook was feeling restless himself, in spite of the fact that he had established a successful farm in Guildhall. He journeyed to the area where Abel had settled, and there he reached an agreement to purchase his son-in-law's plot of land. Abel, who did not want to "be crowded by neighbors," moved twelve miles south to Hart's Location, which lay toward the southern end of the notch; today the Notchland Inn is located there.[6] King George III had granted land there to Thomas Chadbourne in return for Chadbourne's service in the French and Indian War, and Richard Hart had bought it from Chadbourne for ten cents an acre. Ever since, it has been known as Hart's Location.[7]

The site was, if possible, even more stunningly beautiful than Abel's previous homestead at Nash and Sawyer's Location. On both sides, the mountains catapulted to the sky, and directly to the north were dramatic granite cliffs that watched over the valley. Along the Saco River, the bottomland was blessed with rich soil. In a short time, Hannah and the children joined Abel there, and together they poured their hearts and souls into building their farm. Their son Ethan recalled helping his father chop trees, cut underbrush, and clear away boulders in days of work that were so strenuous that "my hands would swell and pain me in the night."[8]

Meanwhile, back at Nash and Sawyer's Location, Rosebrook was building a log cabin that his family would live in for several years. In 1803, the Rosebrooks' financial fortunes took a turn for the better when the state of New Hampshire built a turnpike through the notch that connected the northern and southern parts of the state, generating an upsurge in traffic through the pass and vastly increasing trade between the upper Connecticut and the seaports of Portsmouth, Portland, and Boston. Lines of horse teams that stretched as far back as a half mile hauled all manner of goods through the notch en route to points south, while stagecoaches heading both north and south rattled their way through on the rough road.[9] Sensing an opportunity, Rosebrook built a two-story inn on a famous mound called Giant's Grave. In addition to the hostelry, he constructed a barn, a shack, stables, a sawmill, and a gristmill, and supplemented his income from the inn by farming. Rosebrook's inn was the first accommodation for travelers in the White Mountains and became an immediate success because of its location and the reputation that the Rosebrooks gained for their warm hospitality.

As Rosebrook established his innkeeping business, Abel built a productive farm at Hart's Location and opened his own inn, known as the Crawford House. His son Ethan had grown to the then-enormous height of six feet, two and a half inches, and would forever after be known as the Giant of the Hills. Renowned as much for his superhuman strength as his height, he had, according to one story, carried a five-hundred-pound barrel of salt on his back for a considerable distance.[10] In 1811, Ethan enlisted in the army and, after serving for eighteen months, migrated to the upstate New York town of Louisville, where he planned to buy property and start his own farm. At this point, though, one of the contingencies of frontier life upset his plans, for in 1816, he received an urgent letter from his grandfather Rosebrook, who had developed cancer of the lip and could no longer manage the farmwork. He asked Ethan to return and care for the inn and farm, which Rosebrook would sign over to his grandson if he agreed to help.

Ethan was reluctant to take on the responsibility of caring for his grandfather and the farm, but after injuring himself in an accident, he returned to

3.2. Carrigain map: *The Gap of the White Mountains*. Carrigain's 1816 map shows "the Gap of the White Mountains," now called Crawford Notch, as it appeared during the period when the Crawfords were settling the region. The illustration is highly stylized; the steep cliffs overwhelm the solitary traveler, accentuating the wildness of the region. Courtesy of Dartmouth College Library.

the Rosebrooks' place for a visit, and, after listening to his grandfather's entreaties, agreed to work the farm. In May of that year, a cousin of Abel's named Lucy Howe came to the house to care for her grandfather, whose health had continued to worsen. Lucy was the daughter of Samuel Howe and Mercy Rosebrook, who was Eleazer and Hannah's oldest daughter. Rosebrook passed away in September of 1817, but as Ethan and Lucy had shared the responsibilities of caring for him and managing his farm, they had come to know each other. On November 1, 1817, after a short courtship, they were married.

Ethan took possession of the farm before his grandfather's death, but he also assumed Rosebrook's mortgage and borrowed more funds to make improvements. On July 18, 1818, Lucy gave birth to their first child, but later that night, a candle that had been left burning set fire to the kitchen of the farmhouse and the fire spread rapidly, completely destroying their home. The house had not been insured, leading to a loss of three thousand dollars and making Ethan's financial situation more precarious because payments continued coming due. Undeterred, he built a new, smaller house at the same location, but the fire was the beginning of financial setbacks that would dog him for the rest of his life.[11]

As he cast about for additional income, he realized that he could earn money as a guide, because the reputation of the mountains' beauty was attracting growing numbers of travelers. That summer, as Ethan was rebuilding the house, a Bostonian named Colonel Binney and two other men approached him about guiding them into the mountains, but when they saw how preoccupied he was with rebuilding the house, they continued on to Hart's Location and hired Abel. Ethan later learned from his father that the party had encountered great difficulty in making its way through the thick forests, "sometimes crawling under a thicket of trees, sometimes over logs and windfalls"—and had never reached any of the summits. In September of that year, yet another traveling party hired Abel to lead them to the top of Mount Washington. This time they reached their goal, and at the top of the mountain, they left an inscription that read, "*Altius ibunt, qui ad summa nitunteer*"—"They will go higher who strive to enter heaven."[12]

Meanwhile, Ethan had finished building his new house, which doubled as an inn that accommodated teamsters transporting goods through the notch and travelers who wanted to tour the mountains. In May of 1819, four more men came to visit the mountains and hired Ethan as guide, but as they climbed, they "suffered considerable inconvenience by the thickness of the trees and brush, which would every now and then take hold of their clothes and stop them."[13] It was the third party that had visited the mountains in recent months, signaling that the region's reputation for natural beauty was spreading. To give travelers better access to the mountains and a more direct experience of the wilderness, Ethan and Abel decided to build a footpath through the woods and up the west side of the Presidential Range to the summit of Mount Washington. Cutting the trees and grading the trail was an exhausting task, but when they finally finished, they had created the renowned Crawford Path—the first hiking trail in the United States. Ethan advertised the path in local newspapers, and soon visitors were journeying to the mountains specifically to climb the trail and to enjoy the Crawfords' hospitality.[14]

The Crawford Path was a major milestone, for it marked the birth of wilderness experience as a recreational activity in the White Mountains. Increasing numbers of visitors used the trail, a sign that Americans were beginning to view the mountain wilderness as worthy of exploration for personal, aesthetic, and scientific reasons. As the Crawfords cleared more trails through the White Mountains, they enhanced the intrinsic value of the mountain wilderness by opening up access to it.

In 1820, Ethan served as guide and equipment carrier for a party of seven that included Adrian N. Bracket, John W. Weeks, and Charles J. Stuart. After ascending Mount Washington, they named the surrounding peaks—Adams, Jefferson, Madison, Monroe, Franklin, and Pleasant.[15] One of the members of the party was Philip Carrigain, who, in 1816, created the first definitive map of New Hampshire. Later that summer, some members of the same party returned and measured the heights of the mountains, concluding that Mount Washington rose 6,428 feet above sea level.[16] In 1822, Ethan set to work to, in his words, "see if there could not be a better and more practicable way found to ascend the mountains."[17] He cut a new, shorter trail that followed more even terrain, without all the ups and downs of the Crawford Path, to the summit of Mount Washington, following closely the route by which the cog railway would later ascend the mountain.[18]

On August 31, 1821, three women arrived in the notch to attempt to climb Mount Washington.[19] They were the Austin sisters, accompanied by their brother; by Charles J. Stewart, who was engaged to one of the sisters; and by a local farmer named Faulkner. They hired Ethan as a guide and stayed at a camp that Ethan had set up at the base of the mountain, where visitors could stay overnight and start their ascent early in the morning. The weather had turned miserable by the time they reached camp, and they decided to put up for the night and wait for improved conditions. The next morning, the weather was much improved, and the group eagerly embarked at six o'clock in the morning. By the time they summited, the weather was gorgeous, leading Ethan to exclaim, "What a beautiful sight! We could look over the whole creation with wonder and surprise, as far as the eye could extend, in every direction, and view the wonderful works of God! Every large pond and sheet of water was plain to be seen within the circuit of one hundred miles."[20] In his

3.3. Ethan Allen Crawford carries a bear. As Ethan Allen Crawford's reputation as a guide and woodsman grew, his exploits took on a legendary cast. This woodcut, showing Ethan carrying a bear, was just one of many illustrations and stories that highlighted his heroic deeds. Courtesy of Dartmouth College Library.

simple yet evocative language, he expressed the new sensibility about the beauty of wild nature that was beginning to emerge in the United States.

By 1823, climbing the mountains was beginning to become a fashionable thing to do—an amazing turnaround from the days when the Puritans had viewed the "dismal wilderness" with such distrust. At the same time that Ethan was guiding people up the mountains, he was expanding his accommodations for visitors. In the fall of 1823, he agreed to rent the Old Notch House, which stood a little north of Abel's farm at Hart's Location, and outfit it for travelers and horses. The house, which had been built in 1793, would later be the site of the Willey disaster of 1826. He also decided to enlarge his house at Giant's Grave. At first he was unwilling to make an addition because of the debts he was already carrying, but his friends advised him that the extra space would allow him to profit from the growing numbers of teamsters and foot travelers who tramped through the notch. He hauled lumber from Bethlehem, twelve miles away, and with thirteen other workers built a two-story addition that measured thirty-six feet by twenty feet. He finished in July, and shortly after he hosted a group of southern gentlemen and a painter who "took some beautiful sketches of the hills and likewise of the Notch," foreshadowing the future popularity of the notch as a subject for landscape artists.[21]

In spite of the growing access and accommodations, though, the mountains remained dangerous, as shown dramatically by the Willey disaster in 1826. The catastrophe became a pivotal episode in the growing body of legend and lore about the White Mountains, combining elements of tragedy and resilience in the face of natural catastrophe. Early in the summer of 1826, signs abounded that the mountains lining the notch were geologically unstable, as torrential rains in June had caused several small avalanches. The Willey family had moved into Ethan's Old Notch House at the foot of the mountains earlier that year, and as Mrs. Willey watched boulders and trees tumble down the mountainsides during storms, she begged her husband to take them away from the notch. Mr. Willey reassured her that the family would be safe.

On August 28, the rains came again, even harder. The next morning at Ethan Crawford's home, his small son trundled into the bedroom, shook his father awake, and blurted, "Father, the earth is nearly covered with water, and the hogs are swimming for life."[22] Ethan bolted from his bed, raced from the house, and blanched as he saw that the entire valley was flooded. The Ammonoosuc River had boiled into a white-water torrent that had ripped down bridges and sheds and drowned fourteen sheep. The water had crept within eighteen inches of their house.

Ethan was nearly frantic with worry over the safety of his father and the Willey family, whose homes stood at the bottom of the steepest and most dangerous slopes in the notch. A traveler came from the north who wanted Ethan to take him across the swollen river so that he could continue south into the notch, but the water was too high, the current too strong. By four o'clock that afternoon, though, the river had subsided enough for them to attempt a crossing. Ethan mounted a horse, pulled the traveler up behind him, and set across. The horse struggled against the vicious current, but they finally reached the other side, and the stranger continued walking into the notch while Ethan recrossed the river to their home. When the stranger reached the Willey house, he found it completely deserted except for a dog. The floor of the notch was in complete chaos, the barn badly damaged by an avalanche, two horses lying dead, oxen trapped under broken timber. The house, miraculously, was undamaged, and, seeing an open door, he walked inside and saw clothes strewn about and other signs that the family had left in a panic. On the table in the middle of the room lay an open Bible.[23]

The traveler hurried south until he reached the farm of Abel Crawford, who was safe with his family but had no information about the Willeys. From

3.4. The Willey place after the slide. This woodcut shows the Willey place after the avalanche of 1826, emphasizing the devastation on the floor of the notch. Courtesy of Dartmouth College Library.

there, the stranger traveled on to Bartlett and Conway, where he told residents of the catastrophic scenes in the notch. By Wednesday, the Ammonoosuc and the Saco had subsided, and Ethan and a brother of his named Thomas joined a party to search for the Willeys. Portions of the road into the notch were demolished, and trees were strewn about. As he approached the Willey house, Ethan saw cows with their bags full of milk. After taking the time to guide another traveler north to the head of the notch, Ethan returned to the Willey house. When he arrived, he saw several friends of the Willeys grieving, as they had realized that they would probably not find any of the family alive. The realization of the family's fate made Ethan speechless, and he could only press the hands of friends and express his grief through tears.

Still the rescuers had not found any traces of the family, but then one of the search party noticed that flies were buzzing over a pile of wood. They threw off the wood and discovered the bodies of Mr. and Mrs. Willey, the family's hired man, and the youngest child—all "broken and mangled."[24] The search continued the next day, Saturday, when they located the corpse of another hired man, and on Sunday, when they discovered the oldest daughter, who had been nearly twelve years old. Her body and face had no bruises at all, and they could only conclude that she had drowned. In all, four adults and five children had been killed by the avalanche, although the party never found the bodies of three of the children.

The slides had carried a tremendous amount of debris for miles down the

Ethan Allen Crawford ◉ 57

side of the mountain, but the house itself had been protected by a ledge of rock above, which had divided the landslide into two streams, sparing the house below. "The whole valley," Ethan lamented, "which was once covered with beautiful green grass, was now a complete quagmire, exhibiting nothing but ruins of the mountains, heaps of timber, large rocks, sand, and gravel. All was dismal and desolate."[25]

In addition to the tragic deaths, the storm caused almost unimaginable havoc throughout the notch. Ethan's house and barn incurred a thousand dollars in damage, while his father's farm was almost entirely destroyed. Abel's loss of property was so extensive that his son did not think he could ever rebuild the farm. "Many suffered more or less who lived on this wild and uncultivated stream, as far as Saco," he said.[26] The turnpike through the notch was destroyed in many places, but in an act of generosity, and to preserve the lifeline between the coast and the north country, the people of Portland, Maine, raised fifteen hundred dollars to rebuild the road.

In a cruel irony, the Willey tragedy made the White Mountains more famous than ever. The disaster appealed to the public's fascination with death, but the degree of that fascination was undoubtedly piqued by the fact that German and English Romanticism were then fashionable in the United States. The English Romantic poets exaggerated the tragic aspects of life, populating their verses with doomed heroes, tumultuous storms, mournful forests, and eerie events. The Willey disaster was a perfect embodiment of those aspects of Romanticism, and the catastrophe quickly took its place as the most famous episode in the accumulating mythic narrative of the White Mountains. The tragedy reinforced the perception of the mountains as a wild environment, and now a significant portion of the American public desired to experience that wildness for themselves.

Only two years later, another tragedy unfolded in the notch that shared many of the same tragic elements as the Willey story—the story of Nancy Barton. Like the Willey disaster, the saga of Nancy imbued the White Mountains with an aura of Romantic tragedy. The young woman worked as a servant for Colonel Joseph Whipple, the landowner in Jefferson who had climbed Mount Washington in 1784 as a member of the Belknap-Cutler expedition. Nancy fell in love with another servant of Whipple's, and after a courtship, the prospective husband proposed that they travel together to Portsmouth in the late fall and be married. In expectation of accompanying him on the journey, she entrusted him with all the money she had earned in service. As the day for their departure approached, Nancy traveled on an errand to Lancaster, but when she returned, she discovered that her lover had already left with Whipple for Portsmouth and had taken all her money. Distraught by the betrayal, she started to follow them through a heavy snowstorm. When she reached the town of Jefferson, she was already wet and exhausted, and the people there tried to dissuade her from going farther.

But she would not be deterred. She left Jefferson and trudged through the deepening snow into the notch. The men in Jefferson allowed her to continue in the belief that she would soon turn back. But she did not reappear, and, more and more alarmed, they set off after her. Meanwhile, she continued marching through the snow until she had traveled through a good portion of the notch. She came to a campfire that Whipple and her lover had started but saw no signs of the two men. In spite of her growing fatigue and hunger, her passion drove her on. In all, she covered an incredible twenty-two miles. The men from Jefferson reached the campfire but did not see her there. Continuing on, they came to a brook, crossed it, and found her, frozen, her clothes hardened to ice. When her lover learned of her death, he fell into a fit of conscience-stricken grief from which he never recovered; only a few months later, he died in a mental hospital.[27]

The saga of Nancy Barton added another episode to the mythology of the mountains—an episode that would be memorialized through the naming of Nancy's Brook and Nancy's Hill and that would be told time and time again in White Mountain tourist guides of the nineteenth century. Like the Willey episode, it added an aura of tragedy that draped itself around the mountains. Gradually, with episodes like these, the mountains were acquiring a history, which proved crucial to the growing popularity of the mountains as a travel destination. Perhaps more important, the stories tightened the emotional bond that people felt with the White Mountains. The narratives warned of the dangers of the wilderness—but they also made that wilderness alluring and romantic.

The Crawfords' innkeeping business benefited from the growing fame of the mountains. In 1828, Ethan decided to build a new inn at the northern gateway to the notch. There, visitors could enjoy fine views of the mountains. The new inn, called the Notch House, was managed by Ethan's brother Thomas. When it opened in 1829, it was an immediate success, attracting such luminaries as Timothy Dwight, Nathaniel Hawthorne, Daniel Webster, Henry David Thoreau, Ralph Waldo Emerson, Thomas Starr King, and Francis Parkman.[28]

Meanwhile, Ethan continued working to make the mountains accessible, building a bridle path seven miles through the woods to the base of Mount Washington and clearing a new trail to the top of Mount Pleasant for climbers who did not want the rigors of summiting the taller Mount Washington. To amuse visitors, he found a wolf that seemed to have a more malleable disposition than most of its brethren and tamed it; on cue, it would howl. In addition, the family kept a beautiful peacock and a deer.[29] In keeping with attitudes of the time toward wildlife, they were exerting humanity's control over nature for the purpose of amusing visitors.

As the flow of tourism increased, Ethan hired other guides to take people up the mountains. He had climbed so many times that he did not want to continue as a guide, but he made exceptions in 1829 and 1830 to lead botanists who had asked him to use his knowledge of the region to help them collect specimens of the mountains' unique flora. In 1829, a group of botanists from Boston arrived to collect plant specimens for their own laboratories, for a botanical garden in New York, and for collections as far away as Europe. Ethan led them as they combed every side of Mount Washington and gathered specimens of the rare alpine flora that the mountain nurtured at its highest elevations. At one point they came to what Ethan called "a great gulf" with "plenty of snow"—the Snow Arch in Tuckerman Ravine—and there they gathered a number of mountain flowers. The next summer, he embarked on his own to collect specimens for a botanist in Boston. Having gained considerable knowledge about the flora of the mountains, he collected plants, along with earth to protect the roots, placed them into containers with moss, labeled them, and shipped them to Boston.

The outdoor sports of hunting and fishing were also beginning to draw visitors to the mountains. In the same year that Ethan collected botanical specimens, he guided parties to a nearby pond, where in short order they caught seventy salmon, which they cooked "in real hunter style." Ethan recalled, "I always enjoyed these and similar feasts in the woods, as in such ways I suppose our forefathers lived when they first came over and settled this country."[30] In remembering those times, Ethan put his finger on one reason for the growing appeal of outdoor sports—that they replicated the skill and valor of the outdoorsmen's forefathers. The experiences of hunting and fishing forged a continuity with the past, giving members of the present generation an opportunity to pursue activities in which their ancestors had demonstrated their skills.

In spite of the growing popularity of the White Mountains, the fact remained that earning an adequate income on the edge of the wilderness was a difficult proposition. By 1832, the unending labor, long winters, and financial pressures had all taken their toll, and Ethan Crawford began to experience health problems that would afflict him for the rest of his life. He had rheumatism and, more alarming, had developed a tumor that caused him constant pain. In 1835, as he was riding down Cherry Mountain, his horse stumbled, throwing the afflicted part of his body hard against the pommel of the saddle and causing excruciating pain. Ethan felt so ill that he tried to sell his property, but none of the offers were enough to cover his debts.[31] During this period, he became friends with Dr. Samuel Bemis, a Boston dentist who sum-

3.5. Lucy Howe Crawford. Lucy Howe was the granddaughter of Eleazar Rosebrook. When she moved to the Rosebrook household to care for her ailing grandfather, she met her cousin Ethan Allen Crawford and later married him. She shaped Ethan's and her own experiences into one of the most compelling of all the White Mountain classics, *Lucy Crawford's History of the White Mountains.* New Hampshire Historical Society.

mered at Hart's Location, where he eventually built a stone house, called Notchland, that he lived in until his death in 1881. (The house still stands near the southern end of Crawford Notch and operates today as the Notchland Inn.) Dr. Bemis introduced Ethan to a physician who performed an operation that relieved some of the pain from the tumor.

Although he felt better physically, Ethan's financial woes only worsened. Finally, in March of 1837, he regretfully succumbed to the advice of his friends and family and gave up possession of the farm to his creditors. Horace Fabyan, a businessman from Portland, Maine, purchased the property, renamed the inn the Mount Washington House, and operated it for the next fifteen years.[32] The sale pained Crawford greatly, but he and Lucy moved their family to Guildhall, Vermont, where they tried to make a living by making and selling maple sugar. However, Ethan could not remain separated from the mountains. In 1843, he and Lucy returned, renting a building near where they had lived for twenty years, and they replanted their roots in the region that they had come to love.

As Ethan lived out his final years in the mountains, he watched the region undergo changes in which his family continued to play a significant role. His sister Hannah married Nathaniel T. P. Davis and lived with Abel at Hart's Location, where Davis, who was also interested in attracting travelers to the region, built a horse path from this part of the notch to the summit of Mount Washington—a path that still carries Davis's name. And even as Abel aged, he remained "a stout and athletic man, capable of doing work and business."

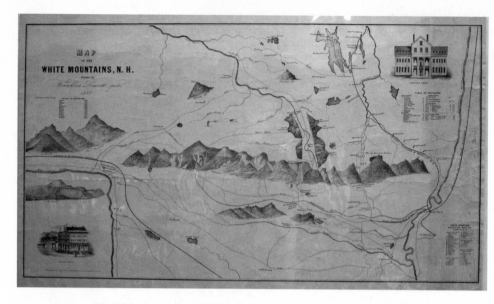

3.6. *Map of the White Mountains, N.H.* (1852), Franklin Leavitt. In 1852, only six years after the death of Ethan Allen Crawford, Franklin Leavitt created a map that showed the beginnings of the tourist industry in the White Mountains. The Crawford House, which was on the plain just north of Crawford Notch, was built in 1850 and 1851. Courtesy of Dartmouth College Library.

In 1840, at the age of seventy-five, he became the first person to ride a horse to the top of Mount Washington.[33]

When Ethan and Lucy Crawford returned to the notch, they embarked on a project that contributed enormously to the region's growing cultural identity. Ethan began to relate to Lucy the episodes of his life, which she shaped into a compelling history that integrated the lives of the Crawfords with the story of the mountains themselves. In 1846, the account was published as *History of the White Mountains,* and in 1860, fourteen years after Ethan had passed away, Lucy published a revised and expanded edition of the book. It was and remains a beloved White Mountain classic—essentially the saga of a modest hero, Ethan Allen Crawford, "a stout athletic man with a great share of courage and fortitude," who was uniquely gifted for life in the mountains. He might have been rough in manners and homely in appearance, but "he possessed a kind heart, and no man was more ready or willing to administer to the suffering or to aid in difficulty than Ethan Allen Crawford was."[34] On countless occasions, he carried people down the mountains on his broad shoulders, and the travelers who accompanied him on expeditions into the wilderness felt secure knowing that this giant of a man was guiding and protecting them. When he passed away on June 22, 1846, William Oakes, who

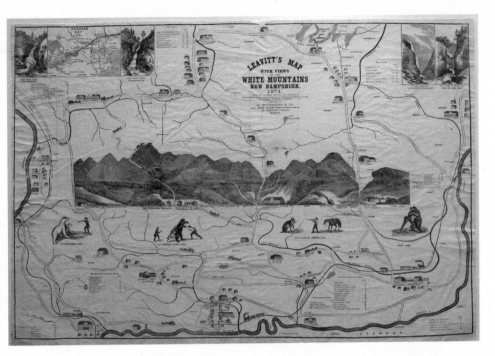

3.7. *Leavitt's Map with Views of the White Mountains, New Hampshire* (1871). Leavitt produced this map in 1871, showing the development of villages in the White Mountains. But even as it showed a region that was becoming civilized, the map celebrated the wilderness experiences by depicting scenes such as Abel Crawford's encounter with a bear. Courtesy of Dartmouth College Library.

would later pen his own classic of the region, *Scenery of the White Mountains,* wrote this memorable inscription for Ethan's grave:

> In memory
> of Ethan A. Crawford
> Who died June 22nd AD 1846
> Aged 54 years
> He built here the first hotel at the
> White Mountains of which he was for
> many years the owner and landlord
> he was of great native talent and sagacity
> of noble, kind and benevolent disposition,
> a beloved husband and father and an
> honest and good man[35]

Lucy Crawford's *History of the White Mountains* falls into the same distinctly American genre of letters as the tales of other pioneers—heroes such as

Daniel Boone, Davy Crockett, and Natty Bumppo of James Fenimore Cooper's *Leatherstocking Tales*. These frontier figures embraced the rugged outdoors and mastered the ways of the woods, signaling an enormous change in American attitudes toward the world of nature. Far from denigrating wild nature, as the Puritans had done, they embraced it. As Ethan's life neared its end, he reflected upon the extraordinary mountain vistas that had so inspired him:

> As you pass along upon the banks of the Ammonoosuc on the westerly side of the mountains, many beautiful little cascades and rivulets come tumbling down from the sides of the small but ragged mountains and continue to increase in magnitude as well as in number as you approach the Notch. . . . In passing down this huge gulf you behold a boundless feast of natural curiosities and the most romantic scenery extant.[36]

With these words, the Giant of the Hills revealed a touch of the poet who had experienced the delights of untrammeled nature. By creating the means—the trails and the shelters—that allowed people to immerse themselves in the beauties of the mountain wilderness, the Crawfords nurtured the growing interest of Americans in nature, wilderness, and mountain climbing and helped to set the stage for artists and writers to celebrate the wildness of nature in the White Mountains. The Crawfords' love for the mountains communicated itself to all who would visit the Whites from then onward. It was an enormous legacy that was critical to the future of the White Mountain landscape—a legacy reflected in the fact that not long after Ethan's death, people were commonly referring to the Notch of the Mountains as Crawford Notch.

Chapter 4

THE ARTIST WHO
REDEEMED THE WILDERNESS

O N A GLORIOUS OCTOBER DAY IN 1828, Thomas Cole, a twenty-seven-year-old landscape artist with a burgeoning reputation in America, stood at the base of Mount Chocorua, the most distinctive peak of the Sandwich Range in the White Mountains. With him was his friend and fellow artist Henry Cheever Pratt; together they had made the long trek from New York City into the north country, following an itinerary written for them by Cole's wealthy patron Daniel Wadsworth. Wadsworth's directions had taken them past Squam Lake and Lake Winnipesaukee and into the White Mountain region.

This was Cole's second visit to the area; his first had been only the year before, when the rugged mountainscape had nearly overwhelmed him with its prodigious beauty. Years later, in a famous lecture to the American Academy of Design in 1835, Cole would recall the grandeur of that landscape as if he were once again seeing it for the first time: "[I]n the mountains of New Hampshire there is a union of the picturesque, the sublime, and the magnificent; there the bare peaks of granite, broken and desolate, cradle the clouds; while the vallies [sic] and broad bases of the mountains rest under the shadow of noble and varied forests."[1]

The two young artists began their ascent of the mountain—a climb that Cole later described in his journal as "more difficult on account of briars and fallen trees than from any abruptness; but we soon entered upon a steep and terribly laborious journey."[2] After the arduous climb, they reached the summit, where they were rewarded with a magnificent view of the entire Sandwich Range. "On every side," Cole rhapsodized, "prospects mighty and sublime opened upon the vision: lakes, mountains, streams, woodlands, dwellings and farms wove themselves into a vast and varied landscape. Of the numerous lakes, some glistened like polished silver, others were dark blue: clouds cast their shadows far and wide, and produced wonderfully fine effects of light and shade."[3]

When Cole returned to his studio in New York that fall, he produced paintings of the White Mountains that remain, today, of unsurpassed beauty. They

4.1. Thomas Cole. One of the founders of the Hudson River School of landscape art, Cole was completely taken by the sublimity of the landscape when he first visited the White Mountains in 1827 and 1828. The extraordinary vibrancy of his White Mountain canvases would do much to spread the reputation of the region's wild landscapes.

Daguerreotype (ca. 1845), Mathew Brady. National Portrait Gallery, Smithsonian Institution/Art Resource, NY.

capture the Whites in all of their wild splendor—a mountainscape of towering crags, lush forests, and roiling storm clouds. In his 1835 lecture, Cole emphasized just how important this uncivilized, pristine quality was to him: "[T]he most distinctive, and perhaps the most impressive, characteristic of American scenery is its wildness."[4] Unlike Europe, he continued, in America "nature is still predominant." The young nation's vast acreage of still-uncivilized land afforded its citizens ample opportunity to experience "scenes of solitude from which the hand of nature has never been lifted." Such magnificent scenes of beauty, he concluded, "affect the mind with a more deep toned emotion than aught which the hand of man has touched."[5]

With these soaring words, Cole issued the manifesto for a radically new attitude toward wilderness—an attitude that he had been expressing through his paintings since the early 1820s. As a cofounder of the Hudson River School of American landscape painting with Asher Brown Durand and Thomas Doughty, Cole was a pivotal figure in revolutionizing American attitudes toward wilderness. And the White Mountain paintings that he created after the two visits in 1827 and 1828 were central to this transformation because they depicted the most rugged, the most uncivilized, the most unpredictable aspects of nature in America. If the Reverends Jeremy Belknap and Manasseh Cutler had made the White Mountains a proper subject for scientific study, and Abel and Ethan Allen Crawford had made the wilderness accessible, then

Thomas Cole made the White Mountain wilderness beautiful; and through his canvases, he taught the American public not only to see the wilderness but to value it and embrace it. Moreover, the paintings helped to establish Mount Washington, Mount Chocorua, and other White Mountain landmarks as highly visible symbols of the American wilderness.

Even before the arrival of Cole and other artists, the earliest images of the White Mountains had begun to establish in the public's mind the untamed beauty of the region. Cartographer Philip Carrigain's map of New Hampshire (1816) featured woodcut images of the White Mountains drawn by J. Kidder of Concord, New Hampshire, and cut by Abel Bowen of Boston. (See the map on page 20.) Robert L. McGrath, professor of art history at Dartmouth College, points out in an essay for Dartmouth's 1980 exhibit of White Mountain art that Kidder probably did not observe the mountains himself but rather relied on the descriptions of others. As a result, the woodcuts functioned more as symbols of the mountains than as accurate depictions of them.[6] These illustrations, McGrath writes, "served to emphasize the idea of soaring height or sharp declivity only dimly suggested by the contours of the map itself."[7] Thus, even the earliest White Mountain images began to create a kind of wilderness symbolism that emphasized the untamed, the daunting, and the dangerous.

The *Gazetteer of the State of New Hampshire* (1823) also featured early images of the White Mountains. In that publication, the author John Farmer wrote that the Whites were perhaps the "loftiest" in the entire United States and that they "furnish a rich profusion of the sublime and beautiful."[8] In using the words "sublime and beautiful," Farmer connected American landscape to the aesthetic theories of European Romanticism, which had a profound influence on Cole.

In the early decades of the nineteenth century, European Romanticism reached across the Atlantic to cause fundamental changes in American attitudes toward nature. In highly vivid language, Wordsworth, Keats, Byron, Shelley, and Coleridge exalted wild nature, associating it with the fundamental goodness of humanity and contrasting its beneficial effects with the corrupting influences of civilization. They also stirred a nostalgic longing for the distant classical past, symbolized by the remains of Greek and Roman architecture that had aged through the centuries to become part of the landscape of Mediterranean lands. And they expressed all these ideas in language and images designed to evoke the strongest possible emotions in readers and viewers. The Romantics had an enduring impact on the generation of artists and writers who, like Thomas Cole, came of age in the second and third decades of the nineteenth century.

In the United States, Romanticism had a particularly nationalist flavor, as writers such as James Fenimore Cooper and artists such as Cole aimed to create a distinctly American art and literature that showcased the continent's natural endowments. Americans began to view the beauty of their land with growing pride; while Europe might be superior in matters of culture, it could not begin to boast the magnificence of America's wilderness. Consequently, as the nation's first generation of landscape artists, led by Cole, celebrated this beauty, the strongly nationalist tenor of the time ensured that they would find a ready market for their canvases.

But while the Romantic spirit of the age provided inspiration, the artists of the period required new aesthetic approaches if they were to adequately capture the magnificence of America's landscape. Three concepts proved to be indispensable: the sublime, the beautiful, and the picturesque. All three fundamentally shaped how Cole and later artists painted landscapes of nature and wilderness—and how Americans viewed and responded to that wilderness.

British statesman Edmund Burke first articulated the concepts of the sublime and the beautiful in 1757 in an influential essay titled *A Philosophical Enquiry into the Origin of Our Ideas of the Sublime and Beautiful*. According to Burke, the primary purpose of a work of art is to inspire emotions, and the most powerful emotions are terror and awe. These feelings are associated with the sublime, as he explained:

> Whatever is fitted in any sort to excite the ideas of pain and danger, that is to say, whatever is in any sort terrible, or is conversant about terrible objects, or operates in a manner analogous to terror, is a source of the sublime; that is, it is productive of the strongest emotion which the mind is capable of feeling. . . . When danger or pain press too nearly, they are incapable of giving any delight, and are simply terrible; but at certain distances, and with certain modifications, they may be, and they are delightful.[9]

A sublime landscape emphasizes powerful and threatening images in nature, such as dark forests, pulsating waterfalls, swirling clouds, and trees blasted by lightning. It also includes natural features of great dimension, such as towering mountains and enormous boulders. Such natural features evoke immediate emotional responses in the viewer, particularly terror and awe. Art historian Donald Keyes, who curated the 1980 exhibit of White Mountain art for Dartmouth College, further notes: "[Cole] introduced imagination as a significant factor in the arts, and with imagination came the importance of individuality and individual emotions."[10]

Beauty, in Burke's aesthetic theory, was an altogether different concept. "By beauty," he wrote, "I mean that quality or those qualities in bodies, by which they cause love, or some passion similar to it."[11] Beautiful natural features are comparatively small and are smooth, with gradual variations and lines that change gradually and subtly. They are delicate, and their colors are "clear and bright" but are not "very strong and glaring."[12] While the sublime causes feelings of awe and terror, beauty instills a sense of peace and calm in the viewer. The power of Cole's art emerged from his ability to blend images of the sublime and the beautiful in single landscapes that created a unified effect.

By emphasizing the importance of emotion, Burke built a theoretical framework for a new and very different kind of landscape that would emerge during the Romantic period of the early nineteenth century. In the neoclassical era of the previous century, landscape artists had emphasized orderliness and harmony, as reflected in the many bucolic landscapes of the British countryside. Such landscapes celebrated the rural values that had led people to transform wilderness into productive farmland.[13] But by articulating the concepts of the sublime and the beautiful, Burke opened the way for a kind of landscape painting that depicted the wild aspects of nature: its turmoil, its dangers, its jarring qualities. The concept of the sublime also helped American artists to overcome the Puritan association of wilderness with the powers of darkness. Where the Puritans had looked at the landscape from a moral point of view, Burke looked at it from an aesthetic point of view. He was saying that the very qualities of wildness of the virgin forest constituted its appeal; they were what made it pleasing.

The other key theory that influenced the landscape arts during this period was the picturesque. Writing about thirty years after Burke, the British critic William Gilpin explained the theory of the picturesque in 1792 in a book titled *Three Essays: On Picturesque Beauty; On Picturesque Travel; and On Sketching Landscape: To Which Is Added a Poem*. Gilpin's writings influenced Cole and other painters.[14]

According to art historian Earl Powell, Gilpin developed the theory of the picturesque in order to "adapt Edmund Burke's theories of the sublime to real world experience."[15] Burke's theory was essentially subjective in that it focused on the viewer's emotional response but did not provide much practical guidance to the artist in how to inspire the desired emotional responses in the viewer. The picturesque, in contrast, gave artists more concrete direction in how to manipulate and organize the natural features in a landscape in order to evoke the desired aesthetic or emotional effect. An artist, for instance, could capture the wild qualities of nature through jagged, uneven lines and surfaces and by juxtaposing light and dark in order to enhance the drama of a scene.[16]

The theory of the picturesque also liberated artists to use their imagination in painting. An artist, for instance, might blend details from different actual vistas in order to create an imaginary landscape that would inspire an emotional response in the viewer. As the theory of the picturesque gained wider circulation, landscape artists felt increasingly free to juxtapose elements from many different actual views and to incorporate myths and legends in their paintings. Theories of the picturesque would become even more influential as the nineteenth century progressed and will be further explored in chapter 6, which will examine the later evolution of White Mountain art.

The theories of the sublime, the beautiful, and the picturesque gave Cole and other American artists of the early nineteenth century an aesthetic foundation for capturing on canvas what they saw before them—a magnificent wilderness of incredible variety and undeniable power. In turn, Cole and the artists who followed taught the American public how to see the beauty of nature in its wildest state. By doing so, they continued the process of redeeming the wilderness from the Puritanical associations with sin and evil—a process that started when Jeremy Belknap and Manasseh Cutler demystified the wilderness with their explorations and that continued when the Crawfords built trails and offered guiding services that allowed Americans to experience wilderness firsthand. Equally important, Cole imbued the mountain wilderness with enormous aesthetic value, which acted as a counterforce against the commercial uses of the land that motivated many of the settlers who migrated into the White Mountain region. Cole's canvases placed the White Mountains at the center of this redemption of wilderness because the region offered, along with New York's Adirondack Mountains, the wildest, most pristine vistas to which the new generation of artists had access.

Born in 1801 in Lancashire, England, to a manufacturer of woolen goods who was never able to make a success in business, Thomas Cole from a young age loved the natural beauty of the English countryside. An introverted boy, his greatest pleasure was to ramble through the countryside, play his flute, and study the shapes and forms of nature. As his friend and biographer Louis Legrand Noble would later write, "The park-scenery, the ivy-mantled walls, and even the sounding rooms of some of the old halls in the vicinity, afforded a range for his eye and fancy."[17] Early on, Cole developed the habit of observing details of nature closely. Perhaps more important, his direct experience of nature inspired emotional responses of pleasure and joy. Even after becoming a well-known artist, he continued to travel extensively into the American wilderness and make sketches, gathering subjects for future canvases and renewing himself emotionally through his contact with nature.

At one point in his youth, Cole read a book that described the natural beauties of North America, which inspired a great desire to see America. He persuaded his father to move the entire family across the Atlantic, and in 1819, they arrived in Philadelphia, where Thomas found employment as a wood engraver. The very next year he traveled with a friend to St. Eustatia in the Bahamas, where he reacted with "love and astonishment" to the scenes of great beauty.[18] During this expedition, he ventured alone into uninhabited areas in order to find scenes of natural beauty. On these short explorations, Cole began to view his surroundings with a painterly eye; according to Noble, he completed a drawing of St. Eustatia that was one of his first artistic efforts.

Cole returned to Philadelphia in 1820 and then followed his family to yet another new start in Steubenville, Ohio. There he assisted in his father's wallpaper business by mixing colors and designing patterns for wall coverings. He also met a traveling portrait painter named Stein who lent Cole an English book on painting that fed the young man's growing desire to become an artist. For the next two years, he wandered the countryside of Ohio as an itinerant portrait painter, bartering his paintings for the bare necessities of life. During this period of wandering, he created his first landscapes, and when he returned to Philadelphia in 1823, he was able to sell a few of his canvases. A talented writer, he also published a short story in the *Saturday Evening Post* and wrote numerous poems that reflected a strong religious orientation that would also influence his paintings. Throughout these years of privation, Cole scratched out a living by painting portraits and taking work as an engraver and designer.[19]

In 1825, Cole moved to New York City, where his father and family were now living. The move placed Cole at the center of the nascent New York art world. He set up a small studio in his father's house on Greenwich Street and began to produce landscapes based on his rambles in the New York and New Jersey area. At the same time, he formed friendships with wealthy patrons of the arts and other young artists, notably John Trumbull, William Dunlap, and Asher Brown Durand—all of whom recognized Cole's rapidly maturing skill.[20]

He traveled into the Catskills for the first time in the fall of 1825, and when he returned to the city, he completed three landscapes of the Catskills and sold them immediately. The poet William Cullen Bryant, a close friend, recalled that, beginning with the sale of these three paintings, Cole "had a fixed reputation, and was numbered among the men of whom our country had reason to be proud. I well remember what an enthusiasm was awakened by these early works of his."[21]

Thus, when Cole first visited the White Mountains in 1827, his reputation as a landscape artist was growing rapidly. When his patron Wadsworth urged Cole to travel to the White Mountains, the young artist must have been intrigued by what he had heard of dramatic mountain vistas and pristine forests. These were tantalizing prospects for landscapes—a region of visual riches that could provide raw material for the young artist's sense of the dramatic and the sublime in nature. He and Henry Pratt stayed at Ethan Allen Crawford's inn, and together they made the dangerous climb to the top of Mount Washington. Cole completed two drawings of the view from the summit.

But perhaps the highlight of their tour was the ascent to the summit of Mount Chocorua. In his journal, Cole vividly described the view that unfolded before them: "Lakes, mountains, streams, forests, villages and farms lay spread beneath us like a beautiful carpet. Some of the numerous lakes shone like silver. . . . The view was sublime but not a scene for the canvass. . . . It was not for pictures I ascended the mountain but for ideas of grandeur, for conceptions, and for these, this was the region."[22] The mountain, with its distinctive cone-shaped summit, took on special, almost mythic, significance for Cole. In his paintings, he would use it more than any other natural landmark of the White Mountains.

After the two visits in 1827 and 1828, Cole produced a stunning series of White Mountain landscapes. Drawing on the theories of the sublime, the beautiful, and the picturesque, he highlighted certain visual qualities over and over: the vast scale of the region's forests and mountains, the drama created by the interplay of its natural features, and the pristine nature of its beauty. In his lecture to the American Academy of Design in 1835, he would recall, "[I]n some regions of the globe nature has wrought on a more stupendous scale, yet she has nowhere so completely married together grandeur and loveliness—there [the viewer] sees the sublime melting into the beautiful, the savage tempered by the magnificent."[23]

A close look at several of his White Mountain paintings reveals not only how Cole captured the visual beauty of the region but also how he created a new perspective toward the wilderness. The painting *View of the White Mountains* (1827) is quite representative. In this lovely scene, a traveler walks along a dirt road that leads out of a vast forest in the background. Art historian Donald Keyes explains that in this painting, "Cole adjusted elements in order to produce an ideal vision that conformed to the Burkean concept of the Sublime."[24] The tree to the right and the boulder both have sharp, irregular edges, heightening the sense of drama. Part of another tree, directly behind the large tree, has either been struck by lightning or blown over; it now lies partly in the road, ahead of the lone traveler. The road on which the traveler is walking, and which also carries two tiny figures in the distance, disappears into the immense, dark forest. In the distance, yet dominating the scene, sits Mount Washington, flanked by the rest of the Presidential Range and wrapped in a mantle of snow. The mountain is both majestic and peaceful, a protective presence in the wilderness.

In this landscape, Cole brought the wilderness alive for an audience that might have heard of Mount Washington but in all likelihood had never seen it. The impression that he created was admiring, even reverential. The scene inspired an emotional response in viewers and established Mount Washington as a recognizable symbol of America's vast wilderness.

4.2. *View of the White Mountains* (1827), Thomas Cole. As the solitary traveler wanders down the road through the forest, the elements of the sublime are evident in the sharp, irregular features of the natural objects and the dark, immense forest. Wadsworth Atheneum Museum of Art, Hartford, CT. Bequest of Daniel Wadsworth.

But perhaps the most important aspect of this painting is its subtle symbols of transcendence, of the immanence of God in nature. Cole, Durand, Jasper Cropsey, and other American landscape artists of the Romantic period were affected profoundly by the Second Great Awakening, the explosion of religious feeling and evangelical preaching that swept the nation in the 1820s and 1830s.[25] Cole had a deep religious faith that led him to respond intuitively to these religious stirrings. In his 1835 lecture, he pointed explicitly to the presence of God in the magnificent scenes of nature that he had observed:

[T]hose scenes of solitude from which the hand of nature has never been lifted, affect the mind with a more deep toned emotion than aught which the hand of man has touched. Amid them the consequent associations are of God the creator—they are his undefiled works, and the mind is cast into the contemplation of eternal things.[26]

The Artist Who Redeemed ⊚ 73

4.3. *Storm Near Mount Washington* (1828), Thomas Cole. Storm clouds threaten Mt. Washington and the small village that lies in the valley, creating a dramatic embodiment of the concept of the sublime.

American landscape painters of this period also inherited a long European tradition of manipulating and juxtaposing the details of nature to create Christian metaphors in their paintings. These visual metaphors included the emanation of light from natural objects, canopies formed by trees to resemble the arches of cathedrals, broken trees that resemble crosses, and such symbols of life and death as rivers, sunsets, lilies, and birds.[27]

In his superb book about White Mountain art, *Gods in Granite*, Robert L. McGrath explains that *View of the White Mountains* "leads the viewer on a spatio-temporal journey that strongly intimates both pilgrimage and spiritual transcendence."[28] Several symbols in the painting contribute to the feeling of transcendence. The two trees to the right form crosses, while the large elm reaches toward heaven. The road into the Ammonoosuc Ravine leads the traveler on a Bunyanesque pilgrimage into the valley of darkness before emerging into the mantle of light that wraps Mount Washington, which itself reaches majestically toward heaven.

In another painting of the same period, *Storm Near Mt. Washington* (1828), Cole used light to suggest the presence of God. In this canvas, which is a highly dramatic embodiment of Burke's concept of the sublime, storm clouds threaten Mount Washington and the tiny settlement in the valley below.[29] Dark clouds clash with lighter ones, while the symmetrical cone of Mount Washington stands in sharp relief to the mountain in the right foreground. Jagged-edged trees ride down the spine of the mountain, while in the foreground is the detritus of nature—trees blasted by lightning that lie strewn chaotically across the floor of the notch.

Yet in the teeth of the threatening storm, Mount Washington stands heroically strong. The mantle of snow reflects the light, which emanates from heaven above, transforming Mount Washington into a beacon of hope for the threatened populace in the valley below. This is a scene of great and dangerous beauty, augmented by visual contrasts that build tension and create a powerful drama. In the wilderness, Cole intimates, we face both beauty and danger, yet the majestic mountain, which reflects the light of heaven, offers protection, hope, and ultimate peace.

Even in paintings that were not explicitly about the White Mountains, Cole used features from the region to evoke the sacredness of nature and the wilderness. *Garden of Eden,* created in 1827, demonstrates how he used actual detail to create an allegorical scene. Cole described the conception behind the painting in a letter to Wadsworth on November 26, 1827:

> The Garden of Eden is the subject. . . . [T]here are in it lofty distant Mountains, a calm expansive lake, wooded bays, rocky promontories—a solitary island, undulating grounds, a meandering river, cascades, gentle lawns, groups of noble trees.[30]

The mountain in the background clearly resembles Mount Chocorua.[31] Adam and Eve face the sun and greet it as it rises; they are surrounded by incredibly lush tropical vegetation. Even in this imaginative painting, Cole incorporated details and features from the White Mountain wilderness and transformed them into metaphors for the presence of God in nature. Such scenes carried moral lessons as well as aesthetic value for the artist. In the 1835 lecture, he would state that poetry and art "carry with them the power to mend our hearts" because they "sublime and purify thought, by grasping the past, the present, and the future—they give the mind a foretaste of its immortality."[32] In conclusion, he would say, "There is in the human mind an almost inseparable connection between the beautiful and the good."[33] By painting canvases of immeasurable beauty, Cole was, in his view, creating a moral drama.

Cole emphasized these moral benefits by the manner in which he depicted humans in his landscapes. The humans—for example, the solitary traveler in *View of the White Mountains*—form a natural part of the landscape. They

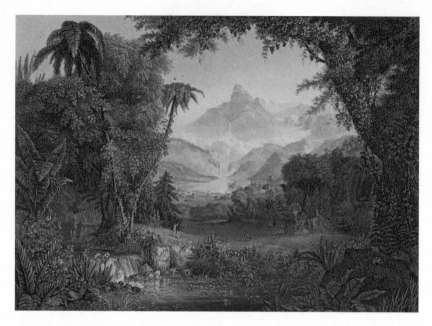

4.4. *Garden of Eden* (1831), engraving by James Smillie, after the work of Thomas Cole. In this allegorical scene, natural details are transformed into metaphors for the presence of God in nature. From *The Holy Bible, containing the old and new testaments* (Boston: Gray and Bowen, 1831, vol. 1, frontispiece). General Research Division, The New York Public Library, Astor, Lenox and Tilden Foundations.

may alter the land to some extent, but they have not violated or destroyed the wilderness; instead, they live in harmony with it. Moreover, they bear witness to the beauty of the land. *Autumn Landscape* (1827–1828) presents another lone traveler who, as a stand-in for the viewer, experiences the aesthetic pleasure and moral benefit of contact with the unsullied wilderness. Mount Chocorua stands calmly in the distance, while the foreground contains a tree that tilts sharply to the right and a small pond; large rocks on the left and right frame the scene. The solitary traveler leans against the boulder in the right foreground. According to art historian Ellwood Parry, the traveler is alone "in a landscape devoid of any other signs of habitation."[34] His pose is reflective, and beneath his elbow is a book—perhaps a book of poetry. The pose gives the painting a Romantic aura and underscores the minimal impact that humans have had on the White Mountain wilderness. Humanity, in its reflective mode, is at home in nature.

Another painting, *Mount Chocorua* (1827), depicts a similarly benign human presence in the White Mountains. A solitary boy fishes in a pond, while Mount Chocorua looks on benevolently in the distance. Other signs of human habitation include a tiny farm on the hillock in the left background, animals in

4.5. *Autumn Landscape (Mount Chocorua)* (1827–1828), Thomas Cole. The solitary traveler rests before Mt. Chocorua, completely at home in the world of nature. The landscape reflects the characteristics of wilderness, with few signs of human habitation. The Warner Collection of the Westervelt-Warner Museum of American Art, Tuscaloosa, AL 35406.

the pond, and logs that have clearly been felled by sawing. Yet this is not a warning of human encroachment on the wilderness. Instead, humanity is living in harmony with nature—a harmony that is visually underscored by the golden glow that suffuses the scene with transcendent warmth. The moral lesson of the painting is clear: humanity benefits from direct experience with nature and wilderness.

Cole often drew on history and legend in his White Mountain canvases. One such painting, produced in 1828, contemplates the aftermath of the Willey disaster of 1826. When Cole visited the region in 1827, the tragedy was a fresh scar on the emotions of those living in the region, and he wrote evocatively about it in his diary:

A strange mystery hangs over the events of that night. We walked among the rocks and felt as though we were but as worms, insignificant and feeble, for as

4.6. *Mount Chocorua, New Hampshire* (1827), Thomas Cole. Amid signs of human habitation, such as the farm on the hill and the animals in the pond, the boy exists in harmony with nature. Mt. Chocorua was popular among White Mountain artists, partly because of its majestic symmetry and partly because of its association with legends such as that of the Native American chief Chocorua. Private collection, courtesy Berry-Hill Galleries.

worms a falling rock could crush us. We looked up at the pinnacles above us and measured ourselves and found ourselves as nothing. How awful must have been the darkness of that night with the crash of falling crags and rushing cataracts. It is impossible for description to give an adequate idea of this scene of desolation.[35]

Moved and fascinated by the tragedy, Cole created a painting titled *Distant View of the Slides that Destroyed the Whilley Family* (1828).[36] The original has been lost, but a lithograph created from it gives a clear idea how Cole approached the subject. It focuses on both Mount Willey and the facing mountain, whose sharply declining side across the foreground of the painting emphasizes the steepness of the mountains in the notch. On the floor of the notch are the signs of destruction: downed trees with their limbs torn off by the power of the storm. The Willey house itself is but a small dot on the side

4.7. *Distant View of the Slides that Destroyed the Whilley Family, The White Mountains* (ca. 1828–1829), Anthony Imbert, lithographer, after the work of Thomas Cole. Cole captures the devastation caused by the avalanche that killed the Willey family. The painting emphasizes the steepness of the walls of the notch and the detritus on the floor. Lithograph, 12 1/2 × 15 1/2 inches. Albany Institute of History & Art; Gift of Edith Cole Hill (Mrs. Howard) Silberstein, great-granddaughter of the artist.

of the mountain. Cole's purpose was to capture the unlimited power of nature through details such as the hovering storm clouds, the steepness of the mountainsides, and the detritus on the floor of the notch.[37] In addition to evoking the sometimes terrible power of nature, Cole also added to the mythology of the White Mountains by memorializing this natural catastrophe, which held such profound implications about the vulnerability of humanity before the dangers of nature.

In other canvases, Cole drew on Native American legends to create a kind of mythic narrative of the White Mountains. For example, in *Chocorua's Curse* (1829), he depicted the climax of the tragedy involving Chocorua, who had killed the family of Cornelius Campbell because the Indian's son had died from eating poison while visiting Campbell's home. Campbell hunted down Chocorua and shot him on the summit of the mountain that bears his name. (The story is told in more detail in chapter 5.) The painting places Chocorua at the peak of the mountain, with Campbell at the level just below, holding a

4.8. *Chocorua's Curse* (1830), from *The Token* (Boston, 1830), George W. Hatch, after a painting by Thomas Cole. The legend of Chocorua is one of the most enduring of White Mountain legends. Courtesy of Dartmouth College Library.

musket and preparing to shoot the chieftain. In his journal, Cole wrote about the incident:

> We came out, at length, to a lonely and deserted clearing, just at the foot of the mountain. The cause of this abandonment is, they say, the poisonous effects of the water upon the cattle; the result, according to tradition, of the curse of Chocorua, an Indian, from whom the peak, upon which he was killed by Whites, takes its name.[38]

In this painting, Cole drew on the Native American history of the region, associating the natural scene with a tragic human event that would deepen the viewer's emotional response to the landscape. Cole accomplished two purposes: he imbued the landscape with moral and spiritual meaning, and he immortalized the episode as a defining event in the history of the White Mountains. Viewers felt the tragedy of the deaths and the senselessness of the chasm between whites and Indians—and have forever associated the tragedy with the summit of Mount Chocorua. McGrath summarizes Cole's achievement when he writes, "Cole's effort to elevate the wilderness to a state of aes-

4.9. Landscape scene from *The Last of the Mohicans* (1827), Thomas Cole. Cole created two paintings on the subject of James Fenimore Cooper's *Last of the Mohicans*. In this rendition, the character of Cora kneels before the Delaware chief Tamenund and pleads for the lives of Alice, Duncan Heyward, Hawkeye, and herself. The balancing rock was a symbol of the spiritual forces at work in nature. Fenimore Art Museum, Cooperstown, NY.

thetic respectability was grounded in a conscious effort to discover accessible myths in Native American history."[39]

In 1828, Cole created two paintings based on James Fenimore Cooper's novel *The Last of the Mohicans* that also incorporated Native American themes. Both canvases portray the scene from the novel in which Cora kneels before the Delaware chief Tamenund and pleads with the chief to help her, her sister Alice, Duncan Heyward, and Hawkeye gain their freedom from captivity by the Huron warrior Magua.[40] The tribe of Delaware gather solemnly in an area that Cooper describes as a "natural rocky terrace," form a large circle, and watch the highly charged interchange between Tamenund and Cora.[41] Even though Cooper had set the novel near Lake George, Cole relocated the story to the White Mountains so that he could incorporate dramatic mountain settings, particularly Mount Chocorua, to heighten the drama of the scene.

One of the most striking details in both paintings is the balancing rock just behind Cora and Tamenund. These "rocking stones," as they were called, fascinated people during the Romantic period, because they pointed to mysterious forces at work in nature. In particular, they were often connected with pagan rituals because they embodied spiritual forces at work.[42] In the paintings, Cole used the balancing rock to signify that this was a sacred place for the Indians.

Chocorua's Curse and the two *Last of the Mohicans* paintings reflect the intersection of Indian culture and white culture during the early decades of the nineteenth century, when many white writers and artists viewed Indians through the prism of Romanticism. To the Romantic sensibility, Indian cultures were comparatively primitive yet appealing because they were so closely integrated with the natural environment. Consequently, Cole drew on the Romantic perception of the relationship between Indian culture and the North American wilderness. In *Chocorua's Curse,* he memorialized the tragic outcome of the conflict between whites and Indians for control of that wilderness. In the paintings based on Cooper, he commemorated a people who were at home in nature, and through symbols such as the balancing rock, he emphasized the sacredness of the connection between the Indians and the wilderness environment in which they had thrived before the arrival of Europeans.

In these paintings, Cole used the White Mountains as the setting for episodes in the creation of an American myth that centers on wilderness. Through the evocative power of his landscapes, he implied that America's vast wilderness holds the potential for humankind's redemption. God is immanent in nature, and when individuals open themselves to the beauties of nature, when they immerse themselves in the sacred landscape, they draw closer to redemption. Cole's view of nature and wilderness was profoundly idealistic, accounting in no small measure for the mysterious power of his landscapes. Moreover, through the power of his art, he performed a transformation—he elevated the White Mountains into the archetypal American wilderness, which they would remain until the emergence of Yosemite Valley and the Western landscape as symbols of American wilderness at the end of the nineteenth century.

For the next ten years, Cole traveled extensively in Europe and through other regions of the United States. But he returned to the White Mountains one more time, in 1839, and the result of this trip was his most famous White Mountain canvas, *The Notch of the White Mountains* (1839). Painted eleven years after his previous visit, it reflects Cole's love for and fascination with this landscape, and he continued to infuse it with unmistakable signs of the sublime. The mountain forms an imposing and majestic presence. It is painted in contrasts, a thick, dark hulk at its base that gradually rises into the light until, at its top, it is clothed in wisps of clouds. The trees to the right are naked,

4.10. *A View of the Mountain Pass Called the Notch of the White Mountains (Crawford Notch)* (1839), Thomas Cole. When Cole returned to the mountains in the 1830s, signs of human settlements were more visible, as evident in the many stumps that dot the floor of the notch. Yet still the landscape has all the elements of the sublime—the soaring mountains, the swirling clouds, and the jagged edges of the forest on the mountain. Andrew W. Mellon Fund, Image © 2005 Board of Trustees, National Gallery of Art, Washington.

their branches sharp, jagged, threatening. Clouds swirl about the mountain and even seem to be exploding through the head of the notch itself. The mountains on each side descend like the teeth of a saw to the floor. The elements of the sublime are present: astonishment, terror, awe. The mountains are beautiful and dangerous, and there is more than a hint of the presence of God in the landscape.

However, this painting also includes unmistakable signs that in the intervening years between Cole's visits, from 1828 to 1839, the settlers in the region have begun to transform the wilderness. A man rides a horse on a well-worn trail toward a simple farmhouse. In the foreground, trees have been cut down with axes, but their stumps have not yet been removed; the land is not yet completely domesticated. The painting captures a moment in time when the White Mountains were teetering on the brink of settlement. The wilderness still has all the elements of the sublime: the magnificent mountain, the swirling clouds, the jagged edges of the forested slopes as they descend to the floor of

The Artist Who Redeemed ◦ 83

the notch. But the wilderness is no longer pristine. Now the mountains exist in juxtaposition with primitive yet unmistakable accoutrements of civilization, which are beginning to impose order on the unharnessed beauty of the wilderness. Keyes points out that when Cole painted this canvas, the White Mountains had accumulated a history, a lore. The Willey tragedy had occurred, Nancy Barton had met her fate, and the Crawfords had left their considerable mark on the region. The mountains had, in Keyes's words, acquired "an almost mythic overtone."[43] Cole himself seemed ambivalent about these signs of encroaching civilization. In his 1835 address to the American Academy of Design, he said:

> [T]here are those who regret that with the improvements of cultivation the
> sublimity of the wilderness should pass away: for those scenes of solitude
> from which the hand of nature has never been lifted, affect the mind with a
> more deep toned emotion than aught which the hand of man has touched.[44]

Yet in the same lecture, he also acknowledged that civilization carries with it certain benefits:

> [T]he cultivated must not be forgotten, for it is still more important to man
> in his social capacity—necessarily bringing him in contact with the cultured;
> it encompasses our homes, and, though devoid of the stern sublimity of the
> wild, its quieter spirit steals tenderly into our bosoms mingled with a thou-
> sand domestic affections and heart-touching associations—human hands
> have wrought, and human deeds hallowed all around.[45]

In these two statements and in *The Notch of the White Mountains,* an ambivalence about wilderness appeared that would be a continuing theme in artistic and literary treatments of wilderness in the United States. We Americans like our wilderness, but we also like the trappings of civilization. Cole attempted to resolve this ambivalence by depicting the full magnificence of wild nature, by portraying humanity in harmony with nature, and by making the accoutrements of civilization noninvasive. As we shall see, the artists who followed Cole to the White Mountains shared the same ambivalence, but they attempted to resolve it in other ways.

In spite of this ambivalence, though, Cole made an enormous contribution in creating a heritage of respect for and love of the American wilderness, and his White Mountains paintings were pivotal in creating this heritage. Through his remarkable skill and his feeling for nature, he showed Americans how beautiful their own unspoiled, untamed land was. He established icons of wilderness, particularly Mount Chocorua, Mount Washington, and Crawford Notch, which became more than just beautiful places. They came to symbolize the power, the majesty, the freedom of America's pristine natural beauty. When, at the end of the nineteenth century, the region came under assault by lumber interests, these icons of wilderness served as vivid and powerful reminders to Americans of how beautiful the White Mountain wilderness was—and still could be.

The period of the 1820s and 1830s in the history of the White Mountains was about to close, and throughout the following two decades, signs of civilization would become gradually more apparent. Towns sprouted in the region's valleys, roads extended their reach into the mountains, and hotels and camps accommodated ever-increasing numbers of tourists. The wilderness was rapidly disappearing, setting the stage for an ongoing conflict between those who shared Cole's love of the pristine wilderness and those who took a more instrumental view of the land. In addition, the concept of what made a beautiful landscape would also change. Images of the White Mountains as a sublime wilderness would become rare, and canvases from the 1850s would tend toward the pastoral, showing people living on farms and in harmony with nature—an artistic evolution that chapter 6 will explore further.

Yet Cole's canvases have remained visually powerful symbols of America's wilderness. Along with the literature of writers such as Thoreau, they have created a powerful countermyth for America. From John Winthrop through Paul Bunyan to John Wayne, the dominant myth of the United States has been one of nation building by taming the vast wilderness and turning it to productive use. But in Cole's canvases, wild nature becomes the hero, while humanity is a secondary character. In these extraordinary paintings, the wilderness fairly leaps off the canvas; it is alive and vibrant; it displays a multitude of moods. Yet the wilderness also holds deep and essential meanings for humanity; it is sacred, and through encounters with nature at its most unspoiled and wildest, the pilgrim experiences the transcendent and journeys toward a spiritual renaissance—toward the mountain wrapped in light and touching the borders of heaven.

Chapter 5

WRITERS AND THE SEARCH
FOR MEANING IN WILDERNESS

D URING THE CHRISTMAS HOLIDAY SEASON OF 1829, subscribers
to an annual magazine titled *The Token: A Christmas and New Year's
Present* immersed themselves in Lydia Maria Child's dramatic retelling of an extraordinary story of the White Mountains—the legend of the
Pequawket sachem Chocorua. The tale begins after Lovewell's Battle, when
most of the Pequawkets had left New Hampshire for Canada. Chocorua,
however, had refused to abandon the Sandwich Range, where, he believed, the
spirits of his ancestors continued to reside. There he raised his young son, Tuamba, and maintained friendly relationships with neighboring white settlers,
including a man named Cornelius Campbell. Tuamba was often at Campbell's homestead, playing with his children.

One year, Chocorua needed to travel to Canada to meet with those of his
people who had migrated north, and he left his son in Campbell's care. The
boy found poison that Campbell had concocted to kill a pesky fox, drank part
of it, and soon died. When Chocorua returned to find his son dead and buried,
he was devastated with grief. Quickly, though, grief turned to rage and a vow
of revenge, and when Campbell returned to his cabin from working in the
fields, he found the slain bodies of his wife and children on the cabin floor.[1]

Now it was the white man's turn for fury and revenge. He pursued Chocorua
to the top of the mountain that now bears his name and shot him there. But
before dying, Chocorua brought down a curse upon Campbell and the other
white settlers in the region:

> A curse upon ye, white men! May the Great Spirit curse ye when he speaks
> in the clouds, and his words are fire! Chocorua had a son—and ye killed him
> while the sky looked bright! Lightning blast your crops! Wind and fire destroy
> your dwellings! The Evil Spirit breathe death upon your cattle! Your graves lie
> in the war path of the Indian! Panthers howl, and wolves fatten over your bones!
> Chocorua goes to the Great Spirit—his curse stays with the white man![2]

According to the legend, Chocorua's curse resulted in the poisoning of several nearby towns' water supply, and cattle that drank the water died. Even-

tually, however, those deaths were traced to the presence of muriate of lime in the water supply.

This tale found its way into countless White Mountain guidebooks in the nineteenth century, and it has remained one of the famous legends associated with the Whites. It is no coincidence that Mrs. Child's retelling of the Chocorua legend appeared in 1829. In the early 1800s, American culture was deeply influenced by European Romanticism, and popular and serious writers of the day reflected those influences, suffusing their works with memorable descriptions of wild nature and with overtones of the mysterious, the tragic, and the supernatural. The legend of Chocorua was prime material for Romantic writers, unfolding as it did amidst the beauties of the Sandwich Range yet also invoking feelings of terror—the very elements of the sublime that Thomas Cole had summoned in his dramatic paintings of the White Mountains. It also served a darker purpose. By reinforcing the stereotype of the violent Native American who could not be trusted to control his passions, the tale reinforced one of the original justifications for appropriating the land from the indigenous inhabitants—that the native people were "heathens" whose culture did not constitute a true civilization. It was only a short step from that stereotype to the full-fledged removal of the Abenaki and other native people from their ancestral lands.

The Romantics had a fascination with dramatic landscapes, and with mysterious events; if such events were tinged with the supernatural, so much the better. These qualities attracted American writers to the White Mountains as a subject because the mountains displayed all these qualities in abundance. Consequently, a literature of the White Mountains began to emerge in the middle decades of the nineteenth century. In addition to inspiring an extensive oral literature of tales and legends, the mountains provided the setting for three important tales by Nathaniel Hawthorne and were the centerpiece of one of the pioneering works of American nature writing: Thomas Starr King's *The White Hills: Their Legends, Landscape, and Poetry*. They also inspired two well-known nature poets of the second half of the nineteenth century: John Greenleaf Whittier and Lucy Larcom.

Because this literature gained wide readership throughout the United States, it had an enormous impact on the attitudes of Americans toward nature and wilderness, in much the same way that the art of Thomas Cole did. The writers celebrated the beauty of the Whites and transformed unique geological formations such as the Old Man of the Mountain and the Flume into beloved landmarks. They also imbued even the wildest mountain landscapes with personal, moral, and spiritual meanings. Consequently, the stories, nonfiction narratives, and poems that flowed from these authors' pens forged an emotional bond between readers and the White Mountains. Visitors who climbed to the summit of Mount Chocorua were usually familiar with the legend of the Pequawket sachem, and for them the climb to the top became more than simply a walk through a pretty forest; it became an ascent through the legend itself, and to stand atop the mountain's summit was to stand where Chocorua himself had made his last stand. The climbing experience gained an emotional resonance that it would not have otherwise had, and this kind of personal connection would become extremely important in leading those who loved the mountains to seek ways to protect them at the end of the nineteenth century.

The earliest examples of White Mountain literature were the vivid tales and legends that settlers in the mountains passed down from one generation to another and told to outsiders who toured the region. Many of these tales were Abenaki in origin, while other narratives had their origins in historical episodes that were enhanced through retelling, such as the raid by Rogers' Rangers on St. Francis, Lovewell's Battle, and the Willey tragedy. Writers saw that a market was emerging for written narratives based on legend, history, or a little bit of both.

A classic example of such a hybrid narrative is *Incidents in White Mountain History,* published in 1856 and written by the Reverend Benjamin G. Willey, the brother of Samuel Willey, whose family had perished in the famous landslide three decades earlier. In twenty-three chapters, Willey spins the first comprehensive narrative of the Whites, beginning with their geological origins, continuing with the early exploration by the Reverend Jeremy Belknap, and concluding with accounts of the founding of the villages of Franconia and Bethlehem. Along the way, he retells a number of Indian legends, but the most interesting aspect of his book is the significance that he assigns to the natural features of the region. According to Reverend Willey, "New England owes to her granite peaks more than to her extensive commerce and flourishing trade. . . . Wealth and health flow from their sides; and liberty is always safe among their passes."[3] In this and similar passages, Willey infused the mountains with moral value, identifying them as sanctuaries promoting health, prosperity, and freedom.

Reverend Willey also used exalted language to highlight geological formations that were growing in popularity among tourists, such as the Flume, the Basin, the Devil's Den, and, most famous of all, the Old Man of the Mountain, which Francis Whitcomb and Luke Brooks had discovered in 1805.[4] Formed by the accidental convergence of geological pressures over thousands of years, the Old Man was perhaps the most outstanding example in the United States of the tendency humans have to assign traits that they admire in themselves to natural phenomena, thus claiming a kind of ownership of those phenomena. Reverend Willey described the Old Man's traits as vividly as they have ever been described:

The expression of the face, as it stands out in bold relief against the sky, is quite stern. The mouth alone betrays any signs of age and feebleness. But the "Old Man of the Mountains" has never been known to flinch. "He neither blinks at the near flashes of the lightning beneath his nose, nor flinches from the driving snow and sleet of the Franconia winter, which makes the mercury of the thermometer shrink into the bulb and congeal."[5]

Here was the character of New England incarnate—stalwart, unflinching, solid with integrity. In the cultural figure of the Old Man, nature acquired symbolic significance as the embodiment of traits that did not even have to be stated to be understood. A purely accidental phenomenon of nature thus ascended to the level of an icon.

Another White Mountain classic in the same vein as *Incidents* is John Hubbard Spaulding's *Guide and Historical Relics of the White Mountains*, published in 1855. Spaulding was the manager of the Tip-Top House on the summit of Mount Washington. His uncle, Samuel Fitch Spaulding of Lancaster, had built the hotel and opened it in 1853, and John wrote his book to revivify White Mountain legends and to entice visitors to the region.[6] *Relics* contains some history but is primarily a guide to various locales in the Whites, sweetened with legends and tales that had been circulating for years. It tells, for instance, the legend of Giant's Grave, in which a Native American stands on the mound and intones, "*No pale-face shall take deep root here; this the Great Spirit whispered in my ear.*"[7] Another story concerns Granny Stalbird's Rock, in Crawford Notch, where Granny, noted for her knowledge of herbs, seeks shelter from a terrible storm by hiding beneath an enormous boulder. Forever after, the boulder has carried Granny's name.

Spaulding spun his stories with lively detail but made little effort to separate fact from legend. However, the point was not to achieve factual accuracy but to create an allure about the mountains that would increase tourism. In retelling these stories, Spaulding was doing exactly what Willey was doing—creating a mythic narrative of the White Mountains that infused nature with moral and spiritual significance. In titling his book *Relics*, he implied that the mountain locales about which he wrote were quasi-religious places in the temple of nature.

In keeping with this theme, he recounted a number of legends in which spirits made themselves visible. In one legend, a white hunter in the mountains sets up camp by a stream and settles down to sleep; the moon rises and spreads its light through the night air, except for a large shadow cast by the nearby mountain. Suddenly the hunter hears a peculiar sound, and, raising his head, sees that the mist hanging over the top of the mountain has solidified into the shape of a large church. Within this church, the hunter can see

5.1. Nathaniel Hawthorne. Hawthorne wrote three tales of the Whites: "The Ambitious Guest," "The Great Carbuncle," and "The Great Stone Face." He also wrote a nonfiction sketch, "Our Evening Party Among the Mountains," about his stay at Ethan Allen Crawford's inn. Like Thomas Cole, he imbued the White Mountain landscape with a sense of mystery and danger and emphasized the wild aspects of the mountains' beauty. Brady-Handy Photograph Collection, Library of Congress Prints and Photographs Division, Washington, D.C.

an altar, around which the smoke of incense curls. Through the smoke, he sees native people "kneeling in profound silence" and hears the notes of a song drift toward him through the frigid night air.[8] Then, just as suddenly as they appeared, the church and its altar vanish, and a group of men descend the mountain "in solemn silence." As they climb down, the hunter sees the shapes of silvery fairies. The vision ends abruptly with the sudden sound of a "loud laugh of brutal triumph," evoking the presence of the supernatural in the mountains.[9]

Nathaniel Hawthorne used wild nature in ways similar to those of Spaulding but with far greater artistic consciousness. He wrote three popular tales about the White Mountains: "The Ambitious Guest," "The Great Carbuncle," and "The Great Stone Face," as well as a nonfiction account of an evening spent at Ethan Allen Crawford's inn, titled "Our Evening Party Among the Mountains." In Hawthorne's hands, the beautiful phenomena of wild nature become literary symbols through which the narrator reveals the moral behavior of his characters; through their symbolic use, the phenomena of nature acquire personal and moral meanings for readers.

Throughout his life, Hawthorne was keenly attuned to his natural surroundings. He spent part of his boyhood visiting relatives on the shores of Maine's Sebago Lake, from which he could see granite-capped mountains in the distance. They held great allure for him, but it was not until 1832 that he

5.2. The old Willey house. Samuel Willey and his family were living in this house in Crawford Notch when an avalanche swept down the mountain on August 28, 1826, and killed the entire family. Nathaniel Hawthorne memorialized the episode in his story "The Ambitious Guest." Horace Fabyan later bought the house and added onto it; the corner of the addition is visible in the photograph. Fire claimed the old house on September 25, 1899. Courtesy of Dartmouth College Library.

visited them, embarking on a trip that took him not only to the Whites but also to Lake Champlain, Lake Ontario, and Niagara Falls. In the Whites, he visited the most famous attractions, including the Old Man of the Mountain, and stayed at Ethan Crawford's inn at the head of the notch. Despondent over setbacks in his writing career, he found that the tour revived his ambition to write, and he came away overflowing with plot ideas.[10]

The most historical of Hawthorne's White Mountain tales is "The Ambitious Guest," based on the Willey disaster, which impressed him deeply when he traveled through the notch. The story begins with the unnamed family, gathered in their cabin in the shadow of the steep mountains. Immediately the narrator establishes a mood of dire expectancy: "This family were situated in the Notch of the White Hills, where the wind was sharp throughout the year, and pitilessly cold in the winter."[11] The passage establishes that nature will be a central character in this tale.

The house is a small inn for travelers, and as the family members sit huddled in their tiny living area, a stranger knocks and enters, seeking shelter for the night. They accept him, and he pulls a chair to the fire, joining the family with its "warmth and simplicity of feeling." The young man begins to talk and makes his ambitions clear. He desperately wants to make something of his life, to be distinguished in some way so that he will not be forgotten when his earthly life ends. But so far, he confesses, he has accomplished nothing: "Were I to vanish from the earth to-morrow, none would know so much of me as you."[12] It is a chilling piece of foreshadowing. The young man's dreams and ambitions provoke similar thoughts in the rest of the family, who express their own ambitions.

But as they share these visions for the future, the wind through the notch takes "a deeper and drearier sound," as if the mountains are alive with spirits. The grandmother of the family, who has been silent up to now, says that while the others have been "wishing and planning," she has been preparing for her inevitable end by laying out her "graveclothes . . . a nice linen shroud, a cap with a muslin ruff, and everything of a finer sort that she had worn since her wedding day." The grandmother remembers a superstition that if anything is amiss in a person's clothes at the moment of death, the corpse will raise its hands and attempt to rearrange the burial costume. She asks the others, when she is dead, to hold a mirror over her face so that she "may take a glimpse at myself, and see whether all's right."[13]

After this gloomy invocation, silence settles over the group, until they suddenly feel the little house tremble, as if "the foundations of the earth" are being shaken. All look wildly at one another and exclaim, "The Slide! The Slide!" It is "the unutterable horror of the catastrophe." All rush from the cottage, seeking "refuge in what they deemed a safer spot," where the family built a barrier. But in a tragic twist of irony, they run directly into the path of the slide, which has been divided by a huge boulder into two branches, parting to spare the house but destroying everything else on the side of the mountain; the entire family perishes. When rescuers arrive at the site of the tragedy the next morning, they find the fire still burning in the hearth and the chairs still gathered in a circle around the fire. But a mystery remains—was there a stranger in the cabin during the avalanche? Some say so, but others deny that there are "sufficient grounds for such a conjecture." The narrator then summarizes the theme of the tale: "Woe for the high-souled youth, with his dream of Early Immortality!"[14]

In this tale, nature is the protagonist; it acts on its own will and determines the fate of the people in the valley. One way in which the author underscores the potency of nature is through personification, when, for example, the father of the family says, "The old mountain has thrown a stone at us, for fear we should forget him."[15] The passage hints at nature's power to affect human hopes and dreams. In such passages, Hawthorne was reversing the relationship between humanity and nature that had been predominant in American culture. Humanity's mission, dating from the colonial period, had been to modify nature by clearing the forests, planting fields, damming rivers, and constructing roads and towns. But through the metaphor of the avalanche that buried the Willey family, the author is saying that, in reality, nature is the awesome force that acts on humanity, and to imagine otherwise reveals a deeply flawed and hubristic view of the relationship between humanity and the natural world.

On the evening that Hawthorne stayed at Ethan Crawford's inn, he heard the legend of a great emerald hidden somewhere in the mountains, which he imaginatively transformed into the story "The Great Carbuncle," an allegory of human greed, self-delusion, and happiness. It relates the tale of a party of adventurers who have traveled to the Crystal Hills in search of the Carbuncle. The party includes six men, all of whom are "selfish and solitary," and a young newlywed couple, Matthew and Hannah. Significantly, the setting of the story is a "remote and solitary region," "a vast extent of wilderness" that "lay between them and the nearest settlement."[16] Far from the trappings of civilization, the wilderness provides a stark, unblinking view of human foibles and makes clear the moral lessons of the tale.

The Carbuncle was a mythical gem sought by countless treasure hunters in the White Mountains during the colonial era. Hawthorne used this historical association to transform the Carbuncle into a symbol of humanity's never-ending quest for inner fulfillment through external means, particularly riches and fame. In this story, the group of adventurers includes the Seeker, who has gone nearly insane because of greed; Ichabod Pigsnort, who is reputed to roll naked every evening in piles of silver; Dr. Cacaphodel, an alchemist who wants to reduce the Carbuncle to its first elements in a quest for scientific knowledge; the Cynic, who wears enormous glasses through which he sees all in a negative light; a poet, whose verses are ethereal and abstract; Lord de Vere, a pretentious Englishman who wishes to hang the Carbuncle in his ancestral castle; and Matthew and Hannah, innocent newlyweds who want to bring the gem back to their cottage, where it will brighten their house and deepen their love.[17]

As the story proceeds, Matthew and Hannah awaken in the morning to find that the others have departed to begin their search for the gem. Before following the others, they take time to cleanse themselves:

> But Matthew and Hannah, after their calm rest, were as light as two young deer, and merely stopped to say their prayers and wash themselves in a cold pool of the Amonoosuck, and then to taste a morsel of food, ere they turned their faces to the mountain-side.[18]

In this passage, the young couple display a high degree of integration with the natural world. They take on the characteristics of the deer of the forests, and in washing themselves in the river, they perform an ablution that leaves them morally and spiritually cleansed. Because they are grounded in the world of nature, they live by authentic values that will guide them to a destiny that is far different from those of the other fortune seekers.

Matthew and Hannah climb the mountain until they arrive at a beautiful lake, where they see the Great Carbuncle. But they are not the first to have reached the spot, and here the narrator tells us of the fate of each of the other fortune seekers, whose destinies flow from their inauthentic values. At the foot of the lake is the Seeker, who found the gem and died immediately, destined never to enjoy the fruits of his greed. Matthew and Hannah then see the Cynic, who claims that he cannot see the Carbuncle. Matthew implores, "Take off those abominable spectacles, and you cannot help seeing it!"[19] But when the Cynic does so and looks, the sight of the Carbuncle blinds him.

When Hannah and Matthew see what has happened to the Seeker and the Cynic, they renounce the Carbuncle. They realize that they have internalized their love for each other and do not need the external validation provided by the Carbuncle. The remaining members of the party meet far different fates. The merchant loses all his wealth. The poet returns to his home with a great piece of ice that he uses for inspiration, but the literary critics claim that his poetry remains cold and distant. Lord de Vere makes his way back to his ancestral home empty-handed and eventually dies. The miserable Cynic wanders blindly throughout the world, looking for light but never finding it. The inauthenticity of their values dooms them to lives of desperation. Dr. Cacaphodel, however, meets a somewhat more hopeful fate. The doctor is not able to take the Carbuncle back to his laboratory to study it, as he intended. Instead, he returns with a large sample of granite, which he grinds to powder, dissolves in acids, melts in a crucible, and burns with a blowpipe. After all these experiments, he publishes his results "in one of the heaviest folios of the day."[20] Perhaps, the author seems to be saying, scientific knowledge may provide a firm foundation for authentic human endeavor.

As in "The Ambitious Guest," Hawthorne turned wild nature into a central character through which a moral lesson was taught. In the story, the Carbuncle is the symbol of each seeker's own projected hopes and illusions. However, the only two people who enrich their lives from the experience are Matthew and Hannah, who have an intimate relationship with the natural world. Their actions show that their values are authentic, that they have no need of the light provided by the Carbuncle. Instead, the light shines inside them, sustaining their enduring love.

The third of Hawthorne's White Mountain tales is "The Great Stone Face," a story of the Old Man of the Mountain that became one of his most beloved short works. In the tale, Hawthorne once again imbues wild nature with

5.3. Enthroned among the clouds, the Old Man of the Mountain. The most iconic of all White Mountain landmarks, it was often portrayed in cloudy, shadowy conditions, accentuating the mood of mystery that surrounded the geographic formation. Hawthorne's story "The Great Stone Face" helped solidify the Old Man as a White Mountain landmark. Courtesy of Dartmouth College Library.

moral significance. The story's setting is Franconia Notch, and its central symbol is the Old Man of the Mountain. At the center of the story is a young boy named Ernest, whose mother tells him of an ancient prophecy that a child will be born whose face resembles the Great Stone Face and who is destined to become the wisest leader of the time. As the story unfolds, a succession of men—a wealthy man, an aging soldier, and a politician—are rumored to be the ones who will fulfill the prophecy. But all three turn out to be pretenders, for none approaches the high moral standards implicit in the moral integrity symbolized by the Great Stone Face.

Ironically, as Ernest searches for the one who will fulfill the prophecy, he himself grows into a wise man with great spiritual gifts. Eventually Ernest becomes a preacher, and as his fame spreads throughout the mountain region, people travel from afar to receive his wisdom. One of these is a well-known poet who grew up in the valley and has returned for a visit. Even though the poet no longer makes the valley his home, he continues to be inspired by its beauty.

Ernest and the poet walk together to a place where Ernest will preach—a "natural pulpit" directly across from the Great Stone Face. To the large crowd that gathers, Ernest speaks from his heart, and his inspiring words are "the words of life, because a life of good deeds and holy love was melted into them." The poet is moved to tears; just at that moment, his gaze falls upon the Great Stone Face, and he immediately sees the likeness between the stone profile and Ernest's face. The poet shouts to the crowd, "Behold! Behold! Ernest is himself a likeness of the Great Stone Face!"[21] We realize that Ernest shares in the divinity of the mountains and of all nature, as symbolized by the Great Stone Face. He remains, however, humble and simply leaves the valley with the poet, hoping that a person better than he will come to the valley and fulfill the prophecy.

Throughout this tale, Hawthorne describes the mountains as a place where angels abide, just as the Abenaki regarded the mountains as the dwelling place of the Great Spirit. At one point, the mists part and reveal the awe-inspiring features of the Great Stone Face, "as if a mighty angel were sitting among the hills." As Ernest enters middle age, his years of meditation endow him with such wisdom "that it seems as though he had been talking with the angels."[22]

In all three of these stories, Hawthorne packs images of nature with symbolic meaning, elevating the significance of those natural phenomena. The Willey slide represents forces outside humanity's control that control our destinies. The Great Carbuncle represents the illusory nature of many of humanity's hopes and dreams. And the Great Stone Face represents qualities that abide within us but that we do not see because we are constantly looking outside ourselves to fill the deficits that we feel so acutely.

Hawthorne's stories elevated the White Mountains as a subject for serious literary expression. With these stories and with the rich oral tradition of legends, the White Mountains were assuming a prominent place in the American imagination. Moreover, by making frequent use of personification, he was implying that the earth is a living, breathing organism. In "The Ambitious Guest," Hawthorne compares the Notch of the Mountains to "a great artery, through which the life-blood of internal commerce is continually throbbing between Maine, on one side, and the Green Mountains and the shores of the St. Lawrence, on the other."[23] In "The Great Carbuncle," the rocky summits of the mountains "throw off their shaggy mantle of forest trees, and either robe themselves in clouds or tower naked into the sky."[24] In "The Great Stone Face," the features of the Old Man of the Mountain are "noble," its expression "at once grand and sweet, as if it were the glow of a vast, warm heart."[25] Through such imagery, nature and wilderness breathe with the vitality of dynamic organisms.

By the middle of the nineteenth century, literary styles were beginning to shift away from Romanticism and toward more realistic modes of expression,

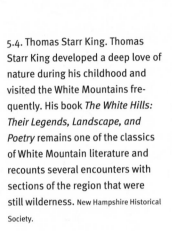

5.4. Thomas Starr King. Thomas Starr King developed a deep love of nature during his childhood and visited the White Mountains frequently. His book *The White Hills: Their Legends, Landscape, and Poetry* remains one of the classics of White Mountain literature and recounts several encounters with sections of the region that were still wilderness. New Hampshire Historical Society.

and writing about the White Mountains reflected this trend, with a greater emphasis on close observation of nature and accuracy of detail. A new kind of nonfiction writing emerged that was inspired by Thoreau's *Walden* and that took as its purpose the education of the American public about the nation's wondrous natural beauties. The White Mountains inspired one of the pioneering works in this genre—Thomas Starr King's monumental *The White Hills: Their Legends, Landscape, and Poetry* (1859), a distinctive blend of nature description, history, scientific knowledge, and philosophical meditation.

Thomas Starr King developed an intense love of nature while growing up as the son of a Unitarian clergyman in Charlestown, Massachusetts. In 1839, when he was only fifteen years old, his father died, leaving his family penniless. But young Thomas, who was a voracious reader and spoke with an eloquence that was far beyond his years, came to the attention of some of the leading literary lights in Boston, including Warren Sawyer, the president of the Mercantile Library Association. Starr King had prepared a lecture on Goethe, and Sawyer asked two friends of his, E. P. Whipple and James T. Fields, to invite the young man to deliver a lecture on the German poet to the association. The young man was reluctant, but they convinced him, and the lecture turned out to be an enormous success.[26] Starr King and Whipple commenced a lifelong friendship, sharing a love of nature in general and of the White Mountains in particular.

Starr King's earliest confirmed visit to the mountains was in 1849, although he may have visited them in 1837 in the company of his father. On the 1849 journey, he traveled past Lake Winnipesaukee and Lake Ossipee, finally arriving at Thomas Crawford's Notch House. While staying in the notch, he and his party of fellow travelers stopped at the Willey house, when a deafening clap of thunder startled all of them, causing a wave of emotion to sweep through the group as they sat astride their horses and contemplated the tragic deaths of the Willey family. The scene, with its poignant juxtaposition of beauty and tragedy, moved Starr King enormously. He rode horseback to the top of Mount Washington, where he admired the magnificent views, and on succeeding days, he visited other well-known sites in the mountains, including Franconia Notch.[27]

With this visit, Starr King fell under the spell of the mountains and was repeatedly drawn back to them. Using the town of Gorham as his base, he explored, observed, took notes, and, in 1853, began to write articles about the mountains for the *Boston Transcript*. Six years later, he had enough material to shape into *The White Hills*, which became an immediate critical and popular success. Even though he left New England soon after for California, the book remained an enduring legacy of his love for the Whites. Starr King's purpose in writing it was to influence Americans' attitudes toward wild nature by fashioning a comprehensive portrait of the mountains that would encompass natural history, philosophy, religion, legend, literature, and science. In addition to his own nature writing, the volume includes poems by John Greenleaf Whittier, William Cullen Bryant, Henry Wadsworth Longfellow, and James Russell Lowell, as well as two chapters that Professor Edward Tuckerman of Amherst College wrote on the historical explorations of the White Mountain region and on the mountains' flora and fauna.

While the book includes lovely descriptions of the region's rural landscapes, its most memorable passages glorify the wildness of the mountains. Nowhere is Starr King's celebration of wilderness more evident than in a wonderful account of an expedition he organized that took a northern route to the summit of Mount Washington, traversing Mounts Madison, Adams, Jefferson, and Clay along the way. He had traveled often on the Cherry Mountain road between Gorham and Jefferson and had noticed a deep ravine that might provide the starting point for a northern route to Mount Washington. He knew intuitively that, in that ravine, he would find "the very spirit of the hills" and "the weirdness, freshness, and majesty which 'carriage-roads' and hurrying feet and 'Tip-Top Houses' are driving or disenchanting from Mount Washington."[28]

The group of four that he recruited included a guide named Gordon, a Boston lawyer who had backcountry experience, a minister, and an artist. They embarked from the northern base of Mount Adams, beyond Randolph Hill, and trekked through a forest before beginning to climb into the ravine itself.

No trail existed, so they followed a stream all the way into the ravine. After climbing through the gorge for several hours, they set up camp for the night at a spot where they could see the "easterly cliff of the gorge," which "glowed with vivid gold." In the wild, Starr King rhapsodized, the smallest pleasures were magnified. Even the tea he drank tasted more delicious than it ever had before, and he wondered, "Was it because it was made of water tapped in its granite service-pipe, half-way between the clouds and the lower earth, that it yielded a flavor more exquisite than the cream of the Alpine House had ever imparted before?"[29]

When the party awoke the next morning, the weather was splendid, and they resumed their climb. For six hours they struggled upward until they finally reached a plateau from which they could see Mount Adams and a magnificent view of "grand rock scenery"—a stunning blend of "strength and beauty."[30] They then came within view of the cone of Mount Madison—"steep, symmetrical, and sharp, with more commanding beauty of form than any other summit of the White Hills has ever shown to my eye." After admiring the immense beauty of the mountain, they pushed onward, for the time was now past noon and they needed to reach Mount Washington's summit, where they would spend the night, by dusk. They traversed Mount Adams, Mount Jefferson, and Mount Clay, arriving finally at Mount Washington's Tip-Top House at seven o'clock that evening.[31] There they were rewarded with an unusually clear view of the surrounding countryside, including Lovewell's Pond, Sebago Lake, Lake Ossipee, Lake Winnipesaukee, and, gleaming in the distance, the Atlantic Ocean.

King was proud of the climb, stating that "there is no approach to Mount Washington, and no series of mountain views, comparable with this ascent and its surroundings on the northerly side."[32] As they descended the next day, he traveled a small distance ahead of the party and experienced an exquisite silence in which he found "perfect peace, perfect stillness, universal brightness, the fullness of vision, and a wondrous glory in all the heaven, and over all the earth."[33] It was a near-mystical experience that signified the power of the wilderness to inspire the human soul to higher aspirations.

Perhaps the most forward-looking aspect of The White Hills was its expression of an early ecological consciousness, which emerged in certain passages that explored the relationships among the mountains, valleys, river ways, and weather of the White Mountains. For example, in one beautifully written section, he explained the critical role that mountains play in the distribution of precipitation:

The uses of mountain ranges, in relation to the supply of water, are so evident that we need not dwell long upon them. It is plain that we could not live upon the globe in any state of civilization, if the surface had been finished as a monotonous prairie. Were it not for the great swells of land, the ridges and crests of rock, the wrinkles, curves, and writhings of the strata, how could springs of water be formed? What drainage could a country have? How could the rains be hoarded in fountains and lakes? Where would be the storehouses of the snow and hail?[34]

Through such passages, Starr King was teaching the American public to look at geographical regions as systems with complex interactions of forces and materials—winds and storms, rocks and soils, vegetation and animals. By examining these complex interactions, he was introducing a new way of looking at America's wildernesses. *The White Hills* represented a major milestone in nature writing not only because it celebrated the beauties of the mountain wilderness but because it helped to build the groundwork for understanding mountains as ecosystems.

Two poets of the same era were no less influential than Starr King in bringing the White Mountains to the attention of the American reading public— John Greenleaf Whittier and Lucy Larcom. Both were from the Boston area, and both spent delicious summers in the White Mountains. They shared a friendship that evolved over the years, from Whittier's initial mentoring of Larcom to the more equal relation of poets who had both attained widespread popularity. Because they wrote so many verses about the Whites, they may have done as much as Starr King did to popularize the region. And though neither of them embraced the wildness of the mountains as passionately as King, they did pen some lovely images of wild nature. Most importantly, though, they shared a sense of the sacredness of the mountains that expressed itself in memorable images of nature's beauty as the reflection of God's beneficence.

Whittier was born on December 17, 1807, on a farm near Haverhill, Massachusetts, the oldest son and second child of John Whittier and Abigail Hussy, who were devout Quakers. He started writing poetry as a child, but it took him time to establish himself as a poet, and he took work as an editor of a number of publications. He also emerged as a leading abolitionist voice after the publication in 1833 of *Justice and Expediency,* an impassioned diatribe against slavery.[35] In 1866, he achieved national fame with the publication of *Snow-Bound,* a portrayal of the rural area around Haverhill that brought him enormous popularity and ensured his financial security for the rest of his life. Because of its success, he had the means to visit the White Mountain region every summer, often staying at Center Harbor on Lake Winnepesaukee.[36] There, he always slept in the southeast room so that he could watch the sun rise.

Whittier believed that contact with nature benefited people by bringing out the noblest aspects of the human character, providing a refuge for healing and inner peace and inspiring meditations on God. According to one of his biographers, "[I]f Whittier's views about art inclined toward moralism, they also inclined toward realism."[37] Particularly in his narrative poems, he depicted rural folk whose lives were integrated organically with the rhythms of the natural world, and he populated his verse with idealized images of rural Americana, such as holidays, feasts, and sleigh rides. Over and over in his poetry, he highlighted the simplicity and forthrightness of rural folk and connected those values to the transformative power of nature. However, at times he also celebrated the raw grandeur of the wilderness. In "Franconia from the Pemigewasset," the poet forged stirring images of the power of a mountain storm:

> Last night's thunder-gust
> Roared not in vain: for where its lightnings thrust
> Their tongues of fire, the great peaks seem so near,
> Burned clean of mist, so starkly bold and clear,
> I almost pause the wind in the pines to hear,
> The loose rock's fall, the steps of browsing deer.
> The clouds that shattered on yon slide-worn walls
> And splintered on the rocks their spears of rain
> Have set in play a thousand waterfalls.[38]

The thunder and lightning have "Burned clean" the "mist," cleansing the mountains, purifying them, loosing the water from the sides and sending it plunging into "a thousand waterfalls." Such images of transformation wrought by nature resonated powerfully with an American public that sought refuge from the wrenching social changes caused by rapidly growing cities, the growth of urban poverty, the soullessness of factory work, and other social ills that accompanied rapid industrialization after the Civil War.

The most powerful sign of the transformative power of nature is Whittier's evocation of the transcendent in wild nature. In his nature poetry, God makes Himself immanent through the mountains, forests, rivers, lakes, and other beauties of the natural world. In "The Last Walk in Autumn," the poet tramps through the woods, which are the "Rich gift of God" made visible through "hues wherewith our Northern clime / Makes autumn's dropping woodlands gay."[39] Whittier further explores the theme of God's presence in the natural world in "Summer by the Lakeside," which captures scenes at Lake Winnipesaukee at noon and in the evening. As the afternoon ends and the shadows of dusk approach, the poet meditates on the approach of death but is comforted by nature:

> Rocked on her breast, these pines and I
> Alike on Nature's love rely;
> And equal seems to live or die.
>
> Assured that He whose presence fills
> With light the spaces of these hills
> No evil to His creatures wills,
>
> The simple faith remains, that He
> Will do, whatever that may be,
> The best alike for man and tree.[40]

Not only is God present in nature, but He cares for the creatures and trees as well as for humanity. The poet is expressing the revolutionary idea that flora and fauna share equal status with humanity in this world. All parts of God's creation are to be valued, and by extension, humanity must care for the trees, flowers, forests, and streams. With these ideas, Whittier and other nature poets of the time were engaged in an astounding project that represented a revolution in attitudes toward nature. They were restoring the sacred to nature, giving it a sense of the divine that had been lost as civilization had been carved out of the wilderness.

Closely connected with Whittier was Lucy Larcom, a native of Beverly, Massachusetts, who, at various times in her life, worked as an operative at the textile mills in Lowell, Massachusetts; authored the best-selling *New England Girlhood from Memory*, a memoir of the mill experience; and became one of the most popular female poets of the mid–nineteenth century. Whittier was her friend and colleague, advising her on poetry and helping her establish herself as a self-supporting author. Like Whittier, she adored the White Mountains, summered there, and wrote numerous poems about the region. Also like him, she introduced the love of nature to a wide readership and deepened the affection that thousands of her readers felt toward the Whites.

To accomplish all this, she had to overcome immense odds. She was born in 1824 to Benjamin Larcom, a retired sea captain, and Lois Barrett.[41] The family lived in Beverly, which was still rural at the time, and there she fell in love with the outdoors. In 1832, Captain Larcom died, leaving the family with no source of income, and after struggling for three more years in Beverly, Mrs. Larcom finally decided in 1835 to move the family to Lowell and keep a boardinghouse for the young women who worked in the mills. The

5.5. Lucy Larcom. While spending her formative years working in the Lowell textile mills, Lucy Larcom began to write for the mill operatives' journal, *The Lowell Offering*. She first visited the White Mountains in 1859, visited them regularly after 1861, and produced many poems featuring scenes from the region. New Hampshire Historical Society.

next year, when she was twelve years old, Lucy went to work as an operative in the mills.

Larcom began to find her voice as a writer through the *Lowell Offering,* the renowned literary magazine that published the writings of mill operatives from 1840 to 1845. Like other young women in the mills, she attended school three months a year, where she learned to read and write. Her older sister Eveline was active in the group that edited the *Offering,* and soon Lucy was contributing poems to the journal. In 1844, Whittier came to Lowell as the editor of the *Middlesex Standard,* and one evening, Harriet Farley, a coeditor of the *Offering,* brought him to a meeting of their "improvement circle." Larcom met Whittier at these meetings and showed him some of her poems, but he left Lowell soon after, and a friendship would not develop between them until their paths crossed again years later. Over the next few years, she completed her education, gained some teaching experience, and returned to Beverly. More confident from her years of independence and education, she now entered Whittier's literary circle and became close friends with his sister, Elizabeth.[42]

In 1859, Larcom visited the White Mountains for the first time and was astounded by their beauty. In a letter to a friend, she wrote how "delightful" it was to "move on naturally and without thought, like sunshine and cloud and breeze, or to be moved as the leaf is by the wind—to be shone on as the flower is by the sun—this is the life—one kind of life, and the Epicurean existence has its charms."[43] Beginning in 1861, she visited the mountains regularly, and her love for them found expression in dozens of poems that were notable for their accurate descriptions of specific locales. As she became more familiar with the mountains, her poetic output grew, and she published in magazines as prestigious as the *Atlantic Monthly.*

As time went on, Larcom spent longer periods in the Whites. Often she would find a spot in the woods, perhaps next to a stream, where she could be alone, absorb the views, and make notes from which she would draw imagery for her poems. In her most effective poems, Larcom produces finely observed natural details that quietly evoke the beauty of the White Mountains. For example, in "Clouds on White Face," she effectively uses contrasting images to explore the varying moods of the mountain:

> So lovingly the clouds caress his head—
>> The mountain-monarch; he, severe and hard,
>> With white face set like flint horizon-ward;
> They weaving softest fleece of gold and red,
> And gossamer of airiest silver thread,
>> To wrap his form, wind-beaten, thunder-scarred.[44]

Larcom portrays the mountain as alive, dynamic, capable of emotion. Even the inanimate phenomena of nature, such as rocks and water, brim with life and meaning. The mountain wears the same mythic bearing that the Old Man of the Mountain does in Hawthorne's story "The Great Stone Face." Her most frequently occurring theme, however, is the intuition of God's presence in nature. She was greatly influenced by Emerson but modified his ideas to suit her own perceptions and beliefs. To Emerson, the Oversoul was a transcendent yet impersonal force that infused its spirit into all living phenomena. To Larcom, the transcendent spirit was a personal God whose spirit permeated nature and was evident in the landscape. An explicit expression of this theme appears in "In a Cloud Rift," in which the poet has climbed to the summit of Mount Washington and feels powerful intimations of God's presence:

> Upon our loftiest White Mountain peak,
>> Filled with the freshness of untainted air,
> We sat, nor cared to listen or to speak
>> To one another, for the silence there
> Was eloquent with God's presence. Not a sound
>> Uttered the winds in their unhindered sweep[45]

The poet and her fellow climbers undergo an experience that approaches mysticism, as the mountaintop brings them closer to God, amid a deep silence that is "eloquent with God's presence." In "The Summit-Flower," Larcom makes even more explicit the theme of spiritual insight attained at the summit of a mountain. As she stands atop Mount Washington, the poet feels the burdens of life's worries:

> The mountains crush me with their savage might;
> Nature's rude strength is more than I can bear.

Then she sees a beautiful yet hardy flower, growing alone on the granite cone of the mountain yet offering her comfort:

> O little white flower on the summit born,
> How tenderly you look into my eyes!

In the next stanza, the poet meditates on the spiritual significance of this little flower:

> I touch your leaf with reverence, little flower!
> I think of spiritual heights beyond your ken,
> Where mightier movements of invisible power
> Mould into God-like grace the lives of men.[46]

In her intuition of the presence of God at the summit of the mountain, Larcom was drawing on the centuries-old archetype of mountains as the intersection of the human and the divine. In *The White Hills,* Thomas Starr King showed that he shared this intuition, as reflected in an ode to the Indian chief Sagamore that concludes with this stirring evocation of the eternal spirit of the mountains:

> Our very works are tombstones to our dust!
> Achilles rears his mound and saith, "I lived!"
> God utters forth a voice, and mountains rise
> And whisper to eternity, "I am!"[47]

In another passage, as King contemplates Mount Kearsarge, he realizes with "a well of joy" that "If the spectacles could be shown as miracles, the first creations of the spirit that quickeneth all things, what wonder and rapture would respond to them!"[48] He then relates a legend about Brahma, who has heard a complaint that while the base of a mountain is mantled with beautiful green forests, its summit is barren of all but cold rock. Brahma responds, "The very light shall clothe thee, and the shadow of the passing cloud shall be as a royal mantle. More verdure would be less light. Thou shalt share in the azure of heaven, and the youngest and whitest cloud of a summer's sky shall nestle in thy bosom."[49]

Such language used by King, Whittier, and Larcom is the language of worship, at an altar formed of mountain and stream, of purple sunsets, of insects with delicately veined wings, and of colors so rich that they embed themselves forever in the eye's memory. It was with such language—and with the sublime images of Thomas Cole's art—that the wild beauties of the White Mountains began to inhabit a sanctified place in the hearts of a significant part of the American population that was beginning to look to nature for solace and inspiration. In such language and through such art, the Whites acquired enormous aesthetic, moral, and spiritual value. The mountains took center stage, along with the Adirondacks, as a place with unique significance in the literary and artistic life of the nation, and it was here that American artists and poets taught their compatriots to love nature and wilderness. When environmental degradation would threaten the mountains only three decades later, those Americans who had learned to love the White Mountains through this wonderful art and literature would feel as if a part of their heart was being ripped out, and they would not hesitate to take action to preserve the beauty of the sublime mountain forests.

Chapter 6

WHITE MOUNTAIN ART AND THE
DOMESTICATION OF WILDERNESS

IN THE EARLY 1840s, Samuel W. Thompson established an inn in North
Conway for the scores of teamsters who drove teams of horses and oxen
through Crawford Notch and Pinkham Notch every week. At first his inn
thrived, but within ten years, railroads had extended their reach into the
mountains and taken away most of the business of transporting raw materials and goods through the notches. The number of customers at Thompson's
inn plummeted, and he feared that he would lose his livelihood. But one
night, a landscape painter came to stay at the inn . . . and then stayed another
night, and another night. By the time he departed, months later, he had painted
a number of canvases that found a ready market. Thompson's son later recalled, "This one man was enthusiastic, others saw his pictures or heard of
them and came to this wonderfully beautiful place. Not many years after that
Champney and Kensett found our beautiful valley."[1] From that point on,
Thompson's inn became a favored haven for artists.

By the middle of the nineteenth century, the popularity of Thomas Cole's
landscapes had inspired dozens of artists like the one who visited Samuel
Thompson's inn to make pilgrimages to the White Mountains and produce
paintings that popularized the dramatic vistas of the region throughout the
United States and Europe. Among the artists sojourning to the Whites were such
pioneers of American landscape painting as Thomas Doughty, Asher Brown
Durand, Benjamin Champney, John F. Kensett, Frederic E. Church, John W.
Casilear, and Albert Bierstadt. Lesser-known artists such as Frank H. Shapleigh, George Loring Brown, and Edward Hill also thrived in the latter decades
of the 1800s. Some of these artists visited the mountains only briefly, while
others established studios in the region or became artists-in-residence at grand
hotels that began to populate the region after the Civil War. These artists' styles
of painting varied widely, but they shared a passion for the mountains' extraordinary vistas. It is no exaggeration to say that the art of this period played
a pivotal role in establishing the White Mountains as a beloved vacation destination for a middle class that was just beginning to discover the pleasures of
tourism.

The artists who traveled into the Whites in the 1840s found a landscape that was rapidly changing. The towns that had been founded in the late 1700s and early 1800s had grown, and the transformation of the landscape described in chapter 2 had continued apace. The roads that connected the towns were more extensive, the land was increasingly parceled off into farms, rivers had been dammed for irrigation and flood control. The farms that had at first struggled on the edge of the wilderness were now firmly established. Every town had several sawmills, which processed increasing numbers of trees into lumber and other wood products. The travelers who had once trickled into the White Mountains were becoming a stream, drawn by the beauty of the region, the popularity of Thomas Cole's paintings, the writings of Hawthorne and Starr King, the publicity that attended such tragedies as the deaths of the Willey family, and the reputation of small inns like those of the Crawfords.

While much of the mountain landscape remained wild, civilization was gradually encroaching upon that wilderness. The best way to observe this gradual evolution in the uses of land in the White Mountains is by examining the art of the region from the 1840s through the 1880s, for the canvases reflect explicitly the changes that were occurring in the mountainscape. But in addition to reflecting these changes in the landscape, the artists of this period defined ideal scenic beauty as a compromise between the wild nature of Thomas Cole's landscapes and the increasingly pastoral countryside. Through this compromise, the White Mountain art of the mid- to late nineteenth century reflected the American desire to settle the land, domesticate it, and put it to good, practical use. Moreover, the art revealed a conflict between the glorification of wilderness and the idealization of the forces of civilization—particularly economic development—that would continue to be apparent in White Mountain history.

In an essay for a comprehensive exhibit of White Mountain art at Dartmouth College in 1980, art historian Donald D. Keyes identified four phases in the evolution of White Mountain art—phases that reflected evolving, and sometimes conflicting, attitudes toward nature. The Romantic period, which was most associated with Thomas Cole, lasted from the 1820s to 1840; the picturesque period extended from 1840 to the Civil War; the mature White Mountain school of art, which was centered in North Conway, dominated after the war; and the final stage saw the decline of White Mountain art at the end of the nineteenth century.[2] The artists who are the focus of this chapter fall into the final three phases of this evolutionary arc.

Thomas Cole had drawn on the aesthetic theories of the sublime to develop an artistic style that emphasized the wild aspects of nature through such visual motifs as craggy cliffs, enormous forests untouched by the hand of humankind, and intense storm clouds gathering over the mountains. However, by the later years of Cole's career, even he could not ignore the signs of settlement in the White Mountains, and in his *Notch of the White Mountains* (1839), he incorporated the consequences of settlement through visual details such as stumps of cut trees and a small cabin on the floor of Crawford Notch.

As the countryside was increasingly transformed by such evidence of human activity, aesthetic theories about what constituted a beautiful landscape began to shift away from the sublime and toward the picturesque, a theory of landscape aesthetics that came out of England at the end of the 1700s but did not reach its peak of influence in the United States until the 1840s and 1850s. During that time, the theory provided artists with aesthetic principles for depicting human changes to the land while still celebrating the extraordinary natural beauty of areas like the White Mountains.[3]

Theories about the picturesque gained popularity in the United States through the writings of two Englishmen, Sir Uvedale Price and Robert Payne Knight, who, with William Gilpin, were instrumental in elaborating ideas about the picturesque.[4] Price was a squire who developed an interest in nature and landscape painting as he wandered the grounds of his family's estate in Herefordshire, England. For him, Burke's theory of the beautiful and the sublime did not account for the visual appeal of scenes that were more serene and orderly than the sublime landscapes that Burke had extolled. In a 1794 publication titled *An Essay on the Picturesque,* Price wrote, "[E]ven when I first read the original work [by Burke], I felt that there were numberless objects which gave delight to the eye and yet differed from the beautiful as from the sublime."[5] He saw the need for a third category of aesthetic qualities that could explain the appeal of certain scenes in nature, and this category he termed the picturesque, which emphasized the painterly qualities of scenic vistas.[6] Price believed that the two qualities that made a natural scene picturesque were variety and intricacy: "I am therefore persuaded, that the two opposite qualities of roughness, and of sudden variation, joined to that of irregularity, are the most efficient causes of the picturesque"[7] The theory of the picturesque was more suited than that of the sublime for rendering a landscape that was filling up rapidly with houses, barns, fences, cultivated fields, and grazing livestock; indeed, the goal was to integrate these signs of human impact without losing the charms of nature.

Price contrasted the picturesque with the Burkean concept of the sublime. The sublime, he wrote, has "greatness of dimension," but "the picturesque has no connection with dimension of any kind."[8] The sublime often creates the illusion of "infinity," as in depictions of the boundless ocean.[9] A picturesque scene, though, is limited by boundaries, which give form and dimension to a scene. Most important, the emotional impact of a picturesque scene is far different from that of a sublime one. The sublime is solemn and inspires terror, while the picturesque emphasizes what Donald Keyes has called "accessible magnificence"—scenes that are contemplative, calm, realistic.[10] The theory of the sublime had been perfect for capturing the wildness of the unspoiled White Mountain landscape; the theory of the picturesque was ideal for depicting a landscape that, while still lovely, was rapidly being populated and cultivated.

A transitional artist who incorporated elements of both the sublime and the picturesque was Asher Brown Durand, who had accompanied Cole on his final pilgrimage to the White Mountains in 1838. Born in 1796 in New Jersey, Durand suffered from fragile health. As a result, he later said, he "received a greater share of maternal solicitude," which developed in him a strong sense of himself as a person apart from others.[11] As a youth, he loved nature and spent countless hours exploring the still-rural countryside of New Jersey.[12] Inheriting artistic talent from his father, who was a watchmaker and silversmith, Durand became an engraver and eventually was a partner in a highly successful New York company that produced banknotes. But he grew increasingly frustrated by the growing commercialism of American life, and his sense of dissatisfaction led to disillusionment with the engraving business.[13]

In 1836, he left the company to devote himself to painting, quickly establishing himself as a portrait painter. But when the Panic of 1837 caused all his commissions to be canceled, he decided to pursue landscape painting, in which he could express his profound feeling for nature. "His love of nature was a passion," Daniel Huntington noted in a memorial address upon the artist's death in 1887, "an enthusiasm always burning within him, but it was like a steady fire, not a sudden blaze quickly sinking to ashes."[14] A deeply religious individual, Durand also found in landscape painting a means to celebrate God and nurture people toward more spiritual values through exposure to nature. "Nature may not cure," he wrote in his journal, "but she will soothe."[15]

Durand traveled incessantly throughout the Catskills, the Adirondacks, Vermont, and New Hampshire until he stopped painting in 1880. His paintings of the White Mountains followed visits to the region in 1855, 1856, and 1857, but although his mentor, Cole, had traveled into a pristine wilderness, Durand ventured into a region that was filling up with farms, towns, mills, railroads, and tourist hotels.[16] By 1851, tourists could ride the Atlantic and Saint Lawrence Railroad to a new station in Gorham, and from there, they had only an eight-mile ride via stagecoach to the base of Mount Washington.[17] Like Cole, Durand incorporated elements of the sublime into his canvases, but he also addressed these new realities. Where Cole was dramatic, Durand was quieter and more subtle. Where Cole exaggerated details in the landscape to achieve the effects of awe and terror, Durand endeavored to depict natural scenes realistically.

6.1. *Mount Chocorua, New Hampshire* (1855), Asher B. Durand. Durand's paintings of the White Mountains portray the land as wild, but in this view he has made the mountain appear more accessible by softening the sharp edges that characterized Cole's treatment of the same mountain. Museum of Art, Rhode Island School of Design, Gift of the Providence Art Association.

These differences are starkly apparent in Durand's *Mount Chocorua, New Hampshire* (1855), a painting that Robert L. McGrath, professor of art history at Dartmouth College, has termed "a nostalgic recreation of the mythic past."[18] Durand portrayed the mountain and valley as land that was still primarily wilderness, but the artist slightly rounded the contours of the mountain and suffused it with a soft light, making the peak less intimidating and more accessible than in Cole's comparable depiction of Chocorua.[19] In the catalogue for the 1980 Dartmouth exhibit on White Mountain art, Donald Keyes wrote:

[*Mount Chocorua, New Hampshire*] . . . is a watershed of the ideals embodied in the Sublime on the one hand and the Picturesque on the other. Representing the primitive state in which there is no overt view of man or his habitations, nonetheless the cleared land reflects the order man has imposed on a part of nature. The space is grand, with the mountain rising magnificently. . . . On

White Mountain Art ๏ 111

the other hand, Durand's space is carefully ordered with precisely rendered forms, all of which are set before a serene Lake Chocorua.[20]

Like Cole, Durand invested the landscape with spiritual significance—a reflection of the artist's Transcendentalism, the Emersonian belief that the infinitely rich details of nature point to higher spiritual realities. According to British historian Simon Schama, "Durand was, in effect, the theologian of the second generation of the Hudson Valley school. By his lights, the whole point of landscape was expressive veneration."[21] In Durand's *Chocorua,* the solitary peak clearly reaches toward heaven while looking benignly over the valley below. The painting expresses a soaring sense of spirituality through the intersection of Chocorua's peak with the heavenly clouds above.

Durand expressed his deeply held beliefs about the relationship between art and faith in his "Letters on Landscape Painting," which he wrote for the respected nineteenth-century literary journal *The Crayon.* In one letter, he wrote, "The voice of nature. . . is the voice of God."[22] In another, he averred that he felt God's presence most powerfully in the outdoors: "I have declined attendance on church service, the better to indulge reflection unrestrained under the high canopy of heaven, amidst the expanse of waters—fit place to worship God and contemplate the wonders of his power."[23] *Mount Chocorua, New Hampshire* is a powerful visual expression of that sense of worship, and it extends Cole's theme of the sacredness of nature and wilderness.

Another of Durand's White Mountain canvases highlights the picturesque integration of details of civilization into vistas of pastoral beauty. *White Mountain Scenery, Franconia Notch, New Hampshire* (1857) presents a scene in which the Pemigewasset River flows calmly across the foreground, while symbols of domestication are readily visible—two grazing cattle and a boat tied to a branch that overhangs the river. In the background, the Franconia Range provides a mountain backdrop for the pastoral scene. According to Professor McGrath, this painting is "another version of the . . . midcentury synthesis of the wild with the cultivated."[24] Its contemplative mood is accentuated by the soft colors that suffuse the air; moreover, the symbols of cultivation occupy the foreground, while the wild beauty of Franconia Notch recedes into the background.

White Mountain Scenery indicates the direction that White Mountain art was taking in the 1850s. American landscape artists were creating indelible images of a rural America in which the Jeffersonian vision of the self-sufficient farmer and the Jacksonian enthronement of the common person reached their apotheosis. The resulting art celebrated the values of individualism and rural democracy.[25] Even though the relationship between humanity and the land was utilitarian, the artists portrayed Americans pursuing those utilitarian goals in harmony with nature.

6.2. *White Mountain Scenery, Franconia Notch, New Hampshire* (1857), Asher B. Durand. By the mid-1800s, signs of human settlement were becoming a regular feature of White Mountain art. In this canvas, two grazing cattle and a boat tied to a branch are visible symbols of civilization. Yet still humanity lives in harmony with nature. Collection of The New-York Historical Society, Stuart Collection, on Permanent Loan from the New York Public Library, negative number 27105, S-105.

The White Mountain artist who best expressed the changing tastes in the American art-buying public was Benjamin Champney, whose paintings achieved enormous popularity in the 1870s and 1880s. In addition to being a leading artist in his own right, he took center stage in what came to be known as the White Mountain school of art by inspiring scores of other artists to make pilgrimages to the mountains. Born in New Ipswich, New Hampshire, in 1817, Champney was the son of Rebecca and Benjamin Champney, who was a lawyer but, in Champney's words, "was unfortunate in business."[26] When Champney's father died suddenly in 1827, his mother, with seven children to support, sent young Benjamin to live with her sister in Lebanon, New Hampshire. There he attended school for twelve weeks a year and worked at a local cotton mill owned by his uncle. From an early age, he enjoyed drawing and sketching.[27]

When Champney was sixteen, he migrated to Boston to work for a shoe dealer. Behind the dealer's store on Washington Street was the Pendleton Lithographic Company, and as he watched the engravers and artists enter and leave

6.3. Benjamin Champney. Benjamin Champney was probably the best known of the White Mountain artists to emerge after the Civil War. He maintained a studio in North Conway that was itself a tourist attraction. New Hampshire Historical Society.

the company's offices, he determined to talk himself into an apprenticeship there. Eventually he did so, and there he acquired his first formal training as a draftsman, doing commercial work. Meanwhile, he began to experiment with color landscapes and worked up the courage to show one of his efforts to Washington Allston, the most prominent artist in Boston at the time. Allston praised the work and encouraged Champney to go to Paris for further study. In 1841, Champney and Robert Cooke, an artist friend, set sail for Europe, where Champney remained until sailing back to Boston in 1846. After returning to the United States, he established his reputation as one of the best young American landscape artists.

Champney had visited the White Mountains briefly as a young man in 1838, and during his long apprenticeship in Europe and Boston, he had never forgotten about the beauty of the Whites. When he finally returned to them in 1850, he lauded the landscape as "something more than terrestrial."[28] During that pivotal summer of 1850, he, John F. Kensett, and a young artist named William Willard immersed themselves in six exhilarating weeks of exploration of every corner of the region, capturing as much of the mountains' beauty as they could on canvas. While other artists of the period usually made pencil sketches of scenes and then turned those sketches into paintings at their studios, Champney painted directly from nature, which gave his efforts a remarkable freshness and spontaneity.[29] In his autobiography, he looked back on these years with great fondness:

> We were delighted with the surrounding scenery, the wild stretch of the intervales, broken with well-tilled farms, the fields just ripening for the harvest, with the noble elms dotted about in pretty groups. . . . We had seen grander, higher mountains in Switzerland, but not often so much beauty and artistic picturesqueness brought together in one valley.[30]

When Champney returned to the Whites the next summer, he found a group of artists, including John Casilear and a nephew of Asher Durand's named John Durand, already ensconced at Samuel Thompson's Kearsarge House in North Conway. According to art historian Charles O. Vogel, "The summer of 1851 proved to be the defining moment in the establishment of New Hampshire's White Mountains as a nationally important artists' destination."[31] The group at Kearsarge House reveled as much in their exploration of the region as they did in their painting. Thompson pointed the artists to scenic areas of the forest that they would never have found on their own. One day he told them of a picturesque waterfall in back of White Horse Ledge; its roar was so loud that it could be heard all the way from the inn. Thompson had only a vague idea of the waterfall's whereabouts but asked his son, William, to lead the group of artists in search of it. For hours they scoured the area but could not locate the falls. Finally, though, Champney and the group made one more try:

> [A]fter traveling through the dense woods for half a mile we found the stream, and following it down heard the rush of waters, and soon caught a glimpse of broken, ledgy rocks. We at once named it Thompson's Falls, and, hastening back to our comrades, we gave them such glowing accounts of our discovery that we all wished to return the next day for sketching, and we did.[32]

They loved the waterfall for its wild scenery and returned to it again and again for sketching and painting. In 1853, Champney married Mary Caroline Brooks, and after their honeymoon, they found a large home just south of North Conway's village center. They purchased it, and Champney immediately set about transforming a carpenter's shop near the house into a studio with windows that opened up wonderfully to the outdoor light. Delighted with the setting, Champney made the home his summer studio for the next half century, completing hundreds of paintings of White Mountain vistas. He exhibited regularly in Boston and New York, and the demand for his landscapes eventually made him a wealthy man; in 1874, he and his wife purchased an ornate mansion in Woburn, Massachusetts, that became their home away from the mountains.

Meanwhile, other artists were pouring into the White Mountain region and establishing working residences at the local hotels and boardinghouses, where they produced paintings for tourists eager to display a bit of mountain heaven in their parlors. Champney remained independent of the hotels, but because of his national reputation and charismatic personality, his summer studio became a magnet that attracted summer tourists and aspiring artists, for whom he was a patient mentor.[33] On July 27, 1880, the *North Conway Idler* took its readers on a tour of the famous artist's studio:

> [There] we love to linger, and look upon the many bright scenes of nature reproduced by the skillful touch of this most gifted artist. Among the most prominent pictures we notice specially a large autumn scene on the Ellis river, on the Glen road. This is truly a perfect gem of art, showing wonderful fine effects in light and coloring, and a perfect blaze of glory through the mountain gorges. . . . [T]his studio is always open to visitors, who will carry away with them recollections of one of the most enjoyable places in North Conway.[34]

The hallmark of Champney's paintings is their pastoral quality. If Cole awes us with scenes of wild beauty, Champney soothes us with what Donald Keyes refers to as a "picturesque, agrarian paradise."[35] A typical painting is *Intervale, North Conway* (undated), which captures a view from North Conway that looks toward Whitehorse Ledge and Cathedral Ledge. In the foreground are a farmhouse, cultivated fields, an orchard, and workers in the fields. Champney downplays the daunting faces of the two cliffs in favor of humanity's productive impact on the landscape. The farmers are working fields that are presumably their own, even as they carry out their fruitful labor in the shadow of the beautiful mountains that surround them. They work with diligence and skill, as reflected in the orderly fields and well-tended orchards. This emphasis on productivity in harmony with nature is a powerful expression of nineteenth-century Americans' view of their nation as a land of small property owners who controlled their own fate through political and economic power, fulfilling the vision of Thomas Jefferson.

Intervale reflects another development in White Mountain painting— de-emphasis of the wild qualities of nature. The catalogue for a 1996 exhibit of White Mountain art sponsored by the New Hampshire Historical Society noted, "Seen from North Conway, the mountains rose from the Intervale far

6.4. *Intervale, North Conway* (undated), Benjamin Champney. Champney's paintings emphasized scenes of rural beauty in the White Mountains. The cultivated fields and the orchards in
this view indicate a well-ordered farm, while the soaring cliffs of Whitehorse Ledge and Cathedral Ledge are de-emphasized. Courtesy, Woburn Public Library, Woburn MA.

enough away to form a compelling view, one that did not intimidate the observer with the mountains' size, height, and wildness."[36] The romantic turbu-
lence of Cole's landscapes was perhaps too wild for the generation of Americans who came of age in the mid-1800s. Romanticism was in decline, and in
American landscape painting, energetic renditions of wild nature gave way to
more sedate visions in which wonders of nature coexisted with signs of civilization, creating a precarious harmony.

Champney's close friend John F. Kensett, who had accompanied him on
his first painting tour of the region in 1850, was also active in North Conway,
and his canvases depict similar images of humanity working and living in
harmony with nature. Kensett's *Mount Washington from the Valley of Conway*
(1851) showcases an idyllic small town as it rests in the arms of a benign Mount
Washington, reflecting what one art historian has referred to as the "poetry of
the commonplace" seen in Kensett and other artists of this period.[37] The
dense forest has been cleared and a tidy space created for human habitation.
The small house and the surrounding trees exist in complete harmony, as the
trees lean toward the house in protective sympathy. Moreover, the clouds

6.5. *Mount Washington from the Valley of Conway* (1851), John Frederick Kensett. Kensett, a close friend of Champney's, also portrayed scenes of bucolic beauty, in which humanity had integrated itself harmoniously with nature. Both Kensett and Champney adapted to a land-scape that was being domesticated from the wild nature of Thomas Cole's time. Oil on canvas, 40⅜ × 60⅜ in. (102.6 × 153.4 cm). Davis Museum and Cultural Center, Wellesley College, Wellesley, MA. Gift of Mr. and Mrs. James B. Munn (Ruth C. Hanford, Class of 1909) in the name of the Class of 1909, 1977.37.

float above the town instead of threatening it, and the mountains, not nearly so wild and tempestuous as in Cole's canvases, gaze approvingly upon the human settlement in the valley, completing a rural paradise.

In *Intervale, North Conway, Mount Washington from the Valley of Conway,* and hundreds of other paintings from this period, art played an important social role, defining humanity's changing relationship with nature and mod-eling how humanity could carve a civilization out of the wilderness while al-lowing the world of nature to continue to thrive. Certain canvases even por-trayed the beneficial effects of life on the edge of the wilderness, transmuting the settlement of the mountains into a moral lesson. Such is the inspiring theme, for example, of *Eagle Cliff, Franconia Notch, New Hampshire,* completed in 1858 by Jasper F. Cropsey, a successful New York architect who had turned to landscape painting in the 1840s. After traveling extensively in Europe from 1847 to 1849, Cropsey returned to America and toured the White Mountains in 1852, 1855, and 1856.[38] Known for his use of rich colors, he painted numer-

6.6. *Eagle Cliff, Franconia Notch, New Hampshire* (1858), Jasper Francis Cropsey. This painting romanticizes the era of the pioneer. The family lives on the edge of wilderness, where they find happiness and spiritual fulfillment. Note the religious iconography, such as the tree branches that form a cross. North Carolina Museum of Art, Raleigh, Purchased with funds from the State of North Carolina.

ous scenes of the stunning autumns in New England. In addition, he was, like Cole and Durand, guided by a strong religious faith that he often expressed by populating his canvases with religious iconography.

In *Eagle Cliff*, the dominant image is of a log cabin that sits resolutely at the edge of the mountain wilderness, while in the foreground stand the cabin's inhabitants, a family of four. The painting celebrates family comity, as the two children hold each other's hands and the husband wraps his arm around his wife. Subtle religious iconography appears in the form of two trees to the left of the cabin that intertwine their branches to form a cross. Professor McGrath notes about this painting, "Cropsey's image functions to retrieve the perceived era of pioneer simplicity."[39] The rustic cabin, which reflects the recent settlement of the region, coexists comfortably with Eagle Cliff and the ubiquitous Mount Chocorua, which Cropsey has transported from the Sandwich Range to Franconia Notch. The painting is an articulate expression of the theme that humans can thrive on the edge of the mountain wilderness and that habitation of the land does not have to ruin the wondrous mountainscape. Moreover, the presence of the family and of religious iconography tells us that life on the

6.7. *Mount Washington and Walker's Pond from Old Barn in Conway, New Hampshire* (1885), Frank Henry Shapleigh. The perspective is from the interior of the barn, as details of domestica-tion are highlighted, while Mt. Washington sits in the distance. This painting shows the degree to which images of domestication were taking precedence over scenes of wild nature by the 1880s. Hood Museum of Art, Dartmouth College, Hanover, New Hampshire; purchased through the Julia L. Whittier Fund.

edge of the wilderness nurtures family love and spiritual integrity. The painting typifies the search for an ideal balance between wilderness and civilization—a search that conservationists would embark on at the end of the nineteenth century as they took action in the face of deforestation of the Whites.

As the domestication of the White Mountain landscape continued apace, canvases appeared that more explicitly approved of the growing human foot-print on the land. A typical example is *Mount Washington and Walker's Pond from Old Barn in Conway, New Hampshire* (1885), by Frank H. Shapleigh, who spent almost every summer in Jackson, New Hampshire, from 1877 until his death in 1906. In this canvas, the artist presents a view of Mount Washington from the interior of a barn, making the mountain visually less prominent than such details of domestication as chickens, hay, and a broom. The proud peak, which so symbolized the sublime mysteries of the wilderness in Cole's paintings, has devolved into a pretty backdrop for rural life. According to art historian Catherine H. Campbell, "The landscape is literally seen through a man-made structure and is limited and defined by it."[40] Indeed, civilization was so well-established in the mountain region that the barn was now "old"—

a fixed part of the landscape. The painting speaks volumes about how the region had changed and how artists were choosing to depict those changes.

While paintings like *Mount Washington and Walker's Pond from Old Barn* indicated the extent to which the White Mountain region had become a pastoral landscape, even more radical changes were coming because of industrialization. Railroads, sawmills, paper mills, and resort hotels were proliferating, and corporate logging operations began to cut down swaths of forest in the 1880s. Donald Keyes pointed out in his essay for the 1980 Dartmouth College exhibit, "As America grew, the concern with carving order out of the wilderness came to be balanced by a new, opposing concern, that of preserving nature unmolested by industrial development."[41] The goal of the White Mountain artists remained the celebration of natural beauty, but now they had to develop an aesthetic means to accommodate the new industrialization. In their canvases, for example, they began to include railroads, which were the most visible symbol of industrialization. Yet as Catherine Campbell pointed out, the artists had difficulty integrating railroads effectively into their landscapes: "They tried to see it [the railroad] as a symbol of progress and improvement, and yet lamented its intrusion into the wilderness and its destruction of all that the wilderness had signified."[42]

Edward Hill's *Echo Lake from Artist's Ledge*, completed in 1887, reflects this ambivalence even as it depicts the impact that industrialization was having on the mountains. The canvas portrays a scene at Echo Lake in Franconia Notch in which a train passes through the woods to the left, a steamboat crosses the lake, and, in the notch itself, a large resort hotel is visible. A solitary man in the foreground, surrounded by logs that have been felled by lightning (left foreground) and saws (right foreground), looks impassively upon the encroachments of industrialization and tourism. Hill attempted to resolve the tension between the beauty of the wilderness and the encroachment of industrialization by integrating the train, the steamboat, and the hotel into the landscape in such a way as to create a harmonious whole. According to Robert McGrath, "A resident of New Hampshire, Hill welcomed the incursions of tourism (together with the resultant monied clientele) into the Notch. Like many of the natives of the region today, Hill was prepared to sacrifice the wilderness to the hope and dream of prosperity."[43] In the distance, though, the mountains remain heavily forested, as majestic as always, despite the radical changes in the land that have been wrought by economic development. Even for an artist like Hill, who integrated images of industrialization into his landscapes, the mountains remained magnificent symbols of wild nature.

Of all the changes in the White Mountains, the most far-reaching was the rapid growth of logging operations, and it was this development that artists had the most difficulty depicting. After the Civil War, logging companies adopted

6.8. *Echo Lake from Artist's Ledge* (1887), Edward Hill. Hill attempted to integrate symbols of industrialization into scenes of natural beauty. Here, a locomotive and a steamboat represent the incursion of industry, while the grand resort hotel in the background reflects the explosion of tourism in the White Mountains. New Hampshire Historical Society.

the methods and large scale of industry to meet the burgeoning demand for wood throughout the United States. Entrepreneurs—some local, such as J. E. Henry and the Brown brothers, others from outside New Hampshire—organized companies that bought huge tracts of forested land and started the practice of clear-cutting, which was the rapid cutting of all trees, irrespective of size or maturity. Clear-cutting was beginning to have a devastating impact on the White Mountain landscape by the 1890s, but instead of documenting such realities, the White Mountain artists served the expectations of their audience by continuing to produce idealized landscapes in which small towns nestled against pretty mountains.

One of the few exceptions to these idealizations was another painting by Edward Hill—*Lumbering Camp in Winter,* completed in 1882. In the scene, a single lumber operator tends to a team of oxen that hauls logs through the forest. To the left is his simple logging cabin, where, in a note of domesticity, his clothes are left out to dry. Meanwhile, in the right foreground, logs lie strewn about, presumably waiting to be hauled to the local mill for processing into lumber. While the artist was portraying a stark reality of the north woods, he also located beauty in the scene, through the brown tones that con-

6.9. *Lumbering Camp in Winter* (1882), Edward Hill. This painting is one of the few works of White Mountain artists that portrays the logging industry in the mountains. The artist found a kind of nostalgic beauty in the scene. New Hampshire Historical Society.

vey a sense of nostalgia, through the simplicity of the cabin with its connotation of rural self-reliance, and through the density of the forest in the background, which continues to thrive in spite of the logging operations.

The scene is an encomium to the small-time logging operator, yet it avoids a head-on confrontation with the reality that, by the 1880s, industrial logging was already beginning to strip away the White Mountain forest and threaten the wilderness characteristics of the region. As the degradation of the mountain environment became more visible in the last decade of the nineteenth century, the pastoral ideal that attempted to find a balance between commerce and wilderness could not hold, and fine-art painting proved to be an inadequate instrument for recording the impact of logging. Instead, the art of photography documented the degradation of the mountain environment: pictures shocked the public with their stark images of denuded mountainsides, rivers clogged with logs, and soil erosion. This photographic record would prove to be enormously important in building public support to prevent the continued clear-cutting of the White Mountain forests.

Art, of course, is not reportage, and it is unfair to expect the artists of the period to have addressed the growing issue of deforestation in the region. But

White Mountain Art ⊚ 123

6.10. *Carter Dome from Carter Lake, New Hampshire* (c. 1880), William Lewis Sonntag, Sr. (American, 1822–1900). While most White Mountain artists continued to produce nostalgic landscapes, Sonntag's landscapes reflected the influence of Impressionism, as light and form took precedence over the realistic portrayal of features of the landscape. Point of brush and black ink, watercolor, gouache, graphite touches on cream wove paper 13 3/16 × 19 1/8 (355 × 485 mm) [irregular]. Cooper-Hewitt, National Design Museum, Smithsonian Institution. Gift of William H. Matthews from the Estate of Frederick A. Moore, 1956–183–1; photo: Scott Hyde.

even in aesthetic terms, White Mountain art by the 1870s and 1880s seemed to be frozen in a quaint sentimentalism. Too many canvases featured the same well-known vistas—Mount Washington, Mount Chocorua, the Saco River, the Flume—and by 1890, the art of the White Mountains was declining in both aesthetic and popular terms. The conservative aesthetic of the White Mountain school left little room for artistic innovation, even as American landscape artists, under the influence of the French Barbizon School, began to experiment with form and light in ways that presaged the arrival of Impressionism in America. For example, William Lewis Sonntag's *Carter Dome from Carter Lake, New Hampshire* (ca. 1880) presented the mountains in less realistic and more impressionistic modes. Another reason for the decline of White Mountain art was that the locus of American landscape painting shifted to the West and the towering peaks of Colorado and California.

Even though the creativity behind the art of the White Mountains dissipated, the legacy of that art was far-reaching. The artists of the nineteenth century

literally taught Americans to see their natural surroundings and to participate vicariously in the wondrous sights in which their nation abounded. The
vistas that the White Mountain artists painted so often—Mount Washington, Mount Chocorua, the Flume, the Saco River—metamorphosed into national symbols of America's incredible natural beauty, which became a source
of immense national pride. And even as the artists depicted an increasingly
domesticated countryside, those scenes of farm and pasture were confined
primarily to the region's valleys.

Though often pushed back to more distant, less threatening horizons, the
mountains remained proud symbols of wild nature; still the pristine forests
draped the mountains' shoulders like magnificent emerald mantles. They
spoke to the American soul, conveying a potent message of individual freedom, self-determination, and power. They represented a part of the land that
remained dangerous and unpredictable—beyond the boundaries of civilization. And as Americans experienced the growing constraints of modern life,
working long hours in factories and living in dirty and crowded cities, they
clung more fiercely than ever to those soaring symbols of wilderness and freedom. Little wonder that during this period, every American household was
said to have two objects: a well-thumbed Bible and a mountain landscape
hanging in the parlor—a visual connection to America's most powerful talis-
mans of individual freedom.[44] Even as the White Mountain region grew more
domesticated during the course of the nineteenth century, the mountains remained powerful symbols of the wild and the beautiful, inspiring thousands
to experience their untrammeled pleasures, inspiring a love that would ultimately save their forests from extinction.

Chapter 7

THE RESORT HOTELS: LUXURY
AT THE EDGE OF WILDERNESS

AFTER THE END OF THE CIVIL WAR, an exhausted American public yearned to return to normalcy. It was a time when the American middle class, trapped by the stresses of urbanization and industrialization, began to look for relief to the pleasures of the summer vacation. No region would feel the effects of this change in the leisure habits of the American people more than the White Mountains. Indeed, it was a golden age for the Whites, when railroads transported thousands of tourists into the mountains, when luxurious grand hotels accommodated those pleasure seekers, and when hunting and fishing and horseback riding and a thousand other activities promised the benefits of physical activity and family togetherness.

One of the major promoters of the White Mountains during this golden era was Moses F. Sweetser, an avid outdoorsman who climbed eighty summits in the region and wrote numerous White Mountain guidebooks that spread the mountains' reputation for wonderful summer vacations far and wide. In his *White Mountains: A Handbook for Travellers* (1881), Sweetser articulately recounted the restorative powers that a week in the mountains could provide:

> When the busy citizen has grown weary under the pressure of business or study, and loses his ability to eat or sleep, or to take pleasure either in present or anticipated comforts, let him visit the mountains and inhale their electric air, forgetting for the month his home-cares, and adapting his thoughts to the ennobling surroundings. The sojourn in a summer-hotel is well and beneficial, but the journey on foot is better, since it gives incessant variety and ever-changing themes of diversion.[1]

In addition to articulating the appeal of a mountain vacation, Sweetser's words captured the tension between two very different attitudes toward nature, which we have already seen evident in White Mountain art—the tension between the experience of untamed nature, which is accessible only by "the journey on foot," and the experience of a tamed and domesticated nature, the nature of the "summer-hotel." After the Civil War, grand resort hotels multiplied throughout the White Mountains and offered experiences that mediated nature for casual tourists by providing guided hikes, horseback rides on carefully maintained trails, and other highly organized activities in the outdoors that ensured the guests' safety and security. Never did the hotels promise the direct experience of wild nature. Nevertheless, the hotels played a transitional but important role in the later popularity of wilderness experiences in the White Mountains. By making the experience of nature safe and accessible, they exposed thousands of Americans to the pleasures of the outdoors. Of these travelers to the northern forest, a hardy minority would gradually develop the yearning for a more direct experience of wild nature, and by the end of the nineteenth century, these adventurers would pioneer new ways to experience the White Mountain wilderness.

After the Civil War, literally hundreds of accommodations were built in the Whites, ranging from simple boardinghouses and campsites to elaborate grand hotels. At the same time, the promotion of the region as a tourist destination became an industry unto itself, as publishers, railroad companies, and hotels issued guidebooks that marketed the region. The *Guide to the White Mountains and Lakes of New Hampshire: With Minute and Accurate Descriptions of the Scenery and Objects of Interest on the Route,* for instance, was published in 1851 by the Concord, New Hampshire, firm of Tripp & Osgood. It emphasized practical advice for travelers, such as the best routes to the mountains, information about inns and hotels, and descriptions of common tourist attractions.

In addition to these nitty-gritty facts, some of the guidebooks extolled the benefits of the summer vacation, giving us insight into the role that recreation was starting to play in American society. Writers such as Sweetser and Henry Burt, who also wrote a number of guides, lauded the ability of nature to heal the psyche of Americans shaken by the rapid pace of change in their lives. For example, Henry Burt's *Guide Through the Connecticut Valley to the White Mountains and the River Saguenay* (1874) praised the psychological relief that a sojourn in the mountains could bring:

> Oh! You man of toil! What will it profit you to wear your very life out in acquiring mere wealth, while the finer instincts of your nature are blotted out, or allowed to run to water? The White Hills should be cherished by us all, as the Mecca of America, to which it should be a religious duty, to make at least one pilgrimage in our life time![2]

Burt's words expressed a backlash against the materialistic values of the Gilded Age, and the splendors of natural beauty became an antidote to the accompanying social pressures. To awaken the public to the solace provided by nature, guidebook writers went to great lengths to describe the magnifi-

7.1. Stereoscopic views. The stereoscope was an optical instrument that created a three-dimensional effect from two photographs of the same scene shown from slightly different perspectives. The photograph is of the Flume, before a huge boulder wedged between the two walls plummeted into the waters below on June 20, 1883. Courtesy of Dartmouth College Library. Photograph by Joseph Mehling.

cence of the White Mountains' natural attractions. In a volume that Sweetser wrote for Chisolm's series of guidebooks, he employed language that bordered on hyperbole to describe White Mountain scenery and to compare it favorably with that of the Swiss Alps, the Sierra Nevada, and Yosemite:

> The foremost charm of the White Mountains is their almost infinite variety of scenery, inexhaustible in its resources and unlimited in its manifold combinations. Each of the outer villages and each of the inner glens commands aspects of the main ranges so distinct and different as to resemble views in separate lands. Every mile of approach or recession on either of the roads opens a new series of prospects, each of which has its own peculiar beauty and attractiveness, and reveals news phases of natural grandeur, new combinations of landscape effects.[3]

Another aspect of marketing the natural splendors of the Whites was the promotion of their cultural, literary, and artistic heritage. By the 1870s, the region had acquired a rich store of evocative stories, legends, and historical episodes, which blended together to form a mythic narrative that became a cornerstone in the marketing of the region. "The traditions of the aborigines and the pioneers," Sweetser wrote, "have been woven about many of the most interesting of its localities; and the pens of poets and dreamers, scientists and historians, have been busy for over two centuries with these mountains."[4] By the late nineteenth century, many of the natural attractions of the White Mountains, such as the Old Man of the Mountain, the Basin, the Flume, the Pool, and the Crystal Cascade, had taken on the status of cultural symbols, and the guidebooks marketed them effectively. Eastman's *White Mountain Guide Book,* for instance, cannily pitched the Old Man as the embodiment of the stalwart New England character, noting, "Every portion of the face is there upon the solid mountain steep. There is the stern, projecting, massive brow, as though stamped with the thought and wisdom of centuries. . . . The chin is well thrown forward, with exact proportionate length, betokening the hard, obstinate character of the 'Old Man.'"[5]

Another benefit of nature that the guidebooks emphasized was its capacity to restore physical health. In the late nineteenth century, American society became obsessed with physical health, strength, and endurance, and the guidebooks accordingly boasted of the health benefits of the mountains. In his *White Mountains: A Handbook,* for instance, Moses Sweetser promoted the physical benefits of the pedestrian tour in words that reflected the cult of masculinity and vigor personified by Theodore Roosevelt:

> The pedestrian tour is of high value to men of sedentary habits, giving them a valuable and needed change of habit, expanding their shrunken lungs, and teaching their limbs pliancy and strength. It is pleasing to see so many of the undergraduates of the New England colleges taking up this form of exercise and visiting the mountains in small squads on active service.[6]

The mountains even had the power to cure diseases. The town of Bethlehem, located 1,450 feet above sea level and featuring crisp, cool air, became a popular mountain resort because it provided relief to hay fever sufferers; it also became the headquarters of the American Hay-Fever Association. Thousands of hay fever sufferers made pilgrimages to the town, especially in August and September, when hay fever was at its worst in the cities.[7]

Just as important as these social developments in stimulating interest in White Mountain vacations was the arrival of the railroads. The first step in bringing train transportation to the Whites occurred on September 6, 1842, when the Concord Railroad connected Lowell and Boston to southern New Hampshire and then gradually extended north.[8] During the 1840s and 1850s, the Boston, Concord, and Montreal Railroad, the Portland and Ogdensburg, and other railroad lines opened up routes and carried ever-increasing numbers of travelers into the White Mountains.

7.2. Artist's sketch of arrival of first train at Fabyan's. In August 1875, the first train, operated by the Portland and Ogdensburg Railroad, pulled into Fabyan's. The completion of the railroad through Crawford Notch was an enormous engineering feat because of the elevation gain through the notch and the ravines that needed to be traversed. Twin Mountain Bretton Woods Historical Society.

The result was an explosion in the number of accommodations and the development of grand resort hotels, which vividly reflected the social mores of the Gilded Age. The purpose here is not to tell an exhaustive story of the White Mountain hotels, which has already been accomplished in superb books such as *The Grand Resort Hotels of the White Mountains,* by architectural historian Bryant F. Tolles, Jr. Instead, we will explore how White Mountain hostelries shaped the experience of nature through the recreational activities that they offered to their guests. The hotels purposely downplayed the wild aspects of nature in order to appeal to the broadest possible clientele, which wanted exposure to nature but also a modicum of comfort and convenience. Consequently, the hotels emphasized highly organized forays into the outdoors, such as guided hikes and pony rides. They also offered activities in which nature formed a backdrop, such as golf and tennis. What the hotels did not offer was a direct experience of wilderness. From the window of a luxuriously appointed hotel room with all the latest amenities, the view of the still-wild sectors of the White Mountains was a faraway one. The hotel owners, consciously or not, mediated the experience of nature for their guests by providing controlled, even insulated, experiences of the outdoors. The beginning of a wilderness movement in the late nineteenth century would be partly a reaction against such mediated experiences.

The best place to follow the evolution of White Mountain hostelries toward comfort and luxury is in Crawford Notch, the birthplace of White Mountain hospitality and the setting for some of the most legendary accommodations that ever nestled into the side of a mountain. The gradual development of inns in the Crawford Notch area shows dramatically how the relationship between hotels and the natural environment changed from the 1820s to 1900, reflecting evolving attitudes toward nature and wilderness. The first inns in the notch were rudimentary accommodations that served the practical needs of teamsters hauling raw materials and goods on the first turnpike through the notch.

As traffic through the notch increased and people started to venture into the mountains to climb to the tops of peaks with the Crawfords as guides, the need for better accommodations became apparent. In 1824, Ethan Allen Crawford added to his inn at Giant's Grave, and he made yet another addition in 1832. This inn came to be known as Crawford's Old Moosehorn Tavern.[9] It was comfortable but simple, as was Abel Crawford's Mount Crawford House, which his son-in-law, Captain Nathaniel T. P. Davis, later managed. One of the charms of the Mount Crawford House was its setting, which remained wild through much of the nineteenth century. According to *Tripp's White Mountain Guide Book:*

> In the rear of the building the Saco winds its way through a channel won
> from the solid granite. In many places the rocky wall rises full twenty feet,
> perpendicular, above the current. Again the bank is smooth and pebbly. At
> one spot the waters foam and boil like a witch's caldron. At another, they float
> lazily along with a cold, blue depth, in which the cunning trout lies hid.[10]

Because of its location, the inn provided superb access for hiking and fishing. Dr. Samuel Bemis, a Boston dentist who bought the property in 1856, was an avid angler who discovered Bemis Pond, about six miles behind his house, and traipsed to it often to fish. The inn was also the starting point for one of the most famous trails in the White Mountains—a bridle path that Captain Davis built up the side of Mount Crawford and eventually to Mount Washington. The Mount Crawford House is a superb example of how innkeepers helped to open up access to the backwoods areas of the White Mountains with simple yet comfortable accommodations.

A few miles north of Crawford Notch, the Giant's Grave bore a succession of hotels that reflected a growing emphasis on luxury as the nineteenth century progressed. When Ethan Allen Crawford returned to Guildhall, Vermont, in 1837, Horace Fabyan leased Crawford's inn and then gained ownership of it in 1841. He renamed it the Mount Washington House and poured money into upgrading the hotel, expanding it in 1847 and 1848 to accommodate the growing numbers of visitors. But in 1853, fire destroyed the Mount Washington House, and the property languished. In 1864, Sylvester Marsh, who later developed the cog railway up Mount Washington, acquired the property and started the construction of a replacement hotel, but it too burned down, in 1868, before being completed.[11] In 1872, Marsh transferred the property to the Mount Washington Hotel Company, in which he was a partner. The company issued stock, raised $200,000, and undertook construction of a luxury hotel on the site of Fabyan's old hotel. To make the site suitable for a large hotel, though, the owners ordered the leveling of the Giant's Grave, which brought howls of protest from locals over the destruction of the famous landmark. Opponents even invoked ancient Native American cautionary tales that white men who lived on that sacred ground would be cursed.[12] Leveling the Giant's Grave sent a clear signal that icons of White Mountain history were not sacrosanct and that the perceived needs of the tourist industry took priority.

When it opened with a grand celebration in 1873, the new Fabyan House offered a highly organized, all-encompassing experience for travelers. It boasted accommodations for five hundred guests, a livery stable, a newsstand, a billiard hall, a bowling alley, a post office, an enormous parlor of 3,500 square feet, and a dining room of almost 6,000 square feet. The hotel also came to be known for its hospitality, especially after 1878, when Asa Barron, who had been operating the Twin Mountain House in the adjoining town of Carroll, leased the hotel and began to operate it with his son, Colonel Oscar G. Barron. Oscar Barron remained connected to the Fabyan House for thirty-five years, where his skill as a hotel keeper and his cordial personality endeared him to generations of tourists.[13]

Three other historic hotels in the Crawford Notch area reflected this same evolution toward luxurious amenities—the White Mountain House, the Notch House, and the Crawford House. The White Mountain House was approximately three-quarters of a mile to the west of the Fabyan House. It was built by a descendant of Eleazer Rosebrook, and when Ethan Allen Crawford returned to the mountains in 1843 from Guildhall, Vermont, he took up residence there. Even though it was one of the oldest hotels in the mountains, it underwent a number of improvements, so that by the 1890s, one guidebook writer wrote about it, "We are assured . . . that every convenience and comfort in the house, delicacy and dainty at the table, and neatness in the arrangement and furnishing of the chambers, may be found here at the 'White Mountain House.'"[14]

Four miles to the south, at the Gate of the Notch, was another historic inn, the Notch House. Abel and Ethan Allen Crawford had planned and built the inn in 1827 and 1828 and opened it to the public in 1829, with Ethan's brother, Thomas J. Crawford, as the proprietor. The inn became a favorite subject for artists because of its beautiful setting, and many canvases of the era show the hotel against the scenic backdrop of the notch. It also was near the renowned Crawford Path, which provided access from the west to the summit of Mount

7.3. Saco Lake, the Crawford House. The Crawford House stood just north of the Gate of the Notch and across the road from Saco Lake. The hotel, one of the most luxurious in the Whites, operated until it burned down in 1977. The AMC's Highland Center now stands on the same site. Courtesy of Dartmouth College Library.

Washington. In 1854, fire destroyed the Notch House, but it remains one of the most familiar of the historic White Mountain inns because it was featured so often in paintings.

To the west of the Notch House rose the other grand hotel in the Crawford Notch area—the Crawford House. In fact, two Crawford Houses have stood on this spot, which is now the location of the Appalachian Mountain Club's Highland Center. The first Crawford House, comfortable yet hardly luxurious, burned down in 1859. The hotel owner, Cyrus Eastman, and his partners resolved to rebuild it as rapidly as possible. They envisioned a grand hotel, and to build it, the engineers had to haul prodigious amounts of lumber from as far away as seventeen miles. Only sixty days after the first Crawford House burned down, the second one opened—on July 13, 1859—with a grand dinner for forty special guests.[15]

Like the Fabyan House, the new Crawford House boasted a magnificent setting and amenities that appealed to America's taste for luxury during the

Gilded Age. The hotel was located on the picturesque watershed between the Saco and the Connecticut rivers and looked south into the magnificent notch. Saco Lake, source of the Saco River, stood like a pristine mirror in front of the hotel. What's more, Moses Sweetser noted, "The rugged forest between the lake and the overhanging mountain has been combed and brushed and perfumed, and otherwise adorned for a summer [garden] so that it has won the happily suggestive name of Idlewild."[16] Apparently the hotel owners had found ways to improve upon nature for the enjoyment of their guests.

In spite of its rugged surroundings, though, the hotel created an all-encompassing environment, a sort of cocoon surrounded by the forests. According to Sweetser, "[T]his is a good hotel of the first class, . . . with broad and almost interminable piazzas, cool and airy halls, post-office, telegraph-office, livery-stable, bowling-alley, gaslights; environs which the landscape-gardener has justly approved; and a dining-room where even Epicurus . . . need not famish."[17] It was also the scene of an active nightlife. After a day of tramping through the mountains, guests returned to an elegant parlor where a band played music and couples danced far into the night.[18]

The hotels did not ignore the outdoors, but they provided supervision and guidance that would protect the safety of those who wished to sojourn into the mountains. The Crawford House, for instance, maintained fifty ponies for riding in the mountains, as well as guides to lead trampers to the summits.[19] One of the most popular excursions was to ride a horse-drawn carriage up Mount Willard to a ledge that afforded a splendid view of the entire notch—a view nearly identical to the one that the same perch affords today.

In spite of the luxurious accommodations provided by hotels such as the Crawford House and the emphasis on supervised experiences of the outdoors, the call to wilderness was not completely ignored. In writing about the Crawford House, Moses Sweetser pointed that even though his readers might be staying in the lap of luxury, they still were very close to the most sublime experiences of wild nature. He pointed out:

> Some miles below, and far secluded in the tangled forest on the west of the railroad, are the splendid phenomena of the Ripley Falls and the Arethusa Falls, the former reached by a good path leading from Avalanche Station, and falling 108 feet, over high and imposing cliffs—while the Arethusa Falls are 176 feet high, and form one of the most magnificent decorations of the hill-country, but are so environed with pathless savagery that they are visited but rarely.[20]

Guests might be resting in utmost comfort, but possibilities remained for the exploration of still-wild regions, and Sweetser was determined to publicize opportunities for such experiences. He was, though, in the minority among guidebook writers in encouraging his readers to venture on their own into wilderness areas of the Whites.

In Franconia Notch, the hotels reflected the same trend toward comfort and luxury. Two early hotels in Franconia Notch were the Lafayette House and the Flume House. The Lafayette House, which was located several hundred feet from the base of Cannon Mountain, was not as large as other grand hotels, but according to one guidebook, it was "equal to any of them in location and objects of interest. It has been entirely refitted and some additions made."[21] The Flume House stood five miles south of the Lafayette House, in the heart of Franconia Notch. The hotel boasted spectacular views of the Pemigewasset Valley on one side and the soaring mountains of Franconia Notch. The driving force behind the construction of the Flume House in 1848 was an energetic entrepreneur named Robert Taft, who had grown up in Barre, Vermont. According to one friend, Taft was a reserved man who inspired the respect of people because of his integrity. Like other successful hoteliers, he devoted himself completely to the attentions of travelers.[22]

The architecture of the Flume House revealed the importance of social relations during the Gilded Age. According to *Tripp's White Mountain Guide Book,* "The lower floor is divided into offices, parlors, a dining hall, etc. Parlors and parlors with bed-rooms attached occupy the second story. The third flight consists of sleeping apartments exclusively."[23] People gathered and conversed in the parlors every evening instead of retreating into their individual rooms. During the Gilded Age, conviviality was a highly valued cultural trait, and in fact, even when outdoor enthusiasts began to organize wilderness expeditions at the end of the nineteenth century, they did so in clubs.

The most luxurious hotel in Franconia Notch was the Profile House, which was located at the highest point in the notch, almost two thousand feet above sea level. The hotel was within walking distance of Echo Lake, where, in the words of Henry Burt, "its great charm is in the wonderful echoes that reverberate among the mountain-fastnesses, on loud shouting, blowing of a horn, or firing of a cannon."[24] In 1852, Robert Taft, George T. Brown, and Ira Coffin started construction of the hotel, which originally had 110 rooms but was continually expanded until it could accommodate five hundred guests.

Like the Crawford House and the Fabyan House, the Profile House's calling cards were luxury, entertainment, and convenience. Every evening, bands played the favorite songs of the day, and couples danced far into the night. Office workers could stay in touch with the city through the telegraph office and daily delivery of mail. The hotel included also a "bric-a-brac shop," billiard and bowling rooms, a livery stable, a barbershop, and, in the words of Moses Sweetser, "a dining-room fit for a conclave of cardinals."[25] Yet in spite

7.4. First sight of the Profile House. The Profile House was the most luxurious hotel in Franconia Notch and had the advantage of a spectacular location—nestled under Cannon Mountain and only a short walk from Profile Lake and the Old Man of the Mountain. From the Profile House, tourists could visit the Flume, the Basin, the Pool, and other natural landmarks of the Whites. New Hampshire Historical Society.

of all these amenities, the Profile House did expose its guests to the surrounding world of nature. In his guidebook, Henry Burt emphasized that one of the Profile House's most appealing features was its proximity to well-known tourist attractions such as the Flume, the Basin, the Pool, and, most famous of all, the Old Man of the Mountain. He advised travelers, "Here can be had an excellent view of the Flume, from one end to the other. It is a pleasant spot for meditation, and all nature around you seems in harmony. You are lost in wonder over the cause which produced such a remarkable scene. Whence came the power that rent these rocks asunder? And how long has this great granite boulder been suspended in its singular position?"[26]

To the east, in Pinkham Notch, accommodations developed to serve travelers to Mount Washington and the other peaks of the Presidential Range, and they, too, became progressively more luxurious. John Bellow opened the first inn in the valley in 1850 but in 1852 sold the establishment to Joseph M. Thompson, who renamed it the Glen House. Thompson's hostelry benefited from increased traffic through the notch because of a stagecoach line that connected Gorham to Conway.[27] He also helped to make the surrounding environment accessible to guests by building trails to the surrounding waterfalls and a trail up Mount Washington.[28]

In 1861, the Mount Washington Carriage Road opened for business, and in fact, the success of the Glen House was inextricably linked to the carriage road and the enduring tourist appeal of Mount Washington. A charter for the construction of a road to the summit of the mountain was granted in 1855, but it took six years to complete the daunting task of building the road, which ran for eight miles; the average gain in elevation was twelve feet for every hundred feet of road, but in places the gain was as much as sixteen feet for every hundred feet of road. When the road was completed, horse-drawn carriages took four hours to ascend to the summit.[29]

Tragically, Thompson drowned in a freshet that swept through the Peabody River in October 1869, and two brothers, Weston Milliken and Charles Milliken, bought the Glen House property in 1871. Three years later, Charles Milliken took sole control of the property, and like other successful hotel entrepreneurs, he moved aggressively to transform the house into a premier resort. The hotel's parlor was huge, covering more than an acre, and the hotel featured a number of other amenities, including a book and picture shop, a post office and telegraph office, a billiard room, tennis courts, and archery lawns. Yet as happened so frequently in the Whites, fire enveloped the Glen House and burned it to the ground in 1884. The owners immediately set about building a replacement hotel—the new Glen House, which was even larger than the hostelry it replaced, accommodating five hundred guests and featuring modern amenities and the distinctive style of an English cottage. But this hotel, too, was doomed; fire swept it away in 1893, leaving only the stables housing the horses and carriages for the Mount Washington Carriage Road.[30]

West of the Glen House, but more than 6,200 feet higher into the atmosphere, more rugged accommodations took root on the summit of Mount Washington. The two summit hotels, the Tip-Top House and the Summit House, were very different from the grand resort hotels. They exposed their guests to nature at its most extreme—the fiercest winds in the world, suffocating snow, dangerously rapid changes in weather. Even as luxury thrived below, the instinct for wilderness adventure survived, and hotel entrepreneurs moved to satisfy the demand by building simple but sturdy accommodation with native materials, such as granite, that made these small hotels appear to be at one with their mountain environment.

The desire for accommodations on the summit grew also because of the opening of the Mount Washington Railway in 1869. Sylvester Marsh was a native of Littleton, New Hampshire, who had a genius for inventing mechanical devices. In 1852, after climbing to the summit of Mount Washington, he conceived the idea of a railroad that would carry passengers to the top of the mountain. Marsh hit upon the use of cogs, which grabbed like gear teeth into parallel cross-pins that ran between tracks and hauled the train up and down the mountain.[31] The first train reached the summit in 1869, running three miles and climbing 3,606 feet. The cog railway climbed more sharply than the carriage road, with a maximum gain of one vertical foot for every three horizontal feet, but it could ascend the mountain in only an hour and a half. It was an immediate hit among travelers.

With the cog railway, the carriage road, and a growing number of climbers, the need for accommodations at the top was apparent. In 1852 and 1853, Lucius M. Rosebrook and Joseph S. Hall constructed the Summit House, a stone building with walls that were four feet thick; to withstand the fierce winds, the entire structure was anchored to the summit by cables that were two inches in circumference. At about the time that the Summit House opened, Samuel F. Spaulding built the Tip-Top House. Its walls were even thicker— six feet—and the structure measured 28 feet by 84 feet. After the Tip-Top House was completed in 1853, it replaced the Summit House as the primary accommodations on the top of Mount Washington, and the Summit House became little more than an adjunct, its space providing additional sleeping rooms. From 1877 to 1884, the Tip-Top House served as the office of *Among the Clouds,* a daily newspaper printed on the summit during the summer season that offered accounts of daily doings on the mountain, but after the paper ceased publication, the building fell into neglect. On June 8, 1908, a fire burned down all the buildings on the summit except the Tip-Top House, which incurred some damage. The stone structure had great sentimental appeal, though,

7.5. Sliding down Mt. Washington Railway. Workers on the Mt. Washington Cog Railway slid down tracks on slide-boards in order to inspect the tracks. But in the early twentieth century, a worker using a slide-board was killed, and the use of the devices ended. Courtesy of Dartmouth College Library.

and the public called for it to be restored and made suitable again for over-night guests. It reopened for business in 1915, but on August 29, only eight days after opening, fire swept through its interior, leaving only the thick outer walls. Finally, in 1980, the state of New Hampshire restored the historic structure and turned it into a museum devoted to the history of Mount Washington.[32]

The Summit House, meanwhile, grew more and more dilapidated until Walter Aiken, who managed the cog railway, decided to build a new and much larger Summit House, which was completed between 1872 and 1873. A wooden structure that measured 220 feet by 40 feet, it accommodated 150 to 200 guests and featured a dining room that served 150 people.[33] The building was heated by steam, which kept temperatures comfortable in even the worst weather. Famous guests included Presidents U. S. Grant and Rutherford B. Hayes, Lucy Larcom, Henry Ward Beecher, Harriet Beecher Stowe, and P. T. Barnum.[34] The spectacular fire that engulfed the summit of the mountain on June 8, 1908, claimed the Summit House, leaving the stone-built Tip-Top House alone atop Mount Washington. While these summit hotels were comfortable, they did not pretend to provide a luxurious experience. Instead, they thrived because they appealed to that percentage of visitors to Mount Washington who craved the challenge and danger that the mountain offered.

As hotels were being built close to the mountains, towns nearby, including Conway, North Conway, Jackson, and Gorham, were becoming desirable travel destinations in their own right. They shared a bucolic charm, ready access to the mountains via carriage or horse, ample opportunities for entertainment, and the presence of artists such as Benjamin Champney. The building and expansion of hotels in the towns continued a land-use pattern in the Whites in which commercial development occurred at the edge of the mountain wilderness. As tourism became an economic engine of the region, it gave rise to an infrastructure of tourism that included not only hotels but taverns, restaurants, carriage shops, "bric-a-brac" shops, supply shops for hunting and fishing, and residences for workers in the tourism industry. Slowly the towns and this infrastructure were reaching like tentacles into the surrounding mountain areas, and more buildings and roads were replacing forestland. This gradual process would eventually lead to intense debates over how best to preserve the wilderness characteristics of the White Mountains while encouraging economic development.

From the earliest days of White Mountain tourism, Conway and North Conway featured a number of inns, including the Washington House, which opened in 1812 in North Conway, the Pequawket House in Conway, the McMillan House in North Conway, and Samuel W. Thompson's Kearsarge House, which expanded in 1872 and offered recreational and social activities to meet the growing demand for entertainment. Among the sports that its guests pursued were baseball, golf, tennis, billiards, horse riding, croquet, and in the evening, music and dance—all highly social activities that reflected American culture's turn toward more organized forms of recreation.[35]

A very different kind of cultural experience developed at Intervale, just north of North Conway, where the Abenaki chief Joseph Laurent founded an Indian camp in 1884 that proved popular among tourists. Laurent had grown up in St. Francis (called Odanak after 1917) and was educated in the English language at St. Francis, where he was mentored by Pial Pol Wzokhilan, a graduate of Dartmouth College and the headmaster of the St. Francis school. Laurent developed an interest in the Abenaki language and, in 1884, published a grammar and vocabulary of the language. During the same year, he came to the scenic location of Intervale, where he met and became friends with William M. Wyman, who owned the Elmwood Inn. Wyman gave Laurent the opportunity to establish a seasonal camp at a site in Intervale along the Saco River, where Laurent built five cabins. By the turn of the century, the camp had expanded to include cabins for cooking and storage, a shop where Laurent sold baskets made by Abenaki people in St. Francis, and a number of

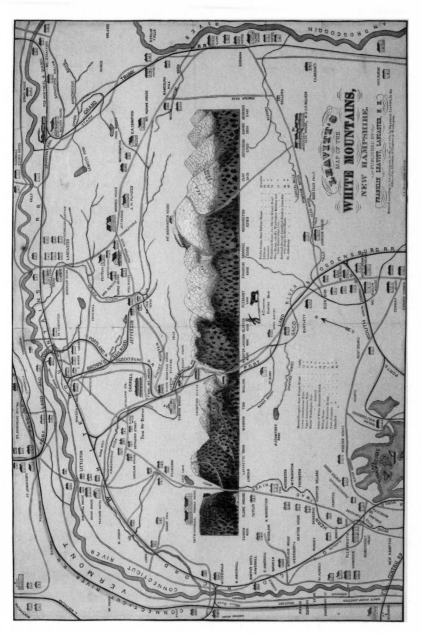

7.6. *Leavitt's Map of the White Mountains, New Hampshire* (1878). This map, which Franklin Leavitt created only seven years after the map on page 63, shows dramatically the rush of civilization into the White Mountains. By the 1870s, railroads had made most sections of the mountains accessible, and numerous hotels dotted the region. Courtesy of Dartmouth College Library.

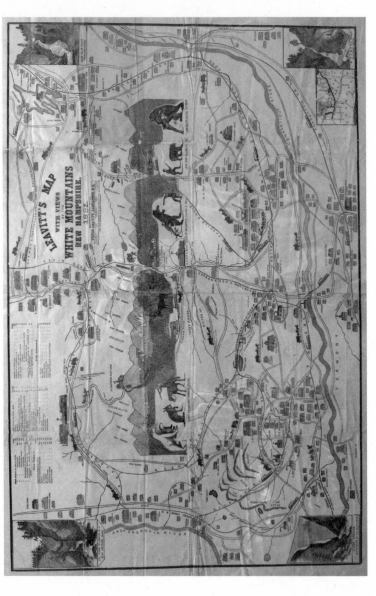

7.7. *Leavitt's Map of the White Mountains, New Hampshire* (1882). Leavitt's 1882 map shows an even more crowded White Mountain region bursting with hotels, villages, roads, and railroads. Yet scenes of confrontation with wild animals are still at the center, keeping alive the wilderness heritage of the White Mountains. Courtesy of Dartmouth College Library.

wigwams. He died in 1917, but his wife operated the camp until 1960, when their son, Stephen, took over the management.[36]

Chief Laurent's mission was the preservation of the Abenaki language and culture. The camp at Intervale, along with five other Indian camps in New Hampshire, sold baskets and other Abenaki handicrafts that became highly desirable collectors' items among white tourists. The popularity of these handicrafts contributed to the tribe's economy, gradually improving the Abenaki people's standard of living. For white tourists, visiting Indian camps and purchasing authentic handicrafts were part of the romanticized experience that they sought during a White Mountain vacation. Tourists felt as if they were experiencing closeness to nature, which was signified by the stereotype of the "noble savage." If they wanted as authentic an experience as possible, they stayed in one of the cabins, but if not, they could return to their luxurious hotels for the evening.[37]

Also visiting Chief Laurent's camp were anthropologists, who gained valuable information about Abenaki lifeways from indigenous people who stayed there seasonally. At the same time, the anthropolgists' research benefited the Abenaki people. According to Stephen Laurent, "[A] significant and extensive contribution of the Abenaki Intervale settlement was the intensive study of their ways, language and traditions by [anthropologists]."[38] The scholars collected stories and other cultural data, which helped to stimulate an Abenaki cultural renaissance and to maintain the people's cultural identity. The Intervale camp became a cultural center to which the indigenous people would make pilgrimages every year, eventually leading to Abenaki resettlement in Conway and other towns.[39] The popularity of Laurent's camp indicates that tourists in the late nineteenth century had a growing, if romanticized, interest in the lifeways of indigenous people, who lived in an authentic relationship with the natural world that seemed like an appealing alternative to the increasingly complex urban world that most tourists lived in.

Bethlehem was an example of a deliberate effort to develop a town into an all-encompassing resort that provided a complete escape from that world. As the village gained a reputation as a haven for hay-fever sufferers, entrepreneurs scrambled to upgrade the accommodations. In 1863, Henry Howard, later the governor of Rhode Island, spent a number of months in Bethlehem recuperating from an injury he had suffered when a stagecoach in which he was riding capsized. While recovering, he checked out the area, noted the town's clear air and pleasant surroundings, and realized that the sleepy village had great economic potential as a summer resort. He proceeded to purchase large lots of land and subdivided them.[40]

Meanwhile, the American Hay-Fever Association established its headquarters in the village, foreshadowing the invasion every July and August of thousands of miserable hay fever sufferers. The relief seekers stayed at the town's original hotel, the Sinclair, and in boardinghouses that dotted the village and its environs. But in 1871, an enterprising Bostonian, Isaac S. Cruft, arrived in town and immediately saw the potential for profit. He purchased a large plot of land about a mile east of Bethlehem Village, and there he built the Maplewood in 1876, destined to become one of the most luxurious of all White Mountain hotels. In addition to its spectacular view of the Presidential Range, the hotel was practically a town unto itself, with its own railroad station, post office, cottages, golf course, and gambling casino. The Maplewood, like other grand hotels in the White Mountains, offered a high degree of organized recreation.

The epitome of hotel building in the mountains, and a fitting transition from the nineteenth century to the twentieth, was the Mount Washington Hotel at Bretton Woods. This world-famous hotel, which opened in 1902, represented the apotheosis of the mediated experience of nature. It offered its prosperous guests a cornucopia of recreational riches, including bridle paths, golf courses, tennis courts, and cross-country ski trails. According to Moses Sweetser, "It is a modern village in its own establishment, standing amid glorious mountain scenery on virgin soil and maintained in the highest degree of excellence."[41] The hotel was the brainchild of Joseph Stickney, a New York businessman who owned the Mount Pleasant House, also in Bretton Woods. Stickney and his partners first started to develop the idea for a grand hotel in the mid-1880s. In the 1890s, John Anderson, who was a part owner of the Mount Pleasant House, entered the picture. Anderson loved the outdoors and wanted to develop a hotel that would include myriad recreational activities. He was the first to identify a potential site for the hotel—the Ammonoosuc plain, which afforded a spectacular view of Mount Washington and the other Presidentials. Stickney, as it happened, owned the land.[42]

Stickney commissioned a New York architect named Charles Alling Gifford to design the new hotel, and Gifford produced a distinctive Spanish Renaissance design. The construction workers, who included skilled Italian stoneworkers, broke ground for the hotel in 1901. The building, which featured a stone foundation and steel posts and girders to make it more resistant to fire, went up rapidly, even though it was the largest structure made primarily of wood that was ever built in New Hampshire.[43] On August 1, 1902, the construction was not completed, but the hotel opened nevertheless with a spectacular ball attended by Ethan Allen Crawford III and his daughter, Lucy Howe Crawford. Work on the hotel continued, but unfortunately, Stickney died in 1903 without seeing the finished building, which was destined to become a landmark.[44]

The completed hotel was immense, with accommodations for six hundred people.[45] What truly set the hotel apart, though, was its appeal to the moneyed classes. In the White Mountains up to this point, the primary appeal had been to middle class visitors, who were willing to pay for comfortable accommodations but were also looking for value. The Mount Washington was different because it set out to attract the growing cohort of millionaires who lived within a day's travel of the mountains. Its very ambience whispered luxury. At night, the hotel glowed with five thousand incandescent lamps, and according to one guidebook, "[T]here is an indoor scene comparable in brilliancy with a reception to the diplomatic corps at the White House or a levee at the Court of St. James."[46]

Hotel guests never needed to step outside to explore the mountains, so complete were the recreational activities: a billiard room, bowling alleys, squash courts, an indoor swimming pool (which no other hotel of the era had), a massage room, Turkish baths, shops, locker rooms for golfers, a bicycle room, and a children's playroom. About the relentless onslaught of recreational activities, one of the guidebooks gushed:

> The younger members of the big summer colony are in an hourly whirl of delicious excitement, golfing, driving, fishing, motoring, disporting in swimming-pools, playing baseball, tennis or squash, rowing, sailing (for you can row and sail in some parts of the Mountains), enjoying picnics and hay rides, "camping out," photographing, sketching, playing croquet, billiards or bridge, enjoying concerts or theatricals—in short, having a good time, as only those who summer in the White Mountains can enjoy one.[47]

The Mount Washington Hotel also helped popularize golf in the north country, boasting the best new eighteen-hole course at a time when only three other hotels in the mountains had eighteen-hole courses: the Maplewood, the Profile House, and the Waumbek House in Jefferson.[48] Golf was exploding in popularity, partly because the sport reinforced the values of business through its intricate rules, good sportsmanship in the face of victory or defeat, and self-discipline; even the sixty caddies at Bretton Woods were renowned for their discipline and professionalism. Moreover, a golf course itself represented a symbolic use of nature, as the designers organized the land into a highly regimented series of challenges and rewards, making a well-designed course a superb example of the subjugation of wild nature.

The Mount Washington Hotel became an economic engine for the entire region by drawing wealthy travelers to the White Mountains, stimulating other hotels to improve their recreational facilities, and providing hundreds of jobs for local inhabitants. In describing the marvels of this wonderful new venue, the White Mountain guidebooks of the era predicted the construction of many more grand hotels.[49] Ironically, though, the opening of the Mount Washington marked an end rather than a continuation of the golden age for resort hotels in the White Mountains. As the twentieth century dawned, the grand hotels began a long period of decline because of slowly declining numbers of guests, enormous fixed costs, and changing social mores. Even the Mount Washington entered uncertain times. It thrived under the management of Joseph Stickney's widow, Carolyn, but when she passed away in 1936, the hotel went through a succession of owners and struggled to make a profit. The hotel did earn enormous cachet during the waning days of World War II, when it served as the site of the World Monetary Fund Conference, popularly known as the Bretton Woods Conference, during the summer of 1944.[50]

These beautiful hotels faded away for a number of reasons, but perhaps the most fatal factor was the emergence of the automobile in the early twentieth century. A family in its own car could mobilize for trips throughout the entire White Mountain region, staying for a night or two at different locations and enjoying much of the region in a single vacation. Hand in hand with this technological factor was the quickening pace of American life, which made a month of vacation at a grand hotel seem anachronistic. The automobile and an expanding rail system also transported northeasterners to Florida, the West, and the Southwest, taking tourist dollars away from the White Mountains.

However, another factor contributing to the decline of the hotels was directly related to changes in Americans' attitudes toward nature. The hotels did open up access to nature for thousands of people, but, as we have seen, that access was often highly organized for the safety and security of patrons. Not all Americans valued the highly mediated experiences of nature that the resort hotels offered. Instead, more adventurous types began to seek encounters with nature at its purest—nature that had not been modified by the hand of humanity. They wanted also to recapture Thoreau's sense of individuality and self-reliance, which were at odds with the atmosphere of a grand hotel operated by a corporation for the comfort of its guests and the profit of its investors.

The quest to reconnect with wild nature led to a wilderness renaissance in the White Mountains. As the next chapter will explore, hiking and camping began a steady climb to popularity as adventurers plunged into the White Mountain backcountry, far from the hotels and the towns. At the same time, the most visionary among these adventurers formed the first hiking clubs in America to provide direct encounters with wild nature, to promote exploration, and to advocate for conservation. In the wilderness, the new adventurers sought not only to observe and understand nature, but to assert their individuality through the experience of nature at its most pristine.

Chapter 8

HIKING CLUBS AND A
WILDERNESS RENAISSANCE

IN APRIL 1863, A GROUP of outdoor enthusiasts gathered in Williamstown, Massachusetts, and organized the first hiking club in America—the Alpine Club of Williamstown. Through the club's two years of existence, its members organized weekly expeditions, including a notable journey to the White Mountains, to explore New England's scenic beauty. In a few short years, other hiking clubs were sprouting up around New England, including the White Mountain Club of Portland, Maine, in 1873 and the Appalachian Mountain Club in 1876.

Hiking clubs grew out of a surge of interest in nature and the outdoors after the Civil War. As we have seen in chapter 7, the White Mountains attracted thousands of vacationers every year, and grand resort hotels opened their doors to accommodate the tourists who flocked to the region. The hotels, though, offered only highly mediated experiences of nature. By the 1870s, a growing cohort of nature lovers had rejected this highly organized approach and yearned to experience nature directly in its wildest forms—nature untouched by the hand of humanity. They sought the exhilaration that came from exploring regions that had never been mapped, blazing new trails to the top of never-before-visited mountains, and camping in solitude in the backwoods. These individualists valued wild nature for the resplendent beauties that it boasted, for the physical regeneration that it stimulated, and for the spiritual insights that it inspired. For this new generation of outdoor lovers, hiking, or "tramping," as it was most often called at the time, became more than simply a form of physical exercise. It became an expression of individuality in an American society that was increasingly dominated by large corporations and big government. From the 1870s to 1900, these pioneers in outdoor recreation continued to redeem wilderness from the Puritan fathers—a process of redemption that had begun with the Crawfords and the Romantic artists and writers.

As the negative connotations of wilderness receded, ideas about the value of wilderness were beginning to formulate. In the West, John Muir was synthesizing his own experiences and encyclopedic knowledge of natural history

8.1. *Camp Fern Under Professor Hopkins* (ca. 1870), probably by Marcia Snyder. Professor Albert Hopkins of Williams College was a driving force behind the Alpine Club of Williamstown, but most of the officers of the club were women, who took an increasing interest in outdoor recreation after the Civil War. Williamstown House of Local History.

to develop ideas about the value of wilderness and the importance of preserving it. In the White Mountains, a group of knowledgeable nature enthusiasts formed hiking clubs, promoted outdoor recreation, and wrote about their personal experiences and their growing knowledge of wild nature for a number of journals published in New England. These enthusiasts formed a grassroots core of wilderness supporters who accomplished two important things. First, they taught the public how to experience wilderness by providing practical advice on hiking and camping, in the process making remote areas more accessible than they had ever been before. Second, they articulated rationales for experiencing wilderness that were the first step in the development of a wilderness philosophy, which would emerge in the twentieth century with the environmental policies and writings of Benton MacKaye, Aldo Leopold, Bob Marshall, Arthur Carhart, and others.

Members of the Alpine Club of Williamstown established precedents for later hiking clubs by exploring natural areas that were far off the beaten path, establishing a formal organization, and writing about their adventures. The primary force behind the club was Albert Hopkins, a professor at Williams College who was described as a "stern-visaged man, which concealed a tender spirit [and] a love of Nature." The other founding members of the club were nine women of Williamstown who had formed a keen interest in nature and outdoor exploration as they had grown up in the shadow of Mount Greylock. The officers of the club were Fanny Dewey, the leader; Carrie Hopkins, the secretary and treasurer; Bessie Sabin, the surgeon; and Fanny Whitman, the bugler. Professor Hopkins was the chronicler—the official recorder of the club's excursions.[1] The prominent role of women in the club reflected women's growing interest in outdoor recreation, where they found opportunities for independence and for pursuing their interests in natural history. When the Alpine Club disbanded, several of the women would become active in the Appalachian Mountain Club.

The club met weekly for expeditions in the vicinity of Williamstown, which afforded numerous opportunities for wonderful hikes, and the chronicler wrote an account of each week's tramp and read it aloud at the club's next meeting. In August of 1863, the members undertook the greatest adventure of the club's existence—a twelve-day walking tour of the White Mountains. The hike was significant because its sense of daring and adventure contrasted so starkly with the types of outdoors experiences that the resort hotels were emphasizing at the time. The members of the White Mountain expedition were Mrs. Mark Hopkins, Carrie Hopkins, Fanny Dewey, Fanny Whitman, Julie Gould, William Tatlock, Edward Griffin, and Samuel Scudder. Scudder, who was the only one of the group who had been to the Whites before, served as leader. The party met at White River Junction, Vermont, on August 22, took a train to Littleton, New Hampshire, and then traveled on to Franconia Notch, where they stayed at the Profile House, with the women taking a room together and the men sleeping on the floor of the hotel's parlor.[2] The next day, they traveled to Crawford Notch, where they visited the Crawford House and climbed the carriage road up Mount Willard to the ledge that overlooks the notch. Then they proceeded to climb Mount Washington, starting on the carriage road but veering onto the trail through Tuckerman Ravine and following that route to the summit, where they stayed overnight.

Once at the top, they determined to head north over Mount Clay, Mount Jefferson, and finally Mount Madison, from which they planned to descend east to Dolly Copp's inn on the road that led from Pinkham Notch to Randolph. Dolly, one of the most colorful innkeepers in the mountains, kept the inn with her husband, Hayes, but most people called it Dolly's place because she was the hostel's most visible face—an extroverted woman who put visitors at ease with her stories and hospitality.[3]

The route that the party intended to follow was roughly the same one that Thomas Starr King had followed, though in reverse. It still snaked through largely unexplored wilderness; the women in the party would be the first females to explore this part of the Presidentials.[4] The group arose early the next morning to a sky that was leaden gray; rain would threaten them through the entire hike. After reaching Mount Clay and then Mount Jefferson, which they summited without incident, they descended and came to the head of King Ravine, where Starr King himself had passed, and then began to climb again, reaching the summit of Mount Madison.

From there they undertook the final descent, heading east toward Dolly Copp's. By now, it was 5:30 in the afternoon. The forest was completely un-mapped territory without any blazed trails, but the stalwarts continued on, crashing through what Scudder describes as a "tangle of scrub, where the strength of our clothing was put to the severest test."[5] Night was falling rap-idly, and soon they were feeling their way forward in pitch-blackness. Scud-der estimated that they were still only halfway down the mountain. For illu-mination they had only matches, which they lit sparingly to read their compasses. After four hours of halting progress through the thick forest, the bugler blew hard on her horn. To their great mutual relief, the trampers heard the answer of a distant horn, and soon after, the faint sounds of dogs bark-ing. At 9:30 that night, they reached Dolly Copp's.

What was most amazing about this hike, aside from the protagonists' derring-do, was the rudimentary nature of their equipment. They carried only matches for light, and without proper maps, they had only a vague sense of obstacles that might force them to change course or even halt their advance during that dark descent. Such experiences whetted the adventurers' appetites for more exploratory tramps into the wild regions of the White Mountains, but they also underscored the need for improved equipment and accurate maps. The club remained active for two more years, sponsor-ing eighteen hikes in 1864 and nineteen in 1865. After 1865, though, the club left no formal records, and its members parted ways from Williamstown to pursue professional opportunities.[6] Though short-lived, the Alpine Club was the beginning of a community of outdoor enthusiasts in New England who would continue to embrace experiences in the still-wild regions of the mountains.

On August 30, 1873, a group of six gentlemen and two guides from Port-land, Maine, stood at the foot of Mount Carrigain, about three miles south-west of Abel Crawford's old homestead at Hart's Location in Crawford Notch, and excitedly discussed the idea of forming a club of their own that would organize formal expeditions to little-known areas of the mountains, study their natural history, and gather scientific data. To their organization they gave the name the White Mountain Club of Portland, and although it lasted only a little longer than its Williamstown predecessor—until 1884—it left an impor-tant legacy of newspaper articles that celebrated the exhilaration of wilder-ness exploration in the Whites.[7]

The club, which met every month at the Portland Society of Natural History, brought together some of the most accomplished citizens of Portland at the time. The driving force behind the club was George Morse, a highly enthusiastic young man who loved the outdoors. Other members included his brother, Edward, who was the director of the Peabody Museum in Salem, Massachusetts, and who became the president of the American Association for the Advancement of Science in 1886; Professor George Vose, who taught at Bowdoin College and M.I.T. and had worked with Professor Charles Hitchcock on the geological survey of New Hampshire; and Abner Lowell, the first president of the club and, later, one of the directors of the Mount Washington Carriage Road. One of the club's members, Edward H. Elwell, was the editor of a weekly newspaper, the *Portland Transcript,* and he published vivid accounts of the group's expeditions in Maine and New Hampshire, bringing the many wonders of the mountains into the living rooms of Portland.[8]

In 1876, only three years after the White Mountain Club started, the most influential and long-lasting of the New England hiking clubs was founded—the Appalachian Mountain Club (AMC). One reason for the club's influence was that its charter members gave the club a clear mission and regularly disseminated information about mountain geography, natural history, geology, botany, zoology, meteorology, hydrology, travel, and exploration. The club collected information about ranges around the world, but its home region remained the White Mountains, about which it would publish numerous articles in its journal, *Appalachia,* which started publication in 1876. In addition to the AMC, which was active throughout the Northeast, a number of local hiking clubs were founded in the White Mountains in the waning years of the nineteenth century, including the Randolph Mountain Club, the Wonalancet Out Door Club, the Chocorua Mountain Club, the Waterville Athletic and Improvement Association, and the North Woodstock Improvement Association. All these clubs built and maintained extensive hiking trails and promoted participation in hiking and the safety of hikers.[9] The emergence of such clubs was a clear indication that a grassroots movement was developing that passionately embraced the experience of nature in all its forms—from day hikes to extended backwoods expeditions and mountain climbing. The AMC and the local clubs built and maintained trails; published their own accounts of mountain and backwoods experiences; studied the flora, fauna, geology, and meteorology of the region; and attracted conservationists who later became leaders in the protection of natural areas in the White Mountains.

The first step in the formation of the AMC occurred on January 1, 1876, when Professor Edward C. Pickering, an astronomer who taught at Harvard and was the director of the Harvard College Observatory for forty-two years,

8.2. Edward C. Pickering (ca. 1910–1920). Pickering, who was a professor at Harvard and the director of Harvard's observatory from 1876 to 1918, sent the invitation to organize the Appalachian Mountain Club and served as the AMC's first president.
Harvard College Observatory.

sent cards of invitation to a select group of fifty outdoor enthusiasts who shared his fascination with mountains. The invitation read:

Dear Sir: You are hereby invited with your friends to attend a meeting of those interested in mountain exploration, to be held at the Institute of Technology on Saturday, January 8th, at 3 P.M.

Yours truly,
E. C. Pickering[10]

Approximately thirty people attended this initial meeting, which generated enough enthusiasm to encourage a follow-up meeting on January 12, at which the charter members began the task of organizing the club. On January 26, the attending members adopted a constitution, and on February 9, the first official meeting of the fledgling club took place. In a decision that would have far-reaching consequences, the founders voted to permit women to join the club, reflecting social changes of the time that acknowledged women's activism in the political world and their growing participation in outdoor recreation.

At the initial organizational meetings, the club organized five departments of special interest, each with its own councillor. The organizational scheme gave the club five designated areas for acquiring and disseminating information and ensured that there would be a balance between the club's scientific and humanistic interests. The five original departments, and their councillors, were T. Sperry Hunt for Natural History, Professor Charles Hitchcock for Topography, Charles E. Fay for Art, L. F. Pourtales for Exploration, and William G. Nowell for Improvements.[11]

The councillors reported regularly in *Appalachia* on the club's initiatives, contributing both reports and articles that added to the body of knowledge about the Whites and other mountain ranges. In addition, the club amassed a collection of books, maps, photographs, sketches, and other materials about mountains. Through its Improvements Department, club members cleared away trees at the summits of mountains so that trampers could obtain unobstructed views, showing how pivotal the appreciation of scenery was to the White Mountain experience. To further enhance the climbing experience, the AMC placed registers at the summits of mountains so that climbers could record their names, dates, and observations.

As hikes like the one by the Alpine Club through the northern Presidentials showed, there simply were not accurate maps of the Whites' more remote areas. In an early meeting of the AMC, Professor Hitchcock proposed that the club conduct an extensive survey of the Whites for the purpose of preparing an official map of the region.[12] The club also planned to survey streams, trails, and roads, from which sketches would be made that could be used in the preparation of the map. Finally, the map would include profiles of various mountains and a table with the elevations of all the mountains. Such efforts led to the publication in 1907 of the club's first *White Mountain Guide*, an indispensable handbook—now in its twenty-seventh edition—that was enormously important in encouraging broader participation in hiking, camping, and backpacking in the Whites.

In 1879, Charles E. Fay, who had been the first councillor of the AMC's Department of Art, was elected the president of the organization and delivered the President's Annual Address—a speech that was notable because it lauded the value of experiencing wild nature. "I purpose," he commenced, "to discuss briefly the various pleasures we experience as we ascend these grand monuments of Nature and stand upon their breezy summits."[13] He extolled the value of mountaineering and other encounters with wild nature, linking the club's philosophy back to the Romanticism of the early nineteenth century but also defining the value of wilderness and mountaineering in modern terms. Fay was, in essence, beginning to articulate a philosophy of wilderness. His address stands as a key document in the evolution of thinking about the value of wilderness.

To Fay, the benefits of contact with wild nature fell into four categories—physical, social, intellectual, and spiritual. Regarding the physical benefits of wilderness, he extolled the opportunities for promoting good health that tramping and climbing provided. Social and intellectual benefits emerged from the individual's growing scientific understanding of the natural world. Fay connected the increasing fascination with mountaineering and the outdoors to the scientific spirit of the age. The interest in mountains, he believed, "was developed simultaneously with modern science and has kept pace with it."[14] He explained further, "The study of natural science inevitably led man face to face with Nature. As a rich reward for him who in the fullness of time turned to her not only with the soul but the understanding, she revealed the glory of her visible forms in forest, wild ravine, and cloud-draped mountain top."[15]

Fay had identified a key argument for the preservation of wilderness: the knowledge to be gained by studying an ecosystem in its pristine state—one that had not felt the impact of humanity. However, he was at his most eloquent in describing the spiritual benefits of contact with wilderness. To put his audience in the proper mind-set, he took them on an imaginary hike up a mountain and described the transcendent moment of reaching the summit, where the individual soul "can hardly fail . . . to be conscious of an influence akin to religious exaltation. We call it the sentiment of the sublime."[16] In using the word *sublime,* Fay connected the growing popularity of mountain climbing and wilderness exploration to the ideas of Edmund Burke and the art of Thomas Cole. In stirring words, he concluded that climbing a mountain provided an "assurance of [the soul's] nobility and perchance a prophecy of what it shall be."[17]

The AMC organized a number of expeditions into areas of the White Mountains that were little known at that time. For example, L. F. Pourtales, the AMC's first exploration councillor, proposed that the club explore the areas north of Dixville Notch; the Pilot Range; the mountains east of Wild River; the country north and east of the Androscoggin River; the valleys of Mount Washington River and Rocky Branch; the area between Sawyer's River and Moat Mountain; the region between Tripyramid, Chocorua, and Black Mountain; the northern slopes between Mount Lafayette and Mount Willard; and the East Branch of the Pemigewasset River. To make these expeditions as scientifically productive as possible, he suggested that trampers keep a journal of each trip, use compasses to make annotations about directions traveled, and measure distances by keeping track of times between landmarks. With his proposals, Pourtales was establishing a protocol for exploring wilderness areas and recording information about them.[18]

One early goal for explorers was Mount Tripyramid, a three-peaked mountain that forms the eastern barrier of Waterville Valley. In August of 1874, Fay himself led a party of two other men to the three summits of Tripyramid. For years they had observed the mountain from afar, and it presented a daunting challenge; no trails were visible that led through the thick forests surrounding the mountains' base. They could see, though, that a landslide down the

South Peak had ripped away trees, leaving a gash that might serve as a kind of path up the mountain. Fay proposed that they traverse this slide to climb the South Peak, walk along the ridge to the Middle Peak, and continue on to the North Peak.[19] He believed that they would be the first white people to venture onto all three peaks.

Just as important as the expedition itself, though, was the account of it that Fay published in *Appalachia* in June of 1876. His narrative, titled "A Day on Tripyramid," embodied the very principles that Fay had articulated in his inaugural address. The goal was to venture off the beaten path, to challenge oneself, to explore regions that had not yet been explored. Fay wrote about the group's venture as a personal experience, filling his account with vivid detail and a pervasive sense of awe at the beauty of the unspoiled nature that the hikers encountered. He conveyed a sense also that his readers, with the proper preparation and precautions, could undertake similar adventures themselves and write about them in the pages of the journal. Fay and the other early leaders of these new hiking clubs were democratizing the wilderness experience by sharing both knowledge and enthusiasm; the implied invitation to readers to embark on their own explorations was impossible to resist.

On that day, the three companions took a carriage from Campton, and as they approached the mountain, Fay observed that it was "clothed . . . in its closely woven garment of dark spruces, save where it is rent from top to bottom by the great land-slide of 1869."[20] They disembarked from their carriage and crossed a farmer's field, passed a series of cascades, and found a handwritten sign emblazoned on a tree that read "To the Slide!" After some searching, they found a path alongside the slide, which formed a rough gouge with V-shaped sides.[21]

They scrambled up alongside the slide, and as they ascended, the angle of the mountain grew steeper, the climb more difficult. They came to a brook, and Fay noted, "Even this slope is too great to be traversed with ease, save barefoot, and unless one be willing to make this sacrifice, he is obliged either to walk along the edge of the brook, supporting himself by his alpenstock against the steeper wall, or take to the inhospitable woods above."[22] With such vivid detail, Fay was revivifying the spirit of adventure that had animated such earlier explorers of the White Mountains as Captain John Evans, Jeremy Belknap, and Thomas Starr King. But he also brought a scientific sensibility to the expedition, as he explained the effects of the great slide:

> The slide occurred at the time of very severe rains. . . . [T]he mass formed a loosely constructed dam in the valley. . . . [S]ome twenty-four acres of the mountain side with its added tons of forest, must have descended into the ravine—a surface more than half that of Boston Common.[23]

By noon they had reached the head of the slide, and after a bit more climbing attained the South Peak, which was covered by dense growth, but they saw immediately that a previous group had cut away some of the trees to gain a better view—a common practice at the time that was considered to be a legitimate way of improving upon nature. The party reveled in the vista, as Fay enthused, "To say that the view is extensive, fine, beautiful, superb even, would probably be no exaggeration. Is there a pinnacle four thousand feet above the sea from which one could gaze and not say as much?"[24] They headed onto the ridge that connected the South Peak to the Middle Peak, and there they encountered true wilderness:

> [Y]ou must make your way among trees of honest size that rise from treacherous foundations, where the plausible, thick mosses artfully conceal the interstices of the rocks, into which the incautious pedestrian plunges, now ankle, now knee deep, or even, as we have sometimes experienced it, so that a whole limb parts company with its competitor, and you stand transfixed like an ungraceful ballet-dancer. Such was the character of the region through which we now began to make our way.[25]

They continued through the thick undergrowth to the Middle Peak, the highest summit, where the trees were tall enough to impede their view but too short to climb. They then descended to a ridge that connected the Middle Peak to the North Peak and continued on. A longer distance separated these two summits, but the ascent of the North Peak was more gradual, and they made their way quickly forward, for the forest was less dense than it had been between the previous two peaks. By three o'clock in the afternoon, they had reached the summit of the northern mountain, but to gain a view of the surrounding countryside, they needed to climb a "withered tree on the easterly side of the summit." There they were rewarded with an extraordinary view:

> It gazes down upon the unbroken wilderness of evergreen stretching northward far as the eye can reach, and is lulled by the "hush" of their murmuring. It looks upon that Prince of the Wilderness, Mount Carrigain, and, with . . . Osceola, worships, looking northward to the throne of the Great Spirit on cloud-capped Agiochook. . . . I scarcely know a more lovely picture.[26]

For their descent, they headed southwest, bushwhacking their way through the forest that clad the side of the mountain. Even in the descent, Fay conveyed a sense of danger and excitement: "Here one would leap six or eight feet down a steep rock, holding on, indeed, by a sapling, but little knowing on what his feet were to alight; then another would lose his foothold, and go sliding, with many a remonstrance, some rods down the steep slope among the under brush until some tree afforded a temporary mooring."[27] Finally they located the brook that they had seen in their ascent of the South Peak, some distance below the V formed by the slide, and retraced their route. Twelve hours after starting, they returned to Campton.

Along the way they passed a hotel owned by a Mr. Greeley, who told them, "You are probably the first persons that ever stood on that north peak." Fay acknowledged that they had seen some trees cut down on the North Peak, indicating that a previous group had summited the mountain, but he concluded that they were the first party to make the tour of all three peaks of the Tripyramid.[28] So ended the first account of a wilderness adventure to appear in the pages of *Appalachia*. Fay's article became a model for numerous accounts that would appear in the journal's pages. It was precise in its descriptions of the flora and fauna, but most important, it featured an accessible style that depicted the exploration of wild nature as a highly desirable experience.

Women who were active in the hiking clubs were soon writing about their own experiences of wild nature in the White Mountains. Fanny Whitman, who had gained valuable tramping experience with the Alpine Club of Williamstown, wrote a number of articles in the 1870s and 1880s. In 1877, for example, she wrote an exciting account of a climb through Tuckerman Ravine. She and her party had been camping in different sites in the mountains for several weeks, and by the middle of August, they had set up camp close to the Peabody River, from which they visited Crystal Cascade and Glen Ellis. On another day, they set out to climb to the Snow Arch in Tuckerman Ravine, well above the timberline, which they reached without incident, savoring the experience of standing under the arch of ice and snow. But as so often happens on Mount Washington, a storm gathered quickly as night approached. According to Whitman, "The winds howled, the clouds thickened and thickened as the storm every moment increased, and the black walls of the Ravine seemed to be shutting us in closer and closer." In her account, she dispassionately described the danger of the situation: "Night was coming on, we could hardly reach the woods before darkness would be upon us, the only implement we had for building a shelter was the knife I wore in my belt, our stock of matches had become wet and dry wood was not to be found." To make matters worse, they were "wet to the skin and shaking with cold."[29]

Another member of the party exclaimed that their only hope was to climb higher—to reach shelter at the summit of the mountain—but they had no idea what route would take them through the ravine. Finally they found a stream and climbed upward alongside it. When they reached the upper wall of the ravine, the storm struck "with its full force, compelling us to cling to each other for support."[30] Night was falling, and they veered toward where they thought the carriage road was but encountered a field of scrub between the ravine and the road. Afraid of being trapped by the full force of the storm, they retreated to the ravine and headed in a different direction—around the head of the ravine and toward the northwest, where they thought they would find the ancient Crawford Path.

Whitman did not know the direction of the summit at this point. The storm increased in intensity, but at one point the clouds parted; they reconnoitered their position and started to believe that they would survive. They continued through the darkness until they reached the Crawford Path—"a ridge of stones apparently thrown up by human hands." By now they were exhausted, and it was so dark that they could not see each other's faces.[31] They found shelter for a time on the side of the mountain and rested, but at that point Whitman's companion remarked that Lizzie Bourne, who had perished on the side of Mount Washington on September 14, 1855, had been closer to shelter on the summit than they were—and still she had died.[32] They summoned what remained of their strength for the final climb, clawing their way over the enormous boulders that line the summit of Mount Washington like marbles thrown down by the gods. Finally they reached the Summit House and burst into the building, where the guests hurriedly gave them dry clothes, food, and drink, and they sent off a telegram to the Glen House to stop a search party that was looking for them.[33] It was an extraordinary account that highlighted the dangers of Mount Washington, as well as the need for safety guidelines and proper equipment for climbing the mountain. At the same time, Whitman celebrated the daring and determination of the climbers.

One of the major missions of the AMC was to make improvements, and, as the original councillor of improvements, William Nowell set an ambitious agenda that would have a far-reaching impact on the Whites. In addition to building and maintaining hiking trails, the AMC would eventually create the world-famous hut system, clear trees from summits to improve views, build campgrounds, and construct cabins—efforts that were similar to those of local hiking clubs in the White Mountains, the Green Mountain Club of Vermont, and the Adirondack Trail Improvement Society. Members of the hiking clubs generally saw exploration and improvements as complementary missions because both would give people greater access to wild nature while increasing safety. According to Laura and Guy Waterman in *Forest and Crag*, "[O]ne reason why the AMC became and remained the dominant mountain club of the Northeast may well be traced to its combining under one organizational roof both the improvers and the explorers."[34]

In the twentieth century, many wilderness lovers would come to believe that such improvements as trails and huts were too successful because they led to overuse that threatened the very qualities of wilderness. On heavily

8.3. Lizzie Bourne's monument. As Fanny Whitman and her companions fought their way through a storm on Mt. Washington, one of her companions noted that Lizzie Bourne had been closer to the summit than they were. On September 13, 1855, Lizzie had started up Mt. Washington with her uncle and his daughter. A storm came up quickly, and they could not find their way to the Tip-Top House. Lizzie perished, and this monument marked the place where she died. Courtesy of Dartmouth College Library.

used trails, for example, hikers might inadvertently tramp down wildflowers and pack down the earth, causing erosion. However, these issues did not surface in the last two decades of the nineteenth century, when hiking club members threw themselves passionately into both exploration and improvements. William Nowell set out a clear protocol for the creation of trails, which were to be six feet to eight feet in width, cleared of underbrush and roots, and marked in systematic ways. "At the entrance of each path," Nowell wrote, "there should be placed at the point where the path leaves the traveled road a sign-board painted with black letters on a white background, and at the point where the path enters the woods a similar board in sight from the first."[35]

In addition, trail workers were to mark trees with two blazes, one facing up the path and one facing down; the one facing the summit was to be a foot higher than the lower one. Blazes made by the AMC were to have three horizontal cuts made by a hatchet. Workers also marked the compass bearings of trails and distances to landmarks and summits, using white arrows that pointed trampers in the right direction. When a trail was completed, the club's Improvements Council inspected and approved it and then marked it with the club's official stamp, an *A*. Above the tree line, AMC workers placed cairns made of four rocks, and at the summits of challenging mountains, they placed record bottles with pencil and paper on which climbers could write their names, date, and information about the climb.[36] By putting in place such protocols, the AMC and the local hiking clubs endowed hiking with sufficient organization to improve safety without robbing the activity of its sense of spontaneous discovery.

With ceaseless energy, Nowell and J. Rayner Edmands, another AMC pioneer in trail construction and improvement, proposed numerous new trails. Nowell proposed trails and the clearing of summits on Mount Cherry, Carter Dome, Mount Carrigain, North Twin, and Tripyramid. The orientation was clear— wild nature was beautiful, but still it could be modified to give people access to the wondrous sights; humanity remained at the center of the natural world.[37]

If growing numbers of people wanted to explore the far corners of the White Mountain wilderness, many also turned to camping as a way to stay in those far corners and steep themselves in wild nature. Camping in the late 1800s was truly a wilderness experience. Yesterday's campers had to locate an appropriate site for a camp, clear it, gather firewood, and cut the boughs of nearby trees to make primitive mattresses for themselves. In 1877, Major John M. Gould, a veteran of the Civil War who had been one of the founding members of the White Mountain Club of Portland, published *How to Camp Out,* which was probably the first camping guide to be issued in the United States. According to Gould, campers regained a sense of self-sufficiency and individuality that was getting lost in post–Civil War America. Even in advising campers on their attire, Major Gould urged his readers to obey only the dictates of their own sensibilities. "Wear what you please," he implored, "if it be comfortable and durable: do not mind what people say. When you are camping you have a right to be independent."[38] Campers re-created the pioneer experience, which resonated powerfully with Americans as part of their nation-building mythology.

The growing popularity of camping and hiking reflected a strain of egalitarianism in American culture. On the trail, all hikers' boots got muddy, no matter what their income and status when they returned to the city. And at the campsite, all campers wore the same rough outfits, had their jobs in camp, and slept on equally rough mattresses made of the boughs cut from nearby trees. Moreover, women were equal partners in the backwoods experience, and just as they enthusiastically joined hikes sponsored by the AMC and other clubs, so did they participate fully in the camping experience. In 1879, Fanny Whitman published an article titled "Camp Life for Ladies," which articulated the reasons for the growing popularity of camping, particularly as an alternative to the resort hotels. According to Whitman, she and her female friends had first started visiting the White Mountains on stagecoaches. "There was then to us," she wrote, "an indescribable charm in the undisturbed wildness of the region passed through, in the lonely grandeur of the summits and the delicious plash of the mountain streams."[39] But as the area became more civilized, the charm of the region decreased, and she and her friends yearned to venture into the uninhabited regions of the mountains:

We loved the mountains, every rock and rill, every ravine and ridge, but we loved them as we first saw them, when little of fashion or sham penetrated so far, and we determined to try some plan by which we might reach less frequented places, continue to enjoy our mountain trips free from those who go only to say they have been, and can only tell you when they return, which hotel sets the best table or where the finest dresses are seen.[40]

Whitman and her friends had heard of the pleasures of camping out, and they decided to try it for themselves, camping first near Conway, where they stayed for three weeks in what was a successful experiment. After that initial experience, they arranged to be "conveyed far into the wilderness, and have trusted to fortune to get out again."[41] They camped throughout the White Mountains—particularly in the Franconia Range and venturing as far north as Dixville Notch, which was still quite remote. In these backcountry forays, Whitman observed, women could do "almost the same mountain work as men, may visit those delightful spots which have hitherto been but a name to them."[42] Her words reflected a search for challenge and for authenticity that could be satisfied only by wilderness.

In those days, two types of camping were common. One type was to walk and carry one's own equipment, and another was to hire a horse and wagon to carry equipment into the backwoods. The second type allowed for more equipment, but it was more expensive because of the need to hire a horse and wagon; this mode of camping was more common among larger groups.[43] In his book, Major Gould discussed both modes of camping but gave more attention to smaller expeditions in which trampers carried their own equipment. However, this type of camping was difficult because of the weight of the rudimentary equipment:

[F]irst we will start into wild and uninhabited regions, afoot, carrying on our backs blankets, a tent, frying-pan, food, and even a shot-gun and fishing-tackle. This is very hard work for a young man to follow daily for any length

8.4. Early backpacking equipment. In the late nineteenth century, multiday hikes through the backcountry were beginning to become popular, but the avid backpacker had quite a load to carry, with a bedroll thrown over the shoulder and a knapsack to carry the camping essentials. From *How to Camp Out,* by John M. Gould (New York: Scribner, 1877).

of time; and, although it sounds romantic, yet let no party of young people think they can find pleasure in it many days.[44]

These early backpackers carried an unimaginable amount of equipment: a knapsack or haversack, a rubber blanket, a wool blanket, underwear, a shirt, socks, collars, a pup tent—then called an A-tent—toilet articles, stationery for writing about one's adventures, and at least one day's supply of food. For cooking, the camper needed a frying pan and a coffee pot, and for cutting wood, a hatchet. Gould was not one to romanticize the camping experience; after advising neophyte campers on their equipment, he tersely stated, "You have the prospect of hard work."[45]

Gould dispensed his advice about backcountry survival in a decidedly military tone that reflected his experience in the Civil War. If a larger group were camping, he recommended organizing the people into four squads, with each person assigned a particular duty so that there would not be any shirkers. "Nothing tends to make ill feeling more than having to do another's work," he warned, "and, where there are many in a party, each one is apt to leave something for others to do."[46] Fanny Whitman agreed on the importance of dividing the labor, noting, "With a little experience women can do all this work without difficulty, and easily arrange many conveniences in and around the tent."[47]

Gould also recommended that the party include people of different ages; a camping party consisting only of young men might court disaster, for "it is hardly possible for a dozen young men to be gone a fortnight on a trip of this kind without some quarreling; and, as this mars the sport so much, all should be careful not to give or take offence."[48] The party should have an acknowledged leader. "Where there are many," the former Civil War officer asserted, "there must be a captain,—some one that the others are responsible to, and who commands their respect."[49]

In setting up camp, the first thing to do was to raise the tent or shelter. Campers during this period used a wide variety of shelters, from wooden lean-tos to simple pup tents. Backcountry trampers sometimes found three-sided, semipermanent bark shelters that fishermen had built. The Pemigewasset wilderness had several such shelters, and the Randolph Mountain Club had built shelters on the northern ridges of the Presidential Range. Usually, though, the party had to bring tents made of canvas, which were ponderously heavy to carry. The smallest and most portable type was the pup tent, which was usually made of canvas but might be made of cotton or silk to reduce its weight.[50] No matter what style of tent a camper used, though, it was a self-built affair. "We have done very much toward the construction of the one we now use," Fanny Whitman wrote, "and have made it a perfect protection and very comfortable. It has walls higher than they are usually made, with a fly extending the length of the tent in front, and a hood reaching far down over the back—the latter being a great protection both from sun and rain."[51]

Although bedrolls—rolled-up bedding—were becoming common in the late 1800s, many campers made do-it-yourself bedding by cutting down boughs from surrounding trees and laying them on the ground. A camper might also create a mattress by carrying a sack and filling it with straw, boughs, or shavings from a tree.[52] During blackfly season, campers put up netting to keep the pesky insects away, and they sometimes even wore veils around their heads while tramping.[53] Blackflies had been a nuisance since the days of the Abenaki, and in his guidebook, Moses Sweetser went out of his way to warn his readers about the harm that blackflies and mosquitoes could inflict upon the flesh of hapless humans:

> The traveller among the deep forests and uninhabited glens is apt to meet terrible and pitiless enemies in the form of black flies and mosquitoes, especially during May, June, and July. They come in such vast numbers, and with such unappeasable hunger, that it is almost impossible to keep them away for a moment, and their stings are so sharp and empoisoned as to wellnigh madden their unfortunate victims.[54]

People used tar and oil on hands, face, and neck to keep the infernal pests off, but these makeshift repellents were uncomfortable to wear and odious in the extreme. The best remedy, in Sweetser's opinion, was to make a smudge, a small fire on which fresh bark or green boughs were placed to produce smoke that kept the tiny but voracious insects away. Once camp was set up, campers settled in for their first night's sleep. Usually—and every source from the period says the same thing—campers slept fitfully on that first night, but after that, according to Fanny Whitman, they slept deeply, "with the aroma of hemlock, and lulled by the rippling of a mountain stream—a sleep that brings strength for the hardest climbs, and better fits us for serious work when vacation is over."[55]

Food during this era of camping was as rudimentary as the sleeping arrangements. According to Major Gould, the most desirable food for camping was baked beans and beef, and he described one common backcountry dish: "Alternate layers of beef, salt pork, and hard bread were put in the pot, covered with water, and baked all night in a hole full of coals."[56] Fanny Whitman, though, seemed to have more expertise in the area of backcountry diet, reporting that she and her party commonly ate from an ample menu that included oatmeal, potatoes, trout, bacon, eggs, johnnycakes, and rice fritters.[57] Fish were a staple of campers' diets. Campers cooked their meals in a frying pan, which, along with a coffeepot, was the only cooking equipment that was absolutely necessary. However, if the party were traveling into the backcountry with a horse and wagon, they often brought along an elaborate stove that provided more flexibility for backcountry chefs. It was a box with rounded corners that measured 21 inches long, 20 inches wide, and 13 inches high. Air to stoke the fire entered through a slide in the bottom, and a funnel carried smoke into the air and away from the campground.[58]

Camping parties carried water in canteens, but they counted on refilling them with water from streams.[59] Campers of that era seemed to have little compunction about drinking from streams, which may account for the frequent references to diarrhea and stomach ailments that run through Gould's book. "I have just said that your stomach is liable to become disordered," he told prospective campers. "You will be apt to have a great thirst, and not much appetite the first and second days, followed by costiveness, lame stomach, and a feeling of weakness and exhaustion." As a remedy, he suggested that hikers eat laxative foods, such as figs—a dubious prescription for treating diarrhea.[60] In his guidebooks, Moses Sweetser was more cautious about water, suggesting that campers and hikers obtain water from springs near summits or in the hollows of rocks after rainstorms. He also recommended carrying a bottle of cold tea, "to be drank [sic] sparingly and at wide intervals." He—in fact, all the guidebook writers—recommended that campers and hikers avoid alcoholic liquors, "which are weakening in their effects when such work as mountaineering is on hand."[61]

Deciding on proper clothing was difficult in the mountains; in summer, temperatures might range from ninety degrees in the valleys to below freezing at the top of Mount Washington. Moreover, nineteenth-century campers did not have the benefit of fabrics that provided lightweight protection from extreme temperatures. For backcountry camping, Major Gould recommended that men wear "Loose woolen shirts, of dark colors and with flowing collar," and they were to "[a]void gaudiness and too much trimming." In an odd detail, he warned that one's shirt "should reach nearly to the knees, to prevent disorders in the stomach and bowels." People at the time must have thought that covering up the stomach could stave off stomachaches.[62] In addition, the trousers were to be "loose, and made of rather heavier cloth than is usually worn at home in summer. . . . They should be cut high in the waist to cover the stomach well, and thus prevent sickness."[63] Again we see the concern with staving off ailments of the digestive system.

For hiking footwear, Gould suggested "brogans reaching above the ankles, and fastening by laces or buttons as you prefer, but not so tight as to bind the cords of the foot."[64] The adventurer, before embarking on the camping trip, should break in the shoes well, lubricate them with neat's-foot oil, and inspect them to be sure "that there are no nails, either in sight or partly covered, to cut your feet." The socks were to be woolen or merino, and the major warned that if you darned your socks, the repairs "should be done smoothly, since a bunch in the stocking is apt to bruise the skin."[65]

Since recreational hiking was relatively new, the experts of the time advised their readers on the art of tramping through the forest. Major Gould favored an overtly military approach, referring to hiking as "marching" and recommending an approach similar to that of soldiers—march for an hour and rest ten minutes. Fortunately, he was not as rigid as first appearances might suggest; he did encourage trampers "to halt frequently for sight-seeing, but not to lie perfectly still more than five or ten minutes, as a reaction is apt

8.5. The Thousand Streams, above Snow Arch, Tuckerman's Ravine. Four trampers of the Gilded Age stood for this photograph at the Thousand Streams, above the Snow Arch in Tuckerman's Ravine. They were attired in long coats, which were decidedly more bulky for climbing than today's lightweight materials. Courtesy of Dartmouth College Library.

to set in, and you will feel fatigue upon rising."[66] Moses Sweetser, though, probably would not have been impressed with Gould's advice, for he objected to the speed with which some pedestrian tours tramped through an area, giving the hikers little opportunity to enjoy the scenery. To Sweetser, these rapid forays were akin to "forced marches which would astonish even defeated raiders, retreating through a hostile country."[67]

A tradition of the era was keeping a journal of one's adventures in the backwoods. Major Gould provided explicit advice to his readers about keeping a journal of one's travels. "Write facts such as what you saw, heard, did, and failed to do," he offered, but, ever the practical military man, he added, [D]o not try to write poetry or fine writing of any kind."[68] The major, himself an inveterate journal writer, passed on to his readers another bit of sensible advice:

> [W]rite what you can, and let it stand with all its blots, errors, and non-sense. And be careful, when you are five years older, not to go through the diary with eraser and scissors; for, if you live still another five years, nothing will interest you more than this diary with all its defects.[69]

In the experiences of John Gould, Charles Fay, Fanny Whitman, and other outdoor adventurers, we see something extraordinary—that wild nature had lost its earlier negative connotations and was evolving into something to be sought after and cherished. Even though these backwoods trampers did not use the word *wilderness,* they expressed a yearning to experience wild nature directly. In journeying into the parts of the White Mountains that remained wild, they found a satisfaction that was visceral—a rush of adrenaline at facing dangers that might lie just ahead, at journeying into regions that had no trails, at using one's wits to confront the challenges that nature offered, and at being amazed by natural vistas of unparalleled beauty. In all their experiences was an expression of individuality that ran counter to the growing organization and complexity of American life. And in their visceral responses was born a love of wild nature that would, in the twentieth century, blossom into sophisticated ideas about the value of wilderness and what it means to the American spirit.

When the individuals who came of age after the Civil War journeyed into the White Mountains and began to form hiking clubs, build trails, and camp in the backcountry, they continued to be influenced by Romanticism through the writings of Thoreau, Starr King, Hawthorne, and Whittier and through the art of Cole, Durand, and Champney. However, they also reflected the attitudes of an age that was more scientific and rational than the Romantic era had been, and they therefore pursued more pragmatic goals to facilitate the enjoyment of nature, such as the construction of trails that would bring people into the backcountry. This generation of outdoor enthusiasts began to build a rationale for experiencing wilderness, a rationale that focused on three core benefits of wild nature:

- The intellectual benefits. Experiencing the solitude of wild nature allowed individuals to renew themselves intellectually by observing and experiencing the delights of nature. Such experiences allowed individuals to contemplate their own values and priorities and to strengthen their sense of individuality.

- The physical benefits. In an age that emphasized luxury and convenience, wilderness gave individuals an opportunity to challenge themselves physically and to build their strength and endurance and to counteract the decadent influences of industrial society.
- The social and spiritual benefits. Experiences of wild nature acted as a counterforce to the growing materialism of American society by exposing people to the inherent joy that comes from contemplating nature—a joy that does not have to be advertised or purchased. In wild nature, the individual could reconnect with a sense of spiritual well-being.

In the twentieth century, conservationists would extend this early thinking about the value of wild nature to develop a philosophy of wilderness centered on outdoor recreation and scientific knowledge. But the pioneering hikers and campers of the late nineteenth century laid a foundation for future thinking about wilderness, and because of that, they were indispensable figures in the evolution of attitudes toward wild nature. The White Mountains played a pivotal role in inspiring these changing attitudes through the incomparable magnificence of their vistas, and they would continue to do so in the twentieth century, when new challenges to the region's beauty would lead to farsighted conservation policies and legislation.

PART III

New Policies toward Wilderness,
1900–2005

At the dawn of the twentieth century, two competing
visions of the White Mountains continue to clash. One
vision stresses economic development, while the other
emphasizes the unique aesthetic, scientific, and recreational value of the mountains. Heavy logging at the turn
of the century threatens to devastate the White Mountain
wilderness, but conservationists win passage of the Weeks
Act in 1911, which gives the federal government the resources
to purchase privately held forestlands for the purpose of
conserving them. The White Mountain National Forest is
established, and the forests begin to regain their ecological
health. After World War II, though, heavy logging resumes,
and environmentalists conclude that the only way to protect the mountains is through the creation of a wilderness
preservation system. Their efforts bring passage of the
Wilderness Act in 1964 and the Eastern Wilderness Act in
1975. These and later legislative acts lead to the creation of
five wilderness areas in the Whites and a recommendation
for a sixth—areas in which the magnificent beauty and the
ecological diversity of the White Mountains are legislatively
protected.

Chapter 9

THE WEEKS ACT AND ITS IMPACT

A S THE YEAR OF 1870 APPROACHED, the picturesque town of Wentworth, on the southwestern edge of the White Mountain region, prepared to celebrate the centennial of its founding. As part of the festivities, one of the village's most illustrious citizens, Dr. Peter Hoyt, wrote a comprehensive account of the town's development titled *History of Wentworth, New Hampshire, from the First Settlement of the Town to the Year 1870.* His chronicle has become one of the most important lenses we have for viewing the development of a White Mountain village and is especially valuable for tracing the region's environmental history, for Dr. Hoyt was, in the words of one colleague who spoke at his funeral, "a great admirer of nature, a lover of the beautiful, and an earnest seeker of the truth."[1]

An amateur botanist, the doctor was a close observer of the natural environment, and as he spun the history of his hometown, he pointed out the impact that timber cutting had had on the mountain forests during his lifetime. After the railroads had reached the mountains in the early 1850s, he noted, speculators had bought up land that was thick with forests, and the cutting of trees became "almost a mania."[2] He continued:

> [T]hese plains and these valleys have been shorn of their primitive forests.
> Those great pines, so majestic and stately, which were the wonder of the early
> travelers from the Merrimack to the Coos county. They have all disappeared.
> The hillsides have been shorn of their great growth of Hemlock, Spruce,
> beech, birch and maple. . . . The very rapid clearing away of the old forest
> growths for wood or lumber purposes is a great feature of the present—
> indeed it is almost cut away, except in almost inaccessible places. Such as on
> the steep sides of the mountain or else so far away as to make its transporta-
> tion too expensive.[3]

By the final decade of the nineteenth century, the timber harvesting that Dr. Hoyt described had taken on a feverish intensity that would eventually have destroyed the White Mountain forests if not for the passage in 1911 of the Weeks Act, named after its sponsor, John Wingate Weeks, who was a Massachusetts congressman, later a senator, and a New Hampshire native. The law was a turning point in U.S. environmental history because, for the first time, the federal government acquired the power and resources to purchase forest-lands from private interests for the purpose of managing and conserving them. Julie Wormser, the director of policy for the Appalachian Mountain Club, said, "Without the Weeks Act, we would have no eastern national forests—not the White Mountain National Forest, but also no national forests in the Green Mountains, the Finger Lakes region, the Alleghenies, or the southern Appalachians. We quite possibly wouldn't have an Appalachian Trail, either, since much of the trail wends its way through national forest lands."[4]

The Weeks Act was, more than anything, a people's act, as groups of con-servationists watched the destruction of the Appalachian forests and forged an effective movement to save them, helping to establish the political viabil-ity of grassroots activism to protect the environment. The victorious battle to push the Weeks bill through Congress signaled a fundamental shift in Ameri-can attitudes toward wilderness. As we have seen, through the first three cen-turies of the nation's history, Americans had viewed the wilderness as an in-finite resource to be exploited by an ever-expanding population. In the late nineteenth century, though, growing numbers of people began to view nature through the eyes of Thoreau and John Muir, who were teaching their readers how important wilderness was to the full nurturance of the human spirit. The increased hiking and camping in the mountains and the development of hiking clubs attest to the broadening love of nature and wilderness. These changing recreational interests and the positive attitudes toward nature that they indicated were critical to the development of a grassroots movement to save the White Mountain forests.

The timber-cutting industry in New Hampshire dated back to colonial days, when representatives of the English Crown marked the tallest white pines to be cut for the masts of ships. Throughout the colonial period, the demand for New England's trees continued to expand. As chapter 2 explained, each town in the White Mountains had its group of sawmills, and the first settlers cut trees in the dense surrounding forests as they built their towns and laid the foundation for economic development in the north country. In her *History of the White Mountains,* Lucy Crawford observed that soon after the town of Con-way was settled in 1776, entrepreneurs "began the lumber business by floating logs and masts down the Saco to its mouth."[5]

Logging in the region increased dramatically after the Civil War, when the demand for wood exploded because of the nation's rapid industrialization and urbanization. The most important step in opening up New Hampshire's northern woods to logging operations was Governor Walter Harriman's de-cision in 1867 to sell 172,000 acres of state-owned forestland, including land in the White Mountains, to private speculators for $26,000.[6] Harriman has

9.1. Logging road in Lincoln, New Hampshire, 1905. Logging increased dramatically after the Civil War, when a rapidly growing economy and the development of chemical processes for making paper from pulpwood fueled demand for timber. This photograph captures some of the obstacles to logging in the north country: rugged terrain and muddy roads. New Hampshire Historical Society.

been much criticized ever since for selling off the land so cheaply, but, in point of fact, he was carrying out a long-standing government policy of dispensing public lands to stimulate settlement and economic development. This policy did not begin to change until the 1860s and 1870s, when the movement to conserve public lands originated in the West and slowly spread east of the Mississippi.

When Harriman sold the public lands in the mountain regions, speculators bought tracts from the state and then sold either the land itself or the cutting rights to the timber that was on it. At the same time, the Boston and Maine Railroad, the Concord Railroad, and smaller railroad companies extended their lines into the mountains and provided an efficient way to ship millions of board feet to the cities to the south.

Fueling the demand for timber in the 1870s was the development of new chemical processes to manufacture paper from wood pulp; previously, manufacturers had made paper from rags. Because the new paper processes used spruce, poplar, and other soft woods, lumber companies started cutting down those varieties in vastly greater numbers. From 1850 to 1890, the income generated by lumber products in New Hampshire increased ninefold, and during the next ten years, from 1890 to 1900, the value of the timber harvest doubled.[7] New Hampshire became the nation's largest supplier of spruce, and the value of the spruce harvested in the state rose from $1,282,022 in 1889 to $7,224,733 in 1899 and $13,994,251 in 1909.[8]

As the market for wood pulp exploded, logging companies turned to the practice of clear-cutting—the rapid cutting of all trees on a tract of land, regardless of the size of the trees. Clear-cutting was especially prevalent on the upper slopes of mountains, where lumber operators found that even if they left younger trees standing, those trees often blew down in strong winds because deeply rooted, mature trees no longer surrounded and protected them. Another reason why lumber companies did not find it profitable to spare young trees for a second cutting was because these trees took so long to reach maturity in the relatively thin soil on mountainsides; according to one estimate, spruce required 126 years to reach a diameter of six inches.[9] As a result, even though the operators would not use trees under six inches or hardwoods, which were not in demand, they cut down all the trees to facilitate the removal of usable trees. The operators then rolled the marketable logs down the sides of the mountains over the smaller logs and the hardwoods. The process denuded the sides of many mountains, leaving them completely shorn of the magnificent trees that were so essential to the beauty and the health of the mountain ecosystems.

By the 1880s, clear-cutting was having a visible impact on the White Mountains, transforming the valleys and the sides of mountains from swaths of healthy green forest into gray wastelands. The devastation caused widespread alarm, and a broad range of publications—from local newspapers to esteemed national publications such as the *Atlantic Monthly, Harper's,* and *The Nation*—began to describe the results. An early voice that warned of the environmental impact was that of Charles Sprague Sargent, the director of the Arnold Arboretum in Boston and a pioneering voice for conservation. In 1888, Sargent cofounded a weekly titled *Garden and Forest: A Journal of Horticulture, Landscape Art and Forestry.* The journal published a series of editorials and articles, some written by Sargent himself, some by other leading conservationists, that warned of the impending destruction of the White Mountain forests.

In the journal's very first issue, on February 29, 1888, the famed historian Francis Parkman vividly conveyed the impact that clear-cutting was having on the White Mountain scenery: "These mountains owe three-fourths of their charms to the primeval forest that still covers them. Speculators have their eyes on it, and if they are permitted to work their will the State will find a most productive piece of property sadly fallen in value."[10] In an editorial later that year, Sargent estimated that lumber operators would cut 6 million board feet of spruce over the next year from the slopes of Mount Washington alone.[11]

But that estimate only skimmed the surface of the problem. In an editorial in 1889, Sargent quoted an article in the *Daily Mirror and American,* a Manchester newspaper, that predicted that in the logging season from 1888 to 1889, the Connecticut River Lumber Company would cut as much as 100 million board feet of spruce; the Brown Lumber Company and the Berlin Falls Company would cut 20 million feet; and the Kilkenny Lumber Company would cut 30 million.[12] The *Mirror's* reporter described in detail the impact that this rapid cutting was having on the mountains:

> With the forests departs much of the beauty, the grandeur and the attractiveness which have made our mountains famous as health and pleasure resorts. When the woods have been cut away, the White Mountains are about as bleak and barren a section of country as we know of, and when there are no timber lots left the charm that was formerly theirs will be wanting. Even the Profile, the Franconia and Crawford Notches and Mount Washington would lose much of their glory and beauty with the destruction of the forests in which they are set, and the territory about them, when stripped of trees, would be one to shun.[13]

But perhaps no article did as much to galvanize public attention as one that appeared in the February 1893 issue of the *Atlantic Monthly*—"White Mountain Forests in Peril," by Julius H. Ward. Ward, who knew the mountains intimately enough to publish a book about them in 1896, painted a picture of the deforestation that was all the more effective because of its combination of passion with a comprehensive marshaling of facts. He estimated that lumber operators were annually cutting approximately 600 million board feet of timber in the White Mountains and along the streams and rivers that ran into the Connecticut River.[14] In the Zealand Valley, J. E. Henry and his sons had cleared away all the timber and set up kilns to make charcoal. According to Ward, Henry and George Van Dyke together owned 100,000 additional acres of forested land in the White Mountains, including tracts on Mount Washington, in North Woodstock, and in the Pemigewasset wilderness. Ward asserted, "They have it in their power, if they shall cut this forest as they have cut the forest in Zealand valley, to spoil the whole White Mountain region for a period of fifty years, to dry up the east branch of the Pemigewasset, to reduce the Merrimac to the size of a brook in summer, and to bring about . . . desolation."[15]

Ward went on to note that the White Mountain forests made a profitable target for timber harvesting because the operators could ship logs easily and

9.2. Logging at Zealand Village. In the late nineteenth century, Zealand Valley was one of the most heavily logged regions in the White Mountains. Lumber operator J. E. Henry's company built an entire village that included residences for loggers and mills for processing lumber.
Twin Mountain Bretton Woods Historical Society.

cheaply via river or railroad to Portland, Boston, and New York. To make the New Hampshire forests even more inviting, a duty on Canadian lumber made it prohibitively expensive for American manufacturers to import timber from the vast forests north of the border. The upshot was that because of the rapid cutting in the White Mountains, "it is freely admitted by the inhabitants of the region and by the lumbermen that within a dozen years they will be so badly hacked that one will hardly know them as they exist to-day."[16] Ward continued:

> A ready illustration of these methods of lumbering is furnished to any one who goes from Fabyan's to the base of Mount Washington, and overlooks what was once a magnificent wilderness, but where now the axe and the fire have combined to leave what looks like a frightful desolation.[17]

The destruction was equally devastating along the banks of the Ammonoosuc River, where "one sees the same frightful slaughter of forest, the trees cut off entirely." Along the road to Whitefield and Jefferson, the Brown Company, one of the other major lumber operators in the region, had completely cut down the forests. And in Gorham and around Berlin Falls, "[T]he destruction of the forests is equivalent to the desolation of the country. It looks as if it had been forsaken and condemned."[18]

9.3. Deforestation in the White Mountains, 1914–1919. Logging on Mt. Carrigain left extensive slash, which was being studied by (*left to right*) Henry S. Graves, chief forester of the U.S. Forest Service; J. J. Fritz, forest supervisor from 1918 to 1923; Franklin Reed, district forester; Philip Ayres, forester for the Society for the Protection of New Hampshire Forests; Allen Chamberlain of the *Boston Transcript* and later director of the AMC; and C. B. Shiffer, district ranger. White Mountain National Forest.

In addition to the destruction of the mountains' legendary beauty, clear-cutting had a number of devastating ecological effects that rippled throughout New England, affecting in particular the region's rivers and streams. Five rivers that carry water throughout New England—the Connecticut, the Androscoggin, the Merrimack, the Kennebec, and the Saco—originate in the White Mountains. Before heavy logging, the pine and spruce trees had grown closely together and kept the ground porous so that it soaked up melting snow and rainwater, which then seeped slowly into the streams and rivers, replenishing them at an even rate. Philip W. Ayres, a social worker and historian who, in 1901, became the forester of the New Hampshire Society for the Protection of Forests and spearheaded the movement to save the White Mountain forests, wrote, "The effect of the forest cover in holding back water is very much the same as that of a great storage reservoir."[19]

But when the mountains' forest canopy disappeared, sunlight hit the soil directly and dried it, destroying the sponge-like quality and decreasing the ability of the soil to retain water. Consequently, during the spring snowmelt and summer storms, water ran off more quickly into rivers and streams, causing freshets, or sudden overflows. Without the forest cover, the ground froze earlier in the autumn and increased the threat of freshets during winter months. In his history of Wentworth, Peter Hoyt wrote that the town experienced destructive freshets as far back as 1785, and they occurred with increasing regularity—in 1818, 1824, and 1826. Hoyt's observations underscored the ecological impact that deforestation was having on the region's streams and rivers:

> Even within my own recollection, the sailing down of whole floats of uprooted trees, accompanied with flood wood of a mean character such as old Stumps, logs etc etc in great abundance upon the swollen waters of the River, constituted a feature in the freshets of those days, which was watched by all with intense interest and curiosity. Beside this, since the clearing of the Lands in the vicinity of the River there has been a gradual lessening of its water[s] in their average flow.[20]

As the forest canopy disappeared and the soil hardened, rain that fell during storms also ran off more quickly into rivers and streams, carrying tons of silt, which became a threat to the navigability of rivers downstream. According to Philip Ayres, sand was constantly forming bars in the Connecticut River between Hartford, Connecticut, and Long Island Sound. At the mouth of the Connecticut River, one could find grit "as hard as diamonds" and "heavier than the alluvial soil" that had been washed down from the mountain forests and into the river.[21]

When lumber operators logged trees that lined riverbanks, the rivers in the region began to change course by cutting farther into the surrounding soil. A good example was the Saco River. Julius Ward explained, "The Saco has been so much diminished by the cutting of the forests near its source that the ability of the land to hold the water back has been lessened within the memory of the oldest inhabitants."[22] Freshets only made the problem worse, washing away soil along the river and further eroding the banks.

But perhaps the most far-reaching ecological impact of clear-cutting was the dramatic increase in forest fires. In 1905, forester Alfred K. Chittenden wrote a pivotal report on the northern forests of New Hampshire. The state of New Hampshire funded the report, which was published by the U.S. Bureau of Forestry and as part of the New Hampshire Forestry Commission Biennial Report. Chittenden warned, "At present fires are the greatest danger threatening the forests of New Hampshire and their dependent industries."[23] When the lumber operators finished cutting a tract of land, they left behind tons of debris such as limbs, twigs, leaves, and trees that were too small to be used. This debris, called slash, formed highly combustible kindling that needed

9.4. Fire on Owl's Head and Mount Bond. In the 1890s, fire destroyed the forests on Owl's Head, in what is now the Pemigewasset Wilderness. Fires in the White Mountains in 1903 were so extensive that clouds of ash drifted south to Nashua. New Hampshire Historical Society.

only a spark from a locomotive, a lightning strike, or a carelessly thrown match to ignite a fire that would spread quickly across acres at a time. In 1888 in Zealand Valley, which had been logged extensively by the J. E. Henry Company, a smoker reportedly dropped a burning match and ignited an inferno that eventually destroyed more than 12,000 acres of forest, plus 2 million board feet of logs that were waiting to be sawed.[24]

The worst conflagrations swept across the region in 1903, when a fifty-two-day drought from April to June made the forests as dry as tinder.[25] That year alone, 554 fires blazed across New Hampshire and burned 84,255 acres of forestland—more than 10 percent of the White Mountain region.[26] Heavy clouds of ash from the fires drifted as far south as Nashua.[27] Fire destroyed 10,000 acres in the Zealand Valley that had not been burned in the 1888 fire, another 18,000 acres in Kilkenny in Berlin, and yet more forests in the Wild River Valley in the Carter Range.[28] Many of these fires were caused by sparks shot off into the surrounding forests by locomotives—a common cause of fire in the north country. In Carroll in July 1903, for instance, one fire started when a speeding train rounded a curve and threw glowing coals as far as eight feet from the tracks, igniting fires in the grass along the tracks that quickly spread into the surrounding forest.[29] In 1907, another epidemic of fires swept through the region, destroying 35,000 acres in the Twin Mountain Range, on

Mount Garfield, and on Mount Lafayette. All three regions had been heavily logged, and the fires leaped through the slash.[30]

In addition to destroying standing forests, fires delayed the growth of replacement trees by burning seeds and the nutrients in the soil that are needed to nurture new growth. According to Chittenden, "The influence of fire on the soil is due almost wholly to the destruction of the humus and other organic matter in it."[31] Humus increased the ability of the soil to retain water and act as a fertilizer for the growth of trees. But when the humus was burned, the nitrogen in the organic material on the forest floor escaped, and the result, according to Chittenden, was to "destroy . . . absolutely the most valuable plant food constituent in the soil."[32] Moreover, humus was the component of the soil that permitted trees to grow on the sides of mountains, but when fires destroyed the humus, storms then washed away the remaining soils and ashes.[33] Spruce and pine would return to the mountainsides only if seeds blew in from surrounding standing forests, but more often, hardwoods took root in areas that had been burned over. Wild red cherry, for example, often sprouted in burned-over areas because its seeds could germinate as soon as the fire had ended.[34] Birch and aspen were other species that took root in burned-over land. As a result, the extensive fires were transforming the mountain forests themselves, with hardwood becoming more common and spruce and pine less predominant, though they eventually grew back in the normal succession of maturing forests.

As forest fires grew in frequency and destructiveness, timberland owners in New Hampshire, various state agencies, and the U.S. Bureau of Forestry urged the state to take steps to improve its fire services. John Anderson, the general manager of the Mount Pleasant Hotel, which overlooked the Ammonoosuc Valley (the site of the Mount Washington Hotel), took action when fire came close to destroying the hotel in 1903. He signed a contract with the Bureau of Forestry to develop a comprehensive plan for fire prevention on various parcels of land totaling 28,000 acres that hotels in the White Mountains owned.[35] The bureau's plan, issued in 1903, recommended, among other steps, the construction of fire lines and trails that would provide ease of access for firefighters to remote sectors of the forest.[36] In his 1905 report, Chittenden urged the state to appoint district fire wardens who would be responsible for detecting and fighting fires. They would post fire notices in forests, require permits for camping and fishing during dry periods, issue permits for local residents to burn brush, organize fire patrols, and have the authority to call out local residents to fight fires.[37]

Under Anderson's leadership, the Mount Pleasant Hotel, along with the Blue Mountain Forest in Croydon and the M. G. Shaw Lumber Company in Maine, adopted pioneering forestry practices intended to conserve the forests and prevent fires. The hotel agreed to cut only enough timber to finance its fire protection measures, and it embarked on an aggressive program of reforestation.[38] In 1910, the New Hampshire Timberland Owners Association built a number of fire lookout towers throughout the state and operated them until the state took them over in 1918.[39] By then, New Hampshire had adopted many of Chittenden's recommendations; the state forester was the director of fire services, fire wardens had been appointed throughout the state, and New Hampshire had taken a national leadership role in providing fire protection for forests.[40]

Stopping the rapid deforestation of the region, though, proved to be at least as challenging as the development of an effective fire detection and prevention program. As early as the 1880s, lovers of the White Mountain wilderness were beginning to sound the alarm that if the unfettered cutting of timber continued, the result would be the devastation of the forests. By the 1890s, a grassroots movement that encompassed local residents, conservationists throughout New England, and progressive timber operators began to formulate strategies for addressing the crisis. As pioneers in the earliest days of the American environmental movement, though, these activists did not have an established blueprint to follow in conserving natural areas, and as a result, they brought forward a variety of proposals, which fell into three categories:

• Negotiate with lumber operators to change their timber-cutting practices.
• Create a White Mountain national park along the lines of Yellowstone National Park, which had been established in 1872.
• Enable either New Hampshire or the federal government to purchase land from private owners for the purpose of creating a forest preserve that would have multiple uses, including the regulated harvesting of timber.

What made the search for a workable strategy especially difficult was the ingrained American reluctance to limit the rights of property owners—rights that had been held inviolate since the American Revolution. For this reason, all the proposals to save the White Mountain forests sought to achieve a balance between serving the public interest by conserving the forests and protecting the rights of the individuals and companies that owned the land on which the forests sat.

Writing in *Garden and Forest* in February 29, 1888, Francis Parkman brought forward one of the earliest concrete proposals to save the forests. Parkman appealed to the economic self-interest of those who lived and worked in the mountains, writing, "The White Mountains, though worth little to the farmer, are a piece of real estate which yields a sure and abundant income by attracting tourists and their money; and this revenue is certain to increase, unless blind mismanagement interposes." He called for the lumber operators voluntarily to adopt cutting practices that would sustain the forests: "The more conservative, and, in the end, the more profitable management, consists in selecting and cutting out the valuable timber when it has matured, leaving the younger growth for future use."[41] Conservative forestry practices, he insisted, would benefit the timber companies by ensuring the long-term supply of trees, while preserving the famed beauty of the mountain scenery for tourists.

In *Garden and Forest* on December 12, 1888, Charles Sprague Sargent urged the state of New Hampshire to take aggressive action by purchasing forest-lands. "The best investment the State of New Hampshire can make," he wrote, "would be to buy up all this forest-region and hold it perpetually as a forest-reservation. The money it would cost would come back many times over in abundant water supply, and in the yearly disbursements of thousands of visitors from beyond the borders of the state."[42]

Sargent repeated his call for the creation of a state reservation several times throughout the 1890s. Writing in November of 1892, he acknowledged the landowners' property rights, conceding that there was "no legal means for arresting the destruction of the mountain forests and the calamities which will surely follow."[43] Even so, he called for the state to use the right of eminent domain to take back control of the forests, though he did not spell out the mechanism by which it might do so. He also stressed the need for a campaign to educate the public about the imminent devastation of the forests, for only the public could press legislators to take action. He pointed out, for example, that J. B. Harrison, secretary of the state's Forest Commission, was building public awareness of the deforestation by traveling throughout the state and talking to people at town halls and schools. Sargent urged newspapers in all corners of the state to build on these efforts by stoking public support for setting aside land in the White Mountains as a reservation. Only a month later, on November 30, he reported, "It is gratifying to observe that the movement to preserve the forests of the White Mountains, of which we gave an account some weeks ago, is meeting with very general endorsement by the papers of New England and the middle states, and that a fund has been started by the *Boston Herald* to aid this campaign of education."[44]

When Julius Ward's article appeared in the *Atlantic Monthly* a few months later, he put forth a number of proposals of his own. The nation, he asserted, needed radically new policies for protecting critical natural resources like the forests of the White Mountains:

> It is plain that in the future, if these great domains are to be maintained in
> their substantial integrity and wholeness, there must be some other arrange-
> ment for their protection and preservation than now exists, so that the charm

of the region as a great national park may not be lost, and the rights of private owners, who have purchased this property in good faith and are entitled to revenues from it, may be preserved.[45]

Like Parkman and Sargent, Ward urged the adoption of sustainable forestry practices, asserting that the best policy would be to cut only healthy, mature trees that measured at least twelve inches at their base. The practice would permit younger trees to reach maturity and ensure a stead supply of timber.[46] But for any changes in forestry practices to occur, conservationists would have to win the support of private landowners, who controlled the vast majority of the forestlands in northern New Hampshire.[47] "In the present condition of the ownership," Ward wrote, "it is for the proprietors to consent to an arrangement by which the trees shall not be cut below a designated size."[48] He argued, as Parkman had before him, that the owners stood to benefit from such a policy because it would ensure a steady supply of timber over the long haul.

Ward also urged that New Hampshire's Forestry Commission be given the power to purchase lands directly and to create a trust fund for future purchases. Realistically, though, New Hampshire was a rural state that would never have the resources to purchase large tracts of land, as New York had been able to do in purchasing the lands that formed Adirondack State Park. And since the state could not purchase large tracts of land, it could not pass laws limiting the size of trees that were cut, since such laws would, in Ward's words, "interfere with private rights."[49] The situation stood in stark contrast to that in Canada, where because the government still owned vast forestlands, it could enforce regulations governing the size of trees that could be cut.

Yet even though most of the forestlands in the White Mountains were privately owned, Ward emphasized that "There is a public interest in them throughout the nation which is not to be denied."[50] Accordingly, he averred, the railroad companies and hotels ought to join with the lumber operators and take voluntary steps to preserve the forests. He then made an innovative proposal—that the state purchase agreements from the lumber operators "that neither they nor their heirs nor their assigns shall ever cut a tree of less size than that determined on."[51] He estimated that such an arrangement would cost New Hampshire between two million and three million dollars, an amount far less than it would cost to purchase the lands outright. Ultimately, he wished for the creation of "a great public park" in the White Mountains, but the strategy that he proposed could be an effective intermediary step toward preserving the forests. He concluded his call to action with these stirring words:

The White Mountain forests constitute one of the finest natural preserves on this continent, and the appeal goes forth to every patriotic American that their beauty and utility and integrity shall be kept inviolate amid all the dangers which threaten their existence.[52]

After Ward's article appeared, other writers continued to publicize the plight of the White Mountains, but by the end of the 1890s, proposals like Ward's, which depended on the voluntary participation of the lumber operators and the limited resources of the state of New Hampshire, had gone nowhere. Gradually, conservationists began to shift their sights toward the federal government and the creation of a national forest reserve in the White Mountains. But even as forest conservationists were coming to the conclusion that only the federal government had the resources to save the eastern forests, they ran up against a hundred years of precedent, during which it had been the policy of the federal government to sell off lands in the public domain. In a 1986 speech commemorating the seventy-fifth anniversary of the Weeks Act, former New Hampshire governor Sherman Adams articulated the power of this precedent: "At the turn of the century, the idea of purchasing land by the federal government was a revolutionary idea. It was a departure from a century-long policy and tradition of disposing of the public domain in order to build the nation"[53]

The situation was far different in the West, where the federal government still owned millions of acres and could create national parks and preserves from that land. But to create forest preserves east of the Mississippi, the federal government would have to buy back privately owned lands, a complicated process that would entail negotiations for fair prices and transfers of deeds. Most members of Congress felt that committing federal money for purchasing private property was an unprecedented expansion of federal power, and they also viewed the White Mountains crisis as a regional problem and, therefore, a problem that the states rather than the national government should address.

In spite of such obstacles, though, conservation groups in the southeastern states started in the late 1800s to urge federal action to preserve their mountain forests. In the southern Appalachians, the environmental damage from timber cutting was just as great as in the White Mountains. Small farmers had cleared the upper slopes of mountains because they could not afford to purchase land in the valleys, and they had planted crops at ever higher elevations, which led to the runoff of silt into rivers and streams in the valleys below.[54] As a result of these ecological and economic effects, conservation forces in the South reached the same conclusion as their counterparts in the North—that the only hope for saving the forests was through federal action.[55] The southern conservationists wanted to create a national park in the southern Appalachians, and in 1899, they formed the Appalachian National Park Association. Two years later, Senator Jeter C. Pritchard of North Carolina introduced legislation permitting the federal government to purchase land for a national park, but his bill did not pass in Congress.[56]

At the same time, a parallel movement in New Hampshire was beginning to press for federal action. In 1901, a group of conservation-minded citizens formed the Society for the Protection of New Hampshire Forests (SPNHF), which would prove to be a key organization in the drive for a federal land reserve. The next year, Philip W. Ayres, the first forester of SPNHF, studied closely the failure of the southern campaign and then developed an innovative plan that brought together a number of different interest groups in New Hampshire. According to Sherman Adams, "He assembled a coalition made up of diverse elements—loggers and pulp manufacturers, nature lovers, hotel owners, political leaders, literary figures and anyone else who could see the economic and environmental advantages to saving the White Mountains"[57] Ayres and the SPNHF focused their efforts on the creation of a national forest, which would allow for multiple uses of the forestlands that would include continued logging, though under far more tightly managed conditions that would allow the forests to return to health. Ayres lectured tirelessly all over New England, using a lantern slide projector to show photographs that shocked viewers with their savage images of the forest devastation.

As the forester of the SPNHF, Ayres authored a number of technical reports that set a new standard for appeals in favor of conservation because of their tightly constructed arguments, which drew on science, economics, and aesthetics to support the creation of a White Mountain reserve. Certainly, he acknowledged, there were powerful aesthetic and moral reasons to save the forests: "The preservation and proper use of the White Mountain forests . . . feed directly the higher life, and for this reason alone are worthy of a supreme effort to save them from denudation."[58] But the main thrust of his argument was economic, for he knew that he needed to persuade pragmatic members of Congress and owners of lumber and paper companies, and they were more likely to be swayed by dollars-and-cents reasoning. He emphasized, for instance, that by destroying the region's scenic beauty, deforestation would devastate the White Mountain tourism industry. In 1899, he noted, tourism generated $4,947,935 in revenues for New Hampshire from 174,280 summer visitors, creating jobs for 12,354 local residents. The White Mountains, he estimated, accounted for about half of these revenues.[59]

Ayres detailed further the economic impact of deforestation on other parts of New England. Freshets, for instance, were having a devastating impact on the mills downstream from the Whites on the Merrimack River. T. Jefferson Coolidge, the president of the Amoskeag Manufacturing Company in Manchester, described that impact in sobering detail:

For some years the manufacturing establishments on the Merrimac River in New Hampshire have suffered seriously from the cutting down of the forests. One freshet, a few years ago, cost the Amoskeag Company more than $100,000. Besides the injury done by the excessive flow of water in Freshets, we suffer also in the same way from absence of water during dry seasons, as the woods no longer retain the water.[60]

In 1903, Ayres, John Anderson, and other parties interested in the future of New Hampshire's forests convinced the New Hampshire legislature to request the federal Bureau of Forestry to conduct a survey of the state's forests, resulting in the Chittenden Report, which was published in the New Hampshire Forestry Commission's biennial report for 1903–1904 and by the Bureau of Forestry in 1905. In a valuable supplement to that report, Chittenden also examined the hydrography (the scientific study of bodies of water) of New Hampshire's streams and rivers. The report described how the destruction of the forest canopy and resulting erosion had built up silt in the rivers and had led to sudden rises and falls in water level, both of which threatened the navigability of the rivers. The hydrographic supplement to Chittenden's report later proved invaluable in buttressing arguments in favor of a White Mountain forest reserve.[61]

Ayres and the SPNHF were far from alone in the battle. In 1902, Edward Everett Hale, the renowned Boston minister and a leading voice for Progressive reform in the early twentieth century, convened a public meeting at Intervale—the lovely valley north of North Conway that provided a splendid view of the Presidential Range. Other important leaders in the conservation movement emerged, including Allen Chamberlain, the director of the Appalachian Mountain Club; Edwin A. Start, the secretary of the Massachusetts Forestry Association; and Thomas E. Will, the secretary of the American Forestry Association. Like Ayres, all of them traveled throughout New England, giving lectures, showing photographs of the devastation, slowly but surely building public awareness of the crisis and support for forest conservation.[62]

As the conservation movement gained momentum, though, its leaders realized that they still needed to persuade reluctant members of Congress that only federal action could save the forests. In the early years of the twentieth century, a few New England legislators did introduce legislation into Congress. On December 10, 1903, for example, Senator Jacob H. Gallinger of New Hampshire submitted a bill appropriating up to five million dollars for purchasing land for a national forest preserve in the White Mountains. Congress never acted on Gallinger's bill, though, or on bills introduced in the House and Senate in the next Congress in 1904. Congressmen from the West, the South, and the Midwest vociferously opposed the bills—and, in fact, were against the whole idea of spending federal money to solve what they viewed as a regional problem.

To overcome such objections, conservation activists in the North and the South joined forces in 1905, with the southern Appalachian supporters shifting their goal from a national park to a national forest. The northern/southern alliance transformed the movement from a regional cause into a national one and paved the way for support from congressmen representing other regions. With the formation of this coalition, momentum began to build for legislation. In 1906, the American Forestry Association proposed a bill that would establish forest reservations in the North and the South. The bill went to the Senate Committee on Forest Reservations and the Protection of Game, which approved it—with an appropriation of $3 million to purchase land—and sent it to the full Senate in 1907. The Senate, though, was still not ready to pass a land acquisition bill and instead approved a bill that allocated $25,000 for the Department of Agriculture to conduct a study of the northern and southern Appalachians. The secretary of agriculture issued a report in 1908 that recommended that the federal government purchase 5 million acres in the southern Appalachians and 600,000 acres in the White Mountains.[63] At last, a concrete proposal had appeared in print, and it gave pro-conservation legislators a specific objective to aim for in drafting legislation.

When the Sixtieth Congress convened in 1908, support for taking action on the Agriculture Department's report had broadened considerably, yet there remained one obstacle—"Uncle Joe" Cannon of Illinois, the powerful Speaker of the House. An unrepentant opponent of the expansion of federal power, Cannon had dismissed supporters of forest reserves by saying, "Men with a forest fad like yours are nuts."[64] On another occasion, he thundered that the government should spend "not one red cent for scenery"[65]

But as support built among the public and in Congress for federal action, Cannon finally began to accept the inevitable. In 1908, he appointed Massachusetts congressman John Wingate Weeks to the House Committee on Agriculture. Weeks, a graduate of the Naval Academy at Annapolis, had developed a highly successful business career in Boston as a partner in the investment firm of Hornblower & Weeks. Weeks also had deep roots in the White Mountains. His grandfather had gone to Congress from the northern district of New Hampshire, and Weeks had grown up in Lancaster; his beloved summer estate in Lancaster remains open to the public at Weeks State Park. Even though Weeks was widely known to support the creation of eastern forest preserves, he had won Cannon's respect because of his success in business, and in Cannon's eyes, Weeks's support lent credibility to the plan to create a forest reserve.[66] When Cannon named Weeks to the Agriculture Committee, the congressman told the Speaker that he would bring conservation legislation forward to the committee, and Cannon answered that if Weeks could produce a bill that was acceptable to himself as a businessman, then Cannon would make his best effort to have it considered in the House.[67]

The path was finally clear to pass a bill, and in 1908, new bills were introduced in both the House and the Senate. The Senate passed its bill handily, but the House bill faced yet another obstacle. The opponents, having lost the conservation argument on its merits, now sought refuge in the Constitution, claiming that it did not explicitly grant the federal government the power to purchase land from private interests. (Thomas Jefferson had agonized over a similar expansion of federal power during the negotiations over the Louisiana Purchase.) The Agriculture Committee referred the issue of constitutionality to the House Judiciary Committee, which ruled in April of 1908 that the federal government would be able to purchase lands only under the interstate commerce clause of the Constitution. In practical terms, this ruling meant that the government could purchase forestlands only for the purpose of protecting the navigability of rivers and streams that carried interstate traffic.

Even with this setback, Weeks remained determined to push a bill through Congress. He, Representative Asbury Lever of South Carolina, and Representative Frank Currier of New Hampshire drafted a new bill that met the Judiciary Committee's standard for constitutionality by drawing on Chittenden's report on the impact of deforestation on New England's major rivers. The three legislators carefully framed the bill to protect forests containing the headwaters of rivers and streams that provided power, were used for navigation, or had the potential to carry traffic. In preparing the bill, Weeks and his cosponsors explained how forests protect rivers used for power and navigation. The drafting of this bill was, in fact, a remarkable achievement because its framers drew on the latest knowledge about forest ecosystems and the interrelationship of trees, soils, and rivers. Equally important, the bill's framers kept the language general; because the law never named the White Mountains or the southern Appalachians, Congress, over the years, has applied it in purchasing lands throughout the eastern half of the nation.

In January 1909, the Agriculture Committee approved the new bill, which now carried Weeks's name in recognition of his leadership on the issue, and it passed the full House on March 1, 1909. But because this bill replaced the one that the Senate had passed earlier, the Senate now needed to approve of the replacement bill. Unfortunately, its Senate supporters failed to bring it to the floor for a vote, and it died at the end of the session.

When the new Congress convened in 1910, Weeks and Lever reintroduced their bill, which again, on June 24, easily passed the House. In the Senate, though, its opponents made one more last-gasp effort to kill the bill, with Senator Theodore Burton of Ohio leading a filibuster and Senator W. B. Heyburn of Idaho ranting against it as the "most radical piece of fancy legislation that has ever been proposed in the Congress of the United States"[68] Conservation organizations and the public turned up the pressure on the Senate, though, and the bill's opponents finally gave way. Ten long years of heroic effort and passionate belief reached their culmination on February 15, 1911, when the Senate approved the bill by a vote of fifty-eight to nine. On March 1, President William Howard Taft signed the landmark bill into law.

The Weeks Act stated its purpose forthrightly: "To enable any State to cooperate with any other State or States, or with the United States, for the protection of the watershed of navigable streams, and to appoint a commission for the acquisition of lands for the purpose of conserving the navigability of navigable rivers." The act established a clear procedure for the federal government to purchase forestlands for the purpose of protecting them:

- The act designated $1 million for fiscal year 1910 and $2 million for each year afterward, through 1915, for the purpose of surveying and acquiring lands containing the headwaters of navigable rivers. A total of $11 million was designated.
- It established a National Forest Reservation Commission to examine and recommend purchases by Congress. The commission consisted of the secretary of war, the secretary of agriculture, the secretary of the interior, two members of the Senate, and two members of the House.
- The secretary of agriculture was responsible for surveying and recommending lands for the commission to purchase. In time, the Forest Service and the chief forester gained significant new powers through these responsibilities.
- The commission could grant rights for cutting timber and for mining on forest reservations even after the federal government had purchased the land. Over the years, the granting of mineral and timber rights led to perhaps the greatest controversies in applying the law.
- The commission could approve the sale of certain lands appropriate for agriculture, so long as the sale of these lands and their use for agriculture would not do "injury to the forests or to stream flow" and the lands were "not needed for public purposes."
- The federal government could provide grants to the states for the purpose of fighting forest fires. Each state had to appropriate a matching amount for fighting fires in order to receive the federal money. The act allotted a total of $200,000 for this program, which led to steady improvement in the firefighting capacities of states.[69]

In an editorial in March 1911, *American Forestry* hailed the law, stating that even though it was "greatly circumscribed," it represented a major step for-

9.5. Weeks and Harding at Mountain View Hotel. Congressman John Wingate Weeks, who had grown up in Lancaster, N.H., championed the bill in Congress that gave the federal government the resources to purchase forest lands and conserve them. Later a U.S. senator, he is shown here (*front and center, right*) standing beside President Warren G. Harding and his wife in front of the Mountain View Hotel in Whitefield. New Hampshire Historical Society.

ward because it made "our national forest policy really national" and was "a notable triumph of enlightened public sentiment over political obstruction."[70] One way in which the law was "circumscribed" became evident almost immediately. The U.S. Geological Survey, which was charged with surveying the lands for acquisition, dragged its heels in beginning its work. In May 1911, a *New York Times* article reported that the director of the USGS had "only just started his field investigators toward North Carolina and Tennessee; his promised examination of the areas in the White Mountains is promised, not performed," jeopardizing the first appropriation of $2 million.[71] This delay and other problems meant that the government ultimately spent only $8 million of the original allotment of $11 million.[72]

In subsequent years, though, the USGS moved more rapidly, identifying 600,000 acres in the White Mountains and 5 million acres in the southern Appalachians for eventual purchase. One young forester who wrote a report on the White Mountain forest cover as part of the USGS survey was Benton MacKaye, who would later propose the creation of the Appalachian Trail. After the original surveys were completed, the USGS recommended and Congress approved the first acquisitions to create the White Mountain National Forest—the northern slopes of the Presidential Range. "By good fortune," Philip Ayres wrote, "but not by design, these woods were the favorite haunts of the Appalachian Mountain Club, and contained their most numerous trails."[73] Other early acquisitions included the southern slopes of the Presidential Range and the Great Gulf, on the northeastern slopes of Mount Washington. By 1915, the federal government had purchased land in the Carter-Moriah Range, Pinkham Notch, the Tamworth Range, the Bethlehem area, the Pemigewasset Valley, and around Mount Moosilauke.

Even as the federal government was purchasing lands for conservation, the Forest Service instituted more sustainable forestry practices, as Ayres described:

> The method of logging pursued by the Federal Government on the National Forests provides for removing the mature trees, clearing up the debris, protection from fire, and preservation of the crown-cover of the forest so that the sun does not beat upon and dry out the soil, protection of the forest trees from wind, insects, and fungous diseases, regard for water flow, for reforestation, and last but not least, for the beauty of trails and roadside in much traveled places.[74]

By 1915, the federal government had purchased 265,000 acres in the White Mountains and a little more than 1 million acres in the southern Appalachians, including forestlands in North Carolina, West Virginia, Virginia, Tennessee, and Georgia.[75] Yet Ayers expressed disappointment at the imbalance in the amount of land purchased between the northern and the southern Appalachians. "To friends of the White Mountains," he wrote, "this . . . appears a disproportionate division, especially to those who realize the close relationship between the mountain forests and the extensive water-powers upon which New England's industry largely depends."[76] Ayres had other problems with the way the federal government had implemented the law. He pointed out that the government had purchased tracts that were already cut over but should also have acquired land with virgin forests on the upper slopes of the mountains. Such a policy, he maintained, "would have more fully carried out the purpose and intention of the Weeks Act."[77]

On balance, though, when the law came up for renewal in 1915, Ayers wrote, "This was an experiment. It has been worked out successfully."[78] The major conservation groups, including the SPNHF and the Appalachian Mountain Club, launched an intensive lobbying effort to ensure that Congress would extend it. On September 23, 1915, the groups met with Agriculture Secretary David F. Houston and persuaded him that while the law had gotten off to an excellent start, it desperately needed to be extended. Houston supported the extension, and in 1916, Congress approved the expenditure of $2 million per year for another five years.[79]

Yet in spite of the new federal efforts, clear-cutting was continuing in the two passes that were, in many ways, the spiritual heart of the White Mountains— Crawford Notch and Franconia Notch. Despite the remarkable cultural and literary heritage of Crawford Notch, the federal government had not moved to purchase lands there, leaving lumber operators free to continue felling trees and allowing dangerous debris to accumulate. Recognizing that one of the most beautiful vistas east of the Mississippi faced devastation, the SPNHF, the AMC, a number of women's clubs, regional newspapers, and local hotel owners began to lobby the state to intervene and protect the notch from logging. After the SPNHF carried out a survey of the current status of the forests in the notch, the New Hampshire House passed a bill in 1911 that allotted $100,000 for the purchase of lands in the notch. The original intent was for the state to issue bonds to finance the purchase of as much forestland as possible, but, in an oversight, the bill went to the governor without the amendment authorizing the issuance of bonds. Consequently, the state was forced to purchase lands out of its operating budget, and it did so in 1912, appropriating $62,000 to purchase the northern part of the notch, from Crawford House south into the notch for six miles. The tract was less than the state had originally intended to purchase, but the most scenic section of the notch was spared from further logging.[80]

Logging operations also continued in Franconia Notch, in spite of its plethora of tourist attractions, from the Old Man of the Mountain to the Flume. Like Crawford Notch, Franconia was not included in purchases by the federal government, leaving lumber operators free to cut seven million board feet of timber and leave behind tons of slash. Ayres watched the continuing devastation and wrote with dismay, "New growth on the thin soil will be very slow, even if a fire does not set it back for several hundred years."[81] The situation reached a crisis when the Profile House burned down in 1923, prompting the owners of the property to put up six thousand acres for sale to logging operators. The threatened sale galvanized a national campaign to raise money to purchase the land. Astoundingly, conservationists raised $200,000, the state of New Hampshire appropriated a matching amount of funds, and in 1928, the state completed the purchase and created Franconia Notch State Park.

In subsequent years, the Weeks Act evolved to reflect the growing knowledge of forest ecosystems and the public's demand for the protection of natural areas. On June 7, 1924, for instance, Congress allowed the Forest Reservation Commission to purchase land for the broader purpose of managing timber. While land still had to be located in watersheds, it did not have to meet the more rigorous test of being located on the upper headwaters of navigable rivers or streams. Given this greater flexibility, the government purchased lands in Michigan, Minnesota, Wisconsin, Louisiana, Florida, Vermont, Kentucky, Mississippi, Oklahoma, and Arkansas. By the end of 1932, the government had purchased or approved for purchase a total of 4,727,680 acres.[82] In only twenty years, the federal purchase of land had evolved from a controversial practice to a widely accepted and highly desirable policy.

The Weeks Act represented a historic step forward by the young environmental movement of the early twentieth century. It affirmed the desirability of federal stewardship of forests and established a legislative precedent that led to the eventual passage of the Wilderness Act in 1964 and other wilderness protection initiatives. Equally important, Philip Ayres and the others who worked so hard to win passage of the Weeks Act gave the public a continuing voice in environmental policies. Before the Weeks Act, the public's voice struggled to be heard; after the law, its voice would never again be ignored.

The Weeks Act was, in many ways, the culmination of three hundred years of White Mountain history. As we have seen, the English colonists viewed the distant Crystal Hills as unchristian wilderness inhabited by wild beasts and by Native Americans whose lifeways seemed uncivilized. During the 1800s, though, settlers and travelers alike came to accept and then embrace the White Mountain wilderness. Artists, writers, scientists, and explorers celebrated the wild nature that thrived in the White Mountains—the rills of pure water, the topography of primordial granite that challenged adventurous souls and rewarded them with vistas of astounding beauty, the rare arctic flora that populated the upper regions of the mountain slopes. As the nineteenth century progressed, a growing portion of the American public embraced the wild parts of the White Mountains, hiking through the outermost reaches of the forests, camping for days or weeks at a time in the heart of the Pemigewasset wilderness, and hunting and fishing.

When clear-cutting and fires threatened the White Mountains, this deep reservoir of love for the mountains' beauty ultimately led to the passage of the Weeks Act and the preservation of the mountain landscape, along with the aesthetic, recreational, social, cultural, and scientific values that it symbolized. Without the mountain forests, much of the fauna would have disappeared, and erosion would have swept the soil from the mountainsides and clogged the sparkling rivers and streams. The mountains would have been shorn of the emerald beauty of summer and the fiery colors of autumn. With the passage of the Weeks Act, forests that had been cut could regenerate and once again support the flora and fauna of the mountains. In short, because of this law, the White Mountains could continue to support wild nature and could continue to provide the solitude of wilderness.

But even as the federal government used the Weeks Act to purchase and conserve forests for conservation, new threats to the ecological integrity of the White Mountains arose—from tourism, consumerism, and renewed pressures for logging. And as these new threats gathered, the very rationale for preserving the White Mountain wilderness would evolve during the new century. During the first half of the twentieth century, a sophisticated philosophy of the inherent value of wilderness would develop, based on increasing scientific knowledge of ecology, the perception that the flora and fauna of the natural world have their own value, and the belief that humanity is closely connected to the phenomena of the natural world. A wilderness ethic was emerging, and once again, the White Mountains would be at the center of this historic development.

Chapter 10

OUTDOOR RECREATION
AND THE BIRTH OF A
WILDERNESS CONSTITUENCY

I N 1910, THE YEAR BEFORE passage of the weeks act, Warren W. Hart, an
indefatigable explorer of the White Mountains who served as the AMC's
councillor of improvements from 1908 to 1910, undertook the restoration
of the historic Davis Path with several other White Mountain enthusiasts.
Nathaniel T. P. Davis had built the trail as a bridle path in 1845, but it had been
abandoned in 1853 and had been virtually unused ever since, prompting Professor W. H. Pickering to comment, "It has become overgrown, and actually
obliterated for all but a very small portion of the way."[1] The path started across
the road from where Abel Crawford's farm had once stood, scaled Mount
Crawford, and continued on for fifteen miles to its terminus at the summit of
Mount Washington.

One of the men who worked with Hart was Joe Bouchard, an experienced
backwoodsman who had an unerring sense of how to locate the old trail.
"Foot by foot," Hart wrote, "he traced it through thicket and swamp, over bare
rocks, and through blowdowns hundreds of acres in extent."[2] As they worked
their way up the side of the mountain, Hart described the views as "wild and
refreshing," and when they rested, they could see a variety of wildlife—Canada
jays, eagles, hawks, partridges, and the tracks of deer, bear, and moose. They
found the remains of a deer but could not tell whether it had been attacked
by an animal or died of natural causes.

By the ninth day, they had run out of supplies, and Hart trekked back to
Rocky Branch Valley for provisions. The next day, though, they finally approached the summit of Stairs Mountain. Darkness was descending, but they
continued cutting trail, until finally Hart was able to crouch through the final
thickets and walk out on Upper Stair, where he witnessed the last traces of the
setting sun and the emerging stars. Finally they had finished, but the grueling
endeavor had taken them twelve days. Even after its opening, the trail exuded
a singular sense of wildness and isolation, inspiring Hart to write, "[N]ature
lovers will find the monotony of a long wilderness trail broken by an intimate

acquaintance with many varieties of birds not as yet over-timid of human beings."[3]

The reopening of this historic trail demonstrated two things about the White Mountains just before World War I—that the interest in hiking into remote areas of the Whites, which had first evidenced itself in the 1890s, continued to grow; and that the volunteers who spent their energies opening up access to those remote areas had a deeply ingrained respect for the historic trails of the White Mountains. This unique blend of yearning for wild nature and respect for the heritage of the region has shaped the strategies for wilderness preservation in the White Mountains, and it was during the first decades of the twentieth century that the groundwork for those preservation efforts was established.

When Hart recounted the labors of his intrepid group of trail builders in the pages of *Appalachia* in 1911, President William Howard Taft had signed the Weeks Act only months earlier. The law seemed to unleash a pent-up demand for access to the wild and remote corners of the White Mountains, and soon after its signing, volunteer organizations and the U.S. Forest Service were constructing hundreds of miles of trails, creating new campgrounds, and developing numerous other facilities for outdoor recreation. Some of the trails were restorations of historic paths like the Davis, while many others were new trails that wound to all corners of the White Mountains.

The next three decades saw a virtual explosion in outdoor recreation in the White Mountains. Along with the creation of a network of hundreds of miles of tails, these years saw the creation of state parks in New Hampshire, the rapid expansion of the scouting movement, the founding of dozens of local hiking clubs, the growth in popularity of camping as a family activity, the development of rugged sports such as rock climbing and white-water rafting, and the growth in popularity of skiing and other winter sports. While Americans during the 1890s had taken short walks in the woods and luxuriated in their hotel surroundings, now they threw themselves into vigorous outdoor recreation, continuing the trend that had started in the late nineteenth century with the creation of hiking clubs and the building of new trails in the mountains.

Now, on the eve of the First World War, it was as if all the cultural influences that had slowly been transforming the experience of wild nature—the celebrations of the Romantic writers and artists, the pioneering ideals of the Crawfords, the legends and lore of the White Mountains, and the adventurous spirit of nineteenth-century hikers—reached a culmination. More and more Americans had a visceral sense that wild nature presented a healthy alternative to their workaday world, which was increasingly materialistic and corporate. Many were searching for ways to reassert their individuality, particularly through physical challenges in which individual accomplishment still counted for something. In outdoor activities that brought them into direct contact with America's unadulterated natural beauties, they found what they wanted—what they needed. A phalanx of outdoor enthusiasts started a wilderness movement that would soon find articulate expression in the words of Benton MacKaye, Robert (Bob) Marshall, and Aldo Leopold, and in the leadership of Arthur Carhart. But before we examine the ideas of those pioneering environmental thinkers in chapter 11, it is essential to understand how thousands of Americans gravitated toward the wilderness experience in the White Mountains in the years between World War I and World War II—and in the process helped to create a constituency for the preservation of wilderness.

In the White Mountains, the passage of the Weeks Act set in motion governmental policies to restore and conserve the region's forests, without which wilderness recreation would have been impossible. Within a month after President Taft signed the law, Congress approved the White Mountain Purchase Unit, and seven years later, on May 16, 1918, the Department of Agriculture officially created the White Mountain National Forest (WMNF) by merging the original White Mountain Purchase Unit with the more recently acquired Androscoggin Purchase Unit (1913) and the Kilkenny Purchase Unit (1913), which together totaled 950,114 acres. In 1929, the Forest Service excluded the Androscoggin Purchase Unit from the WMNF, leaving the forest with a total of 801,900 acres in New Hampshire and 53,300 acres in Maine.[4]

The Weeks Act had an enormous impact on other parts of the country, too, as the federal government purchased 1.2 million acres in seven southern Appalachian states, including the two Virginias, the two Carolinas, Tennessee, Georgia, and Alabama, as well as a small tract of land in Arkansas.[5] Congress appropriated $600,000 in 1919 to continue purchasing lands and to maintain the continuity of government personnel—the foresters and other expert staffers—who had been evaluating forests for purchase. This continuity was critical to the development of an effective national forest system. As Philip Ayres explained, "It takes an expert to buy forest land anywhere, but when the purchases are made under varying conditions in ten widely separated States, the necessary force becomes highly trained, and if scattered by a lapse of funds, cannot be reestablished without years of expensive practice."[6]

In 1920, Congress voted to renew the Weeks Act, which was due to expire that year, but there was never any real danger that the House or the Senate would fail to extend the legislation, which had come to be regarded as highly beneficial to the nation. In fact, in 1924, Congress passed the Clarke-McNary Act, which greatly expanded the conditions under which the federal government could purchase land from private owners. In addition to providing for better fire protection, restoration of deforested lands, and extension of national forests, the law also permitted the government to purchase lands that comprised watersheds of navigable streams and rivers or that could be used for the production of timber. This was a much more liberal definition of purchasable lands, since the Weeks Act had required lands for purchase to be located near the headwaters of potentially navigable or power-producing streams and rivers.[7]

By the end of 1932, the government had purchased or approved for purchase forty-two tracts of land in twenty states east of the Mississippi, for a total of 4,727,680 acres. The Weeks Act entered a new stage in the spring of 1933, when the federal government decided to purchase lands in the East that would provide employment for the Civilian Conservation Corps (CCC). On May 20, 1933, President Franklin D. Roosevelt approved emergency funds of $20 million for further purchase; this appropriation constituted 80 percent of all the funds that the federal government had already spent for the purchase of forestlands since 1911.[8]

Now that the federal government owned and was responsible for managing these forestlands, a series of questions arose. How would forestlands that had been heavily cut, such as those in the White Mountains, be restored? And what would the restored forests look like? One possible model was Germany, which had been managing its forests for centuries and had adopted a pattern of reforestation that was highly geometric—and distinctly unwild. Somehow, it seemed that such an approach to forest regeneration would never quite fit the American temperament. Finally, who would benefit more from the forests— the industries that wanted to cut millions of acres of trees or a generation of Americans who had a growing appetite for outdoor adventure?

Answering these questions fell to the U.S. Forest Service, which had been formed in 1905 from the old Bureau of Forestry. The Forest Service was in the Department of Agriculture, where it often engaged in bureaucratic competition with the National Park Service, which was in the Department of the Interior and which managed some of America's best-known natural areas, including Yellowstone National Park and the Grand Canyon. Yet the Forest Service managed a far vaster reach of land that, according to Philip Ayres, encompassed a total of 155 million acres.[9] The Forest Service benefited from the political skills of its first chief forester, Gifford Pinchot, friend and hunting companion of the greatest ally that the outdoors ever had in the White House, President Theodore Roosevelt. Pinchot was a skillful political player who established the guiding vision of the Forest Service as the management of the nation's forests to provide "the greatest good for the greatest number." In practical terms, the Forest Service was to manage the national forests for multiple uses, maintaining a balance between recreational uses and economic uses, particularly timber, minerals, and grazing. Since its founding, the chal-

10.1. Gifford Pinchot. Pinchot was the first chief forester of the U.S. Forest Service and a close friend of President Theodore Roosevelt's. His vision for the nation's forests was to provide "the greatest good for the greatest number." The Granger Collection, New York.

lenge facing the Forest Service has been to find the appropriate balance between conservation and production, and this balance has varied from one presidential administration to another, depending on whether the chief executive is more sympathetic to the interests of conservationists and recreational users or to the imperatives of industry and the needs of an economy that has a voracious appetite for wood and minerals.

In managing the WMNF in the years following the passage of the Weeks Act, the Forest Service restored forests that had been cut over, established forestry practices that would provide lumber on a sustainable basis, and expanded recreational facilities in the mountains.[10] In achieving these goals, and especially in making the WMNF an effective "working forest," the Forest Service had to maintain a delicate balance among competing interests that included vacationers, residents, the AMC and other hiking clubs, the Society for the Protection of New Hampshire Forests, timber and paper companies, hotel owners, merchants, and, as the twentieth century progressed, owners of ski resorts. It was a diverse group of interests, but many of these interests had already worked together in the coalition that advocated passage of the Weeks Act. One important advantage in favor of the WMNF was New England town government and its tradition of participatory democracy, in which competing interests discussed their differences and reached consensus on policies that would benefit the region as a whole. Consensus, though, proved more and more elusive as the twentieth century progressed, and the region's popularity led to overuse and increasing ecological pressures on sections of the WMNF.

The Forest Service's first priority was to replant forests that had been cut over during the clear-cutting of the late 1800s and early 1900s. After only a remarkably short time—as early as 1920—Philip Ayres hiked through the White Mountains and saw obvious signs of forest regeneration. The state of New Hampshire's forest surveys indicated that 29 percent of the forestland was, in his words, "in splendid, promising growths."[11] "The new forest," he elaborated, "is springing into life wherever fire has not destroyed the soil. A new patriotism fills [the hiker's] heart."[12] Yet when he passed a red boundary post for the WMNF and walked out of the national forest, the scene changed dramatically. "The sound of many axes greets the ear," Ayres reported. "The sight of men and horses and confused logs meets the eye. [The hiker] is on private land that is being stripped clean. Great black patches on the steep slopes mark recent fires that follow the lumber slash over thousands of acres."[13] The sight only reinforced how critical it was for the federal government to continue purchasing lands for the WMNF. Except in areas protected by state or federal government, Ayres lamented, timber continued to be cut rapidly. Ayres concluded that while a significant part of New Hampshire's forests were healthy, fully one-third of the state's forests were still in "waste condition."[14]

On the lands that the federal government had purchased, the Forest Service instituted practices that would provide a steady supply of timber but would also sustain the forests and maintain their aesthetic integrity; finding the appropriate balance between the production of lumber and the protection of the forests' ecological and aesthetic integrity would be a continuing challenge. The Forest Service instituted a sophisticated system of silviculture, or forestry practices, in which loggers harvested mature trees chosen either individually or in designated groups, leaving younger trees to reach maturity to provide future supplies of timber. Yet even as the Forest Service instituted sustainable methods, clear-cutting and other wasteful forestry practices remained all too common on privately held forestlands. According to Ayres, loggers in New England were cutting 50,000 to 75,000 acres of forestland every year, but only half the acreage grew back to healthy forests.[15]

Financially, the purchase and management of working forests paid off for both the federal government and local governments. Ayres estimated in 1923 that timber from the WMNF would generate $1 million more in revenues than the federal government had paid for the land.[16] Furthermore, local governments in New Hampshire and Vermont benefited from the harvesting of timber. Federal law required the government to return 25 percent of the income from the sale of trees and other forest products to local governments as compensation for the loss of taxes, which local governments had collected based on the value of land with timber. In addition, local governments benefited from the roads and other infrastructure built by the Forest Service, which was obligated to spend 10 percent of its budget on infrastructure improvements.[17]

While the Forest Service and volunteer groups were replanting trees and nurturing the forests back to health, the White Mountains experienced dramatic growth in recreation after World War I. The upsurge in use of the White Mountains was the culmination of a steady increase in outdoor recreation that, as we have seen, experienced a significant boost at the end of the nineteenth century with the founding of hiking clubs and the building of hiking trails. In the 1920s, the new generation embraced a whole constellation of outdoor activities that were increasingly strenuous. They climbed cliffs, took long backpacking trips through the most remote sectors of the WMNF, established primitive camps, went white-water canoeing, and pursued a variety of winter outdoor activities. The common thread in all these activities was that they took place in natural settings that had the characteristics of wilderness. Climbing and backpacking took adventurers away from the heavily used trails and into more remote sections of the mountains, while white-water canoeing involved an element of danger in rivers that had not been harnessed by dams. These experiences brought Americans back in touch with their pioneer roots—a heritage that was central to the growing interest in wilderness in the years following World War I. While leading environmental thinkers such as Benton MacKaye, Bob Marshall, Aldo Leopold, and Arthur Carhart deserve full credit for articulating the value of wilderness, it was these thousands of outdoor adventurers who built the grassroots foundation for the appreciation of wild nature. That appreciation eventually evolved into a powerful movement to preserve wilderness.

In the White Mountains, the lifeblood of the newfound devotion to outdoor recreation was the hiking trails—some gentle and gradual, some dauntingly steep and strewn with boulders, and all giving weekend adventurers a feeling of being connected with America's wilderness as they tramped through regions of the mountains that were still remote and undeveloped. The AMC and local hiking clubs had already cut many trails in the White Mountains, but after the establishment of the WMNF, the emphasis shifted to creating a unified system of trails that would permit extended, multiday hikes within the mountain region and through-hiking from one end of the Whites to the other. The extension of the White Mountain trail system fulfilled a growing desire for hikers to have access to wilderness areas that had, up to that point, been inaccessible except to the hardiest trekkers. In the late 1800s and early

10.2. Hikers at high elevation. After the passage of the Weeks Act, the AMC and local hiking clubs such as the Randolph Mountain Club and the Wonalancet Out Door Club worked to connect and extend trails to accommodate hikers like these. Courtesy of Dartmouth College Library.

1900s, local hiking clubs such as the Randolph Mountain Club, the Wonalancet Out Door Club, the Chocorua Mountain Club, the Dartmouth Outing Club, and clubs in Dublin, Gorham, Intervale, North Woodstock, and Waterville Valley had built loop trails for specific sections of the mountains. Because of the slow transportation in preautomobile days, hikers were looking for loop hikes that would minimize the need to travel from one section of the mountains to another.

But the coming of the automobile and paved roads changed all that. Now hikers could be dropped off at one trailhead and picked up at another, allowing extended, multiday hikes through remote areas of the mountains. Moreover, during a week or two of vacation, hikers could drive to a wide variety of trailheads.[18] This improved access fed the desire to knit all the trails in the White Mountains into an interconnected whole. Four men who were active in the AMC took the initiative to expand and connect the White Mountain hiking trails—Paul R. Jenks, Charles W. Blood, Nathaniel L. Goodrich, and Karl P. Harrington. These men spearheaded a flurry of trail building from 1912 to 1930 that gradually connected the different parts of the mountains and extended trails into areas that had been previously inaccessible.[19]

Providing a strong impetus for the development of a network of trails was the New England Trail Conference, which first met in Boston in the fall of 1916 and was formally established on March 16, 1917.[20] The conference brought together the various New England outdoors and hiking clubs to promote cooperation in the creation and maintenance of White Mountain trails and to share information about their condition. Among the participating organizations were the AMC, the Boy Scouts, local hiking clubs from all corners of the White Mountains, and the Forest Service. The conference published a map and guidebook titled *A Tour Afoot in the White Mountains*, which was distributed to members of the conference and other interested hikers.[21]

With this new level of coordination, trail building could continue apace. Volunteers built a network of trails near the East Branch of the Pemigewasset, allowing overnight hikers and campers to explore the Pemigewasset wilderness for days at a time. They opened up access to the Kinsman Ridge and, for the first time, built a trail through the entire Mahoosuc Range in Maine, which had been the least explored section of the White Mountains.[22] Volunteers built fifteen lean-to shelters in the mountains, which, along with the AMC huts at Lakes-of-the-Clouds, Madison Spring, Pinkham Notch, and Carter Notch, provided shelter for the night or from bad weather. Volunteers also built trail bridges and shared information about techniques for constructing and maintaining trails, the construction of camps, and methods for encouraging trail building.[23] As the trail system expanded, the maintenance of trails, which had once cost a few hundred dollars a season, now cost several thousand dollars, and where volunteers had once put up five or six new trail signs every year, now they were putting up more than a hundred. Trail crews worked all summer, with a foreman leading skilled workers who had experience in building trails and shelters. By 1926, Karl P. Harrington reported that "the White Mountain trails of the Appalachian Mountain Club have been thoughtfully coordinated" and that they were developing into a true system of trails.[24] These wonderful new trails, Harrington concluded triumphantly, allowed the modern city dweller to "break away from honking cars and jingling telephones for a week or two, and breast the breezes, mount the cliffs, and rest beside some lovely lake in the manner of the simple life."[25] He was touching on a theme— the stresses and strains of modern society—that would become central to arguments for the preservation of wilderness.

During this era, trail building itself acquired a romantic aura of physical challenge that harked back to the days of the pioneers. Nate Goodrich made the process seem particularly attractive. He identified three stages in trail building: "There is dreaming the trail, there is prospecting the trail, there is making the trail." His greatest joy was in prospecting, in plotting out the route of the trail. "It has a suggestion of the thrill of exploration," he exclaimed. "No one of us but loves still to play explorer."[26] His words forged a link to the ex-

10.3. Old Mizpah Spring shelter. As the AMC, local hiking clubs, and the Forest Service extended and connected the trails in the White Mountains, backpackers could go on multi-day hikes through the region and use shelters like this one, which stood near the Webster Cliff Trail and the Mount Clinton Trail, on the eastern slope of Crawford Notch. The AMC replaced this shelter with the Mizpah Spring Hut in 1965. Courtesy of Dartmouth College Library.

ploring and pioneering heritage of the White Mountains, but they were also an expression of individuality and empowerment. Where else in the complex American society of the 1920s could an individual utter the words, "There should be a path to the top of that mountain"—and then go out and turn those words into reality?

Not that trail building was easy work; to the contrary, it was very strenuous. Given a week to complete a hiking path, the trail builders spent the first day laying out the route, and then they set down to the physical work. "There is," Goodrich wrote, "an edge, a tenseness about this work. The day is a long strain of keen concentration, of quick decisions, of driving through scrub and blow-downs. The unexpected may appear at any minute—an outlook, a spring, a trail."[27] It was the wilderness experience revisited, complete with the feeling of discovery in blazing a trail through uncharted territory. Moreover, these modern pioneers experienced a strong sense of camaraderie in their endeavors, bonding together as they forged their trail through the woods. During their lunches, they lit their pipes and admired the views. Yet by the end of the day, they were exhausted and pulled themselves—with all muscles aching—tiredly into camp.[28] "We all remember how much of character crops out in that close association," Goodrich wrote, "how much of sympathy, helpfulness, enthusiasm."[29]

In the end, the reward of completing a trail was the exhilaration of giving people access to sublime scenery. When Goodrich's team reached the timberline in building the trail on Mount Garfield, he took the time to observe the surrounding country and exclaimed, ""[W]hat is timberline? It . . . is the sweep of vast spaces, the drift of cloud-shadows, the infinite gradations of distant color. It is the hiss of wind in the firs, the strain against bitter gusts, the keen concentration to hold the trail through dense and drifting fog."[30] His soaring language of celebration reminds us of Starr King, maintaining a continuity with the past that is such a pivotal element of the White Mountain experience.

As the trails expanded to previously inaccessible parts of the White Mountains, weekend adventurers used them with the full knowledge that they were traveling on lesser-known paths to sectors that, even in the 1920s, were not well known. They were, in essence, searching for as pure a wilderness experience as they could find in the White Mountains. In 1928, T. P. Chandler II wrote of the unadulterated joy of hiking on "untraveled paths." One path that he and his companions explored was the recently completed Mahoosuc Range Trail. They started at Gorham and were ferried across the Androscoggin River.[31] After camping at Mascot Pond, they followed the trail over Mount Hayes and Cascade Mountain, heading steadily northeast. Like their path-finding White Mountain predecessors Manasseh Cutler and Starr King, they took the time to observe closely the flora and fauna at this more northerly latitude. Balsam replaced pine, and other plants were "northern cousins" to the ones at lower latitudes—oak fern and beech fern. They climbed over Mount Success, reaching the Maine state line, where they picked up additional supplies, which had been brought in by truck. From there they ascended three more mountains—Mount Carlo, Goose Eye, and North Peak.

In describing the hike, Chandler stressed the group's embrace of the wilderness experience, but he did so with a consciousness that was thoroughly modern. "Above all, we are well out of civilization," he exclaimed. "No longer can we hear the whistle of the [Boston and Maine]; no village sounds get in here. The feel of chairs and tables is quite forgotten; the camp laundry habits of each individual have become apparent—we are in the woods, and of the woods, in so far as we are able."[32] His words reflected the conscious effort that he and his companions were making to escape from civilization temporarily and to renew themselves physically, intellectually, and spiritually. They finally reached Mahoosuc Notch, where they found the going exceedingly difficult. The trail went "around the boulders and over them and under them, through holes and caves that scrape your pack unmercifully or make you unsling it altogether and push it through ahead of you or pull it after."[33]

While they were in the notch, they faced the challenge of rock climbing. One of the hikers, Hank, set his sights on the northwest side of the notch, which consisted of enormous slabs of rock that catapulted up to a ledge. After inching up the vertical rise, he eventually reached the top and was rewarded with an extraordinary sight—a peregrine falcon—"the falcon that was the pride of kings and made falconry the sport in the days of yore."[34] The group slept well that night at Speck Pond—the highest elevation of any pond in Maine. The next day they swam in the pond—and found that it was also the coldest pond in Maine. Their final climb, and the climax of the trip, was the ascent of Old Speck, which, at 4,170 feet, represented the highest peak that they encountered; the summit offered magnificent views of the Rangeley Range in Maine and the Presidentials in New Hampshire. In reflecting on his experience, the author extolled the value of tramping along paths that had not been traveled before. "The frontier always widens," he wrote with a sense of exhilaration, "and when we think we have exhausted it the Red Gods laugh and point to new fields they have prepared."[35] Chandler's words were a celebration of the value of embarking on new journeys into little-known regions, and the sentiments he expressed would be repeated by hundreds of other backwoods trampers.

Chandler's article was one of dozens that White Mountain hikers, campers, and climbers wrote in the 1920s and 1930s for *Appalachia, Granite Monthly,* and other regional publications that gave outdoor enthusiasts outlets for recounting their adventures and sharing knowledge about the geology, flora, and fauna of the mountains and about the rapidly expanding enterprise of mountaineering. The hundreds of outdoors lovers who described their experiences in these journals formed a community of people who were bound together by a quest for authentic experiences of wilderness in which they could test themselves, study nature, and express their visceral enjoyment of the wondrous scenery. For the most part, their accounts were secular and did not have the religious overtones of the writings of Thomas Starr King, Lucy Larcom, and John Greenleaf Whittier. But they shared with those literary predecessors a heightened sensitivity to nature, and they extended the mythic narrative of the White Mountains by taking readers on vicarious journeys into the backcountry and highlighting the beauty of untrammeled nature. Such narratives helped create a constituency that would ultimately advocate for the protection of wilderness in the White Mountains.

A first-person account by Helen Emerson Anthony, published in *Appalachia* in 1924, was an outstanding example of such a narrative, and it stands out today for two reasons: the author effectively contrasted the civilization of the valleys with the wildness of the mountains, and she created anew the familiar experience of climbing Mount Washington. Anthony, who climbed the mountain in June with a female friend, communicated a sense early in her narrative that even though Mount Washington had been climbed thousands of times before, each new climber approached it afresh and discovered for himself or herself the joys and dangers of the mountain. Even well-traveled parts of the Whites retained a sense of wildness about them; every experience on the mountain was a new one because of the different weather conditions and challenges that one might face. The author underscored the sense of anticipation by writing, "It had been said that the trail had not been opened this season, implying solitude was to be reckoned with; also, bears were occasionally seen in the mountains."[36] In her words we sense the nervous excitement that made the mountain an enduring symbol of nature at its rawest and most primitive.

She and her companion rode to the base of the mountain in a carriage, and on the way, they crossed "[o]ver the famous golf links"—though mentioned only briefly, the detail about the golf course became a symbol of the civilized world that they were leaving behind. They began to climb, and as they rose higher, "[T]he appearance of the mountain-side had changed and it began to look wilder"; the forest evolved from hardwoods to balsam and spruce, which grew shorter and shorter and were covered with lichen.[37] During their ascent, the author closely observed the extraordinary flora that populated the sides of the mountain:

> Dispensia grew in tufted mats, the solitary blossom standing upright from the stiff leaves; the low sweet blueberry was there in its mountain form, the small white bells half-hidden by the pale green leaves; Lapland Rose Bay, a tiny rhododendron with petal just falling, was as perfect in its form and character, with a height of only four inches, as were its tall relatives in the Carolina mountains, which boast many feet in height.[38]

After they reached the summit, the narrative took a surprising turn that reflected the two adventurers' orientation toward striking out on one's own and following the path less traveled. Anthony and her companion studied their maps and located an alternative trail that headed down on the other side of the mountain but would eventually join the trail on which they had made their ascent. They started descending on this alternative trail and came to the old Crawford Path and then to a little-used side trail. Embracing the sense of exploration, they forged ahead on the unknown route. "More and more obstructed it grew—what was to be done?" she wondered. "To go back was out of the question—to go forward looked equally so."[39]

They remained calm, though, and observed that even though the trail ahead was clogged with vegetation, it was somewhat more open near the ground, "kept so by some of the smaller wild animals of the mountains." Bending low, they pressed ahead. They came to a thick tangle of brush but bulled their way through and saw with great relief that they had rejoined their original path. From there they resumed their descent and reached the bottom without any more problems. "A few minutes more," she wrote, "and there was the road, and there the golf links, and our day was over." She reflected that it had been "a day of exhilaration and joy, of beauty, of detachment, and contentment; yet not over, for an abiding memory would remain."[40] Her account, with its satisfying denouement, expressed a desire for intense individual experience, the reliance on one's own competence, and the pleasure gained from finding new perspectives on familiar sights. From the crucible of such experiences, a wilderness philosophy was born.

The sense of adventure and exploration even found its way into children's books published during the 1920s and 1930s. Walter Prichard Eaton, a former drama critic in New York, moved in 1910 to the Berkshire Hills of Massachusetts, where he and his wife purchased a farmhouse and a couple hundred acres of land. Although Eaton often wrote about gardening, he also celebrated the pleasures of escaping from the strictures of civilization and striking out on one's own into wilder regions.[41] Because the Boy Scout movement was riding a wave of popularity during the 1920s, Eaton penned a series of books that recounted the fictional adventures of Scouts in a variety of outdoor settings, including *Boy Scouts in the White Mountains; or, The Story of a Long Hike,* published in 1914. Other books in Eaton's series narrated the outdoor adventures and ingenuity of Boy Scouts on Mount Katahdin, on the Long Trail in Vermont, at the Grand Canyon, and in the Berkshires. The series was a kind of sharing of wilderness adventures for young people.

The popularity of scouting reflected another outdoor activity that exploded in popularity after World War I—primitive camping. The surge in the number of campers reflected a desire for self-sufficiency and direct contact with wild nature, and to aid the new cohort of campers, publishers issued camping guides that were far more comprehensive than Major John Gould's had been in the 1870s. For example, Horace Kephart's *Camping and Woodcraft,* published in 1930, was a virtual encyclopedia of practical information about all kinds of camps, from permanent camps set up for the entire summer to transient camps in the backwoods. Kephart covered the gamut of equipment— furniture, tools, tents, bedding, clothing, provisions—and he taught all the skills that one would ever need in the woods, such as building a fire, keeping pests away from the campsite, and dressing game and fish.

Kephart, though, paid special attention to backpacking, which was coming into its own as an outdoor activity. "[B]ack-packing," he averred, "is the cheapest possible way to spend one's vacation in the wilderness."[42] He described a pack harness that was practical—albeit heavy—for long-distance hikers, suggesting that backpackers start with forty or fifty pounds of equipment, which would naturally grow lighter as the hiker ate provisions. The heaviest single object was the sleeping bag, which could weigh as much as eight pounds. The most common type consisted of an "inner bag of woolen blanketing, an outer one of knotted wool batting, and a separate cover of . . . khaki or Tanalite."[43] He also imparted instructions for hiking efficiently and conserving energy:

> The toes are pointed straight forward, or even a trifle inward, so that the inside of the heel, the outside of the ball of the foot, and the smaller toes, all do their share of work and assist in balancing. Walking in this manner, one is not so likely, either, to trip over projecting roots, stones, and other traps, as he would be if the feet formed hooks by pointing outward.[44]

Throughout his guide, Kephart lauded the pleasures of wilderness hiking, particularly as a solitary experience. His emphasis on the individual's direct experience of untamed nature stood in stark contrast to the social interaction that had characterized tourists' experiences at the White Mountain resort hotels during the Gilded Age. According to Kephart, "[M]any a seasoned woodman can avow that some of the most satisfying, if not the happiest, periods of his life have been spent far out of sight and suggestion of his fellow men."[45] The advantages of solitary camping were many. Camping alone simplified the routine of living in the woods; the adventurer could cook what he liked and clean up easily. But most of all, solitary camping created an exquisite sense of freedom. "Any time, anywhere," the author averred, such a camper "can do as he pleases" without having to worry about whether others are having a good time.[46] Finally, Kephart observed that solitary backpackers left less of a footprint on the wilderness than did groups of campers. The solitary camper could sit in the wild and observe nature quietly, without disturbing the animals and birds in the surrounding forest. Nor was a feeling of loneliness inevitable, for "Whoever has an eye for Nature is never less alone than when he is by himself."[47]

Another backcountry experience that grew in popularity during the 1920s and that brought people into contact with wilderness was rock climbing. Two popular sites for climbing in the Whites were the cliff on Cannon Mountain in Franconia Notch and the Pinnacle in Huntington Ravine. Climbing equipment was basic, the technique rudimentary, but climbing offered the invigorating challenge of testing one's mettle. Because it forced the individual to draw on reserves of skill and courage, it served as an antidote to the monotony and anonymity of a society in which large institutions were increasingly dominant.

In an article published in *Appalachia* in 1928, for example, R. L. M. Underhill described an ascent of the cliff on Cannon Mountain that gave a vivid picture of what rock climbing was like at the time.[48] On May 27, 1928, Underhill's party, which included three other men and two women, made a partial ascent of the cliff on Cannon Mountain but had to retreat because of the lateness of the day. On September 18 of that same year, several members of the same party returned, determined this time to reach the top of the cliff. They climbed 150 feet to a terrace and continued for 100 feet more to a second terrace. The cliff above them was too sheer to climb, but they crept to the right, where they found broken slabs of rock that were climbable. There they hoisted themselves up another 50 or 60 feet.

At that point, they reached two vertical cracks that were the only possible route to the top. But the cracks were about six feet apart, and the climbers had to transfer themselves from one crack to another to continue up. Since there were no holds between the cracks, they pounded a wooden stake into the crack they were leaving, looped a rope over it, and grasped the wooden stake to swing themselves over to the larger crack. After doing so, they were able to inch up the main crack by wedging their feet into the fissure and pushing up, using their hands and forearms to maintain their hold. Pulling themselves up in this manner, they ascended several more slabs of granite until they finally reached the top of the cliff—parallel to the nose of the Old Man of the Mountain. In this successful ascent, they approached the climb as a technical problem, reflecting the growing emphasis that outdoor enthusiasts put on physical challenges, technical skills, and individual achievement. Yet, in the end, attaining a beautiful vista remained an integral part of the experience.

During the 1920s, outdoor enthusiasts also turned to white-water canoeing, which, like rock climbing, emphasized the challenge of facing unpredictable forces in nature and the satisfaction of developing technical skills. But perhaps the most significant change in White Mountain recreation was the explosive growth of winter sports—downhill skiing, cross-country skiing, snowshoeing. Cross-country skiing and snowshoeing opened up the backcountry to winter expeditions, and winter camping started to catch on. According to one avid practitioner, "In the wintertime there are no insect pests, the bare trees and the clear air make for wonderful views, . . . and one has the woods to himself with no tourists and automobiles."[49]

To meet the growing demand for these outdoor activities, and in an effort to increase tourism, the Forest Service worked with the AMC and local hiking clubs to improve access to the mountains and upgrade facilities. In 1916, for instance, the Forest Service purchased the Dolly Copp homestead and surrounding property with the intention of transforming it into a summer colony, in which vacationers would purchase one-acre lots. But the prospec-

10.4. Winter climbing. After World War I, a new breed of outdoor enthusiast appeared, looking for challenges and direct contact with the most extreme elements in nature. Outdoor enthusiasts would join together to form a constituency for the preservation of wilderness. Courtesy of Dartmouth College Library.

tive colony aroused little interest, and in 1921, the Forest Service turned the property into a campground, which it has operated ever since. During the Depression, the Civilian Conservation Corps established seventeen work camps in the WMNF, where CCC workers constructed ski trails, hiking trails, mountain shelters, roads, parking areas, and recreational campgrounds. They also salvaged lumber after the 1938 hurricane that devastated New England.[50]

A significant milestone in the history of the White Mountain National Forest occurred when, in response to the ballooning interest in backcountry hiking, camping, and other wilderness activities, the Forest Service began to manage the Great Gulf as a primitive area. This five-thousand-acre forested area in the steep-sided valley between Mount Washington and the northern Presidential peaks remained relatively unscathed by logging, and there, the Forest Service attempted to preserve the characteristics of wilderness by limiting timber harvesting and not constructing roads, campsites, shelters, campgrounds, or any of the other amenities that were proliferating throughout the rest of the Whites. However, the Great Gulf and primitive areas in other na-

10.5. "Greetings from the White Mts., New Hampshire." By the 1930s, the White Mountains were a well-established vacation resort, attracting millions every year. But as tourism grew, it placed new pressures on the White Mountain wilderness. Postcard, ca. 1930. Lake County (IL) Discovery Museum/Curt Teich Postcard Archives.

tional forests did not enjoy statutory protection as wilderness and so remained vulnerable to logging and the development of recreational facilities. Such primitive areas played a key role in the White Mountains—and in all the national forests—by serving as experiments in the preservation of wilderness.

The very idea that the national forests should have primitive areas or designated wilderness grew directly out of the development after World War I of a grassroots constituency that increasingly sought encounters with a natural world that had not been modified by the hand of humanity. This constituency included hikers who loved backpacking deep into the remote areas of the White Mountains, campers and snowshoers who sought self-sufficiency and unimpeded observation of nature, trail builders who wanted to blaze new paths to the farthest corners of the mountains, climbers who challenged themselves to strenuous ascents of sheer cliff walls, white-water rafters who craved the experience of natural forces at their most unpredictable, and other outdoor enthusiasts who yearned for authentic contact with the beauties of wild nature.

In the types of recreation that people pursued after World War I, we see the maturing of trends that began to gather force at the end of the nineteenth century. Those early pioneers in hiking and camping had been motivated by a desire to test themselves, to pursue new experiences of nature, and to develop their individual powers and their self-reliance. These were still the motivations of people who sought encounters with wild nature in the years following World War I, but members of the new generation exhibited a greater assertiveness and assurance in their pursuits. In rock climbing and whitewater canoeing, they sought greater risks, and in backpacking treks through wilderness areas, they welcomed the rewards of solitude and the challenges of extended primitive camping. At the same time, they displayed a growing understanding of and respect for the powers of nature. Instead of manipulating nature, they welcomed nature in its wildest forms.

However, even as the myriad possibilities for outdoor recreation drew millions of vacationers to the White Mountains and to the other national forests, a group of pioneering environmental thinkers began to grow concerned that the very popularity of outdoor activities would ultimately threaten and eventually destroy the characteristics of wilderness that had made these natural areas so attractive in the first place. Their concerns grew sharply as they saw logging and extractive industries once again threaten forest ecosystems. Out of those concerns, and out of their love of wild nature, a philosophy of wilderness gradually coalesced that would be articulated most eloquently by Benton MacKaye, Bob Marshall, Arthur Carhart, and Aldo Leopold. Their ideas about wilderness brought together many of the strands of thought and action that lovers of the White Mountains expressed in the years after World War I: the beauty of wild nature, the quest for independence and self-reliance in the backwoods, the possibilities for personal growth through exposure to wilderness, and the unique beauties of the mountains' flora and fauna. These themes would come together in a powerful philosophy of wilderness that would ultimately lead to the protection of wilderness in the White Mountains.

Chapter 11

TOWARD WILDERNESS PRESERVATION: THE DEVELOPMENT OF A PHILOSOPHY

S OON AFTER WORLD WAR I ENDED, outdoor enthusiast Perceval Sayward published a short essay in *Appalachia* in which he pleaded for the
preservation of the primitive areas in the eastern mountains in which
he loved to tramp. The article, titled "Sanctuary," celebrated the ways in which
wild nature provided a temporary respite from the strains and stresses of
everyday life. In words that echo those of Thoreau, he urged his readers to
find such sanctuaries and to know them as well as possible:

> [T]the most precious of all is the region or district of which we know some-
> thing. . . . We know its character well enough to love it positively and as-
> suredly in advance, and because it contains no railroads, or "good" roads by
> the map, except on the edges, if it contains roads at all, and because no one
> refers to it, we know it is unspoilt by the ways (wise or unwise) of the city
> bred. It is just as it is—a wilderness, a semi-wilderness, an abandoned farm
> section, or whatever your fancy may have lighted on for your sanctuary.[1]

But such sanctuaries, he warned, were "in grave danger" because the mul-
titudes were chugging their automobiles into the mountains on newly paved
roads, where they found ubiquitous signs announcing trailheads that made
the wilderness ever more accessible.

The passionate words of this outdoor adventurer reflect the fact that in the
years between World War I and World War II, a wilderness constituency was
emerging that hungered after direct contact with wild nature. Many of these
outdoor adventurers were inspired by the pioneers who had ventured forth
into the wilderness regions of the United States. But for many, the attraction
to wilderness also signaled a deep-seated reaction against a society that had
abandoned its Jeffersonian roots, that seemed increasingly conformist and
timid, that was increasingly at the beck and call of large corporations. Striking out into the wilderness became an affirmative assertion of the integrity of
the individual.

Most outdoor enthusiasts could not afford the time or expense of journeying to America's spacious wildernesses of the West, but if they lived in the populous cities of the East, they could afford to spend a week or two in the White Mountains, and for that reason, the Whites took on new importance as one of the remaining regions in the East that still featured rugged landscapes, undeveloped backwoods, and dangerous mountains that catapulted weekend adventurers into the challenges of the wilderness experience. At the same time, though, there was a never-ending drive to make the entire region accessible by blazing new hiking trails, constructing campsites, establishing picnic sites, and building roads, all of which threatened to strip away the remaining vestiges of wildness. As the century progressed, growing numbers of conservationists would conclude that significant areas of the White Mountains required permanent protection as wilderness if they were to retain the primitive beauty and ecological diversity that had made them so extraordinary in the first place.

To justify such protection, conservationists needed a well-thought-out system of ideas—a philosophy—that would authoritatively define wilderness and articulate a rationale for its preservation. Fortunately, during the period between the two world wars, four visionary environmental thinkers developed just such a philosophy: Benton MacKaye, Robert (Bob) Marshall, Arthur Carhart, and Aldo Leopold. All four formulated sophisticated ideas about the importance of wilderness in American society and its place in America's national parks and forests. They prized wilderness for its benefits to humanity, but they also recognized that in wilderness could be found critically important ecosystems that nurtured thousands of species. Although only one of these pioneering environmentalists, Benton MacKaye, had extensive youthful experiences in the White Mountains, all of them profoundly influenced the history of the Whites in the twentieth century because their vision of protected wildernesses led directly to the passage of laws that resulted in the eventual designation of five protected wildernesses in the White Mountain National Forest: the Great Gulf, the Presidential Range–Dry River, the Pemigewasset, the Sandwich Range, and the Caribou–Speckled Mountain. (In 2005, the Forest Service recommended the addition of a sixth wilderness, the Wild River.)

Benton MacKaye's roots ran deep in the White Mountains, and his experiences there helped to inspire him to propose the Appalachian Trail and to develop a philosophy of land use in which the idea of protected wildernesses played a significant role. Although he was born in Stamford, Connecticut, on March 6, 1879, he considered his spiritual home to be the one that his family moved to when he was nine years old—the village of Shirley, Massachusetts, some thirty-five miles northwest of Boston. Young Benton fell in love with the rural countryside and explored it incessantly, becoming intimately familiar with its flora, fauna, and geology. In 1891, he and his friends Ned Stone and Warren Brown formed the Rambling Boys' Club for the purpose of studying the local landscape.[2] As Benton matured, he reflected on these forays into the countryside, which he referred to as expeditions. When, after the ninth expedition, he expressed his ideas about the unspoiled Shirley countryside in unusually sophisticated and articulate terms, his older brother James referred ever after to such adventures as "expedition nining."[3]

After finishing his secondary education, MacKaye scored just well enough on Harvard's entrance exam to be accepted, and he started there in the fall of 1896. The two professors who influenced him the most were Nathaniel Southgate Shaler, a pioneer in the field of geology who had written on the uses of leisure in modern society and the importance of experiencing solitude in nature, and William Morris Davis, who taught geology and physical geography. Davis led students to see that landforms of physical geography, such as mountains, have life histories, or cycles, just as organic life-forms do. By way of example, he pointed out how the landscapes of central Massachusetts and southern New Hampshire were in the late stages of their geological cycles, as evidenced by low mountains such as Mount Wachusett and Mount Monadnock, which had been rounded into the shape of mounds by millions of years of erosion.[4] From these two professors, MacKaye learned that the visible landscape resulted from the complex interplay of forces within and upon the land—an insight that he would extend in his mature years by examining the interactions between humans and the natural environment.

While at Harvard, young Benton still felt the impulse to explore, and in August of 1897, when he was eighteen, he and two friends, Draper Maury and James Sturgis Pray, embarked on an expedition to the White Mountains that, according to MacKaye biographer Larry Anderson, exposed him for the first time to wild nature and shaped his future thinking about the value of wilderness.[5] After riding their bicycles north from Shirley, they reached the southern apron of the Whites in mid-August. On August 14, they crossed the Swift River near the Albany Intervale, prompting Benton to write in his journal, "We have said 'good-bye' to the bicycles and civilization and will now pursue our way on foot through the White Mountains."[6]

From the Swift River, they hiked north across the Albany Intervale toward Owl Cliff and Mount Tremont, and after covering two and a half miles, they set up camp. On the next day, they came to a blowdown—an area where many of the trees had been blown down by hurricane-force winds—and struggled through the mélange of trees lying in twisted chaos on the ground. "Over these we must crawl over and under," he wrote in his journal, "balancing ourselves on a 4 inch fallen tree which at the same time we must ascend and which suddenly gives way under its 200 lbs. pressure and leaves us five to ten feet below on our backs."[7] They continued on to Mount Tremont, which lies between Sawyer Pond and the town of Bartlett, and decided to climb the

11.1. James Sturgis Pray, Benton MacKaye, and Draper Maury. In 1897, Benton and his two hiking companions gathered at Albany Intervale, N.H., to embark on a month-long expedition into the White Mountains. It was MacKaye's first extended exposure to wilderness. Courtesy of Dartmouth College Library.

mountain even though storm clouds were gathering. The clouds let loose a driving thunderstorm, but the young adventurers continued and spent the night on the mountain. MacKaye described the experience in words that conveyed his awe at the power of nature:

> I saw the sun rise over the mountains making one side of them day and the other, night. Several hundred feet below in the valleys there were white clouds and occasionally parts of them would rise and chase themselves by me.
>
> On one side Mt. Washington would emerge now and then from a cloud, on another, to the northwest, the Franconia range was seen through Carrigain Notch; to the northeast I could see over into Maine, and on the south away in the distance I could make out the hills of old Massachusetts. I felt then how much I resembled in size one of the hairs on the eye tooth of a flea.[8]

They ventured on to Crawford Notch, where they stayed overnight at the Crawford House and met another friend, Rob Mitchell, and Sturgis Pray's father. After resting at the Crawford House for several days, they headed up the venerable Crawford Path toward the summit of Mount Washington, but another round of storms forced them to return to the Crawford House. They then took a train north to Gorham and tramped south to Pinkham Notch, where they climbed the east side of Mount Washington and spent the night at the Summit House. After hiking to Crawford Notch, they took a train to Franconia Notch and stayed at the Profile House. The company that was then logging along the East Branch of the Pemigewasset took them on one of the company's logging railroads to a camp from which they climbed Mount Osceola.

The next day, which was September 1, they headed to Waterville Valley and ascended Mount Tripyramid. They had hoped to reach shelter for the night, but heavy rain and another blowdown stood in their way, and they spent the night trying to get a few winks of sleep. The following morning, they passed Sabbaday Brook and Sabbaday Falls and soon after completed their giant loop through the mountains, completing their odyssey on September 2, 1897. By the end they were exhausted, but the experience had been both exhilarating and transformative, for it was Benton's first extended experience in the backwoods.[9]

After graduating from Harvard in 1900, MacKaye returned to the university in 1903 to study forestry. In the summer between the first and second years of the program, he worked as a counselor at Camp Moosilauke and, with co-counselor Knowlton Durham, led eight boys on a ten-day trek through the White Mountains, in which he deepened his familiarity with the Whites. The expedition resulted in his first published article, "Our White Mountain Trip: Its Organization and Methods," which appeared in the annual *Log of Camp Moosilauke* in 1904. The two counselors' mission was to teach the boys how to survive in the outdoors. They tramped single file, hiking every other day with their backpacks and covering anywhere from six miles to eighteen and a half miles a day. Along the way, they made side trips to the Flume, Mount Carrigain, Mount Willey, and other legendary White Mountain sites. MacKaye wrote about the boys with a sly sense of humor, observing one night, "The boys turned in one by one as sleep dictated, and after each had had the necessary verbal 'scrap' with his nearest neighbor regarding his resting accommodations, quiet reigned, and snores alone interrupted the crackling of the fire."[10]

As they trekked through the Presidential Range, they came to the AMC's Madison Spring Hut, where MacKaye was appalled to see that hikers had left refuse everywhere. "In return for this courtesy," he lamented, "the people using the hut have strewn the ground all about it with hundreds of tin cans and broken glass jars. The wood-box inside has been used for this same purpose."[11] Printed instructions in the hut had reminded backpackers to take their rubbish with them, but they had paid no attention. MacKaye saw immediately the need to educate the public about proper stewardship of the backwoods. As he, Durham, and their young charges continued on, they found evidence of further disregard for the environment. Along the East Branch of the Pemigewasset River, they were shocked to see an area that had been ruthlessly cut over by a lumber company. MacKaye, who had been unaware of the practice of clear-cutting during his first expedition in the mountains, took close notice of it now:

> The method of lumbering is the primitive one of "shaving" the slopes and leaving them in the ruined condition, as regards the lumber supply and water conservation, which such methods always cause. The beauty of this region, the wildest of the White Mountains, was in great part destroyed, the slashes of the lumbermen branding the mountains like unsightly scars on a beautiful face.[12]

On this expedition, the pleasures of hiking and camping in environments of pristine beauty contrasted sharply with the damage caused by careless backwoods users and heedless lumber operators, and both scenes warned MacKaye that the beauty of natural environments was fragile and faced potential destruction. Already he was beginning to formulate a philosophy of land use in which wilderness protection would play a key role and stewardship of the environment would be a core value. He concluded his account by writing, "The duty of the camper, as one with greater opportunities in this respect than the average citizen, is to preserve the resources which nature has bestowed and to cherish the land as he would his home."[13]

While studying forestry at Harvard, MacKaye lived with his older brother James, a utopian thinker and socialist who nudged Benton's thinking toward socialism. Benton, though, was never a doctrinaire in matters of politics. What attracted him to socialism was an instinct for cooperation rather than competition in community life and a deeply felt commitment to reforms that would ameliorate social and economic inequities.[14] After completing his master's degree in forestry, he struggled to gain his footing in the profession, eventually landing a position as a forestry assistant with the newly formed U.S. Forest Service in 1905 and then teaching a course in forestry at Harvard.[15] The college, though, did not invite him back to teach in 1910, possibly because of his rather limited involvement in left-wing politics.[16]

Meanwhile, he had been writing a forestry textbook, the manuscript of which helped him to win a permanent position with the Forest Service as a forest examiner in 1911. Because of his familiarity with the White Mountain terrain, one of his first assignments was to determine the impact of deforestation on stream flow in each of the major watersheds in the White Mountains. The study was part of the process that the U.S. Geological Survey was going through to determine which lands the federal government should purchase under the auspices of the Weeks Act. Using a complex series of measurements, he was able to produce a series of tables that demonstrated that loss of forest cover through logging was affecting the flow of streams, with the

Zealand River, the Ammonoosuc River, and a number of smaller brooks showing significant reductions in stream flow.[17]

As an employee of the Forest Service, MacKaye had opportunities to study forests in different parts of the country, touring the cutover lands of northern Wisconsin, Minnesota, and Michigan in 1914 and observing not only the depletion of those once-grand forests but also the poverty that gripped people in small towns of the Upper Midwest. In October 1916, he published "Recreational Possibilities of Public Forests" in the *Journal of the New York State Forestry Association,* in which he called for two reforms in how national forests were managed: the expansion of outdoor recreational opportunities and the preservation of wildernesses within the national forests. The article contained shades of what would become his signature idea—the Appalachian Trail—and it also pointed toward the Wilderness Society, of which he would be a cofounder in 1935 with Bob Marshall, Aldo Leopold, and other pioneering environmentalists.[18]

In addition to the environment, Benton's ideas extended to social problems. As he toured the Upper Midwest in 1914, he saw firsthand what happened to people in the towns when the once-abundant forests were cut down. In these cutover regions, the lumber industry, which had been the economic lifeblood of the region, fell on hard times, throwing hundreds of people out of work and devastating the region economically. While staying in Madison, Wisconsin, he met other reformers who were active in Progressive politics, and his thinking about social issues and conservation issues continued to evolve in tandem. Gradually, he began to develop ideas about shifting away from the individualism of American society toward a more cooperative social organization of communities that would create, in MacKaye's words, "an exact diagram of play and work and commercialism."[19] Two ideas were most prominent in MacKaye's social thinking: (1) the need for cooperation in solving the social problems of American life; and (2) the necessity to create communities that would balance work, recreation, and business, so that personal fulfillment rather than economic aggrandizement would form the core values.

Although these years brought intellectual ferment to Benton's life, they also brought professional uncertainty. He left the Forest Service for the Department of Labor in 1918 but departed a year later from the federal bureaucracy and returned to his beloved Shirley, where he wrote editorials for the *Milwaukee Leader,* a socialist newspaper. During these years, he essentially created an innovative career for himself in regional planning—the coordination of employment, recreation, transportation, aesthetics, and natural resources to develop a more integrated and humane environment.[20] A friend, Charles Harris Whitaker, invited Benton to spend time at his small estate in New Jersey, and it was there that MacKaye wrote his landmark article proposing the Appalachian

Trail (AT); the article appeared in the October 1921 issue of the *Journal of the American Institute of Architects.*

MacKaye's proposal is justifiably famous because it led to the creation of the AT, which remains one of the most remarkable feats of coordination for the purposes of outdoor recreation that has ever been achieved in the United States. However, the idea for the trail comprised only one part of MacKaye's vision, which was nothing less than an alternative mode of living and working in America. That MacKaye envisioned a new kind of community was apparent from the very beginning of the article: "Something has been going on in this country during the past few strenuous years which, in the din of war and general upheaval, has been somewhat lost from the public mind. It is the slow quiet development of a special type of community—the recreation camp."[21]

One of his major goals was to encourage greater cooperation in American society. "All communities face an 'economic' problem, but in different ways," he observed. "The camp faces it through cooperation and mutual helpfulness, the others through competition and mutual fleecing." In addition to promoting cooperation, camping stood out as a model of self-sufficiency. "We should seek the ability not only to cook food," he wrote, "but to raise food with less aid—and less hindrance—from the complexities of commerce." The end result would be to enrich people's lives so that "Leisure and the higher pursuits will thereby come to form an increasing proportion of our lives."[22]

Central to this vision was the protection of wilderness areas, especially those that were accessible to people living in cities. "Camping grounds, of course, require wild lands," he wrote. "They are the undeveloped or underdeveloped areas."[23] By a great stroke of good fortune, the Appalachians had "a fairly continuous belt of under-developed lands," which the federal government had purchased through the Weeks Act. The trail that he proposed would follow the skyline of this belt of undeveloped land, beginning at Mount Washington in the White Mountains, where "good work in trail building has been accomplished by the Appalachian Mountain Club," and ending at Mount Mitchell in North Carolina.[24] In this proposal, the White Mountains were to be connected with something larger—in a physical sense, to a forest reserve of mountain wildernesses that, in MacKaye's words, "preserved much of the primal aspects of the days of Daniel Boone."[25] The Whites would form part of a system of interconnected wild areas that would rejuvenate the nation's physical and spiritual energies.

After setting out the rationale for the trail, MacKaye described three types of alternative communities that volunteers would establish along the trail:

1. Shelter camps. The model for these camps was the AMC shelters in the White Mountains. They were to be located a day's hike apart from one

another, and while all would have sleeping facilities, only some would also serve meals.

2. Community camps. On or near the trail would be small communities of like-minded people living on approximately one hundred acres of land to be held in common. The people would engage in a variety of economic activities, though none would be industrial.

3. Food and farm camps. These would be camps devoted to growing food and would comprise one specific type of community camp.[26]

In bringing his historic proposal to a conclusion, MacKaye gave full expression to his utopianism: "The camp community is a sanctuary and a refuge from the scramble of every-day worldly commercial life. It is in essence a retreat from profit. Cooperation replaces antagonism, trust replaces suspicion, emulation replaces competition."[27]

After the article appeared, MacKaye traveled throughout the Northeast and publicized the plan, but aside from one section that was completed in New York, there was not much progress in other states in creating the trail. However, on March 1–3, 1925, the first Appalachian Trail Conference (ATC) convened in Washington, D.C. There, Judge Arthur Perkins of Hartford, Connecticut, and Myron Avery, a lawyer in Washington, D.C., entered the picture, and the trail started to become a reality. Perkins and Avery were both effective organizers, and when Avery became acting chairman of the ATC in 1931 and the permanent chairman in 1932, he pushed the AT ahead with a take-charge approach that sometimes rubbed people the wrong way but got results.

However, MacKaye's grand vision for building an alternative society along the AT disappeared as the focus narrowed to the recreational aspect of the original proposal—to build a wilderness trail connecting Mount Washington and Mount Mitchell. MacKaye and Avery clashed repeatedly over the philosophy behind the AT, but Avery, to his credit, managed to push the project through to completion.[28] In New Hampshire, the AT took shape relatively easily because of the work that Blood, Goodrich, Harrington, Jenks, and scores of other trail builders had done to create the extensive network of trails. All that needed to be done was to complete an eighteen-mile link between the Long Trail in Vermont and the Dartmouth Outing Club's trails in the vicinity of Hanover, New Hampshire.[29]

After the proposal for the AT, MacKaye continued to develop his ideas for land use and regional planning. As his thinking matured, wilderness remained a key to creating an environment that would nourish people's physical, mental, and spiritual health. In 1928, he published a remarkable book, *The New Exploration*—his most comprehensive statement of the philosophy of regional planning. The new exploration, he wrote, was "the actual restoration of the primeval American environment"—the restoration of the wilderness.[30] Mac-Kaye's ideas about land use grew directly out of the experiences that he had had in rural Massachusetts, the White Mountains, and other natural environments, and those ideas always reflected the unique geography of New England, where regions of great natural beauty lay only a short distance from cities. He developed a vision of regional planning that was suited to the specific needs of the Northeast, with its density of population, easy access to natural areas, and blend of different types of environments within a limited geographic area. At the center of this vision were three "elemental environments," which would be linked to one another and would form a sound regional plan. In MacKaye's words, they were:

The Primeval—the environment of life's sources, of the common living-ground of all mankind.

The Rural—the environment of agriculture, of local common interests and all-around human living.

The Urban—the environment of manufacturing and trade, of the community of group interest and specialized living.[31]

The primeval—or wilderness—was "the America of the 'indefinite past,' the America which 'was roaring here' when 'Columbus first sought this continent.'" MacKaye acknowledged the legacy of the indigenous population, for whom the primeval environment had been "a land in which to live."[32] By implication, he recognized the ways in which the Abenaki and other Algonquian people had adapted their lifeways to the conditions of the eastern forests. According to MacKaye, people desiring to restore the primeval American environment would do well to base their restoration on a similarly intimate knowledge of the land.

MacKaye's overall objective was to prevent the metropolitan world from completely swallowing up the primeval and the rural, both of which constituted what he called "indigenous environments." As a key step in protecting these indigenous environments, he proposed the establishment of protected wildernesses:

The outstanding topographic feature consists of the range of hills and mountains encircling the locality. . . . This could be reserved as a common public ground, serving the double purpose of a public forest and a public playground. It might be called a "wilderness area." It would form a linear area, or belt, around and through the locality, well adapted for camping and primitive travel (by foot or horseback).[33]

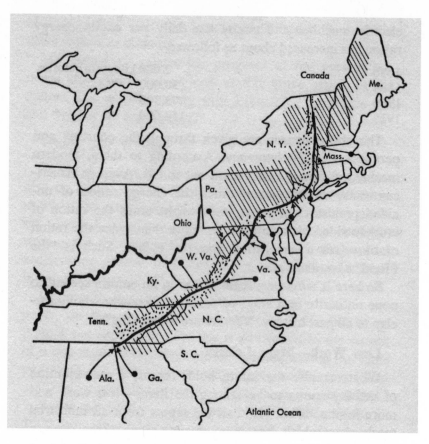

11.2. Population flow in the Appalachian valleys. In his book *From Geography to Geotechnics*, MacKaye included this map showing how wilderness could exist in close proximity with cities in the East. The dots are cities, the arrows show the movement of people, the dark line represents highway transportation, which roughly paralleled the proposed AT, and crosshatched areas are wilderness. From *From Geography to Geotechnics*, by Benton MacKaye, edited by Paul T. Bryant (Urbana: University of Illinois Press, 1968).

These protected wildernesses, which he referred to as "dams" and "levees," would prevent the continued expansion of metropolitan areas and would give city dwellers ready access to wilderness. Such reservations would open up possibilities for the development of people's spiritual and cultural lives, nurturing the possibilities for "true living" rather than mere "mechanical *existence*."[34] There would be a variety of reservations, including state parks, state forests, town forests, and bird sanctuaries.

In MacKaye's vision, protected wilderness would encompass both the vast pristine forests of the West *and* smaller areas of wild nature that were within reach of eastern city dwellers. What Benton was talking about was exactly what the five protected wildernesses of the White Mountains became—easily accessible regions that retained their primitive characteristics and did not have roads, ski lodges, downhill ski trails, RV campsites, hotels, or motels. Because of his New England background, MacKaye, perhaps more than other wilderness thinkers, understood the need for protected wilderness that was accessible to the millions living in nearby cities. Like a true native son, he returned again and again for inspiration to New England's greatest nature writer: "And so we begin to realize Thoreau's dream and prophecy, and to take part each in our humble path in affecting the quality itself of our common mind and day."[35]

Like Benton MacKaye, Bob Marshall was a northeasterner whose youthful experiences in the outdoors—in his case, the Adirondacks—shaped his ideas about wilderness. One of the founding members of the Wilderness Society, he developed rationales for protecting wilderness that were central to the later campaigns for passage of the Wilderness Act of 1964 and the Eastern Wilderness Act of 1975. His thinking is fundamental to understanding how and why we have protected wildernesses in the White Mountains today.

Marshall was born on January 2, 1901, in New York City, the son of a prominent lawyer who was deeply involved in civil liberties and nature conservation— a legacy that Marshall built on through a lifelong commitment not only to conservation but to socialist causes, to which he gravitated during the wrenching years of the Great Depression. Eventually he came to believe that the only way to preserve the nation's forests was to place them into the public domain. As a young person, he spent his summers in the Adirondacks, where his family owned shares in a summer camp. He did much exploring of the natural environs, loved the thrill of exploring new places, and, with his brother George, eventually climbed all the 4,000-footers in the Adirondacks.[36]

It was a propitious time to be a young person exploring the wilds of the Adirondacks, because the region had only recently gained protection from logging and other economic interests. In 1885, New York State passed a law creating a Forest Preserve in the Adirondacks and stipulating that the forests should be preserved as wild lands.[37] The law, though, did not have effective provisions to protect trees, and logging continued in the Adirondacks. In 1894, a state constitutional convention in Albany included an article in its revised constitution that read, "The lands of the State, now owned or hereafter acquired, constituting the Forest Preserve as now fixed by law, shall be forever kept as wild forest lands."[38] In the fall of 1894, the state's voters overwhelmingly approved the new constitution, extending to the forests a degree of protection that was the strongest in the nation. In this atmosphere of wilderness protection, Bob Marshall came of age. Deeply affected by these formative years spent in the forests and on the mountains of the Adirondacks, he committed early to a career in forestry and enrolled at the New York State College of Forestry in Syracuse. When he completed his undergraduate degree, he wanted to work for the U.S. Forest Service in Alaska, which he found immensely seductive because of its enormous wilderness, but instead he was assigned to Carson, Washington.[39]

From 1924 to 1925, he continued his studies in forestry at Harvard's experimental forest in Petersham, Massachusetts, where he learned the value of selective cutting and the principles of sustained-yield forestry, which had the goal of harvesting trees at a rate that would ensure the continuous regeneration of forests and the production of timber.[40] Armed with a master's degree in forestry from Harvard, he went to work for the Northern Rocky Mountain Forest Experiment Station in Missoula, Montana, where his commitment to the preservation of wilderness deepened. In addition, he came to know the firefighters and lumbermen who were on the front line in the forests of the northern Rockies, and he observed the dangerous conditions in which they worked and their appallingly low pay. From that point on, his ideas about conservation would develop in tandem with his commitment to improving the conditions of the men and women who worked in the nation's forests.[41] In this regard, he shared Benton MacKaye's blending of environmental concerns with social concerns.

While in the Rockies, Marshall began to feel a gnawing dissatisfaction with the direction in which the Forest Service was moving under Chief Forester William Greeley, who was developing a more cooperative relationship with the lumber industry. Marshall became aware, in the 1920s, of Forest Service experiments with wilderness protection at the Gila National Forest in New Mexico, and of Aldo Leopold's ideas about the importance of protecting wilderness. In 1927, Marshall conceived a study to determine how much of the nation's forests were still roadless and, in 1936, produced a map that charted those areas.[42] He also began to speak out and write about the value of wilderness. In 1928, for instance, he rebutted an article by Manly Thompson that opposed the preservation of wilderness because only a small minority—only one-half of one percent—ventured into wilderness. In his rebuttal, which appeared in an issue of *Service Bulletin* in 1928, Marshall wrote, "The real question is whether this minority, whatever its numerical strength, is entitled to enjoy the life which it craves."[43] As Marshall was learning about America's wilderness, he was beginning to develop a rationale and strategies for protecting it.

He returned east in 1928 to study for a Ph.D. in plant physiology at Johns Hopkins University in Baltimore. As he pursued his doctorate, he published a landmark article in *Scientific Monthly* titled "The Problem of the Wilderness," in which he made an eloquent case for the preservation of wilderness by emphasizing the opportunities for adventure that primitive areas offered and the psychological sense of freedom that they gave. In addition to building this rationale, he also described what protected wildernesses might look like. He started with an explicit definition of wilderness: "For the ensuing discussion, I shall use the word *wilderness* to denote a region which contains no permanent inhabitants, possesses no possibility of conveyance by any mechanical means and is sufficiently spacious that a person in crossing it must have the experience of sleeping out."[44] Wilderness was to be an area without roads, without transportation by means of power, without permanent shelters, without logging operations. The only human-made appurtenances that it would have would be foot trails for hiking and fire protection, telephone lines for fire protection, and simple structures for temporary shelter.

Marshall had a visceral reaction against the ugliness of modern industrial civilization. "[F]actories belched up great clouds of smoke," he mourned, "where for centuries trees had transpired toward the sky, and the ground-cover of fresh sorrel and twinflower was transformed to asphalt spotted with chewing-gum, coal dust and gasoline." To offset this defilement, wilderness offered three kinds of benefits—physical, mental, and aesthetic—which echoed those that Charles E. Fay had written about in the 1880s. The physical benefits resulted from the exertion of "toting a fifty-pound pack over an abominable trail, snowshoeing across a blizzard-swept plateau or scaling some jagged pinnacle."[45] In wilderness was the expression of the individual's power, as he or she developed survival skills without depending on the infrastructure of modern civilization. Marshall was giving expression to the feelings of hundreds of weekend adventurers who, as we saw in chapter 10, had taken White Mountain recreation in a far more strenuous direction by venturing into the region's rugged backcountry.

Marshall then explored the mental benefits of wilderness. Spending time in a primitive natural environment stimulated independent thought, for by escaping from the incessant din of civilization, the individual was far more able to think creatively and to venture outside the confines of convention. He noted that some of America's greatest thinkers and writers, from Thomas Jefferson to John Muir and William James, had withdrawn into solitude at critical points in their lives. "In a civilization which requires most lives to be passed amid inordinate dissonance, pressure and intrusion," he asserted, "the chance of retiring now and then to the quietude and privacy of sylvan haunts becomes for some people a psychic necessity."[46]

Finally, Marshall lauded the aesthetic rewards of wilderness. He stood in awe of its "sheer stupendousness," using language that echoes the sublimity of Thomas Cole's landscapes: "Any one who has stood upon a lofty summit and gazed over an inchoate tangle of deep canyons and cragged mountains, of sunlit lakelets and black expanses of forest, has become aware of a certain giddy sensation that there are no distances, no measures, simply unrelated matter rising and falling without any analogy to the banal geometry of breadth, thickness and height."[47]

Moreover, the beauty of wilderness was dynamic, as the cycles of nature brought perpetual change to the landscape. "[S]ome ancient tree blows down," he observed, "and the long-suppressed plant suddenly enters into the full vigor of delayed youth" and matures until it, too, falls and decays on the forest floor. Bob Marshall's love of wilderness was positively sensual. He reveled in tramping through the forest and smelling the pines and the balsams, feeling "the stiff wind of mountaintops or the softness of untrodden sphagnum."[48] Its beauty was splendidly unified, for it was uninterrupted by the works of humanity and the distractions of civilization.

Yet, he noted, the preservation of wilderness as strictly pristine did have certain drawbacks. Without adequate protection, entire forests could quickly be destroyed by fire, and unexploited mineral and timber resources would be lost to the national economy. In response, though, Marshall thought that good planning and some degree of compromise would answer such objections. For fire protection, wilderness should include trails, lookout towers, and telephone lines. Compensating for the loss of the natural resources in wildernesses was, he admitted, an even more difficult problem. He suggested that conservationists create wilderness reserves from areas such as mountains, where the difficult terrain made mining and timber harvesting expensive. By his calculations, clear-cutting and other poor forestry practices had ruined the productivity of American forests, which he claimed produced only 22 percent of the timber that they could if logging companies would use selective cutting practices to ensure a sustainable supply of timber.

In conclusion, Marshall noted that the National Conference on Outdoor Recreation, which President Calvin Coolidge had convened in 1924 and 1926, had identified twenty-one wildernesses across the nation that warranted preservation. The Forest Service was beginning to set aside primitive areas, but such areas lacked legal protection from logging, road building, and other forms of economic development. Over the next several years, Marshall continued to urge the preservation of wilderness in a variety of books and magazine articles. In 1932, he wrote the section on recreation for *A National Plan for American Forestry*, which was commissioned by New York senator Royal Copeland and came to be known as the Copeland Report. The section he wrote, titled "The Forest for Recreation," delineated seven types of recreational areas that warranted preservation: superlative areas, which were areas of extraordinary scenic beauty; primeval areas, which contained old-growth timber and were virtually untouched by human activities; wildernesses, which had the char-

11.3. Robert Marshall with backpack. Bob Marshall's passion for wilderness and his ideas about protecting the nation's forests came directly out of his experience as a backpacker, climber, and forester. The Bancroft Library, University of California, Berkeley, CA.

acteristics that he had spelled out in his article in *Scientific Monthly;* roadside areas; campsite areas; residence areas; and outing areas.[49] In the report, he recommended that protected wildernesses have a minimum of 200,000 acres.[50]

As Marshall's ideas about wilderness matured, they attracted national attention. In 1933, Gifford Pinchot asked him to ghostwrite a letter of recommended forest policies for incoming President Franklin D. Roosevelt, and in it, Marshall strongly recommended that the federal government acquire vast amounts of forestland from private owners. Marshall made the proposal the centerpiece of his next project, *The People's Forests* (1933), a book for popular audiences in which he argued for public ownership of all timberlands.

Until the 1930s, thinkers about wilderness had communicated with one another in informal ways, but no one had ever taken steps to create a formal association that would advocate for wilderness. All that changed in 1934, when Marshall, Benton MacKaye, and other foresters gathered in Knoxville, Tennessee, for the annual meeting of the American Forestry Association. On October 19, Marshall, MacKaye, Harvey Broome, and Bernard and Miriam Frank were taking a field trip to visit a Civilian Conservation Corps camp near Knoxville. Broome was an attorney in Knoxville and a leader of the Smoky Mountains Hiking Club, which was instrumental in the creation of the Appalachian Trail. Bernard Frank was a forester on the staff of the Tennessee Valley Authority who specialized in the management of watersheds. In the car, they started tossing around ideas for an association that would dedicate itself to the preservation of wilderness in the United States, and the conversation became so lively, the ideas came so quickly, that they pulled over to the side of the road, got out, clambered up a small rise by the side of the road, and excitedly proceeded to map out plans for the organization that they would call the Wilderness Society.[51]

They sent letters to six other conservationists whom they invited to become founding members of the society: Harold Anderson, Robert Sterling Yard, Aldo Leopold, Ernest Oberholtzer, John Collier, and John Campbell Merriam. Leopold, who was well known in environmental circles, had just been named professor of game management at the University of Wisconsin. Anderson was an accountant in Washington, D.C., and a leader of the Potomac Appalachian Trail Club, which had successfully fought the building of an automobile drive along the Appalachian skyline. Yard had led the formation of the National Parks Association, a watchdog group formed in 1919 to ensure that the federal government maintained high standards of quality at the national parks. Oberholtzer had led the movement to preserve the Quetico-Superior lake country in far northern Minnesota. Both Collier, who was the director of the Bureau of Indian Affairs, and Merriam, who was a paleontologist and the director of the Carnegie Institution, declined to participate. But the other invitees came aboard, and on January 20 and 21, 1935, Anderson, Broome, MacKaye, Marshall, and Yard convened in Washington, D.C., to organize the Wilderness Society. Their mission was to persuade the federal government to set aside large areas of the national forests as wilderness, commencing a long battle for legislative protection that culminated in the passage of the Wilderness Act of 1964 and the Eastern Wilderness Act of 1975.[52]

When the Wilderness Society was formed, Bob Marshall did not assume the presidency of the fledgling organization, but he was, in many ways, its spiritual leader. In one of its first campaigns, in 1935, the society entered on-going negotiations with the Forest Service over the fate of Washington's Olympic Peninsula, which boasted extensive stands of old-growth timber. The Forest Service and the National Park Service were battling over control of Mount Olympus and several hundred thousand acres that surrounded it. After studying the issue, Marshall realized that each agency had its own institutional patterns that tended to compromise wilderness. The Park Service, with its commitment to opening up natural areas to tourists, built too many roads, in Marshall's opinion. The Forest Service, on the other hand, did not protect virgin stands of forests, because of its commitment to sustainable forestry.[53] Marshall asked for the plans from each agency and heard back from both in April 1936, and after comparing the two plans, he decided that the Park Service plan should receive the support of the Wilderness Society because it had fewer roads and preserved stands of virgin forest that the Forest Service would have logged. In May, he testified to a House subcommittee in favor of a bill to establish the Olympic National Park, and it eventually passed, creating the first national park to be managed as a wilderness.[54]

In 1937, Marshall became director of the Forest Service's Division of Recreation and Lands and developed strategies for opening up wilderness to racial minorities and people with lower incomes. These were his final contributions, for on November 10, 1939, at the age of thirty-nine, he passed away while riding a train to New York City. The cause of Marshall's death was not clear; many have speculated that he died of heart failure, but his biographer, James Glover, reported that an autopsy indicated a form of leukemia or hardening of the arteries. In any case, the wilderness movement had lost a towering figure.[55]

Bob Marshall's ideas had an enormous impact on the protection of wilderness in the White Mountains. Although the five wildernesses in the Whites fall short of the 200,000-acre minimum that Marshall recommended, they reflect his thinking in most other ways. They are large enough that backpackers can spend several days in them, completely immersing themselves in an environment in which wild nature is dominant and the works of humanity are only occasionally visible in the form of trails and fire lookouts. They are essentially roadless, except for access roads for fire protection. And they are off-limits to logging for commercial purposes. In short, Bob Marshall's thinking about wilderness proved eminently practical in establishing a direction and specific policy goals for the establishment of protected wildernesses.

The rationale that Benton MacKaye and Bob Marshall developed for protecting wildernesses focused on the ways in which wild nature could enhance people's quality of life. Aldo Leopold brought a different kind of thinking to the conversation about wilderness by emphasizing the health of ecosystems and the ways in which overdevelopment threatened their integrity, and he explained the ecological significance of wilderness in eloquent language that found a wide public. His most famous work was *A Sand County Almanac*, published a year after his death in 1948, but he wrote numerous other essays, which reveal a fascinating evolution in his thinking from an early emphasis on the utilitarian management of public lands toward a far more idealistic vision of environmental stewardship. Like MacKaye and Marshall, he trained as a forester, helped to found the Wilderness Society, and developed reasons for the preservation of wilderness that were critically important to protecting the White Mountains.

Born in Burlington, Iowa, on January 11, 1887, Aldo was the oldest of four children. He attended Sheffield Scientific School at Yale, graduated in 1908, and then earned a master's degree in forestry from the Yale Forestry School in 1909.[56] That year, he joined the Forest Service and was assigned to the Apache National Forest in southeastern Arizona, the beginning of an influential tenure in the American Southwest. Leopold had grown up as an avid hunter and a devoted naturalist, and when he graduated from Yale and joined the Forest Service, he adopted the essentially utilitarian approach of Gifford Pinchot toward the uses of natural areas. But as his biographer, Curt Meine, noted, Leopold emphasized the inherent value of wilderness more and more as his ideas about the environment matured.

In 1911, the Forest Service appointed him the deputy supervisor at Carson National Forest, north of Santa Fe.[57] While there, he read and was greatly influenced by the book *Our Vanishing Wild Life*, by William Temple Hornaday, which made the case for the protection of wild game. Influenced by this and other experiences, Leopold believed that the national forests should be stocked with game for hunters. He also considered it essential to control predators, such as wolves, coyotes, and bears. In fact, in an unsigned piece published in 1915 titled "The Varmint Question," he wrote, "It is well known that predatory animals are continuing to eat the cream of the stock-grower's profits, and it hardly needs to be argued that, with our game supply as low as it is, a reduction in the predatory animal population is bound to help the situation."[58] Leopold's attitudes toward predators would change greatly through the years as his thinking about wilderness evolved.[59]

Leopold eventually rose into management in the Forest Service, and on August 1, 1919, he became the assistant forester in charge of operations for the national forests in the Southwest. That year, he went to the annual meeting of district foresters in Salt Lake City, and there, Carl Stahl, another district forester, told him about a landscape architect named Arthur Carhart, who was based in Colorado. Carhart had received an assignment to conduct surveys as a preliminary step in building summer homes around Trappers Lake, a gorgeous lake in northwestern Colorado with crystal blue waters that were ringed dramatically by mountains. In a surprising move, though, Carhart concluded that building cottages around the lake would be a huge mistake—that the area should be preserved in its primitive condition.[60] Carhart's proposal reverberated throughout environmental circles.

On his way home to Albuquerque, Leopold stopped off to meet Carhart, whom he encouraged to write a memo elaborating on the need for wilderness preservation on lands that the federal government owned, and the result was one of the key documents in the growing movement for wilderness preservation. Carhart wrote, "The problem spoken of . . . was how far shall the Forest Service carry or allow to be carried man-made improvements in scenic territories, and whether there is not a definite point where all such developments, with the exception perhaps of lines of travel and necessary sign boards, shall stop."[61]

Carhart's initiative for wilderness preservation, which he would later extend in successful efforts to preserve the wild canoe waters of northern Minnesota, was in line with Leopold's own thinking about the leadership role that the Forest Service should take. On October 22, 1922, Leopold presented his own proposal for protected wilderness—the Gila Wilderness Area, a vast and unspoiled stretch of forestland in western New Mexico that would, in Leopold's words, provide a place "where pack trips shall be the dominant play."[62] The Forest Service accepted the proposal and on June 3, 1924, designated the forest as the first wilderness area in the United States. It was to remain roadless; the only logging would be for local uses; and limited grazing was permitted, so long as no roads were built.[63] The Gila Wilderness Area became a model for the primitive areas that the Forest Service established in the 1930s and 1940s, including the Great Gulf primitive area in the White Mountains.

Two years later, Leopold accepted a position with the U.S. Forest Products Laboratory in Madison, Wisconsin, but he found that he did not agree with the laboratory's emphasis on the industrial production of timber products and left government service altogether, taking a series of consulting positions with outdoor-recreation associations. Meanwhile, he continued publishing articles on ecology, game management, and conservation. In 1933, the University of Wisconsin created a faculty position for him in game management, and six years later, he assumed the chair of the newly formed Department of Wildlife Management at Wisconsin.

Leopold had first explored ideas about wilderness in a 1921 essay titled "The Wilderness and Its Place in Forest Recreational Policy," in which he sent forth the following famous definition of wilderness: "By 'wilderness' I mean a continuous stretch of country preserved in its natural state, open to lawful hunting and fishing, big enough to absorb a two weeks' pack trip, and kept devoid of roads, artificial trails, cottages, or other works of man."[64]

11.4. Aldo Leopold. Leopold's vision of wilderness developed during his tenure in the U.S. Forest Service in the Southwest. His ideas about the protection of ecosystems and the development of a land ethic influenced conservationists throughout the United States, including those who won protection for the eastern forests. AP Images.

Four years later, he published "Wilderness as a Form of Land Use," an essay influential enough that Benton MacKaye referred to it in *The New Exploration*. According to Leopold, wilderness was a resource that contained natural commodities, such as timber and minerals, but also supported important social values, such as individualism, organizing ability, problem-solving abilities, and informal social interactions that kept alive the egalitarianism of the American frontier. "Public wildernesses," he averred, "are essentially a means for allowing the more virile and primitive forms of outdoor recreation to survive the receding economic fact of pioneering."[65] In addition to activities such as hiking and camping, he regarded hunting and fishing as important and entirely appropriate wilderness activities. This early essay reflected the utilitarianism that marked his thinking about land use at this point in his career, as he stressed the goal of balancing different demands on the land:

> To preserve any land in a wild condition is, of course, a reversal of economic tendency, but that fact alone should not condemn the proposal. A study of the history of land utilization shows that good use is largely a matter of good balance—of wise adjustment between opposing tendencies. The modern movements toward diversified crops and live stock on the farm, conservation of eroding soils, forestry, range management, game management, public parks— all these are attempts to balance opposing tendencies that have swung out of counterpoise.[66]

Yet, Leopold warned, America's wildernesses were a resource that could disappear because of overuse. Consequently, he maintained, "Our wilderness environment cannot, of course, be preserved on any considerable scale as an economic fact. But, like many other receding economic facts, it can be preserved for the ends of sport"—"sport" meaning the entire sphere of physical and aesthetic activities that people pursued through contact with nature.[67] Leopold argued that if we view wilderness as a resource, we begin to recognize its value and to realize that its supply is limited.

Leopold proposed the protection of many different types of wilderness, suggesting that "wilderness exists in all degrees, from the little accidental wild spot at the head of a ravine in a Corn Belt woodlot to vast expanses of virgin country." Furthermore, he thought, the wildernesses worth preserving might "vary in degree from the wild, roadless spot of a few acres left in the rougher parts of public forest devoted to timber-forest, to wild, roadless regions approaching in size a whole national forest or a whole national park."[68] Wildernesses could also vary in purpose and use:

> The retention of certain wild areas in both national forests and national parks will introduce a healthy variety into the wilderness idea itself, the forest areas serving as public hunting grounds, the park areas as public wildlife sanctuaries, and both kinds as public playgrounds in which the wilderness environments and modes of travel may be preserved and enjoyed.[69]

Over the next ten years, Leopold continued to publish articles that explored the value of wildernesses. In 1935, he helped to found the Wilderness Society, and that same year, he bought a shack on the Wisconsin River where he would, for the rest of his life, conduct experiments in restoring the depleted land that surrounded his little house. However, a turning point in Leopold's ideas about wilderness came in 1936, when he studied forestry in Germany. There, he was struck by the extent to which the Germans had practiced forest management by adopting methodical approaches, such as planting trees in rows, which eliminated any sense of wildness about the forests.[70] After his tour of Germany, he went on a hunting trip to Mexico that took him into the Sierra Madre and the Rio Gavilan in the state of Chihuahua. These mountains existed in a pristine state ecologically. Perhaps most important for Leopold's own evolving ideas was the common sight of predators—mountain lions, wolves, coyotes—and he noted that they prevented the overpopulation of small game.[71]

Leopold visited Mexico once again in 1937, and as Curt Meine noted in his biography of Leopold, "These two trips would have a positive and profound effect on his thinking about land."[72] He began to develop a new paradigm for humanity's relationship with the land, which formed the core of a book that he began writing in the mid-1930s. Several publishers passed on the book proposal, but finally, in 1947, Oxford University Press accepted the manuscript for *A Sand County Almanac*, which was published in 1949. Unfortunately, though, it was issued posthumously, as Leopold died of a heart attack on April 21, 1948, while helping to fight a fire on a neighbor's farm.

At the center of *A Sand County Almanac* was the concept of the land ethic, in which the land and its organisms form a biotic community that must be treated with the same ethical considerations as the human community:

> All ethics so far evolved rest upon a single premise: that the individual is a member of a community of interdependent parts. . . . The land ethic simply enlarges the boundaries of the community to include soils, waters, plants, and animals, or collectively: the land.[73]

The only healthy relationship between humanity and the natural world, Leopold argued, is one based on respect and ethical treatment, not on economics. Moreover, conservation efforts had fallen short because they had called for no sacrifice or obligation on the part of humanity and had been founded on economic arguments. But, he explained, "One basic weakness in a conservation system based wholly on economic motives is that most members of the land community have no economic value."[74] He pointed out, for example, that Wisconsin had twenty-two thousand native species of plants and animals, but only 5 percent of those species had economic value. Yet those species were part of the ecosystem and, therefore, deserved to live and to thrive.[75]

Another reason for the preservation of wilderness was its value as a model of land at its healthiest, from which environmental scientists could learn lessons about how to revive ecosystems that had been harmed by urbanization, pollution, and other forces of modern society. Wilderness was, in a sense, a laboratory for understanding the complex interactions of organisms in the biotic community:

> Paleontology offers abundant evidence that wilderness maintained itself for immensely long periods; that its component species were rarely lost, neither did they get out of hand; that weather and water built soil as fast or faster than it was carried away. Wilderness, then, assumes unexpected importance as a laboratory for the study of land-health.[76]

Possibly the greatest shift in Leopold's thinking regarded predators. He came to believe that it was shortsighted to systematically eliminate wolves, mountain lions, bears, and other large predators. Consequently, these carnivores' prey, particularly deer and elk, had overpopulated wildernesses, leading the Forest Service to hire hunters to kill the excess animals. The government, in turn, built new roads to carry hunters into the forests, and soon, roads were crisscrossing yet another wilderness area. To prevent this from happening, foresters in wildernesses should permit predators to reinhabit their native habitats. As Leopold put it, "Of what use are wild areas destitute of their distinctive faunas?"[77] Indeed, one of the most moving passages in *A Sand County Almanac* occurs when the narrator recounts an incident from his younger days in which he and his hunting companions shot a wolf:

> We reached the old wolf in time to watch a fierce green fire dying in her eyes. I realized then, and have known ever since, that there was something new to me in those eyes—something known only to her and to the mountain. I was young then, and full of trigger-itch; I thought that because few wolves meant more deer, that no wolves would mean hunters' paradise. But after seeing the green fire die, I sensed that neither the wolf nor the mountain agreed with such a view.[78]

By developing an ethical basis for wilderness preservation, Leopold moved the argument for wilderness protection to a new realm based on the inherent value of nature and the integrity of complex ecosystems. This ethical foundation was critically important to the movement to protect wilderness in the White Mountains, which would have its beginnings in the 1940s and would flower in the 1950s and 1960s. MacKaye, Marshall, and Carhart had articulated reasons for the protection of wilderness that were founded on the physical, social, aesthetic, and spiritual benefits of wilderness to humanity. However, Aldo Leopold placed these reasons into a larger context by redefining the relationship between humanity and the natural world. In Leopold's view, humanity was part of—not separate from—the world of nature and, therefore, bore an ethical responsibility for maintaining the health of the ecosystems that it inhabited. His views bore similarities to the ways in which the Abenaki and other Native American people perceived the relationship between themselves and the environment. The ethical foundation for environmental protection that Leopold articulated would become central to the success of the movement to protect the White Mountain wilderness.

As important as Benton MacKaye, Bob Marshall, Arthur Carhart, and Aldo Leopold were to the formation of the movement to protect wilderness, they also built on a wilderness heritage that the explorers, pioneers, artists, writers, and outdoor adventurers of the White Mountains helped to create. The history of this magnificent region, as we have seen, has encompassed the explorations of Jeremy Belknap and Manasseh Cutler, the pioneering spirit of the Crawfords, the sublime landscapes of Thomas Cole and other artists, the mystical ruminations of Thomas Starr King, the trail builders of the Appalachian Mountain Club, and the outdoor adventures of early hikers and campers who created a constituency for the protection of wilderness. These White Mountain figures—some famous, others obscured by the years—helped to created a cultural environment in the United States that gradually doused the old Puritan prejudices against wilderness and replaced them with a vision of the wonders of wild nature that inspired the MacKayes, the Marshalls, the Leopolds. Our final step, then, is to see how this new commitment to wilderness turned from vision to practical reality—how it led to legislative protection of the White Mountain wilderness.

Chapter 12

PRESERVING THE WHITE
MOUNTAIN WILDERNESS

GERALD S. WHEELER, who was the forest supervisor for the White Mountain National Forest in the late 1950s and early 1960s, communicated regularly in *Appalachia* about plans and policies for the WMNF. In 1960, he announced changes in how the Forest Service would manage the Great Gulf, the glacial valley between Mount Washington and the northern peaks of the Presidentials. "For many years," he wrote, "the Great Gulf, on the northeast slope of the Presidential Range in New Hampshire, has been maintained in its natural condition by the Forest Service."[1] Wheeler announced that he had recommended to the Forest Service that the Great Gulf be reclassified as a "wild area" and managed according to Regulation U-2, which meant that the primitive conditions of the Great Gulf would be maintained. All told, the wild area would comprise some 5,400 acres.

The fact that Forest Supervisor Wheeler recommended that the Great Gulf be managed as a wild area shows dramatically how far policies regarding wilderness had evolved in the years since the end of World War II. In those years, ideas about the value of wild nature would reach their full maturity. From its inauspicious debut, *A Sand County Almanac* would become a best seller in paperback, winning adherents around the world for Aldo Leopold's ideas about environmental ethics and wilderness values. In 1962, Rachel Carson's *Silent Spring* would galvanize Americans' attention by exposing the impact of DDT on the environment. Edward Abbey, in eloquent and vivid prose, would decry the impingement of humanity on the steadily shrinking wildernesses of the West.

Furthermore, outdoor recreation would go through an exciting revolution as members of the post–World War II generation, using vastly improved equipment, threw themselves into activities that were both challenging and strenuous: technical climbing, backpacking, winter camping, cross-country skiing, snowshoeing, ice climbing, and white-water rafting. And, as the world speeded up, technology became more dominant, and the media grew ever more frenetic, solitude in nature would hold greater appeal than ever. In a single tent in the deep woods, the solitary adventurer could confront the essentials of life, observe the creatures of the forest, and listen to the beat of his or her own life. Benton MacKaye, Bob Marshall, Arthur Carhart, and Aldo Leopold, who had all worked for the U.S. Forest Service, had developed the concept of wilderness. Now a movement to protect wilderness was bursting forth like a butterfly from its cocoon.

The desire to preserve wilderness found full expression in the vast spaces of the West, but the desire burned fiercely in the Appalachians, too, stoked by trends in the East in general and in the White Mountains in particular. However, protecting wilderness in the White Mountains faced obstacles that grew out of two geographic facts about the mountains. First was the reality that since the advent of the automobile, the Whites had become easily accessible to one-quarter of the population of the United States, resulting in millions of annual visitors who embraced the full range of outdoor activities, from multi-day backpacking to more sedate activities such as autumn leaf-peeping. Visits to national forests rose from 45.5 million in 1955 to 52.5 million in 1956 and to 61 million in 1957.[2] The total number of visits to the White Mountains in 1956 was 6,565,550, generating revenues of $53 million a year, which represented 40 percent of New Hampshire's total for recreation.[3] All these visitors used the ample recreational facilities in the mountains and spurred the creation of more facilities. By the mid-1950s, the WMNF boasted one thousand miles of hiking trails—the most complete system of trails in the East and probably in the nation—as well as sixty miles of ski trails and hundreds of miles of paved roads.[4] The WMNF also maintained eleven campgrounds and seven picnicking and bathing areas, and according to counts of automobile traffic, there was a dramatic increase in pleasure driving in the mountains.[5] The Forest Service was at the center of all this recreational activity, as it supervised concessionaires who operated inns, lodges, fishing camps, and marinas.[6] Fishing and hunting remained popular, as they had been for three centuries, though many streams were overfished.

The second fact of geography that made preservation difficult was the continued development of the patchwork quilt of land use that environmental historian William Cronon identified in his book *Changes in the Land*—a pattern that first emerged in the early nineteenth century. The quilt then had consisted of farms and small towns in the valleys, interspersed with the forests that carpeted the sides of the mountains. Agriculture declined in the region as the nineteenth century proceeded, but the emergence of the travel industry in the late nineteenth century led to the construction of dozens of grand resort hotels and the development of a tourism infrastructure that transformed White Mountain towns. These trends only accelerated in the twentieth century, as the towns grew to accommodate motels, restaurants, shops, factory outlets, and gas stations—all of which were direct effects of the automobile.

Adding further to this increasingly complicated landscape was the construction of second homes and condominiums that provided weekend getaways for people in Massachusetts, New York, Connecticut, Rhode Island, and other states, and these new home owners demanded the infrastructure that they were used to in cities, such as water, transportation, and sewage. Finally, skiing exploded in popularity in the mid-1930s, prior to World War II, and soon ski resorts were sprouting up throughout the region, including the Wildcat Mountain ski area in the late 1950s, Cannon Mountain, Waterville Valley, and Loon Mountain. These ski resorts increased the pressures of development, and their lodges, ski runs, chair lifts, and gondolas now dotted the sides of mountains. Without question, the ski industry was an economic boon for northern New Hampshire, but ski resorts also impinged on wilderness in the region.[7] Consequently, what Cronon described as a patchwork quilt was turning into a sometimes-chaotic puzzle of towns, shops, homes, roads, tourist attractions, and ski resorts.

Yet amazingly enough, in the midst of this economic development, the White Mountains stood as beautiful as ever, thanks to the precious protections that resulted from the Weeks Act and the creation of the White Mountain National Forest. The regeneration of the forests, which had started after the 1903 fires and gathered momentum after the passage of the Weeks Act in 1911, bore fruit, and an emerald carpet of second- and third-growth forests bedecked the mountains. Even in the face of catapulting numbers of casual vacationers, wilderness trekkers could still find solitude, challenge, and primitive nature. The mountains boasted more than nine square miles of treeless summits, giving the region a strong alpine flavor.[8] It was still possible to wander areas such as Wild River, the Mahoosuc Range, parts of the Sandwich Range, and the northern Presidentials and encounter wild nature directly. In the coming years, advocates for wilderness would focus on preserving the wilderness characteristics in these and other sectors of the White Mountains.

But there was a cloud on the horizon—a sharp increase in the demand for wood and pulp that began during World War II and continued during the postwar years. With that boom came heavy pressure on the Forest Service to increase logging in the White Mountains and other national forests, and once again logging operators began to clear-cut in the Whites. In an address in 1986 commemorating the seventy-fifth anniversary of the passage of the Weeks Act, former New Hampshire governor Sherman Adams recalled what happened:

For quietly, without public debate, the U.S. Forest Service adopted even aged silviculture with clear-cutting as its principal means of harvesting throughout the country. . . . After decades of using locally-modified selective and selection cutting programs, the Forest Service had by 1962 incorporated in a wholesale, indiscriminate manner this aesthetically disruptive and, in forest conditions such as those prevalent in the White Mountains, scientifically questionable system.[9]

As the economy boomed and demand for wood spiked upward, some feared that the United States would not have enough timber to satisfy its needs. From Adams's point of view, the Forest Service had permitted clear-cutting because, in his words, it was "cheaper and easier to control and administer."[10] To be sure, foresters warned that it was difficult to generalize that clear-cutting was always ecologically harmful, because conditions varied so much from one forest environment to another. However, many tourists reacted very negatively when they saw the results of clear-cutting along hiking trails, from ski slopes, and along roads. In 1956, the Forest Service's chief forester, Richard McArdle, tried to reassert the balanced-use philosophy of the Forest Service and pushed for passage of the Multiple Use–Sustained Yield Act of 1960, which would have reinforced the multiple-use function of the national forests.[11] By the 1960s, an important additional use, in the eyes of environmentalists, was environmental protection. In view of the new demands on the forests, McArdle saw the law as a way to counteract the focus on more aggressive timber production and reemphasize management of the national forests for "*the greatest good of the greatest number in the long run.*"[12]

The renewed clear-cutting met staunch opposition from preservationists, who were already in a high state of alarm over similar situations in the Monongahela National Forest in West Virginia and in the Bitterroot National Forest in Idaho. In both of those forests, the Forest Service implemented clear-cutting without public involvement.[13] Clear-cutting in the Whites, the Monongahela, the Bitterroot, and other national forests led wilderness advocates to the conclusion that the only way to preserve the primitive quality of substantial tracts of the nation's forests was to protect them legislatively as wildernesses.

The resumption of clear-cutting had political implications as well for the Forest Service. Until the 1950s, most conservationists believed that the agency had, for the most part, found a successful balance among the many uses of the national forests for recreation, timber, mining, and scientific study. But the resumption of clear-cutting changed conservationists' attitudes toward the Forest Service.[14] Paul Bofinger, who was the president and forester of the Society for the Protection of New Hampshire Forests from 1965 to 1996, said, "The Forest Service made it easy for groups like the Wilderness Society to criticize them. The [forest] base was small enough that they should have been able to manage the forest without clear-cutting. They were up against people who were angry. As a result, there was a lot of political support for wilderness by the 1960s and certainly by the 1970s."[15] The consequence was to undermine environmentalists' confidence in the ability of the Forest Service to manage the nation's forests for aesthetic and ecological integrity. At the same time, the Forest Service had to follow three imperatives that often clashed with one another:

1. Managing the replenishment of timber and water resources that were critical to the economic development of the region;
2. Managing the forests for the outdoor recreation of millions of people whose expectations ran the gamut from roadside picnics to extended backpacking trips; and
3. Protecting the forest ecosystems.

Moreover, the strong advocacy for wilderness after World War II may have caught the Forest Service's management off guard. In any event, the agency had to engage in a balancing act that would have been difficult for any organization, let alone a large government bureaucracy. In fairness to the Forest Service, it has engaged in self-reflection unusual for government bureaucracies through the publication of histories of the wilderness movement, such as David E. Conrad's *The Land We Cared For: A History of the Forest Service's Eastern Region* and Dennis M. Roth's *The Wilderness Movement and the National Forests: 1964–1980,* which tell the straightforward story of the Forest Service's role in the development of wilderness legislation. From these books and from conversations with foresters, one senses that the period of renewed clear-cutting may have been as painful to a certain cohort of Forest Service foresters as it was to wilderness advocates.

By the mid-1950s, three trends were converging that catalyzed the movement to protect wilderness legislatively: (1) the commitment to wilderness by thousands of recreationists, (2) the development of a philosophy that buttressed that commitment, and (3) the threat to wilderness posed by industrial interests that were slow to recognize the hallowed place that wilderness was taking in the hearts and minds of its advocates. At the national level, Howard Zahniser, the executive secretary of the Wilderness Society, who had inherited the strong commitment to wilderness from Bob Marshall, spearheaded the development and writing of legislation for wilderness protection. On May 24, 1955, Zahniser delivered a speech titled "The Need for Wilderness Areas" to the National Citizen's Planning Conference on Parks and Open Spaces for the American People. Zahniser put forward a plan for a national wilderness preservation system to be formed from the primitive areas, such as the Great Gulf, that the federal government was already administering.[16] On June 7, 1956, Senator Hubert Humphrey of Minnesota submitted the first wilderness bill to the Senate, followed four days later by the submission of a bill in the House by Representative John P. Saylor of Pennsylvania. In addition to estab-

12.1. Howard Zahniser, 1946. As the executive secretary of the Wilderness Society, Zahniser was a highly persuasive advocate for the preservation of wild nature. The waterfall behind Zahniser is in the High Peaks Wilderness of the New York State wilderness system. From the Paul Schaefer Collection of Wilderness Archives. Courtesy of the Adirondack Research Library of the Association for the Protection of the Adirondacks, Niskayuna, NY. Courtesy of Alice B. Zahniser.

lishing protected wilderness, the bills would have eliminated mining and prospecting from wildernesses.[17]

The bills did not pass in Congress, but the next year, Humphrey introduced a new bill, which attracted as cosponsors ten senators and four representatives from both parties. According to Marjorie Hurd, who reported on the progress of the bill for *Appalachia*, "Two facts are recognized: our wilderness area has been shrinking throughout our history; we have valid need for wilderness, both open spaces in their natural condition. . . . To preserve such regions in their present natural state is the purpose of this bill."[18] The new bill was stronger than Humphrey's 1956 bill. It would have established a National Wilderness Preservation System encompassing lands administered by the National Park Service, the Forest Service, the Fish and Wildlife Service, and the Bureau of Indian Affairs. The wildernesses would have included fifty areas in national parks, eighty in national forests, twenty in wildlife refuges, and fifteen on Indian lands, though Native Americans would have had to approve of any lands included in the wilderness system.[19] Hurd concluded, "This is a real advance and a very definite gain for conservation; the preservation of wilderness is recognized not as a starry-eyed dream but as a national policy."[20] During the same time period, groups involved in the wilderness movement—including the Sierra Club, the Wilderness Society, the American Planning and Civic Association, the Federated Western Outdoor Clubs, the Izaak Walton League, and the National Parks Association—convened the Fifth Biennial Wilderness Conference to continue developing policies regarding wilderness.[21]

Humphrey's 1957 bill demonstrated that broad-based support existed for wilderness legislation, and in reaction, opponents began to gather their forces and formulate arguments against legislative protection of wilderness. The Forest Service indicated that it favored the overall goals of the legislation, but the agency wanted to have the final decision in what was designated wilderness. Water engineers wanted to retain the right to build dams and harness rivers for hydroelectric power. However, the strongest opposition came from the lumber industry, mining interests, and ranchers with livestock. In his book *The Politics of Wilderness Preservation*, Craig W. Allin identified five arguments of those who opposed wilderness bills. First, opponents claimed, wilderness legislation was not needed at all and, in fact, would be taking land and resources out of use that were needed for a growing population and an expanding economy. Second, wilderness areas already enjoyed sufficient protection. The Forest Service, for instance, was already administering a number of primitive areas. Third, special interests—an elite minority—were behind the advocacy for wilderness legislation. McArdle testified in congressional hearings that while wilderness comprised 8 percent of the lands managed by the federal government, only 1 percent of the visits to national forests were to wildernesses. Fourth, wilderness preservation would weaken the nation and undermine the national defense by taking essential natural resources out of the economic equation. Finally, wilderness legislation went against the doctrine of multiple use that had been the basis for the administration of the national forests since the days of Gifford Pinchot.[22]

In response, wilderness advocates, led by Howard Zahniser, mounted spirited and thoughtful rebuttals to all these points. In answer to the first and second points—that wilderness already had sufficient protection—advocates asserted that the resumption of clear-cutting in national forests proved that there was a need for wilderness legislation, which would prevent further logging. To the argument that wilderness appealed to only a minority of outdoor enthusiasts, Zahniser responded that the users of wilderness comprised a far greater percentage of the population than could be counted by visits to federal wilderness areas over a limited period of time. He drew an analogy to visits to art galleries, explaining that while a small minority of art lovers might visit an art gallery at any one time, over a period of months or years, the number of visitors would accumulate and would represent a higher percentage of the population than was apparent at first. To the argument that wilderness would be removed from economic uses, Zahniser responded that wilderness bills would have minimal impact on economic development, because proposed areas comprised less than 2.5 percent of the land area of the United States.[23]

Wilderness advocates also reminded the public that wilderness provided a respite from the increasing dominance of technology in life and served as a scientific laboratory for studying ecosystems that have felt little human impact. Finally, wilderness advocates argued that wilderness legislation would not end the philosophy of multiple use but instead would ensure that environmental protection would remain one of the multiple uses of national forests. Besides, advocates were not proposing to turn all of the national forests into wilderness, and millions of acres would remain open to logging and other economic uses.[24]

Without question, these debates helped wilderness advocates to sharpen their arguments in favor of wilderness legislation and to continue to build grassroots support for wilderness. When John F. Kennedy was elected president in 1960, the political atmosphere began to tilt in favor of wilderness. In February 1961, soon after taking office, Kennedy endorsed a Senate wilderness bill, and momentum began to build toward passage. The Senate passed a bill on September 6, 1961, and sent it to the House. Representative Saylor introduced a bill into the House, where, according to Craig Allin, the full House would probably have voted in favor of the legislation, but the Interior Committee, chaired by Wayne Aspinall of Colorado, killed the legislation.[25] Throughout the early 1960s, Aspinall repeatedly threw up roadblocks to the passage of wilderness legislation.

When the Eighty-eighth Congress convened in January of 1963, the Senate quickly repassed wilderness legislation, and a number of representatives introduced wilderness bills in the House. The passage of some kind of wilderness legislation seemed assured, but the key issue now was whether the power to add wilderness in the future would reside in the executive branch or the legislative branch of the federal government. Giving the power to the executive branch meant that the designation of future wilderness areas would depend on the degree to which each presidential administration favored conservation. On the other hand, placing the power with Congress did not seem promising; the difficulty in passing basic wilderness protection through Congress did not augur well for the approval of wildernesses in the future. In the end, though, the two House bills that had the best chance for passage—one introduced by Saylor and one by Representative John Dingell of Michigan— kept the authority for adding wildernesses with Congress.

In April of 1964, Howard Zahniser spoke at the final congressional hearing in favor of wilderness, but, unfortunately, he died soon after of a heart attack at the age of fifty-eight, before he could see the final passage of the wilderness act for which he had worked so passionately. On June 2, 1964, the Interior Committee sent Saylor's bill to the floor of the House, but the committee had weakened the bill considerably by attaching several amendments, including one that gave the executive branch the power to remove protection from primitive areas before they could be considered for wilderness designation.[26] However, on the floor of the House, Saylor succeeded in strengthening the bill in several ways. First, he added protection for California's San Gorgonio Wild Area, where developers wanted to build a ski resort. Second, he added an amendment that prevented the executive branch from unilaterally removing primitive areas from protection. This amendment was important because it ensured that Congress, rather than the executive branch, would retain power over the designation of wildernesses. The House passed the bill by a 374 to 1 vote, and on September 3, 1964, President Lyndon Johnson signed the National Wilderness Preservation Act.[27]

The act extended wilderness designation to 9.1 million acres of land that the Forest Service had classified as wilderness, wild, or canoe areas, and it protected the wild characteristics of primitive areas until Congress decided whether to extend wilderness protection to such areas. It defined wilderness as "an area where the earth and its community of life are untrammeled by man, where man himself is a visitor who does not remain."[28] Such an area retains "its primeval character and influence, without permanent improvements or human habitation." The act then went on to specify that such land:

(1) generally appears to have been affected primarily by the forces of nature, with the imprint of man's work substantially unnoticeable; (2) has outstand-

12.2. The Wilderness Act of 1964. While signing the Wilderness Act on September 3, 1964, President Lyndon B. Johnson gave pens to Mrs. Howard Zahniser and Mrs. Olaus J. Murie.
National Park Service. Photograph by Abbie Rowe, National Park Service photographer.

ing opportunities for solitude or a primitive and unconfined type of recreation; (3) has at least five thousand acres of land or is of sufficient size as to make practicable its preservation and use in an unimpaired condition; and (4) may also contain ecological, geological, or other features of scientific, educational, scenic, or historical value.[29]

A key provision prohibited certain uses. There was to be "no commercial enterprise and no permanent road within any wilderness area designated by this Act." The only temporary roads were to be those required for "emergencies involving the health and safety of persons within the area." Finally, there was to be "no use of motor vehicles, motorized equipment or motorboats, no landing of aircraft, no other form of mechanical transport, and no structure or installation within any such area."[30] The Forest Service would study areas to be proposed as wilderness, but only an act of Congress could create future wildernesses.

The only area in the White Mountains that received immediate wilderness protection was the Great Gulf—5,552 acres that had been administered for

12.3. The Great Gulf. The Great Gulf, which lies between Mt. Washington and the northern peaks of the Presidential Range, was the only area in the White Mountains that the Forest Service managed as a primitive area, and it became the first protected wilderness in the Whites when the Wilderness Act passed Congress in 1964. Courtesy of Dartmouth College Library.

decades as a primitive area and had retained many of its primitive characteristics. Ironically, though, the wilderness designation immediately led to increased use. David Govatski, a forester who worked for many years for the Forest Service and who now conducts historical and ecological tours throughout the region, noted that he remembered going to the Great Gulf soon after the passage of the Wilderness Act and finding the area more crowded with hikers than it had ever been before. Eventually the Forest Service began to issue permits to limit the number of backpackers and to alleviate overcrowding. The immediate popularity of the Great Gulf Wilderness demonstrated clearly that there was a pent-up demand for wilderness in the White Mountains.

Yet that demand was frustrated throughout the 1960s because of the way in which the Forest Service applied the Wilderness Act, especially in the eastern forests. The problem in the East, as the White Mountains demonstrated, was that most of the forests had been cut over once, leading to the question of whether they constituted wilderness, since they had been affected substantially by human activity. Thus, in evaluating which forests would be recommended to Congress for future protection as wilderness, the Forest Service implemented what has come to be known as the "purity policy," which stemmed from the definition of wilderness as "primeval" areas in which signs of human activity were virtually absent. The Forest Service, the Fish and Wildlife Service, and the Park Service interpreted the policy to mean that if an area had second growth, old roads, or abandoned mines, it could not qualify as wilderness. The interpretation created a problem in the White Mountains, where most of the area had second- or even third-growth forests. The purity policy, which essentially was a way for the Forest Service to maintain control of forest management in the eastern forests, set up an inevitable clash between the agency and advocates of wilderness, who were enthusiastically studying and recommending more wilderness protection than had been expected when the legislation had passed. Moreover, Congress was looking favorably on the proposals that were being made for protection.[31] Consequently, the Wilderness Society, the Sierra Club, and grassroots conservation groups continued to press for more wilderness designation.

The Wilderness Act required the Forest Service and other land agencies to evaluate roadless areas regularly for wilderness potential. In the early 1970s, the Forest Service initiated a study of roadless areas known as RARE I (Roadless Area Review and Evaluation).[32] Chief Forester Edward Cliff said that the Forest Service conducted RARE I because "Every time we made a move into a roadless area we ran into opposition which generally materialized in the form of a lawsuit or a wilderness proposal by a congressman."[33] In 1971 and 1972, the Forest Service studied 1,449 roadless areas that had 55.9 million acres. However, almost all of the areas were west of the Mississippi, with only two in the East and one in Puerto Rico, greatly dismaying environmentalists in the East. Both the Wilderness Society and the Sierra Club were highly critical of RARE I, partly because the process ignored roadless areas in the East.[34]

Concurrent with these events, the Forest Service was trying to determine how to manage its primitive areas in the East in response to the growing pressure for wilderness protection. According to Forest Service chief historian Dennis M. Roth, "Public pressure for the designation of wilderness areas in the East had developed slowly after the passage of the Wilderness Act," and in response, the Forest Service concluded that it needed to show leadership regarding wilderness preservation. As a result, the agency proposed a new category, "wild areas," which would consist of areas that had been logged or used in other ways but now demonstrated many of the characteristics of wilderness. In wild areas, future commercial logging, mining, and grazing would be banned. However, the Wilderness Society did not want the creation of a new wilderness category and, instead, favored expanding the Wilderness Act to encompass eastern forests. The Wilderness Society's lobbyists, Doug Scott, Harry Crandell, and Ernie Dickerman, persuaded the Nixon administration to come out in favor of the creation of eastern wildernesses within the framework of the current wilderness system.[35]

Even so, the proposal for the new category of wild areas remained alive, and in September 1972, the Senate passed the National Forest Wild Areas bill, which distinguished between wild areas in the East and wildernesses in the West.[36] To head off the creation of the new system, the Wilderness Society hurriedly wrote an alternative eastern wilderness bill and recruited Senator James Buckley of New York and Senator Frank Church of Idaho to sponsor it; eventually they were joined by Senator Henry Jackson of Washington, and the bill was introduced into Congress in January 1973.[37]

At the same time, not all environmentalists in the East favored the creation of eastern wildernesses. Dennis Roth explained, "Some northeasterners had become skeptical about the wisdom of wilderness designations after observing the heavy use of the Great Gulf Wilderness in New Hampshire."[38] In addition, the AMC, which had worked well with the Forest Service over the years, feared that it would have to take down existing trail shelters if areas encompassing the shelters were designated as wilderness. Roth hypothesized also that New Englanders' independence may have played a role in their attitude toward the passage of federal wilderness legislation, and he noted that New Englanders looked with pride on their tradition of conservation and were suspicious of federal interference that might come with the passage of wilderness legislation.[39] Joseph Penfold, who was the conservation director of the Izaak Walton League, also worried about watering down the criteria for the creation of eastern wildernesses. He warned, "Even if the line can be held rigorously against the invasion by commercial development—and pressures for such are unrelenting—there still remains the growing and nearly irresistible pressure of recreationists themselves who, with snowmobiles, outboard, ATV and other gadgetry, or sheer numbers lean their weight against every wilderness boundary."[40]

Even in the face of such skepticism, though, the Wilderness Society, which had become the most potent force pressing for legislative protection of wilderness, pursued the designation of eastern wilderness areas. The leaders of the Wilderness Society believed that they had inherited a legacy of commitment to wilderness from Howard Zahniser, and they did not want to dilute that legacy through the creation of two systems for preserving wild nature.[41] Ernie Dickerman explained, "In our opinion it is preferable to put into the System an area which may contain some minor work of man than it is to reject the entire area or a significant portion of it in order to avoid such minor features. After all, the objective is to preserve wilderness, not seek reasons for rejecting its preservation."[42] The leaders of the Sierra Club, however, favored the wild areas legislation because they felt that it was the best way to protect eastern wildernesses areas in the face of resistance by the Forest Service.[43]

In December of 1972, Doug Scott and Ernie Dickerman of the Wilderness Society invited environmental leaders, including local leaders of the Sierra Club, to a meeting in Knoxville, Tennessee, at which Scott and Dickerman argued the case for working within the current system of wilderness protection rather than creating a second system of wild areas. They made two important points—that splitting wilderness advocates into two camps would undermine the unity of the wilderness movement and that the creation of wild areas would give credence to the Forest Service's purity argument. Dickerman also maintained that the proposal for wild areas stoked the Forest Service's hopes that it could resist proposals for wildernesses throughout the West. The Sierra Club eventually supported the Wilderness Society's position, but the disagreement led to some hard feelings between leaders of the two organizations.[44]

By early fall of 1973, the Forest Service had abandoned the proposal for two systems of wilderness protection, and momentum started to build toward the designation of eastern wildernesses. The purity principle had successfully been repudiated, meaning that an area could be designated wilderness even if it showed signs of nonconforming uses, such as logging, grazing, or mining. The House Interior Committee approved a bill creating eastern wildernesses on December 16, 1974, and two days later, the full House approved the bill and passed it on to the Senate, which quickly passed it. On January 3, 1975, President Gerald R. Ford signed the bill, which was untitled but has come to be known as the Eastern Wilderness Act (1975). It established fifteen wildernesses immediately, increasing the amount of wilderness in the East by five times, and established seventeen areas to be studied as potential wildernesses.[45] In the White Mountains, the act created the Presidential Range–Dry River Wilderness—an area of 27,380 acres that extended south from Mount Washington to the southeastern section of the Presidential Range and included parts of the Dry River and Rocky Branch. The wilderness was a significant addition in that much of the area had been heavily logged, but under the conditions of the Eastern Wilderness Act, it retained enough of its primitive character to be considered wild.

Even with the passage of the Wilderness Act and the Eastern Wilderness Act, though, foresters inside and outside the Forest Service continued to express concerns as to whether setting aside forests as wilderness was the best policy for either the economic interests of the north country or the long-term ecological health of the forests. Jay H. Craven, who was a regional forester, said, "I am pleased that we helped identify and evolve the . . . System, but I will continue to raise the question of how much do we need and what can we better achieve for the greatest number in the long run through multiple use management."[46] Craven's words went right to the heart of the wilderness debate—how much land set aside as wilderness was enough? In his address on the seventy-fifth anniversary of the Weeks Act, former governor Adams noted that *wildness* with a small *w* had become *Wilderness* with a capital *W*. Adams warned:

> But I trust that most of you will also share my concern that the heavy-handed big "W" wilderness may be overused and abused. Especially in New England, where we have both the tradition of multiple use and the pressure of nearly one-fifth of the nation's population on less than 5 percent of the nation's land mass, we need to make this meager land base accommodate the optimum variety of uses.[47]

Despite such reservations, the Eastern Wilderness Act represented a significant change in federal policy. First, the idea of wilderness was broadened to include areas that, even though they had been previously cut or mined, had regenerated to the point where they had regained much of their primitive character. The broadening of the concept of wilderness also led to the protection of smaller wild areas that were nearer cities. The concept now came closer to Benton MacKaye's original thinking about ideal metropolitan areas, in which cities, farms, and wildernesses would be linked and exist in proximity to one another. MacKaye's vision of wilderness had always seemed well suited to the realities of the East, with its heavy population centers. The term "multiple use" was also being broadened to encompass environmental protection and multiple recreational uses, while excluding the harvesting of timber or minerals.[48]

The next stage in wilderness protection in the White Mountains occurred in 1977, when President Jimmy Carter initiated a new study of the roadless areas in national parks and forests with RARE II, which differed greatly from RARE I by including the public and by including eastern areas. The purpose was to identify roadless areas that could be recommended to Congress for possible protection as wilderness.[49] According to Supervisor Mike Hathaway of the WMNF, RARE II led to the consideration of twenty potential wildernesses in the late 1970s and early 1980s:

> When the New England people sat down and reached consensus, they wanted 77,000 acres of new wilderness added to the existing wilderness. The Wilderness Society wanted more and there were a couple of areas that were omitted. The Wilderness Society appealed the plan over those new areas because they wanted the lumber interests to stay out of those areas.[50]

Yet, like RARE I, RARE II ran into problems. As RARE II identified road-less areas, wilderness opponents used scare tactics to build political opposition to setting aside lands as wilderness. A group in the southern Appalachians filed suit, alleging that through RARE II, the Forest Service was reclaiming the power to designate wilderness from Congress, which had been granted that power by the Wilderness Act.[51] Finally, the Ninth Circuit Court of Appeals in California declared that the Forest Service was carrying out RARE II improperly. With that injunction, the Forest Service did not proceed with forest planning, which brought timber harvesting in national forests to a halt.[52]

Consequently, in the early 1980s, the Forest Service faced heavy pressure to develop a Forest Management Plan that would include wilderness study areas and plans for future logging in the national forests.[53] For the first time, the process included extensive public participation. The AMC, regional chapters of the Sierra Club, and hiking groups such as the Wonalancet Out Door Club brought forward proposals for wilderness study areas in the White Mountains. In the early 1980s, the Forest Service selected three areas for further study in the Whites: the Sandwich Range, the Pemigewasset Valley, and an expansion of the Presidential Range–Dry River Wilderness.

The expansion of the Presidential Range–Dry River Wilderness was perhaps the most obvious choice, because the area being studied for inclusion encompassed some of the most visible landmarks in the Whites—the northern ridge of the Presidentials formed by Mounts Clay, Jefferson, Adams, and Madison. In the Sandwich Range, the Forest Service examined 60,000 acres, bounded on the north by the Kancamagus Highway; on the west by the col between Loon Mountain and Scar Ridge; on the south by Tripoli Road, Waterville Valley, Mad River Road, and the national forest boundary; and on the east by White Ledge, east of Mount Chocorua. Also included were the Greeley Pond Scenic Area and the Bowl Natural Area.[54] The Sandwich Range consisted of uplands that were still relatively remote, with steep ridges and high passes, and it featured six 4,000-foot mountains. What set the range apart was its capacity for diverse wilderness experiences, which ranged from moderate hikes to steep climbs that rewarded trekkers with breathtaking views. In addition, the range could absorb quite a few people, yet because of the area's size and the number of trails, a hiker could usually find solitude.

The Sandwich Range had never been considered before as a wilderness. But in the mid-1970s, George Zink, Ralph Weymouth, and Ted Sidley—all of whom had been involved in the Wonalancet Out Door Club and the maintenance of trails—advocated for the designation of the range as wilderness.[55] They began planning for the wilderness proposal during the development of the Kancamagus and Waterville Valley Unit Plans. The campaign for the

Sandwich Range is a prime example of the role that grassroots support came to play in wilderness protection.

The other study area was the Pemigewasset ("the Pemi"). For the proposed Pemi Wilderness, the Forest Service studied approximately 100,000 acres of land bounded on the north by the lower slopes of Garfield Ridge, North Twin Mountain, and Sugarloaf; on the west by Franconia Notch; on the south by the Kancamagus Highway; and on the east by Zealand Road, Crawford Notch, and Mount Tremont.[56] The area was, at first glance, an unlikely tract to be designated wilderness. It had been logged until the 1940s, and the human footprint was apparent through the remains of logging camps, railroad trestles, old railroad switches, and seventy-two miles of railroad grades. Karl Roenke, a historian and archaeologist for the WMNF, said:

> People tend to discount areas that have these cultural artifacts, but this doesn't mean that an area doesn't have value as wilderness. In the Pemi, there is a blend of the natural and the cultural. Does the presence of these cultural artifacts make a wilderness any less of a wilderness? Even in the large wilderness areas of the West, you can see evidence of human activity. For example, the Selway-Bitterroot Wilderness in Idaho had been a working National Forest for some twenty years. That's why it is important to research and understand the history of a region as we decide what areas should be wilderness.[57]

The Pemi also had some AMC shelters, which led the AMC to initially oppose wilderness designation, but after boundaries were redrawn to exclude the AMC shelters, the organization supported creation of the wilderness.

In the early 1980s, the White Mountain National Advisory Committee, which had been disbanded by the Carter administration, was reactivated as the White Mountain Ad Hoc Advisory Committee to help formulate a final recommendation about the specific size and boundaries of White Mountain wildernesses to propose to Congress. The chair of this committee was Paul Bofinger of the SPNHF, who was a logical choice because the organization had historically been able to work with the Forest Service, environmental groups, and timber interests in affecting forestry policy and the management of the WMNF. The formation of the Ad Hoc Advisory Committee was the start of an intricate political process intended to build a coalition that would present a realistic proposal for wilderness designation that would be acceptable to all interested parties. Bofinger brought the different groups together, including the AMC, the local chapter of the Sierra Club, the SPNHF, timber operators, and snowmobilers.

Bofinger realized that the committee also needed a strong wilderness advocate, which was how George Zink became a member. Zink, a teacher who owned a home on the southern apron of the Whites, had a long-standing interest in wilderness and believed that the Sandwich Range had the potential to be a wilderness.[58] As a longtime member of the Wonalancet Out Door Club—and eventually its president—he also was involved in trail maintenance in the region. He, Ralph Weymouth, and Ted Sidley were active in the Friends of the Sandwich Range (not to be confused with the second-generation Friends of the Sandwich Range that later advocated for the expansion of the Sandwich Range Wilderness). The original Friends of the Sandwich Range had been formed by local residents who belonged to the New England chapter of the Sierra Club. As active members of the Friends, Zink, Weymouth, and Sidley began to advocate for the designation of a Sandwich Range Wilderness. They wrote, printed, and distributed a four-page flyer titled *A Last Chance for Wilderness*. Zink and Weymouth read papers at the New England Trail Conference. Zink spoke to the New Hampshire Snowmobile Association. And all three engaged in innumerable other advocacy efforts.

A few years before, Zink had articulated a rationale for wilderness that was uniquely suited to the needs of the White Mountains and that served as a guidepost in the group's advocacy. In June of 1978, Tom Deans, the executive director of the AMC, had challenged wilderness advocates to articulate positive reasons for creating wildernesses in the WMNF. The challenge led Zink to write an extended explanation of the positive reasons. He began by distinguishing between the uses of nature for commodities and for amenities; commodities are tangible products such as timber and minerals, while, in his words, "Amenities are those values for which market prices cannot be established, but which give meaning to people's lives. Sunsets and sunrises, a moonlit landscape, a view of a distant mountain range, hearing the vireos calling at dusk, the smell of balsam fir boughs, are all classified as amenities."[59] He pointed out that because amenities are not tangible—because we cannot hold them and sell them—they are often overlooked in determining the value of a landscape. Zink then went on to articulate five positive values of wilderness that stemmed from its use as amenities:

1. Its educational value, as seen in the wilderness activities that organizations such as Outward Bound and the National Outdoor Leadership Schools provide for young people.
2. Its value as wildlife habitat for such fauna as the pileated woodpecker, the eastern cougar, the black bear, and the peregrine falcon.
3. Its value as a laboratory for the evolutionary development of organisms in an environment that has had little impact from human civilization and technology. "A most important value of wilderness," Zink wrote, "lies

in the genetic experimentation which takes place there, continuing unbroken the evolutionary processes."

4. Its value as a healthy ecosystem in which can be studied the life processes of flora and fauna. Zink pointed out, by way of example, that the protection of wilderness had permitted the study of grizzly bears and their habitats.

5. Its value for recreation, from backpacking to rock climbing, which had been gaining popularity in the Whites since the 1920s.[60]

Emphasizing the positive aspects of wilderness designation helped move the political process forward. The Ad Hoc Advisory Committee was charged with examining the wilderness study areas in the White Mountains and making specific recommendations that they could take to New Hampshire's congressional delegation, who would then propose the wildernesses in a bill in Congress. Bofinger explained that, in addition to conservation groups and hiking clubs, "The committee worked with lumber industry leaders. The Brown Company was still a big deal. They were tough, but they were also citizens of the state, and they recognized that management of the forests was a political process."[61]

Two people from the New England office of the Sierra Club, Abigail Avery and Wilma Fry, were very active in the campaign.[62] Fry coordinated the identification of proposed wilderness areas, spending a year talking to people in Tamworth and other surrounding communities to find out what their different perspectives on wilderness were. This was an important step because, according to Zink, "There was local resistance in New Hampshire to wilderness because of fears of lost jobs, particularly from the recreational vehicle industry, which is big, and the snowmobiling groups."[63] According to Paul Bofinger, Abigail Avery talked to different people to get their points of view, which helped enormously in formulating a plan that met many different needs.[64]

In the end, according to Bofinger, "[T]hey all got their maps out and decided what the boundaries of the wilderness areas would be."[65] The Ad Hoc Advisory Committee worked out a compromise and decided not to recommend all of the area that had been identified as potential wilderness during RARE II. Instead, the committee recommended 45,000 acres in the Pemi (out of a possible 100,000), 25,000 acres in the Sandwich Range (out of a possible 60,000), and an addition to the Presidential Range–Dry River Wilderness. The Sandwich Range proposal was gerrymandered to exclude a snowmobile trail, a trail to Flat Mountain Pond that accommodated disabled people, and cross-country ski trails operated by Waterville Valley ski resorts.[66] In the classic New England mode, local groups that had an interest in the future of the

White Mountains had talked to one another and forged a compromise that many sides could live with but that still extended protection to substantial areas of the White Mountain wilderness.

However, after the local groups had worked out this compromise, the Wilderness Society and the national Sierra Club considered the proposal to be inadequate because it did not set aside enough wilderness. According to Bofinger, though, Abigail Avery knew what she had been able to get by working out compromises among the lumber companies, the recreational groups, and the wilderness advocates. He said, "The national director of the Sierra Club came to one meeting, and it was an eye-opener for him to see how these groups had worked together."[67] Avery, Bofinger, and others wanted to maintain the coalition in order to protect the level of appropriations for the WMNF and to sell the wilderness proposals to the local town selectmen, the congressional delegation, and the governor.[68]

Consequently, members of the Ad Hoc Advisory Committee traveled to Washington and testified to Congress on behalf of their proposal. Soon after, Congress passed the New Hampshire Wilderness Act of 1984, which created the Pemi Wilderness, the Sandwich Range Wilderness, and the expansion of the Presidential Range–Dry River Wilderness. Two years later, in his address commemorating the seventy-fifth anniversary of the Weeks Act, former governor Adams wrote about the consensus reached in 1984, which, he said, was "nearly torn apart when Washington groups, led by the Wilderness Society, unrelentingly attacked the legislation."[69] The SPNHF and the AMC fought successfully to save the compromise so that the wilderness legislation would pass in Congress. Through the long and difficult campaign, Adams explained, the process of building consensus resembled "the respectful give-and-take of a New England town meeting."[70] The entire process showed dramatically how politically charged the battle to protect wilderness had become. Yet the process did give opportunities for involvement to the people and interests who cared deeply about the future of the White Mountains. The experience demonstrated that the New England tradition of dialogue and compromise could work very effectively.

Of all the new wildernesses, the Pemigewasset—now one of the largest wildernesses east of the Mississippi River—presented perhaps the greatest management challenge to the Forest Service. The Pemi Valley had at one time contained the most extensive system of logging railroads in the White Mountains, but the trees, a mixture of northern hardwoods and spruce-fir, had grown back, and the area had experienced limited erosion. On the other hand, though, signs of human activity, including railroad ties, concrete bridge abutments, piles of scrap metal, and railroad grades, were still visible.[71] Yet, according to the Forest Service's *Pemigewasset Wilderness Plan*, "To the casual observer 99% of the area appears natural."[72] Parts of the area had heavy use in the summer months, and cross-country skiing and winter camping were growing in popularity. Even so, backpackers could still find ample solitude because the trails spread out in different directions and were separated by large tracts of land.[73]

Given the unique characteristics of the Pemi, the WMNF divided it into three zones: primitive/pristine, semiprimitive, and education. The first zone contained less frequently traveled trails and was ideal for bushwhacking, while the second zone was regularly used by backpackers. In both of these zones, the Forest Service developed plans to restore wilderness conditions. The education zone had the greatest use, and it also had unacceptably high rates of improper fecal waste disposal, trampling of the forest undergrowth, and compacting of soil. Consequently, in addition to taking steps to restore wilderness conditions, the Forest Service began to promote wilderness values and outdoor skills. For example, it published a brochure titled *Pemigewasset Wilderness*, which emphasized the importance of leaving no trace when hiking, backpacking, or camping. It also contained guidelines for wilderness behavior, such as carrying out what was carried in, packing food in reusable containers, burying human waste at least two hundred feet from water, and moving quietly through the woods.[74]

With the creation of the Sandwich Range Wilderness and the Pemi Wilderness, the White Mountains now had four wildernesses, but all were in New Hampshire. Maine, with 45,000 acres of national forest, did not yet have any protected wilderness, and in the late 1980s, wilderness advocates in the state began making the case to create the Caribou–Speckled Mountain Wilderness. They proposed 16,000 acres, with Evans Notch as the northern boundary and Speckled Mountain as its highest point. There were public hearings in the area of Bethel, Maine, because passage of the act would eliminate logging. While the public looked favorably on the proposal, the lumber mills opposed it because they wanted to continue logging beech, birch, and maple trees to manufacture rolling pins, clothespins, dowels, and other wood products.[75]

Eventually the interests involved reached a compromise by which the proposed wilderness would contain 12,000 acres located primarily along the ridges of the mountains; only 4,000 of these 12,000 acres contained timber that the lumber mills could have logged efficiently.[76] Maine's legislators took the proposal to Congress, which passed the Maine Wilderness Act in September of 1990. The new wilderness had human-created structures that the Forest Service removed, including a shelter on Mount Caribou and a fire lookout on Speckled Mountain. The Forest Service applied its rules to preserve the primitive characteristics of the area, so that off-road vehicles, including mountain bikes, were banned; people could not set up camps within two hundred feet of trails; and no hiking groups could be larger than ten people.[77]

4000-FOOTER CLUB OF THE WHITE MOUNTAINS
APPALACHIAN MOUNTAIN CLUB

4 0 0 0 A M C

I have climbed to the summits of all the official peaks of the 4000-Footer Club of the White Mountains

Howard S. Poore

General Outings Committee

President

12.4. "4000-Footer Club of the White Mountains" (front of certificate). As the White Mountains gained wilderness protection, the recreational emphasis in the region changed. The AMC sponsored a 4000-Footer Club, blending the perennial attraction of the mountains with a new emphasis on the challenging aspects of climbing. Reproduced with permission of the Appalachian Mountain Club (AMC), the AMC Four Thousand Footer Committee, and the Family of Howard Sumner Poore.

In 2004 and 2005, the Forest Service considered several proposals for more wilderness protection in the Whites, including an expansion of the Sandwich Range by approximately 10,000 acres. There were also several proposals to create a Wild River Wilderness, which would comprise thousands of acres surrounding the beautiful Wild River, located east of Pinkham Notch and west of the Caribou–Speckled River Wilderness. During RARE II, the AMC had advocated for designating the Wild River region as wilderness, but at the time, the Forest Service had not proposed it. But after the creation of the Caribou–Speckled Mountain Wilderness, attention focused once again on the Wild River for a number of reasons.

According to Dan Yetter, an active member of the Friends of the Wild River, which worked hard for the creation of the new wilderness, "What makes Wild River unique is that it is a watershed. It's a lowland bowl the size of Boston, surrounded by magnificent mountains."[78] The forest around Wild River had been heavily logged, and although there is a road on the east side of the river, no road runs through the entire area. The Friends of the Wild River wanted to prevent further road building, and designating the area as a wilderness was the only way. According to Dan Yetter, "There were volunteers on the ground who suggested boundaries, drew maps, and surveyed trails for evidence of wildlife. We had resources and help from the Wilderness Society, Eastern Mountain Sports, Recreational Equipment International (REI), and the AMC. We also worked with the Friends of the Sandwich Range, a second generation of volunteers working to expand the existing Sandwich Range Wilderness."[79] Proponents also thought that this wilderness designation would economically benefit the northern reaches of the White Mountains because the word *wilderness* has become such a draw for outdoor enthusiasts and for those relocating to areas that promise an enhanced quality of life.

In 2004, the Forest Service presented four proposals and invited public comment. Alternative 2, which added 10,000 acres to the Sandwich Range Wilderness and set aside 23,700 acres to create a new Wild River Wilderness, received the support of the Friends of the Wild River, the Friends of the Sandwich Range, the SPNHF, and other environmental groups in New Hampshire. In late 2005, the WMNF released its Forest Plan, which recommended the addition of approximately 10,500 acres to the Sandwich Range Wilderness and the creation of the Wild River Wilderness, encompassing approximately 24,000 acres.

As of this writing, the White Mountain National Forest has grown to a size of nearly 800,000 acres in New Hampshire and Maine, with 112,000 acres of protected wilderness. If Congress approves the addition of the Wild River Wilderness and the expansion of the Sandwich Range Wilderness, the WMNF will have a total of 145,000 acres of wilderness, comprising nearly 20 percent of the total national forest. When we look back at the history of the White Mountains, the existence of this amount of protected wilderness is nothing short of miraculous. The Whites have been the central character in a four-centuries-long drama that has seen the gradual evolution of attitudes toward wilderness—attitudes that greatly affected actions and policies. In these four centuries, the Whites have made unique contributions to evolving ideas about wilderness that are central to the environmental history of the United States:

- White Mountain artists and writers of the Romantic period in the early nineteenth century played a pivotal role in redeeming the concept of wilderness from the negative attitudes of the Puritans and the strictly utilitarian attitudes of the first settlers. They did so by celebrating the wild beauty of the mountains, but also by making metaphorical uses of the mountains that forged an emotional bond between the region and the people who came to love it.
- Pioneers like the Crawfords and other early guides were the prototypes of wilderness explorers as they climbed mountains, cut trails, built shelters, ventured into unknown regions, and welcomed the challenge and danger that would forever be a part of the wilderness experience.
- Through the early development of hiking clubs and hiking as a recreational activity, outdoor lovers began to turn in large numbers to the exploration of wild nature. White Mountain hiking clubs played an immensely important role by making those experiences widely accessible and by inspiring a conservation ethic in its members.
- Through the passage of the Weeks Act and other pioneering legislation, the idea began to gain acceptance that through collective effort, people can take action to protect the nation's most precious natural resources before they are lost forever.
- Finally, the creation of protected wildernesses in the White Mountains has fulfilled the vision of Benton MacKaye's for humane regional planning—that wilderness can and ought to exist in close proximity to large urban areas. Wilderness does not belong only in the vast spaces of the West or Alaska but has an important place in the East.

Yet in spite of all these positive developments, challenges remain. Attacks on wilderness have reached a crescendo, especially in the West and in Alaska. Even within the environmental movement, there is a continued questioning of the meaning and uses of wilderness. In 1995, environmental historian William Cronon sent out a challenge to the wilderness movement in the form of an essay titled "The Trouble with Wilderness, or Getting Back to the Wrong Nature." The essay made a number of provocative points: That wilderness is a cultural invention that is at times "unnatural." That wilderness advocates have tended to laud the ideal of the primitive at the expense of civilization and human accomplishment. That nostalgia for the frontier, which the concept of wilderness may help to reinforce, reflects an "ambivalence, if not downright hostility, toward modernity."[80] That wilderness advocates are perhaps a little too enamored of rugged individualism and the Theodore Roosevelt model of masculinity. That wilderness represents a way for the nation's wealthiest citizens to escape from the realities of urban America. That the perception of wilderness as virgin land ignores the history and culture of Native Americans, who created a civilization on that land. That wilderness tends to make us think that "nature, to be natural, must be pristine."[81] That the attractions of wilderness tend to make people denigrate rural landscapes and lifeways. That the idealization of wilderness can lead people to ignore the small traces of wilderness that are immediately around them.

These are all fair warnings, yet the history of the White Mountain wilderness demonstrates a steady amelioration of the tendencies that Professor Cronon is appropriately warning us about. The land that we refer to as "wilderness" in the White Mountains has long had a human footprint—for eleven thousand years, the footprint of the Paleo-Indians and later the Abenaki people, the footprint of the first settlers who built rustic inns in Crawford Notch, the footprint of the AMC when it built shelters at the highest elevations to make the mountains safer and more accessible to those who yearned to absorb their beauties.

Ever since the Romantic artists and writers began to celebrate scenes of wild nature in the nineteenth century, the struggle in the White Mountains has been to achieve a balance between wilderness and civilization, between an instrumental view of the land and a view of the land as inherently valuable. Even now, when we hike through the Pemi Wilderness and see traces of human history—a railroad tie, perhaps, or the remains of a bridge—we are reminded of this struggle and of the human impact on the environment. Yet at the same time, we are seeing faith-restoring evidence that environments harmed in the past can be restored to a condition in which wild nature once again reigns supreme in all its beauty and magnificence. It is this realization that is perhaps the greatest contribution made to America's environmental history by the people who have loved the White Mountains and have fought to preserve their legendary beauty, their ecological integrity, and their redeeming wildness.

Notes

Introduction (pp. 1–6)

1. Lucy Crawford, *Lucy Crawford's History of the White Mountains*, ed. Stearns Morse (Boston: Appalachian Mountain Club Books, 1978), 6.
2. Henry David Thoreau, "Walking," in *Walden and Other Writings of Henry David Thoreau*, ed. Brooks Atkinson, 613–616 (New York: Modern Library, 1950).
3. Max Oelschlaeger, *The Idea of Wilderness* (New Haven: Yale University Press, 1991), 105.
4. Gene Daniell and Jon Burroughs, comp. and ed., *White Mountain Wilderness Guide, Twenty-sixth Edition* (Boston: Appalachian Mountain Club Books, 1998), xx.

Chapter 1. Abenaki Homeland, European Wilderness, and Early Exploration (pp. 9–31)

1. Giovanni Verrazzano, qtd. in Frederick Kilbourne, *Chronicles of the White Mountains* (Boston: Houghton Mifflin Company, 1916), 17.
2. Neal Salisbury, *Manitou and Providence: Indians, Europeans, and the Making of New England, 1500–1643* (New York: Oxford University Press, 1982), 10.
3. Colin G. Calloway, *Dawnland Encounters: Indians and Europeans in Northern New England* (Hanover, New Hampshire: University Press of New England, 2003), 3.
4. Joseph Bruchac, *Bowman's Store: A Journey to Myself* (New York: Dial, 1997), 184.
5. A. Irving Hallowell, "Ojibwa Ontology, Behavior, and World View," in *Culture in History: Essays in Honor of Paul Radin*, ed. Stanley Diamond (New York: Columbia University Press, 1960), 42–43.
6. David Stewart-Smith, "The Pennacook Indians and the New England Frontier, circa 1604–1733" (PhD diss., The Union Institute, 1998), 17.
7. Ibid., 4.
8. Gary W. Hume, "Joseph Laurent's Intervale Camp: Post-Colonial Abenaki Adaptation and Revitalization in New Hampshire," in *Algonkians of New England: Past and Present*, ed. Peter Benes (Boston: Boston University Scholarly Publications, 1991), 110.
9. Bruchac, *Bowman's Store*, 41.
10. Stewart-Smith, "The Pennacook Indians," x and 26.
11. Ibid., 16–17.
12. Joseph Bruchac, *Lasting Echoes: An Oral History of Native American People* (New York: Avon, 1997), 2.
13. Salisbury, *Manitou and Providence*, 33.
14. Gordon M. Day, "The Indian as an Ecological Factor in the Northeastern Forest," in *In Search of New England's Native Past: Selected Essays by Gordon M. Day*, ed. Michael K. Foster and William Cowan (Amherst: University of Massachusetts Press, 1998), 36.
15. Ibid., 42.

16. William Wood, *New England's Prospect,* edited with an introduction by Alden T. Vaughan (Amherst: University of Massachusetts Press, 1977), 90.

17. Colin G. Calloway, *The Abenaki* (New York: Chelsea House, 1989), 22–23.

18. Charles Edward Beals, Jr. [William James Sidis], *Passaconaway in the White Mountains* (Boston: Richard G. Badger, 1916), 23.

19. Wood, *New England's Prospect,* 100–101.

20. Joseph Bruchac, "Native Cultures and the Formation of the North American Environmental Ethic," *From Perspectives to New Realities* (http://www.fs.fed.us./eco/eco-watch/ ew920123), 1 of 6.

21. John Cotton, qtd. in Alan Heimart, "Puritanism, the Wilderness, and the Frontier," *New England Quarterly* 26 (1953): 361.

22. John Winthrop, qtd. in Heimart, "Puritanism, the Wilderness, and the Frontier," 361.

23. John Winthrop, "A Modell of Christian Charity," in *American Sermons: The Pilgrims to Martin Luther King Jr.,* ed. Michael Warner (New York: Library of America, 1999), 42.

24. Roderick Nash, *Wilderness and the American Mind* (New Haven: Yale University Press, 1982), 35.

25. Heimart, "Puritanism, the Wilderness, and the Frontier," 362.

26. Peter Carroll, *Puritanism and the Wilderness: The Intellectual Significance of the New England Frontier, 1629–1700* (New York: Columbia University Press), 11.

27. William Bradford, *Of Plymouth Plantation, 1620–1647* (New York: Modern Library, 1981), 227.

28. Edward Johnson, *Wonder-Working Providence of Sion's Savior in New England, 1628–1651* (New York: Scribner, 1910), 51.

29. Ibid., 71–72.

30. Ibid., 234.

31. Sir Ferdinando Gorges, *A Brief Narration of the Original Undertakings of the Advancement of Plantations into the Parts of America,* in *Sir Ferdinando Gorges and His Province of Maine,* ed. James Phinney Baxter (Boston: The Prince Society, 1890), 19:8.

32. Ibid., 19:9.

33. Elizabeth Forbes Morison and Elting E. Morison, *New Hampshire: A Bicentennial History* (New York: Norton, 1976), 8–9.

34. Jere R. Daniell, *Colonial New Hampshire: A History* (Millwood, New York: KTO Press, 1981), 21.

35. John Ward Dean, "Memoir of Capt. John Mason," in *Capt. John Mason: The Founder of New Hampshire,* ed. John Ward Dean (Boston: The Prince Society, 1887), 17:11.

36. Sir Ferdinando Gorges, *A Brief Relation of the Discovery and Plantation of New England,* in *Sir Ferdinando Gorges and His Province of Maine,* ed. James Phinney Baxter (Boston: The Prince Society, 1890), 18:226–227.

37. Ibid., 18:229.

38. Ibid., 18:230.

39. Ibid., 18:231.

40. Daniell, *Colonial New Hampshire,* 26.

41. Dean, "Memoir of Capt. John Mason," 21.

42. Daniell, *Colonial New Hampshire,* 24.

43. Christopher Levett, *A Voyage into New England, Begun in 1632 and Ended in 1624*, in *Maine in the Age of Discovery: Christopher Levett's Voyage, 1623–1624, and a Guide to Sources* (Portland: Maine Historical Society, 1988), 42.

44. Daniell, *Colonial New Hampshire*, 24.

45. John Ward Dean, "Mason's Plantations on the Pascataqua," in *Capt. John Mason: The Founder of New Hampshire*, ed. John Ward Dean (Boston: The Prince Society, 1887), 17:56–57.

46. Daniell, *Colonial New Hampshire*, 27.

47. Ibid.

48. Dean, "Mason's Plantations on the Pascataqua," 17:70.

49. Daniell, *Colonial New Hampshire*, 29.

50. Ibid., 36–38.

51. John Winthrop, *The History of New England from 1630 to 1649*, 3 vols. (Boston: Phelps and Farnham, 1825–1826), 2:67.

52. Frederick Tuckerman, "Early Visits to the White Mountains and Ascents of the Great Range," *Appalachia* 15, no. 2 (1921): 117.

53. Charles E. Fay, "The March of Captain Samuel Willard," *Appalachia* 2, no. 4 (December 1881): 336.

54. Tuckerman, "Early Visits to the White Mountains," 119.

55. Henry R. Andrews, Jr., "The Royal Pines of New Hampshire," *Appalachia* 27, no. 2 (1948), 188.

56. Beals, *Passaconaway in the White Mountains*, 207.

57. Andrews, "The Royal Pines of New Hampshire," 196–197.

58. John H. Spaulding, *Historical Relics of the White Mountains* (1862; repr., Littleton, N.H.: Bondcliff Books, 1998), 33–35.

59. Frederick W. Kilbourne, *Chronicles of the White Mountains* (Boston: Houghton Mifflin, 1916), 26.

60. Russell M. Lawson, *Passaconaway's Realm: Captain John Evans and the Exploration of Mount Washington* (Hanover, New Hampshire: University Press of New England, 2002), 50.

61. William Parker Cutler and Julie Perkins Cutler, *Life, Journals, and Correspondence of Rev. Manasseh Cutler, LL.D.* 2 vols. (Cincinnati: Robert Clarke, 1888), 1:97.

62. Jeremy Belknap, *Journal of a Tour to the White Mountains in July 1784* (Boston: Massachusetts Historical Society, 1876), 9.

63. Cutler and Cutler, *Life, Journals, and Correspondence*, 1:102.

64. Belknap, *Journal of a Tour*, 9.

65. Cutler and Cutler, *Life, Journals, and Correspondence*, 1:103.

66. Ibid.

67. Ibid., 1:103–104.

68. Ibid., 1:105.

69. Laura Waterman and Guy Waterman, "Reverends, Soldiers, Scientists: The Belknap-Cutler Ascent of Mount Washington, 1784," *Appalachia* 45, no. 1 (Summer 1984): 46.

70. Cutler and Cutler, *Life, Journals, and Correspondence*, 1:104–105.

71. Ibid., 1:107.

72. Ibid., 1:108–109.

73. Ibid., 1:109.

74. Jeremy Belknap, *The History of New Hampshire*, 3 vols. (Dover, New Hampshire: O. Crosby and J. Varney, 1812), 3:39.

75. Belknap, *Journal of a Tour*, 15.

76. Belknap, *History of New Hampshire*, 3:40.

77. Ibid., 3:39.

Chapter 2. First Settlers and the Taming of the Wilderness (pp. 32–46)

1. Simeon Bolles, *The Early History of the Town of Bethlehem, New Hampshire* (Woodsville, New Hampshire: Enterprise Printing House, 1883), 9–13.

2. William Cronon, *Changes in the Land: Indians, Colonists, and the Ecology of New England* (New York: Hill and Wang, 1983), 35.

3. Albert Boyden, *Stevenson House, Tamworth, New Hampshire: Tradition, History, and Random Reminiscence* (Tamworth, New Hampshire: privately printed, 1946), 8.

4. Bolles, *The Early History of the Town of Bethlehem*, 7–8.

5. Timothy Dwight, *Travels in New-England and New-York*, 4 vols. (London: William Baynes and Son, 1823), 2:128.

6. Ibid., 2:129.

7. Bolles, *The Early History of the Town of Bethlehem*, 18.

8. Ibid., 19.

9. Cronon, *Changes in the Land*, 35.

10. Ibid., 53.

11. George N. Cross, *Randolph Old and New: Its Ways and Its By-Ways* (Boston: Pinkham Press, 1924), 16.

12. Cronon, *Changes in the Land*, 74.

13. Cross, *Randolph Old and New*, 17.

14. George N. Cross, "Randolph Yesterdays," *Appalachia* 14, no. 1 (1916–1917): 49.

15. William Little, *History of the Town of Warren, N.H. from Its Early Settlement to the Year 1854* (Concord, New Hampshire: McFarland & Jenks, 1854), 62.

16. Cross, *Randolph Old and New*, 23.

17. Little, *History of the Town of Warren*, 9.

18. Frederick B. Lehr, *Carroll, New Hampshire: The First Two Hundred Years, 1772–1972* (Littleton, New Hampshire: Courier Printing Company, 1972), 16.

19. Cronon, *Changes in the Land*, 115.

20. Ibid., 127.

21. Cross, *Randolph Old and New*, 22.

22. Cronon, *Changes in the Land*, 139.

23. Ibid., 139.

24. Ibid., 128.

25. Ibid., 146.

26. Ibid., 147.

27. Ibid., 148.

28. Ibid., 150.

29. Little, *History of the Town of Warren*, 153.

30. Cronon, *Changes in the Land*, 138.

31. Little, *History of the Town of Warren*, 42.

32. Cronon, *Changes in the Land*, 112.

33. Lehr, *Carroll, New Hampshire*, 58.

34. Cronon, *Changes in the Land*, 117–118.

35. Dwight, *Travels in New-England and New-York*, 2:97.

36. Cronon, *Changes in the Land*, 122.

37. Little, *History of the Town of Warren*, 48.

38. Sarah N. Welch, *History of Franconia, New Hampshire* (Littleton, New Hampshire: Courier Printing Company, 1972), 37.

39. Ibid., 38–39.

40. Ibid., 52.

41. Ibid., 38–39.

42. Ibid., 52.

43. Peter L. Hoyt, *Hoyt's History of Wentworth, New Hampshire, from the First Settlement of the Town to the Year 1870*, transcribed by Francis A. Muzzey (Littleton, New Hampshire: Courier Printing Company, 1976), 108.

44. Ibid.

45. Little, *History of the Town of Warren*, 62.

46. Ibid., 63.

47. Ibid., 63–65.

48. Cronon, *Changes in the Land*, 132.

49. Boyden, *Stevenson House*, 8–9.

50. Cross "Randolph Yesterdays," 51.

51. Little, *History of the Town of Warren*, 81.

52. Dwight, *Travels in New-England and New-York*, 2:129.

Chapter 3. Ethan Allen Crawford and the Wilderness Experience (pp. 49–64)

1. Lucy Crawford, *Lucy Crawford's History of the White Mountains*, ed. Stearns Morse (Boston: Appalachian Mountain Club, 1978), 9.

2. Ibid., 13.

3. Frederick W. Kilbourne, *Chronicles of the White Mountains* (Boston: Houghton Mifflin, 1916), 75.

4. Timothy Dwight, *Travels in New-England and New-York*, 4 vols. (London: William Baynes and Son, 1823), 2:145.

5. Kilbourne, *Chronicles of the White Mountains*, 72.

6. Crawford, *Lucy Crawford's History*, 22.

7. Frances Ann Johnson, *Crawford Notch: Southwestern Approach to the White Mountains of New Hampshire* (copyrighted 1965 by the author), 19.

8. Crawford, *Lucy Crawford's History*, 26.

9. Johnson, *Crawford Notch*, 31.

10. Ibid., 21.

11. Crawford, *Lucy Crawford's History,* 30.

12. Ibid., 39–40.

13. Ibid., 41.

14. Ibid.

15. Ibid., 5.

16. Kilbourne, *Chronicles of the White Mountains,* 78.

17. Crawford, *Lucy Crawford's History,* 45.

18. Kilbourne, *Chronicles of the White Mountains,* 79.

19. Crawford, *Lucy Crawford's History,* 50.

20. Ibid., 51.

21. Ibid., 65–66.

22. Ibid., 86.

23. Ibid., 88–89.

24. Ibid., 91.

25. Ibid., 93.

26. Ibid., 94.

27. Ibid., 98–100.

28. Johnson, *Crawford Notch,* 7; Frederick B. Lehr, *Carroll, New Hampshire: The First Two Hundred Years, 1772–1972* (Littleton, New Hampshire: Courier Printing Company, 1972), 18–19.

29. Crawford, *Lucy Crawford's History,* 123.

30. Ibid., 127.

31. Ibid., 150–154.

32. Kilbourne, *Chronicles of the White Mountains,* 163–164.

33. Crawford, *Lucy Crawford's History,* 165.

34. Ibid., 181.

35. Ibid., 223.

36. Ibid., 195.

Chapter 4. The Artist Who Redeemed the Wilderness (pp. 65–85)

1. Thomas Cole, "Essay on American Scenery, 1835," in *American Art, 1700–1960: Sources and Documents,* ed. John W. McCoubrey (Englewood Cliffs, New Jersey: Prentice Hall, 1965), 103.

2. Thomas Cole, qtd. in Louis Legrand Noble, *The Life and Works of Thomas Cole* (Hensonville, New York: Black Dome Press, 1997), 65.

3. Ibid.

4. Cole, "Essay on American Scenery, 1835," 102.

5. Ibid.

6. Robert L. McGrath, "The Real and the Ideal: Popular Images of the White Mountains," in *The White Mountains: Place and Perceptions,* curated by Donald D. Keyes (Hanover, New Hampshire: University Press of New England, 1980), 59.

7. Ibid.

8. John Farmer and Jacob B. Moore, *Gazetteer of the State of New Hampshire* (Concord, New Hampshire: Jacob B. Moore, 1823), 12.

9. Edmund Burke, *A Philosophical Enquiry into the Origin of Our Ideas of the Sublime and the Beautiful,* ed. David Womersley (New York: Penguin, 1998), 86.

10. Donald D. Keyes, "Perceptions of the White Mountains: A General Survey," in *The White Mountains: Place and Perceptions,* curated by Donald D. Keyes (Hanover, New Hampshire: University Press of New England, 1980), 41.

11. Burke, *A Philosophical Enquiry,* 128.

12. Ibid., 151.

13. Roderick Nash, *Wilderness and the American Mind* (New Haven: Yale University Press), 30–31.

14. Earl A. Powell, *Thomas Cole* (New York: Abrams, 2000), 20.

15. Ibid., 22.

16. Ibid., 23.

17. Noble, *The Life and Works of Thomas Cole,* 4.

18. Ibid., 8.

19. Ibid., 28.

20. Ibid., 35.

21. Ibid., 36.

22. Thomas Cole, qtd. in Marcia Clark, "A Visionary Artist Who Celebrated Wilds of America," *Smithsonian* (September 1975): 95.

23. Cole, "Essay on American Scenery, 1835," 103.

24. Keyes, "Perceptions of the White Mountains," 42.

25. James F. Cooper, *Knights of the Brush: The Hudson River School and the Moral Landscape* (New York: Hudson Hills Press, 1999), 38.

26. Cole, "Essay on American Scenery, 1835," 102.

27. Cooper, *Knights of the Brush,* 38.

28. Robert L. McGrath, *Gods in Granite: The Art of the White Mountains of New Hampshire* (Syracuse, New York: Syracuse University Press, 2001), 62.

29. Ibid., 63.

30. Elwood C. Parry III, *The Art of Thomas Cole: Ambition and Imagination* (Newark: University of Delaware Press, 1988), 70.

31. Ibid.

32. Cole, "Essay on American Scenery, 1835," 98.

33. Ibid., 99.

34. Parry, *The Art of Thomas Cole,* 58–59.

35. Thomas Cole, qtd. in Clark, "A Visionary Artist," 92.

36. McGrath, "The Real and the Ideal," 60.

37. Ibid.

38. Thomas Cole, qtd. in Parry, *The Art of Thomas Cole,* 86.

39. McGrath, *Gods in Granite,* 37.

40. Parry, *The Art of Thomas Cole,* 65.

41. James Fenimore Cooper, *The Last of the Mohicans* (New York: Dodd, Mead, 1951), 301.

42. Parry, *The Art of Thomas Cole,* 64–65.

43. Keyes, "Perceptions of the White Mountains," 42.

44. Cole, "Essay on American Scenery, 1835," 102.

45. Ibid., 100.

Chapter 5. Writers and the Search for Meaning in Wilderness (pp. 86–106)

1. Frederick W. Kilbourne, *Chronicles of the White Mountains* (Boston: Houghton Mifflin, 1916), 11–12.

2. Lydia Maria Childs, qtd. in Kilbourne, *Chronicles of the White Mountains,* 12.

3. Benjamin Willey, *Incidents in White Mountain History* (Boston: Nathaniel Noyes, 1856), 30–31.

4. Kilbourne, *Chronicles of the White Mountains,* 101.

5. Willey, *Incidents in White Mountain History,* 37.

6. Kilbourne, *Chronicles of the White Mountains,* 231.

7. John H. Spaulding, *Historical Relics of the White Mountains* (Littleton, New Hampshire: Bondcliff Books, 1998), 17.

8. Ibid., 38.

9. Ibid., 39.

10. Kilbourne, *Chronicles of the White Mountains,* 115.

11. Nathaniel Hawthorne, "The Ambitious Guest," in *The Complete Novels and Selected Tales of Nathaniel Hawthorne,* ed. Norman Holmes Pearson (New York: Modern Library, 1937), 990.

12. Ibid., 991–992.

13. Ibid., 994.

14. Ibid., 995.

15. Ibid., 991.

16. Nathaniel Hawthorne, "The Great Carbuncle: A Mystery of the White Mountains," in *The Complete Novels and Selected Tales of Nathaniel Hawthorne,* ed. Norman Holmes Pearson (New York: Modern Library, 1937), 927.

17. Ibid., 928.

18. Ibid., 932–933.

19. Ibid., 934–935.

20. Ibid.

21. Nathaniel Hawthorne, "The Great Stone Face," in *The Complete Novels and Selected Tales of Nathaniel Hawthorne,* ed. Norman Holmes Pearson (New York: Modern Library, 1937), 1171.

22. Ibid., 1177–1178.

23. Hawthorne, "The Ambitious Guest," 990.

24. Hawthorne, "The Great Carbuncle," 927.

25. Hawthorne, "The Great Stone Face," 1171.

26. Georgia D. Merrill, comp., *History of Coos County, New Hampshire* (Syracuse, New York: W. A. Fergusson, 1888), 424.

27. Kilbourne, *Chronicles of the White Mountains,* 129–130.

28. Thomas Starr King, *The White Hills: Their Legends, Landscape, and Poetry* (Boston: Crosby, Nichols, 1860), 352.

29. Ibid., 354–356.

30. Ibid., 360.

31. Ibid., 365.

32. Ibid., 366.

33. Ibid., 368–369.

34. Ibid., 100.

35. Edward Wagenknecht, *John Greenleaf Whittier: A Portrait in Paradox* (New York: Oxford University Press, 1967), 3–4.

36. Ibid., 7.

37. Ibid., 126.

38. John Greenleaf Whittier, "Franconia from the Pemigewasset," in *The Poetical Works of Whittier,* ed. Hyatt H. Waggoner (Boston: Houghton Mifflin, 1975), 156.

39. John Greenleaf Whittier, "The Last Walk in Autumn," in *The Poetical Works of Whittier,* ed. Hyatt H. Waggoner (Boston: Houghton Mifflin, 1975), 150.

40. John Greenleaf Whittier, "Summer by the Lakeside," in *The Poetical Works of Whittier,* ed. Hyatt H. Waggoner (Boston: Houghton Mifflin, 1975), 147.

41. Shirley Marchalonis, *The Worlds of Lucy Larcom, 1824–1893* (Athens: University of Georgia Press, 1989), 14.

42. Ibid., 77.

43. Lucy Larcom, qtd. in Marchalonis, *The Worlds of Lucy Larcom,* 127.

44. Lucy Larcom, "Clouds on White Face," in *The Poetical Works of Lucy Larcom* (Boston: Houghton Mifflin, 1884), 19.

45. Larcom, "In a Cloud Rift," in *The Poetical Works of Lucy Larcom* (Boston: Houghton Mifflin, 1884), 243.

46. Larcom, "The Summit-Flower," in *The Poetical Works of Lucy Larcom* (Boston: Houghton Mifflin, 1884), 301.

47. King, *The White Hills,* 28.

48. Ibid., 175.

49. Ibid.

Chapter 6. White Mountain Art and the Domestication of Wilderness (pp. 107–125)

1. S. D. Thompson, qtd. in Donald D. Keyes, "Perceptions of the White Mountains: A General Survey," in *The White Mountains: Place and Perceptions,* curated by Donald D. Keyes (Hanover, New Hampshire: University Press of New England, 1980), 44.

2. Donald D. Keyes, "Perceptions of the White Mountains: A General Survey," in *The White Mountains: Place and Perceptions,* curated by Donald D. Keyes (Hanover, New Hampshire: University Press of New England, 1980), 41.

3. Ibid., 43.

4. Ibid.

5. Uvedale Price, *An Essay on the Picturesque* (London: J. Robson, 1794), 39.

6. Keyes, "Perceptions of the White Mountains," 43.

7. Price, *An Essay on the Picturesque*, 44–45.

8. Ibid., 80.

9. Ibid.

10. Keyes, "Perceptions of the White Mountains," 43.

11. Asher B. Durand, qtd. in David B. Lawall, *Asher Brown Durand: His Art and Art Theory in Relation to His Times* (New York: Garland, 1977), 2–3.

12. Lawall, *Asher Brown Durand*, 51–52.

13. Ibid., 106.

14. Daniel Huntington, *Asher B. Durand: A Memorial Address* (New York: The Century, 1887), 46.

15. Asher B. Durand, qtd. in Lawall, *Asher Brown Durand*, 206.

16. Keyes, "Perceptions of the White Mountains," 48.

17. Robert L. McGrath, *Gods in Granite: The Art of the White Mountains of New Hampshire* (Syracuse, New York: Syracuse University Press, 2001), 151.

18. Ibid., 46.

19. Ibid., 45.

20. Keyes, "Perceptions of the White Mountains," 48–49.

21. Simon Schama, *Landscape and Memory* (New York: Vintage Books, 1996), 197.

22. Asher B. Durand, qtd. in Lawall, *Asher Brown Durand*, 51–52.

23. Asher B. Durand, qtd. in Lawall, *Asher Brown Durand*, 84.

24. McGrath, *Gods in Granite*, 117.

25. Keyes, "Perceptions of the White Mountains," 43.

26. Benjamin Champney, *Sixty Years' Memories of Art and Artists* (Woburn, Massachusetts: The News Print, 1900), 1.

27. Ibid., 6.

28. Benjamin Champney, qtd. in Charles O. Vogel, "'Wanderings after the Wild and Beautiful': The Life and Career of Benjamin Champney," in *Beauty Caught and Kept: Benjamin Champney in the White Mountains,* special issue, *Historical New Hampshire* 51, nos. 3–4 (1996): 78.

29. Vogel, "'Wanderings after the Wild and Beautiful,'" 78.

30. Champney, *Sixty Years' Memories of Art and Artists*, 102–103.

31. Vogel, "'Wanderings after the Wild and Beautiful,'" 78.

32. Champney, *Sixty Years' Memories of Art and Artists*, 104–105.

33. Vogel, "'Wanderings after the Wild and Beautiful,'" 81.

34. *North Conway Idler,* qtd. in Vogel, "'Wanderings after the Wild and Beautiful,'" 86.

35. Donald D. Keyes, "The Great Gallery of Nature: Benjamin Champney in the Development of White Mountain Art," in *Beauty Caught and Kept: Benjamin Champney in the White Mountains,* special issue, *Historical New Hampshire* 51, nos. 3–4 (1996): 96.

36. Hillary Anderson and Donna-Belle Garvin, "Catalogue of Paintings Exhibited, 'Beauty Caught and Kept': Benjamin Champney in the White Mountains," in *Beauty Caught and Kept: Benjamin Champney in the White Mountains,* special issue, *Historical New Hampshire* 51, nos. 3–4 (1996): 111.

37. Milton Brown et al., *American Art* (Englewood Cliffs, New Jersey: Prentice Hall, 1985), 199.

38. Catherine H. Campbell, "Catalogue of the Exhibition," in *The White Mountains: Place and Perceptions,* curated by Donald D. Keyes (Hanover, New Hampshire: University Press of New England), 88.

39. McGrath, *Gods in Granite,* 128.

40. Campbell, "Catalogue of the Exhibition," 110.

41. Keyes, "Perceptions of the White Mountains," 43.

42. Campbell, "Catalogue of the Exhibition," 90.

43. McGrath, *Gods in Granite,* 125.

44. James F. Cooper, *Knights of the Brush: The Hudson River School and the Moral Landscape* (New York: Hudson Hills Press, 1999), 38.

Chapter 7. The Resort Hotels: Luxury at the Edge of Wilderness (pp. 126–146)

1. Moses F. Sweetser, *The White Mountains: A Handbook for Travellers* (Boston: James R. Osgood and Company, 1881), 34.

2. Henry F. Burt, *Burt's Guide Through the Connecticut Valley to the White Mountains and the River Saguenay* (Springfield, Massachusetts: New England Publishing Company, 1874), 229.

3. Moses F. Sweetser, *Chisholm's White Mountain Guide Book* (Portland, Maine: Chisholm Brothers, 1898), 16.

4. Ibid., 18.

5. Edson D. Eastman, *The White Mountain Guide Book* (Boston: Lee & Shepard, 1879), 127–128.

6. Sweetser, *The White Mountains,* 34.

7. Frederick W. Kilbourne, *Chronicles of the White Mountains* (Boston: Houghton Mifflin, 1916), 333.

8. Ibid., 221–223.

9. Bryant F. Tolles, Jr., *The Grand Resort Hotels of the White Mountains: A Vanishing Architectural Legacy* (Boston: Godine, 1998), 30.

10. *Tripp's White Mountain Guide Book, or Guide to the Mountain and Lake Scenery of New-Hampshire* (Boston: Redding; New York: E. H. Tripp, 1882), 97.

11. Tolles, *The Grand Resort Hotels,* 110–111.

12. Sweetser, *Chisholm's White Mountain Guide Book,* 48.

13. Kilbourne, *Chronicles of the White Mountains,* 336.

14. *Tripp's White Mountain Guide Book,* 100.

15. Tolles, *The Grand Resort Hotels,* 35.

16. Sweetser, *Chisholm's White Mountain Guide Book,* 42.

17. Ibid.

18. Burt, *Burt's Guide,* 247.

19. *Tripp's White Mountain Guide Book,* 99.

20. Sweetser, *Chisholm's White Mountain Guide Book,* 45.

21. *Tripp's White Mountain Guide Book,* 108.

22. Kilbourne, *Chronicles of the White Mountains,* 167–168.

23. *Tripp's White Mountain Guide Book,* 108.

24. Burt, *Burt's Guide*, 232.

25. Sweetser, *Chisholm's White Mountain Guide Book*, 78.

26. Burt, *Burt's Guide*, 242.

27. Tolles, *The Grand Resort Hotels*, 51.

28. Kilbourne, *Chronicles of the White Mountains*, 171.

29. F. Allen Burt, *The Story of Mount Washington* (Hanover, New Hampshire: Dartmouth Publications, 1960), 266–267.

30. Kilbourne, *Chronicles of the White Mountains*, 339–340.

31. Ibid., 238–239.

32. Tolles, *The Grand Resort Hotels*, 60–61.

33. Ibid., 115.

34. Ibid., 116.

35. Ibid., 80.

36. Gary W. Hume, "Joseph Laurent's Intervale Camp: Post-Colonial Abenaki Adaptation and Revitalization in New Hampshire," in *Algonkians of New England: Past and Present*, ed. Peter Benes (Boston: Boston University Scholarly Publications, 1991), 103–105.

37. Ibid., 106.

38. Stephen Laurent, qtd. in Hume, "Joseph Laurent's Intervale Camp," 110.

39. Ibid.

40. Kilbourne, *Chronicles of the White Mountains*, 332.

41. Sweetser, *Chisholm's White Mountain Guide Book*, 47.

42. Tolles, *The Grand Resort Hotels*, 214.

43. Ibid., 216.

44. *The White Mountains of New Hampshire: In the Heart of the Nation's Playground* (Boston: General Passenger Department, Boston & Maine Railroad, 1910), 19.

45. *New England Vacation Resorts: A List of Hotels and Boarding Houses Located on the Boston & Maine Railroad* (Boston: General Passenger Department, Boston & Maine Railroad, 1907), 62.

46. *The White Mountains of New Hampshire: In the Heart of the Nation's Playground*, 19.

47. Ibid., 26–27.

48. Ibid., 27.

49. Ibid., 19–20.

50. Tolles, *The Grand Resort Hotels*, 222.

Chapter 8. Hiking Clubs and a Wilderness Renaissance (pp. 147–168)

1. Samuel H. Scudder, "The Alpine Club of Williamstown, Mass.," *Appalachia* 4, no. 1 (1884): 46.

2. Ibid., 51.

3. Julie Boardman, *When Women and Mountains Meet: Adventures in the White Mountains* (Etna, New Hampshire: Durand Press, 2001), 27–29.

4. Scudder, "Alpine Club," 52.

5. Ibid., 53.

6. Ibid., 54.

7. Charles B. Fobes, "The White Mountain Club of Portland, Maine, 1873–1884," *Appalachia* 30, no. 3 (June 1955): 381.

8. Ibid., 392.

9. Laura Waterman and Guy Waterman, *Forest and Crag: A History of Hiking, Trail Blazing, and Adventure in the Northeast Mountains* (Boston: Appalachian Mountain Club Books, 2003), 444.

10. "Proceedings of the Club," *Appalachia* 1, no. 1 (1876): 58.

11. "Introductory," *Appalachia* 1, no. 1 (1876): 5.

12. Charles H. Hitchcock, "Reports of the Councillors for the Spring of 1876: Topography," *Appalachia* 1, no. 1 (1876): 38.

13. Charles E. Fay, "The Annual Address of the President," *Appalachia* 2, no. 1 (1879): 1.

14. Ibid., 5.

15. Ibid., 6.

16. Ibid., 8.

17. Ibid., 11.

18. L. F. Pourtales, "Reports of the Councillors for the Spring of 1876: Exploration," *Appalachia* 1, no. 1 (1876): 49–50.

19. Charles E. Fay, "A Day on Tripyramid," *Appalachia* 1, no. 1 (1876): 15.

20. Ibid., 15.

21. Ibid., 16.

22. Ibid., 17.

23. Ibid., 18–19.

24. Ibid., 20.

25. Ibid.

26. Ibid., 22.

27. Ibid., 22–23.

28. Ibid., 23.

29. M. F. Whitman, "A Climb Through Tuckerman's Ravine," *Appalachia* 1, no. 3 (1877): 134.

30. Ibid., 135.

31. Ibid.

32. Lucy Crawford, *Lucy Crawford's History of the White Mountains*, ed. Stearns Morse (Boston: Appalachian Mountain Club, 1978), 188–191.

33. Whitman, "Climb," 137.

34. Waterman and Waterman, *Forest and Crag*, 200.

35. William Nowell, "Reports of the Councillors for the Spring of 1876: Improvements," *Appalachia* 1, no. 1 (1877): 55.

36. Ibid., 56.

37. Nowell, "Reports of the Councillors for the Spring of 1876: Improvements," 56.

38. John M. Gould, *How to Camp Out* (New York: Scribner, 1877), 12.

39. M. F. Whitman, "Camp Life for Ladies," *Appalachia* 2, no. 1 (1879): 44.

40. Ibid.

41. Ibid.

42. Ibid.

43. Waterman and Waterman, *Forest and Crag*, 256–257.

44. Gould, *How to Camp Out,* 14.

45. Ibid., 22.

46. Ibid., 27.

47. Whitman, "Camp Life," 48.

48. Gould, *How to Camp Out,* 27.

49. Ibid., 26.

50. Waterman and Waterman, *Forest and Crag,* 256.

51. Whitman, "Camp Life," 48.

52. Gould, *How to Camp Out,* 62.

53. Whitman, "Camp Life," 46.

54. Moses F. Sweetser, *The White Mountains: A Handbook for Travellers* (Boston: James R. Goode and Company, 1881), 47.

55. Whitman, "Camp Life," 48.

56. Gould, *How to Camp Out,* 47.

57. Whitman, "Camp Life," 47.

58. Gould, *How to Camp Out,* 41.

59. Ibid., 51.

60. Ibid., 5.

61. Sweetser, *The White Mountains,* 47.

62. Gould, *How to Camp Out,* 35.

63. Ibid., 37.

64. Ibid., 36.

65. Ibid., 37.

66. Ibid., 50.

67. Sweetser, *The White Mountains,* 35.

68. Gould, *How to Camp Out,* 109.

69. Ibid., 108.

Chapter 9. The Weeks Act and Its Impact (pp. 171–194)

1. Peter Hoyt, *Hoyt's History of Wentworth, New Hampshire, from the First Settlement of the Town to the Year 1870,* transcribed by Francis A. Muzzey (Littleton, New Hampshire: Courier Printing Company, 1976), 5.

2. Ibid., 132.

3. Ibid., 178–182.

4. Julie Wormser, director of policy for the Appalachian Mountain Club, interview by the author, November 18, 2002.

5. Lucy Crawford, *Lucy Crawford's History of the White Mountains,* ed. Stearns Morse (Boston: Appalachian Mountain Club, 1978), 168.

6. Julius Ward, "White Mountain Forests in Peril," *Atlantic Monthly,* February 1893, 248. Iris Baird indicated in a letter to the author that the sale of the state-owned forest land was, in her words, "much more obscure and confusing than Ward and others present it." She has examined the deeds files at the registries in Coos, Carroll, and Grafton counties and found no record of the sales in Grafton or Carroll. She found one in

Coos County regarding the sale of the summit of Mount Washington. The ownership of the summit of Mount Washington was in dispute for years because of differences among surveys of the land. According to Baird, the land at the summit of Mount Washington did not belong to the state.

7. Alfred K. Chittenden, *Forest Conditions of Northern New Hampshire*, Bureau of Forestry Bulletin No. 55 (Washington, D.C.: U.S. Department of Agriculture, 1905), 89.

8. Frederick W. Kilbourne, *Chronicles of the White Mountains* (Boston: Houghton Mifflin, 1916), 380.

9. Philip W. Ayres, *Commercial Importance of the White Mountain Forests* (Washington, D.C.: U. S. Department of Agriculture), 10.

10. Francis Parkman, "The Forests of the White Mountains," *Garden and Forest* 1 (February 29, 1888): 2.

11. Charles Sprague Sargent, "The Forests of the White Mountains in Danger," *Garden and Forest* 1 (December 12, 1888): 493.

12. Charles Sprague Sargent, "Destruction of Forests in New Hampshire," *Garden and Forest* 2 (February 20, 1889): 86.

13. *Daily Mirror and American*, qtd. in Charles Sprague Sargent, "Destruction of Forests in New Hampshire," *Garden and Forest* 2 (February 20, 1889): 86.

14. Ward, "White Mountain Forests in Peril," 249.

15. Ibid.

16. Ibid.

17. Ibid., 248.

18. Ibid.

19. Ayres, *Commercial Importance*, 28.

20. Hoyt, *Hoyt's History of Wentworth, New Hampshire*, 63.

21. Ayres, *Commercial Importance*, 30.

22. Ward, "White Mountain Forests in Peril," 250.

23. Chittenden, *Forest Conditions*, 96.

24. Ibid., 62.

25. Ibid.

26. Ibid., 70.

27. Kilbourne, *Chronicles of the White Mountains*, 381.

28. Ibid., 382.

29. Chittenden, *Forest Conditions*, 70.

30. Kilbourne, *Chronicles of the White Mountains*, 382.

31. Chittenden, *Forest Conditions*, 66.

32. Ibid.

36. Ibid.

34. Ibid., 67.

35. Ayres, *Commercial Importance*, 6.

36. Iris W. Baird, *Looking Out for Our Forests: The Evolution of a Plan to Protect New Hampshire's Woodlands from Fire* (Lancaster, New Hampshire: Baird Backwoods Construction Publications, 2005), 4.

37. Chittenden, *Forest Conditions*, 96–97.

38. Baird, *Looking Out for Our Forests*, 8–9.

39. Ibid., 21.

40. Kilbourne, *Chronicles of the White Mountains*, 383.

41. Parkman, "The Forests of the White Mountains," 2.

42. Sargent, "The Forests of the White Mountains in Danger," 493–494.

43. Charles Sprague Sargent, "The White Mountain Forests," *Garden and Forest* 5 (November 2, 1892): 518.

44. Charles Sprague Sargent, "The Movement to Preserve the Forests of the White Mountains." *Garden and Forest* 5 (November 30, 1892): 565–566.

45. Ward, "White Mountain Forests in Peril," 251.

46. Ibid., 250.

47. Chittenden, *Forest Conditions*, 15.

48. Ward, "White Mountain Forests in Peril," 251.

49. Ibid., 252.

50. Ibid.

51. Ibid., 253–254.

52. Ibid., 255.

53. Sherman Adams, *The Weeks Act: A 75th Anniversary Appraisal* (New York: The Newcomen Society of the United States, 1986), 5.

54. Baird, *Looking Out for Our Forests*, 5.

55. Charles D. Smith, "Gentlemen, You Have My Scalp," *American Forestry*, February 1962, 17.

56. Karl Roenke, "Why We Have a National Forest," *The Citizen* (Laconia, New Hampshire), February 16, 2004.

57. Adams, *The Weeks Act*, 12.

58. Ayres, *Commercial Importance*, 30.

59. Ibid., 31.

60. T. Jefferson Coolidge, qtd. in Ayres, *Commercial Importance*, 17.

61. Baird, *Looking Out for Our Forests*, 4.

62. Smith, "Gentlemen, You Have My Scalp," 18.

63. Kilbourne, *Chronicles of the White Mountains*, 392.

64. Joseph Cannon, qtd. in Smith, "Gentlemen, You Have My Scalp," 16.

65. Cannon, qtd. in Adams, *The Weeks Act*, 6.

66. Smith, "Gentlemen, You Have My Scalp," 19.

67. Baird, *Looking Out for Our Forests*, 7.

68. W. B. Heyburn, qtd. in "Passage of the Appalachian Bill," *American Forestry*, March 1911, 165.

69. "Passage of the Appalachian Bill," 167.

70. "Editorial: The Appalachian Bill," *American Forestry*, March 1911, 168.

71. "Prompt Action Needed," *New York Times*, May 11, 1911, 10.

72. Philip W. Ayres, "New England's Federal Forest Reserve," *American Forestry*, July 1915, 803.

73. Ayres, "New England's Federal Forest Reserve," 806.

74. Ibid.

75. Ibid., 804.

76. Ibid., 804–805.

77. Ibid., 806.

78. Ibid., 803.

79. "Editorial: The Weeks Law Hearing," *American Forestry*, February 1916, 113.

80. Kilbourne, *Chronicles of the White Mountains*, 401–403.

81. Ayres, "New England's Federal Forest Reserve," 810.

82. L. F. Kneipp, "Uncle Sam Buys Some Forests: How the Weeks Law of Twenty-Five Years Ago Is Building up a Great System of National Forests in the East." *American Forestry*, October 1936, 446.

Chapter 10. Outdoor Recreation and the Birth of a Wilderness Constituency (pp. 195–213)

1. Warren W. Hart, "The Davis Path Reopened," *Appalachia* 12, no. 3 (July 1911): 263.

2. Ibid.

3. Ibid., 265–266.

4. David W. Conrad, *The Land We Cared For: A History of the Forest Service's Eastern Region* (Milwaukee: USDA–Forest Service, Region 9, 1997), 46.

5. Philip W. Ayres, "Forest Preservation in the Eastern Mountains," reprint of article in *American Review of Reviews*, April 1920, 4. Page references are to the reprint.

6. Ibid., 5.

7. Conrad, *The Land We Cared For,* 34.

8. L. F. Kneipp, "Uncle Sam Buys Some Forests: How the Weeks Law of Twenty-Five Years Ago Is Building up a Great System of National Forests in the East," *American Forestry*, October 1936, 483.

9. Ayres, "Forest Preservation in the Eastern Mountains," 3.

10. Sherman Adams, *The Weeks Act: A 75th Anniversary Appraisal* (New York: The Newcomen Society of the United States, 1986), 14.

11. Philip W. Ayres, "Reforestation of Water-Sheds," *Journal of the New England Water Works Association* 37, no. 2 (1923): 141.

12. Philip W. Ayres, "Forest Preservation in the Eastern Mountains," reprint of article in *American Review of Reviews*, April 1920, 1. Page references are to the reprint.

13. Ibid.

14. Ayres, "Reforestation of Water-Sheds," 141.

15. Ibid.

16. Ibid., 140.

17. Conrad, *The Land We Cared For,* 140–141.

18. Laura Waterman and Guy Waterman, *Forest and Crag: A History of Hiking, Trail Blazing, and Adventure in the Northeast Mountains* (Boston: Appalachian Mountain Club Books, 2003), 375.

19. Ibid., 397–398.

20. Paul R. Jenks, "New England Trail Conference," *Appalachia* 14, no. 3 (June 1918): 280.

21. Ibid., 283.

22. Karl Harrington, "Appalachian Mountain Club Trail System," *Appalachia* 16, no. 3 (February 1926): 313–314.

23. Jenks, "New England Trail Conference," 283.

24. Harrington, "Appalachian Mountain Club Trail System," 313.

25. Ibid., 314.

26. Nathaniel Goodrich, "The Attractions and Rewards of Trail Making," *Appalachia* 14, no. 3 (June 1918): 247.

27. Ibid., 248.

28. Ibid., 250.

29. Ibid., 251.

30. Ibid., 253.

31. T. P. Chandler II, "Untraveled Paths: I. The Mahoosuc Range Trail, September 1–9, 1928," *Appalachia* 17, no. 2 (December 1928): 128.

32. Ibid., 130.

33. Ibid.

34. Ibid., 131.

35. Ibid., 128.

36. Helen Emerson Anthony, "A Day on a Mountain," *Appalachia* 16, no. 1 (December 1924): 71.

37. Ibid., 72.

38. Ibid., 73.

39. Ibid., 74.

40. Ibid., 74–75.

41. Melanie L. Simo, *Forest and Garden: Traces of Wildness in a Modernizing Land, 1897–1949* (Charlottesville: University of Virginia Press, 2003), 79.

42. Horace Kephart, *Camping and Woodcraft: A Handbook for Vacation Campers and for Travelers in the Wilderness,* 2 vols. (New York: Macmillan, 1930), 2:143.

43. Ibid., 2:144.

44. Ibid., 2:137.

45. Ibid., 2:147.

46. Ibid., 2:148.

47. Ibid.

48. R. L. M. Underhill, "Rock Climbing: White Mountains," *Appalachia* 17, no. 2 (December 1928): 169–170.

49. Clark S. Robinson, "Winter Camping," *Appalachia* 17, no. 2 (December 1928): 156.

50. Conrad, *The Land We Cared For,* 46.

Chapter 11. Toward Wilderness Preservation: The Development of a Philosophy (pp. 214–238)

1. Perceval Sayward, "Sanctuary," *Appalachia* 15, no. 3 (December 1922): 302.

2. Larry Anderson, *Benton MacKaye: Conservationist, Planner, and Creator of the Appalachian Trail* (Baltimore: The Johns Hopkins University Press, 2002), 22.

3. Lewis Mumford, "Introduction," in Benton MacKaye, *The New Exploration: A Philosophy of Regional Planning* (Harpers Ferry: Appalachian Trail Conference; Urbana: University of Illinois Press, 1990), ix.

4. Anderson, *Benton MacKaye,* 32–33.

5. Ibid., 34.

6. Larry Anderson, "Benton MacKaye and the Art of Roving: An 1897 Excursion in the White Mountains," *Appalachia* 46, no. 4 (December 15, 1987): 89–90.

7. Ibid., 90.

8. Benton MacKaye, qtd. in Anderson, "Benton MacKaye and the Art of Roving," 93.

9. Ibid., 94–95.

10. Benton MacKaye, "Our White Mountain Trip: Its Organization and Methods," in *Log of Camp Moosilauke, 1904* (Wentworth, New Hampshire: Camp Moosilauke, 1904), 10.

11. Ibid.

12. Ibid.

13. Ibid.

14. Anderson, *Benton MacKaye*, 57–58.

15. Ibid., 60.

16. Ibid., 63.

17. Benton MacKaye, "The Forest Cover on the Watersheds Examined by the Geological Survey in the White Mts., New Hampshire, April 1913" (manuscript from White Mountain National Forest, Laconia, New Hampshire), 39.

18. Anderson, *Benton MacKaye*, 97.

19. Benton MacKaye, qtd. in Anderson, *Benton MacKaye*, 81.

20. Ibid., 129.

21. Benton MacKaye, "An Appalachian Trail: A Project in Regional Planning," *Journal of the American Institute of Architects* 9 (October 1921): 325.

22. Ibid.

23. Ibid., 326.

24. Ibid., 328.

25. Ibid., 326.

26. Ibid., 328.

27. Ibid., 329.

28. Laura Waterman and Guy Waterman, *Forest and Crag: A History of Hiking, Trail Blazing, and Adventure in the Northeast Mountains* (Boston: Appalachian Mountain Club Books, 2003), 492.

29. Ibid., 503.

30. Benton MacKaye, *The New Exploration: A Philosophy of Regional Planning* (Harpers Ferry: Appalachian Trail Conference, and Urbana: University of Illinois Press, 1990), 56–57.

31. Ibid., 56.

32. Ibid., 57.

33. Ibid., 179.

34. Ibid., 180.

35. Ibid., 214.

36. Paul S. Sutter, *Driven Wild: How the Fight Against Automobiles Launched the Modern Wilderness Movement* (Seattle: University of Washington Press, 2002), 199.

37. Paul Schneider, *The Adirondacks: America's First Wilderness* (New York: Henry Holt, 1997), 224.

38. Ibid., 227.

39. Sutter, *Driven Wild*, 202.

40. James J. Glover, *A Wilderness Original: The Life of Bob Marshall* (Seattle: The Mountaineers, 1986), 60–61.

41. Sutter, *Driven Wild*, 203.

42. Ibid., 208.

43. Robert Marshall, qtd. in Glover, *A Wilderness Original*, 94.

44. Robert Marshall, "The Problem of the Wilderness," *Scientific Monthly* 30, no. 2 (February 1930): 141.

45. Ibid., 142.

46. Ibid., 143.

47. Ibid.

48. Ibid., 145.

49. Glover, *A Wilderness Original*, 147.

50. Sutter, *Driven Wild*, 222–223.

51. Ibid., 4.

52. Ibid., 5–6.

53. Glover, *A Wilderness Original*, 192.

54. Ibid., 199.

55. Ibid., 271.

56. Curt Meine, *Aldo Leopold: His Life and Work* (Madison: University of Wisconsin Press, 1988), 80.

57. Ibid., 14.

58. Aldo Leopold, "The Varmint Question," in *The River of the Mother of God and Other Essays by Aldo Leopold*, ed. Susan L. Flader and J. Baird Callicott (Madison: University of Wisconsin Press, 1991), 47.

59. Meine, *Aldo Leopold*, 135.

60. Ibid., 177.

61. Arthur Carhart, qtd. in Meine, *Aldo Leopold*, 178.

62. Aldo Leopold, qtd. in Meine, *Aldo Leopold*, 205.

63. Sutter, *Driven Wild*, 71–72.

64. Aldo Leopold, "The Wilderness and Its Place in Forest Recreational Policy," in *The River of the Mother of God and Other Essays by Aldo Leopold*, ed. Susan L. Flader and J. Baird Callicott (Madison: University of Wisconsin Press, 1991), 79.

65. Aldo Leopold, "Wilderness as a Form of Land Use," in *The River of the Mother of God and Other Essays by Aldo Leopold*, ed. Susan L. Flader and J. Baird Callicott (Madison: University of Wisconsin Press, 1991), 138.

66. Ibid., 136.

67. Ibid., 137.

68. Ibid., 136.

69. Ibid., 141.

70. Meine, *Aldo Leopold*, 359.

71. Ibid., 367.

72. Ibid., 368.

73. Aldo Leopold, *A Sand County Almanac with Essays on Conservation from Round River* (New York: Ballantine, 1970), 239.
74. Ibid., 246.
75. Ibid.
76. Ibid., 274.
77. Ibid., 268.
78. Ibid., 138–139.

Chapter 12. Preserving the White Mountain Wilderness (pp. 239–264)

1. Gerald S. Wheeler, "Great Gulf Wild Area," *Appalachia* 33, no. 1 (June 1960): 126.
2. David E. Conrad, *The Land We Cared For: A History of the Forest Service's Eastern Region* (Milwaukee: USDA–Forest Service, Region 9, 1997), 151.
3. Gerald S. Wheeler, "Land-Use Planning for the W.M.N.F.," *Appalachia* 31, no. 4 (December 1957): 477.
4. Conrad, *The Land We Cared For,* 137.
5. Wheeler, "Land–Use Planning," 476.
6. Conrad, *The Land We Cared For,* 152.
7. Ibid., 200.
8. Wheeler, "Land–Use Planning," 476.
9. Sherman Adams, *The Weeks Act: A 75th Anniversary Appraisal* (New York: The Newcomen Society, 1986), 16–17.
10. Ibid., 17–18.
11. Conrad, *The Land We Cared For,* 142.
12. Ibid., 143.
13. Ibid., 231.
14. Adams, *The Weeks Act,* 17–18.
15. Paul Bofinger, interview by the author, September 7, 2005.
16. Craig Allin, *The Politics of Wilderness Preservation* (Westport, Connecticut: Greenwood Press, 1982), 104.
17. Ibid., 107.
18. Marjorie Hurd, "Conservation: The Bill for a National Wilderness Preservation System," *Appalachia* 31, no. 3 (June 1957): 421.
19. Ibid., 421.
20. Ibid., 422.
21. Ibid.
22. Allin, *The Politics of Wilderness Preservation,* 108–114.
23. Ibid., 112–114.
24. Ibid., 115.
25. Ibid., 124.
26. Ibid., 135.
27. Ibid.
28. Ibid., 278.
29. Ibid.

30. Ibid., 281.
31. Ibid., 158.
32. Dennis M. Roth, *The Wilderness Movement and the National Forests, 1964–1980* (Washington, D.C.: United States Forest Service, 1984), 36.
33. Ibid.
34. Ibid., 38.
35. Ibid., 38–40.
36. Ibid., 40.
37. Ibid., 40.
38. Ibid., 42.
39. Ibid.
40. Joseph Penfold, qtd. in Roth, *The Wilderness Movement*, 42.
41. Ibid.
42. Ernie Dickerman, qtd. in Roth, *The Wilderness Movement*, 43.
43. Ibid.
44. Ibid., 46.
45. Ibid.
46. Jay H. Craven, qtd. in Conrad, *The Land We Cared For*, 250.
47. Adams, *The Weeks Act*, 18–19.
48. Conrad, *The Land We Cared For*, 244.
49. Ibid.
50. Mike Hathaway, qtd. in Conrad, *The Land We Cared For*, 244.
51. Ibid., 246.
52. George S. Zink, interview by the author, September 6, 2005.
53. Conrad, *The Land We Cared For*, 247.
54. "Sandwich Range Wilderness Study Area (Proposed)," newspaper article from files of White Mountain National Forest.
55. Zink, interview.
56. "Pemigewasset Wilderness Study Area (Proposed)," newspaper article from files of White Mountain National Forest.
57. Karl Roenke, interview by the author, September 7, 2005.
58. Zink, interview.
59. George Zink, "Wilderness Values," manuscript given to the author on September 6, 2005.
60. Ibid., 2.
61. Paul Bofinger, interview by the author, September 7, 2005.
62. Zink, interview.
63. Ibid.
64. Bofinger, interview.
65. Ibid.
66. Zink, interview.
67. Bofinger, interview.
68. Ibid.
69. Adams, *The Weeks Act*, 20.
70. Ibid., 21.

71. U.S. Department of Agriculture, *Pemigewasset Wilderness Plan, White Mountain National Forest* (Washington, D.C.: Government Printing Office, 1989), 2.

72. Ibid., 3.

73. Ibid., 4.

74. *Pemigewasset Wilderness* brochure, from the files of the White Mountain National Forest (Washington, D.C.: U.S. Department of Agriculture).

75. *Maine Sunday Telegram*, "Preserve Opponents Work Out a Compromise," September 30, 1990.

76. Ibid.

77. Ed Parsons, "Hiking Outdoors: Caribou-Speckled Mountain," *Conway Daily Sun*, October 17, 1997, 14.

78. Dan Yetter, telephone interview by the author, August 29, 2005.

79. Ibid.

80. William Cronon, "The Trouble with Wilderness, or Getting Back to the Wrong Nature," in *The Great New Wilderness Debate*, edited by J. Baird Callicott and Michael P. Nelson (Athens: University of Georgia Press, 1998), 480.

81. Ibid., 487.

Bibliography

Primary Sources

Adams, Sherman. *The Weeks Act: A 75th Anniversary Appraisal.* New York: The Newcomen Society of the United States, 1986.

American Forestry. "Appalachian Forests: Putting the New Law into Operation." May 1911, 288–293.

———. "Editorial: The Appalachian Bill." March 1911, 168–171.

———. "Forest Reserves Purchased." August 1915, 879.

———. "Passage of the Appalachian Bill." March 1911, 164–167.

———. "Weeks Bill in Congress." August 1910: 463–480.

———. "Weeks Law Conference." October 1915, 1004–1005.

———. "Weeks Law Hearing." February 1916, 112–113.

Anthony, Helen Emerson. "A Day on a Mountain." *Appalachia* 16, no. 1 (December 1924): 71–75.

Ayres, Philip W. *Commercial Importance of the White Mountain Forests.* Washington, D.C.: U.S. Department of Agriculture, 1909.

———. "Forest Preservation in the Eastern Mountains." Reprint of article in *American Review of Reviews,* April 1920.

———. "Mountain Trails in New England." *American Review of Reviews,* July 1917, 79–82.

———. "New England's Federal Forest Reserve." *American Forestry,* July 1915, 803–812.

———. "Reforestation of Water-Sheds." *Journal of the New England Water Works Association* 37, no. 2 (1923): 127–144.

Baxter, James Phinney. *Memoir of Sir Ferdinando Gorges.* In *Sir Ferdinando Gorges and His Province of Maine,* edited by James Phinney Baxter, 18:1–198. Boston: The Prince Society, 1890.

Belknap, Jeremy. *The History of New Hampshire.* 3 vols. Dover, New Hampshire: O. Crosby and J. Varney, 1812.

———. *Journal of a Tour to the White Mountains in July 1784.* Boston: Massachusetts Historical Society, 1876.

Blood, Charles W. "With the Trail Gang." *Appalachia* 17, no. 3 (June 1929): 246–251.

Boyden, Albert. *Stevenson House, Tamworth, New Hampshire: Tradition, History, and Random Reminiscence.* Tamworth, New Hampshire: privately printed, 1946.

Bradford, William. *Of Plymouth Plantation, 1620–1647.* New York: Modern Library, 1981.

Bruchac, Joseph. *Bowman's Store: A Journey to Myself.* New York: Dial, 1997.

———. *Lasting Echoes: An Oral History of Native American People.* New York: Avon, 1997.

———. "Native Cultures and the Formation of the North American Environmental Ethic." *From Perspectives to New Realities.* http://www.fs.fed.us/eco/eco-watch/ew920123 (accessed April 25, 2004).

Burke, Edmund. *A Philosophical Enquiry into the Origin of Our Ideas of the Sublime and the Beautiful.* Edited by David Womersley. New York: Penguin, 1998.

Burt, Henry M. *Burt's Guide Through the Connecticut Valley to the White Mountains and the River Saguenay.* Springfield, Massachusetts: New England Publishing Company, 1874.

Caribou-Speckled Mountain Wilderness Plan. Evans Notch, New Hampshire: Evans Notch Ranger District of the White Mountain National Forest, 1993.

Chamberlain, Allen. "Public Reservations of New England." *Appalachia* 13, no. 2 (October 1914): 170–181.

Champney, Benjamin. *Sixty Years' Memories of Art and Artists.* Woburn, Massachusetts: The News Print, 1900.

Chandler, T. P., II. "Untraveled Paths: I. The Mahoosuc Range Trail, September 1–9, 1928." *Appalachia* 17, no. 2 (December 1928): 128–131.

"Charter of the Province of Maine Granted to Sir Ferdinando Gorges." In *Sir Ferdinando Gorges and His Province of Maine,* edited by James Phinney Baxter, 19:123–148. Boston: The Prince Society, 1890.

Chittenden, Alfred K. *Forest Conditions of Northern New Hampshire.* Bureau of Forestry Bulletin No. 55. Washington, D.C.: U.S. Department of Agriculture, 1905.

Cole, Thomas. "Essay on American Scenery, 1835." In *American Art, 1700–1960: Sources and Documents,* edited by John W. McCoubrey, 98–110. Englewood Cliffs, New Jersey: Prentice-Hall, 1965.

Comey, Arthur C. "Progress on the Appalachian Trail in New England." *Appalachia* 16, no. 1 (December 1924): 89.

Cooper, James Fenimore. *The Last of the Mohicans.* New York: Dodd, Mead, 1951.

Crawford, Lucy. *Lucy Crawford's History of the White Mountains.* Edited by Stearns Morse. Boston: Appalachian Mountain Club, 1978.

Cutler, William Parker, and Julie Perkins Cutler. *Life, Journals, and Correspondence of Rev. Manasseh Cutler, LL.D.* 2 vols. Cincinnati: Robert Clarke, 1888.

Danforth, Samuel. "A Brief Recognition of New-Englands Errand into the Wilderness." In *American Sermons: The Pilgrims to Martin Luther King Jr.,* edited by Michael Warner, 151–171. New York: Library of America, 1999.

Dean, John Ward. "Mason's Plantations on the Pascataqua." In *Capt. John Mason: The Founder of New Hampshire,* edited by John Ward Dean, 17:53–130. Boston: The Prince Society, 1887.

———. "Memoir of Capt. John Mason." In *Capt. John Mason: The Founder of New Hampshire,* edited by John Ward Dean, 17:1–32. Boston: The Prince Society, 1887.

Dwight, Timothy. *Travels in New-England and New-York.* 4 vols. London: William Baynes and Son, 1823.

Eastman, Edson D. *The White Mountain Guide Book.* Boston: Lee & Shepard, 1879.

Farmer, John, and Jacob B. Moore. *Gazetteer of the State of New Hampshire.* Concord, New Hampshire: Jacob B. Moore, 1823.

Fay, Charles E. "The Annual Address of the President." *Appalachia* 2, no. 1 (1879): 1–14.

———. "A Day on Tripyramid." *Appalachia* 1, no. 1 (1876): 14–25.

———. "The March of Captain Samuel Willard." *Appalachia* 2, no. 4 (December 1881): 336–344.

———. "Reports of the Councillors for the Spring of 1876: Art." *Appalachia* 1, no. 1 (1876): 45–48.

Gilpin, William. *Three Essays: On Picturesque Beauty; On Picturesque Travel; and On Sketching Landscape, To Which Is Added a Poem.* London: R. Blamire, 1792.

Goodrich, Nathaniel. "The Attractions and Rewards of Trail Making." *Appalachia* 14, no. 3 (June 1918): 246–256.

Gookin, Daniel. *Historical Collections of the Indians in New England.* Boston: Apollo Press, 1792.

Gorges, Sir Ferdinando. *A Brief Relation of the Discovery and Plantation of New England.* In *Sir Ferdinando Gorges and His Province of Maine,* edited by James Phinney Baxter, 18:203–240. Boston: The Prince Society, 1890.

———. *A Brief Narration of the Original Undertakings of the Advancement of Plantations into the Parts of America.* In *Sir Ferdinando Gorges and His Province of Maine,* edited by James Phinney Baxter, 19:1–81. Boston: The Prince Society, 1890.

Gould, John M. *How to Camp Out.* New York: Scribner, 1877.

Guide to the White Mountains and Lakes of New Hampshire: With Minute and Accurate Descriptions of the Scenery and Objects of Interest on the Route. Concord, New Hampshire: Tripp & Osgood, 1851.

Harrington, Karl. "Appalachian Mountain Club Trail System." *Appalachia* 16, no. 3 (February 1926): 313–322.

Hart, Warren W. "The Davis Path Reopened." *Appalachia* 12, no. 3 (July 1911): 262–266.

Hawthorne, Nathaniel. "The Ambitious Guest." In *The Complete Novels and Selected Tales of Nathaniel Hawthorne,* edited by Norman Holmes Pearson, 990–996. New York: Modern Library, 1937.

———. "The Great Carbuncle: A Mystery of the White Mountains." In *The Complete Novels and Selected Tales of Nathaniel Hawthorne,* edited by Norman Holmes Pearson, 927–937. New York: Modern Library, 1937.

———. "The Great Stone Face." In *The Complete Novels and Selected Tales of Nathaniel Hawthorne,* edited by Norman Holmes Pearson, 1170–1184. New York: Modern Library, 1937.

———. "Our Evening Party Among the Mountains." In *Mosses from an Old Manse,* 425–429. Columbus: The Ohio State University Press, 1974.

Hitchcock, Charles H. "Reports of the Councillors for the Spring of 1876: Topography." *Appalachia* 1, no. 1 (1876): 38–45.

Hoyt, Peter L. *Hoyt's History of Wentworth, New Hampshire, from the First Settlement of the Town to the Year 1870.* Transcribed by Francis A. Muzzey. Littleton, New Hampshire: Courier Printing Company, 1976.

"Introductory." *Appalachia* 1, no. 1 (1876): 1–5.

Jackson, Howard, and Frank S. Mason. "A.M.C. Ice-Creepers." *Appalachia* 13, no. 2 (October 1914): 160–167.

Jenks, Paul R. "New England Trail Conference." *Appalachia* 14, no. 3 (June 1918): 280–283.

Johnson, Edward. *Wonder-Working Providence of Sion's Savior in New England, 1628–1651.* New York: Scribner, 1910.

Josselyn, John. *New-Englands Rarities Discovered.* Boston: Massachusetts Historical Society, 1972.

————. *Two Voyages to New-England.* Boston: William Veazie, 1865.

Kalm, Peter. *Peter Kalm's Travels in North America: The English Version of 1770.* Edited by Adolph B. Benson. 2 vols. New York: Wilson-Erickson, 1937.

Kephart, Horace. *Camping and Woodcraft: A Handbook for Vacation Campers and for Travelers in the Wilderness.* 2 vols. New York: Macmillan, 1930.

King, Thomas Starr. *The White Hills: Their Legends, Landscape, and Poetry.* Boston: Crosby, Nichols, 1860.

Knowlton, Elizabeth. "Down the Piscataquog." *Appalachia* 17, no. 3 (June 1929): 221–223.

Larcom, Lucy. *The Poetical Works of Lucy Larcom.* Boston: Houghton Mifflin, 1884.

Leopold, Aldo. *A Sand County Almanac with Essays on Conservation from Round River.* New York: Ballantine, 1970.

————. "The Varmint Question." In *The River of the Mother of God and Other Essays by Aldo Leopold,* edited by Susan L. Flader and J. Baird Callicott, 47–48. Madison: University of Wisconsin Press, 1991.

————. "Wilderness." In *The River of the Mother of God and Other Essays by Aldo Leopold,* edited by Susan L. Flader and J. Baird Callicott, 226–229. Madison: University of Wisconsin Press, 1991.

————. "The Wilderness and Its Place in Forest Recreational Policy." In *The River of the Mother of God and Other Essays by Aldo Leopold,* edited by Susan L. Flader and J. Baird Callicott, 78–81. Madison: University of Wisconsin Press, 1991.

————. "Wilderness as a Form of Land Use." In *The River of the Mother of God and Other Essays by Aldo Leopold,* edited by Susan L. Flader and J. Baird Callicott, 134–142. Madison: University of Wisconsin Press, 1991.

Levett, Christopher. *A Voyage into New England, Begun in 1632 and Ended in 1624.* In *Maine in the Age of Discovery: Christopher Levett's Voyage, 1623–1624, and a Guide to Sources,* 33–68. Portland: Maine Historical Society, 1988.

Little, Daniel. "Mr. Little's Tour of the White Mountains, July 23–July 27, 1784." Typescript of unpublished account. Kennebunkport, Maine: Brick Store Museum.

MacKaye, Benton. "An Appalachian Trail: A Project in Regional Planning." *Journal of the American Institute of Architects* 9 (October 1921): 325–330.

————. *Expedition Nine.* Washington, D.C.: The Wilderness Society, 1969.

————. "The Forest Cover on the Watersheds Examined by the Geological Survey in the White Mts., New Hampshire, April 1913." Manuscript from White Mountain National Forest, Laconia, New Hampshire, 1913.

————. *From Geography to Geotechnics.* Edited by Paul T. Bryant. Urbana: University of Illinois Press, 1968.

————. *The New Exploration: A Philosophy of Regional Planning.* Harpers Ferry: Appalachian Trail Conference; Urbana: University of Illinois Press, 1990.

————. "Our White Mountain Trip: Its Organization and Methods." In *Log of Camp Moosilauke, 1904,* 4–12. Wentworth, New Hampshire: Camp Moosilauke, 1904.

————. "Progress Toward the Appalachian Trail." *Appalachia* 15, no. 3 (December 1922): 244–252.

Maine Sunday Telegram. "Preserve Opponents Work Out Compromise." September 30, 1990.

Marshall, Robert. *The People's Forests.* Iowa City: University of Iowa Press, 2002.

———. "The Problem of the Wilderness." *Scientific Monthly* 30, no. 2 (February 1930): 141–148.

Mason, Captain John. "A Briefe Discourse of the New-Found-Land, 1620." In *Capt. John Mason: The Founder of New Hampshire*, edited by John Ward Dean, 17:143–158. Boston: The Prince Society, 1887.

Mather, Cotton. *Magnalia Christi Americana*. Books I and II. Cambridge: The Belknap Press of Harvard University Press, 1977.

———. *The Present State of New-England*. Boston: Samuel Green, 1690.

———. *The Wonders of the Invisible World*. London: John Russell, Smith, 1862.

Mather, Increase. *A Brief Relation of the State of New England from the Beginning of That Plantation to This Present Year, 1689*. London: Richard Baldwine, 1689.

Morton, Thomas. *The New English Canaan*. In *The New English Canaan of Thomas Morton*, edited by Charles Francis Adams, Jr., 14:106–345. Boston: The Prince Society, 1883.

Mourt, G. *A Journal of the Pilgrims at Plymouth: Mourt's Relation*. Ann Arbor: University Microfilms, 1966.

Mumford, Lewis. "Introduction." In Benton MacKaye, *The New Exploration: A Philosophy of Regional Planning*, vii–xxii. Harpers Ferry: Appalachian Trail Conference; Urbana: University of Illinois Press, 1990.

New York Times. "Buys Up Watershed." September 9, 1913, 9.

———. "Dr. Smith's Attitude on Forest Reserves." June 22, 1911, 6.

———. "House for Forest Reserves." June, 25, 1910, 3.

———. "Nation May Buy Biltmore Lands." September 17, 1912, 5.

———. "Not a 'Fancy Piece' of Lawmaking." February 20, 1911, 6.

———. "Not a Rubber Stamp." June 23, 1911, 10.

———. "Prompt Action Needed." May 11, 1911, 10.

———. "Strategic Forests." February 13, 1911, 10.

Nowell, William G. "The Mt. Adams Path." *Appalachia* 1, no. 3 (1877): 174–180.

———. "Reports of the Councillors for the Autumn of 1876: Improvements." *Appalachia* 1, no. 2 (1877): 109–117.

———. "Reports of the Councillors for the Spring of 1876: Improvements." *Appalachia* 1, no. 1 (1877): 51–57.

Oakes, William. *Scenery of the White Mountains: With Sixteen Plates from the Drawings of Isaac Sprague*. Boston: Crosby, Nichols, 1848.

Parkman, Francis. "The Forests of the White Mountains." *Garden and Forest* 1, no. 1 (February 29, 1888): 2.

Parsons, Ed. "Hiking Outdoors: Caribou-Speckled Mountain." *Conway Daily Sun,* October 17, 1997, 14.

Pemigewasset Wilderness. Washington, D.C.: U.S. Department of Agriculture (undated brochure).

Pickering, E. C. "The Annual Address of the President." *Appalachia* 1, no. 2 (1877): 63–70.

Playground and Recreation Association of America. *Camping Out: A Manual on Organized Camping*. New York: Macmillan, 1924.

Pourtales, L. F. "Reports of the Councillors for the Spring of 1876: Exploration." *Appalachia* 1, no. 1 (1876): 49–50.

Price, Uvedale. *An Essay on the Picturesque.* London: J. Robson, 1794.

"Proceedings of the Club." *Appalachia* 1, no. 1 (1876): 58–62.

Ringland, Arthur. "National Conference on Outdoor Recreation." *Appalachia* 16, no. 2 (June 1925): 164–166.

Robinson, Clark S. "Winter Camping." *Appalachia* 17, no. 2 (December 1928): 156–163.

Roenke, Karl. "Why We Have a National Forest." *The Citizen* (Laconia, New Hampshire), February 16, 2004.

Rosier, James. *A True Relation of the Most Prosperous Voyage Made This Present Year 1605 by Captain George Waymouth.* Ann Arbor: University Microfilms, 1966.

Sargent, Charles Sprague. "Destruction of Forests in New Hampshire." *Garden and Forest* 2 (1889): 86.

———. "The Forests of the White Mountains in Danger." *Garden and Forest* 1 (1888): 493.

———. "The Movement to Preserve the Forests of the White Mountains." *Garden and Forest* 5 (November 30, 1892): 565–566.

———. "The White Mountain Forests." *Garden and Forest* 5 (November 2, 1892): 518.

Sayward, Perceval. "Sanctuary." *Appalachia* 15, no. 3 (December 1922): 301–303.

Scudder, Samuel H. "The Alpine Club of Williamstown, Mass." *Appalachia* 4, no. 1, (1884): 45–54.

———. "The Annual Address of the President." *Appalachia* 1, no. 4. (1878): 206–243.

Spaulding, John H. 1862. *Historical Relics of the White Mountains.* Reprint: Littleton, New Hampshire: Bondcliff Books, 1998.

Sweetser, Moses F. *Chisholm's White Mountain Guide Book.* Portland, Maine: Chisholm Brothers, 1898.

———. *The White Mountains: A Handbook for Travellers.* Boston: James R. Osgood and Company, 1881.

Thoreau, Henry David. *Walden.* In *Walden and Other Writings of Henry David Thoreau,* edited by Brooks Atkinson, 3–297. New York: Modern Library, 1950.

———. "Walking." In *Walden and Other Writings of Henry David Thoreau,* edited by Brooks Atkinson, 597–632. New York: Modern Library, 1950.

Tripp's White Mountain Guide Book, or Guide to the Mountain and Lake Scenery of New-Hampshire. Boston: Redding; New York: E. H. Tripp, 1892.

Underhill, R. L. M. "Rock Climbing: White Mountains." *Appalachia* 17, no. 2 (December 1928): 169–172.

Upham, Warren. "The East Branch of the Pemigewasset." *Appalachia* 1, no. 1 (1876): 29–35.

U.S. Department of Agriculture. *Pemigewasset Wilderness Plan, White Mountain National Forest.* Washington, D.C.: Government Printing Office, 1989.

Waldron, Holman D. *With Pen and Camera Thro' the White Mountains.* Portland, Maine: Chisholm Brothers, 1896.

Ward, Julius H. "White Mountain Forests in Peril." *Atlantic Monthly,* February 1893, 247–255.

Wheeler, Gerald S. "Great Gulf Wild Area." *Appalachia* 33, no. 1 (June 1960): 126–128.

———. "Land-Use Planning for the W.M.N.F." *Appalachia* 31, no. 4 (December 1957): 472–478.

———. "White Mountain National Forest." *Appalachia* 33, no. 3 (June 1961): 413–417.

The White Mountains of New Hampshire: In the Heart of the Nation's Playground. Boston: General Passenger Department, Boston & Maine Railroad, 1910.

Whitman, M. F. "Camp Life for Ladies." *Appalachia* 2, no. 1 (1879): 44–48.

———. "A Climb Through Tuckerman's Ravine." *Appalachia* 1, no. 3 (1877): 131–137.

Whittier, John Greenleaf. *The Poetical Works of Whittier*. Edited by Hyatt H. Waggoner. Boston: Houghton Mifflin, 1975.

Willey, Benjamin G. *Incidents in White Mountain History*. Boston: Nathaniel Noyes, 1856.

Winthrop, John. *The History of New England from 1630 to 1649*. 2 vols. Boston: Phelps and Farnham, 1825–1826.

———. "A Modell of Christian Charity." In *American Sermons: The Pilgrims to Martin Luther King Jr.,* edited by Michael Warner, 28–43. New York: Library of America, 1999.

Wood, William. *New England's Prospect*. Edited with an introduction by Alden T. Vaughan. Amherst: University of Massachusetts Press, 1977.

Woolson, A. A. *Reminiscences of Lisbon, N.H.* Littleton, New Hampshire: Courier Printing Company, 1912.

Zink, George. "Wilderness Values." Undated manuscript given to author on September 6, 2005.

Secondary Sources

Adams, Charles Francis, Jr. *Thomas Morton of Merry-Mount*. In T*he New English Canaan of Thomas Morton,* edited by Charles Francis Adams, Jr., 14:1–98. Boston: The Prince Society, 1883.

Allin, Craig W. *The Politics of Wilderness Preservation*. Westport, Connecticut: Greenwood Press, 1982.

Anderson, Hillary, and Donna-Belle Garvin. "Catalogue of Paintings Exhibited, 'Beauty Caught and Kept': Benjamin Champney in the White Mountains." In *Beauty Caught and Kept: Benjamin Champney in the White Mountains*. Special issue, *Historical New Hampshire* 51, nos. 3–4 (1996): 101–132.

Anderson, Larry. "Benton MacKaye and the Art of Roving: An 1897 Excursion in the White Mountains." *Appalachia* 46, no. 4 (December 15, 1987): 85–102.

———. *Benton MacKaye: Conservationist, Planner, and Creator of the Appalachian Trail*. Baltimore: The Johns Hopkins University Press, 2002.

Andrews, Henry M., Jr. "The Royal Pines of New Hampshire." *Appalachia* 27, no. 2 (1948): 186–198.

Armes, Ethel. *Midsummer in Whittier's Country: A Little Study of Sandwich Center*. Birmingham, Alabama: Advance Press, 1905.

Baird, Iris W. *Looking Out for Our Forests: The Evolution of a Plan to Protect New Hampshire's Woodlands from Fire*. Lancaster, New Hampshire: Baird Backwoods Construction Publications, 2005.

Beals, Charles Edward, Jr. [William James Sidis]. *Passaconaway in the White Mountains*. Boston: Richard G. Badger, 1916.

Bellfy, Phil. "Savage, Savages, Savagism." In *Encyclopedia of North American Indians,* edited by Frederick E. Hoxie, 568–570. Boston: Houghton Mifflin, 1996.

Boardman, Julie. *When Women and Mountains Meet: Adventures in the White Mountains.* Etna, New Hampshire: Durand Press, 2001.

Bolles, Simeon. *The Early History of the Town of Bethlehem, New Hampshire.* Woodsville, New Hampshire: Enterprise Printing House, 1883.

Brower, David, ed. *Wilderness: America's Living Heritage.* San Francisco: Sierra Club, 1961 (conference proceedings).

Brown, Donna. *Inventing New England: Regional Tourism in the Nineteenth Century.* Washington, D.C.: Smithsonian Institution Press, 1995.

Brown, Milton, et al. *American Art.* Englewood Cliffs, New Jersey: Prentice-Hall, 1985.

Bruns, Paul E. *A New Hampshire Everlasting and Unfallen.* Concord, New Hampshire: Society for the Protection of New Hampshire Forests, 1969.

Burt, F. Allen. *The Story of Mount Washington.* Hanover, New Hampshire: Dartmouth Publications, 1960.

Caduto, Michael. *A Time Before New Hampshire: The Story of a Land and Native Peoples.* Hanover, New Hampshire: University Press of New England, 2003.

Callicott, J. Baird, and Michael P. Nelson, eds. *The Great New Wilderness Debate.* Athens: University of Georgia Press, 1998.

Calloway, Colin G. *The Abenaki.* New York: Chelsea House, 1989.

———. *Dawnland Encounters: Indians and Europeans in Northern New England.* Hanover, New Hampshire: University Press of New England, 1991.

———. *The Identity of the Saint Francis Indians.* Ottawa: National Museums of Canada, 1981.

———. *The Western Abenakis of Vermont, 1600–1800: Ways, Migration, and the Survival of an Indian People.* Norman: University of Oklahoma Press, 1990.

Campbell, Catherine H. "Catalogue of the Exhibition." In *The White Mountains: Place and Perceptions,* curated by Donald D. Keyes, 79–148. Hanover, New Hampshire: University Press of New England, 1980.

———. *New Hampshire Scenery.* Canaan, New Hampshire: Phoenix Publishing, 1985.

Carroll, Peter. *Puritanism and the Wilderness: The Intellectual Significance of the New England Frontier, 1629–1700.* New York: Columbia University Press, 1969.

Clark, Marcia. "A Visionary Artist Who Celebrated Wilds of America." *Smithsonian,* September 1975, 90–97.

Conrad, David W. *The Land We Cared For: A History of the Forest Service's Eastern Region.* Milwaukee: U.S. Forest Service Region 9, 1997.

Conroy, Rosemary G., and Richard Ober, eds. *People and Place: Society for the Protection of New Hampshire Forests, the First 100 Years.* Concord, New Hampshire: Society for the Protection of New Hampshire Forests, 2001.

Cooper, James F. *Knights of the Brush: The Hudson River School and the Moral Landscape.* New York: Hudson Hills Press, 1999.

Cronon, William. *Changes in the Land: Indians, Colonists, and the Ecology of New England.* New York: Hill and Wang, 2003.

———. "The Trouble with Wilderness, or, Getting Back to the Wrong Nature." In *The Great New Wilderness Debate,* edited by J. Baird Callicott and Michael P. Nelson, 471–499. Athens: University of Georgia Press, 1998.

Cross, George N. *Dolly Copp and the Pioneers of the Glen.* Baltimore: Press of Day Printing Company, 1927.

———. *Randolph Old and New: Its Ways and Its By-Ways.* Boston: Pinkham Press, 1924.

———. "Randolph Yesterdays." *Appalachia* 14, no. 1 (1916–1917): 49–58.

Daniell, Jere R. *Colonial New Hampshire: A History.* Millwood, New York: KTO Press, 1981.

Davis, Abner. "Jefferson." In *History of Coos County, New Hampshire,* compiled by Georgia D. Merrill, 399–425. Syracuse, New York: W. A. Fergusson, 1888.

Davis, Bailey K. *Traditions and Recollections of Berlin, N.H.* Berlin, New Hampshire: Smith-Poley Press, n.d.

Daniell, Gene, and John Burroughs, comp. and ed. *White Mountain Guide, Twenty-sixth Edition.* Boston: Appalachian Mountain Club Books, 1998.

Day, Gordon M. "English-Indian Contacts in New England." In *In Search of New England's Native Past: Selected Essays by Gordon M. Day,* edited by Michael K. Foster and William Cowan, 65–71. Amherst: University of Massachusetts Press, 1998.

———. "Historical Notes on New England Languages." In *In Search of New England's Native Past: Selected Essays by Gordon M. Day,* edited by Michael K. Foster and William Cowan, 102–108. Amherst: University of Massachusetts Press, 1998.

———. "The Identity of the Sokokis. " In *In Search of New England's Native Past: Selected Essays by Gordon M. Day,* edited by Michael K. Foster and William Cowan, 89–97. Amherst: University of Massachusetts Press, 1998.

———. "The Indian as an Ecological Factor in the Northeastern Forest." In *In Search of New England's Native Past: Selected Essays by Gordon M. Day,* edited by Michael K. Foster and William Cowan, 27–48. Amherst: University of Massachusetts Press, 1998.

———. "Indian Place-Names as Ethnohistorical Data." In *In Search of New England's Native Past: Selected Essays,* edited by Michael K. Foster and William Cowan, 195–201. Amherst: University of Massachusetts Press, 1998.

———. "The Name *Algonquin.*" In *In Search of New England's Native Past: Selected Essays by Gordon M. Day,* edited by Michael K. Foster and William Cowan, 123–126. Amherst: University of Massachusetts Press, 1998.

———. "Oral Tradition as Complement." In *In Search of New England's Native Past: Selected Essays by Gordon M. Day,* edited by Michael K. Foster and William Cowan, 127–135. Amherst: University of Massachusetts Press, 1998.

———. "Western Abenaki." In *In Search of New England's Native Past: Selected Essays,* edited by Michael K. Foster and William Cowan, 202–222. Amherst: University of Massachusetts Press, 1998.

———. *Western Abenaki Dictionary.* 2 vols. Hull, Quebec: Canadian Museum of Civilization, 1995.

Dummer Bicentennial Committee. *History of Dummer, New Hampshire, 1773–1973.* Littleton, New Hampshire: Courier Printing Company, 1973.

Eastman, Benjamin D. *North Conway: Its Surroundings, Its Settlement by English People.* North Conway, New Hampshire: Reporter Press, 1880.

Flader, Susan L., and J. Baird Callicott. "Preface and a Brief Chronology." In *The River of the Mother of God and Other Essays by Aldo Leopold,* edited Susan L. Flader and J. Baird Callicott, ix–xv. Madison: University of Wisconsin Press, 1991.

Fobes, Charles B. "The White Mountain Club of Portland, Maine, 1873–1884." *Appalachia* 30, no. 3 (June 1955): 380–395.

Frome, Michael. *Battle for the Wilderness.* Salt Lake City: University of Utah Press, 1997.

Fuller, Henry Morrill. *Sir Ferdinando Gorges (1566–1647): Naval and Military Commander.* New York: Newcomen Society, 1952.

Glover, James J. *A Wilderness Original: The Life of Bob Marshall.* Seattle: The Mountaineers, 1986.

Gove, Bill. *J. E. Henry's Logging Railroads: The History of the East Branch & Lincoln and the Zealand Valley Railroads.* Littleton, New Hampshire: Bondcliff, 1998.

Hallowell, A. Irving. "Ojibwa Ontology, Behavior, and World View." In *Culture in History: Essays in Honor of Paul Radin,* edited by Stanley Diamond, 19–52. New York: Columbia University Press, 1960.

Hardy, Ruth Gillette. "Club Establishes a Conservation Committee." *Appalachia* 26, no. 3 (June 1947): 410.

———. "Conservation: Record of the 84th Congress." *Appalachia* 31, no. 2 (December 1956): 274–275.

Hart, Warren W. "Darby Field." *Appalachia* 11, no. 4 (June 1908): 360–366.

Heffernan, Nancy Coffey, and Ann Page Stecker. *New Hampshire: Crosscurrents in Its Development.* Hanover, New Hampshire: University Press of New England, 2004.

Heimart, Alan. "Puritanism, the Wilderness, and the Frontier." *New England Quarterly* 26 (1953): 361–379.

Hipple, Walter John. *The Beautiful, the Sublime, and the Picturesque in Eighteenth-Century British Aesthetic Theory.* Carbondale: Southern Illinois University Press, 1957.

Hubbard, William. *A General History of New England, from the Discovery to MCDLXXX.* The Collections of the Massachusetts Historical Society, series 2, vol. 5. Boston: Little, Brown, 1815.

Hume, Gary W. "Joseph Laurent's Intervale Camp: Post-Colonial Abenaki Adaptation and Revitalization in New Hampshire." In *Algonkians of New England: Past and Present,* edited by Peter Benes, 101–113. Boston: Boston University Scholarly Publications, 1991.

Huntington, Daniel. *Asher B. Durand: A Memorial Address.* New York: The Century, 1887.

Hurd, Marjorie. "Conservation: The Bill for a National Wilderness Preservation System." *Appalachia* 31, no. 3 (June 1957): 421–422.

Hussey, Christopher. *The Picturesque: Studies in a Point of View.* Hamden, Connecticut: Archon Books, 1967.

Jefferson, New Hampshire, Anniversary Committee. *Historical Memories of Jefferson, New Hampshire.* Littleton, New Hampshire: Courier Printing Company, 1971.

Johnson, Frances Ann. *Crawford Notch: Southwestern Approach to the White Mountains of New Hampshire.* Copyrighted 1965 by the author.

Jorgenson, Neil. *Guide to New England's Landscape.* Barre, Massachusetts: Barre Publishers, 1971.

Josephy, Alvin M., Jr. *500 Nations: An Illustrated History of North American Indians.* New York: Knopf, 1994.

Keyes, Donald D. "The Great Gallery of Nature: Benjamin Champney in the Development of White Mountain Art." In *Beauty Caught and Kept: Benjamin Champney in the White Mountains.* Special issue, *Historical New Hampshire* 51, nos. 3–4 (1996): 91–100.

————. "Perceptions of the White Mountains: A General Survey." In *The White Mountains: Place and Perceptions,* curated by Donald D. Keyes, 41–57. Hanover, New Hampshire: University Press of New England, 1980.

————. curator. *The White Mountains: Place and Perceptions.* Hanover, New Hampshire: University Press of New England, 1980.

Kilbourne, Frederick W. *Chronicles of the White Mountains.* Boston: Houghton Mifflin, 1916.

Kirsch, George B. *Jeremy Belknap: A Biography.* New York: Arno Press, 1982.

Klyza, Christopher McGrory, and Stephen C. Trombulak, eds. *The Future of the Northern Forest.* Hanover, New Hampshire: University Press of New England, 1994.

Kneipp, L. F. "Uncle Sam Buys Some Forests: How the Weeks Law of Twenty-Five Years Ago Is Building up a Great System of National Forests in the East." *American Forestry,* October 1936, 443+.

Lancaster, New Hampshire, Bicentennial Sketchbook Committee. *Two Hundred Years: Lancaster, New Hampshire, 1764–1964.* Lancaster, New Hampshire: Democrat Press, 1964.

Landau, Elaine. *The Abenaki.* New York: Franklin Watts, 1996.

Lawall, David B. *Asher Brown Durand: His Art and Art Theory in Relation to His Times.* New York: Garland, 1977.

Lawson, Russell M. *Passaconaway's Realm: Captain John Evans and the Exploration of Mount Washington.* Hanover, New Hampshire: University Press of New England, 2002.

Lehr, Frederic B. *Carroll, New Hampshire: The First Two Hundred Years, 1772–1972.* Littleton, New Hampshire: Courier Printing Company, 1972.

Lindsell, Robert. *Rail Lines of Northern New England.* Pepperell, Massachusetts: Branch Line Press, 2000.

Little, William. *History of the Town of Warren, N.H. from Its Early Settlement to the Year 1854.* Concord, New Hampshire: McFarland & Jenks, 1854.

Macinnes, C. M. *Ferdinando Gorges and New England.* Bristol, England: Bristol Branch of the Historical Association, 1965.

Marchalonis, Shirley. *The Worlds of Lucy Larcom, 1824–1893.* Athens: University of Georgia Press, 1989.

Marcou, Jane Belknap. *Life of Jeremy Belknap, D.D.: The Historian of New Hampshire.* New York: Harper, 1847.

Marsh, George Perkins. *Man and Nature.* Edited with an introduction by David Lowenthal. Seattle: University of Washington Press, 2003.

Marx, Leo. *The Machine in the Garden: Technology and the Pastoral Ideal in America.* New York: Oxford University Press, 1964.

McGrath, Robert L. *Gods in Granite: The Art of the White Mountains of New Hampshire.* Syracuse, New York: Syracuse University Press, 2001.

————. "The Real and the Ideal: Popular Images of the White Mountains." In *The White Mountains: Place and Perceptions,* curated by Donald D. Keyes, 59–77. Hanover, New Hampshire: University Press of New England, 1980.

Meine, Curt. *Aldo Leopold: His Life and Work.* Madison: University of Wisconsin Press, 1988.

Merrill, Georgia Drew, comp. *History of Coos County, New Hampshire.* Syracuse, New York: W. A. Fergusson, 1888.

Miller, Perry. "Errand into the Wilderness." In *Tensions in American Puritanism*, edited by Richard Reinitz, 135–154. New York: Wiley, 1970.

———. *The New England Mind: The Seventeenth Century*. New York: Macmillan, 1939.

Molloy, Anna Marie. *Peeling-Fairfield, Woodstock, New Hampshire, Celebrates 200 Years, 1763–1963*. North Woodstock, New Hampshire: Glen Press, 1963.

Moody, Robert E. *A Proprietary Experiment in Early New England History: Thomas Gorges and the Province of Maine*. Boston: Boston University Press, 1963.

Morison, Elizabeth Forbes, and Elting E. Morison. *New Hampshire: A Bicentennial History*. New York: Norton, 1976.

Morrison, Kenneth M. *The Embattled Northeast: The Elusive Ideal of Alliance in Abenaki-Euroamerican Relations*. Berkeley: University of California Press, 1984.

Nash, Alice. "Odanak in the 1920s: A Prism of Abenaki History." Translated into English by Claude Gélinas. Originally published as "Odanak durant les années 1920: un prisme reflétant l'histoire des Abénaquis," in *Recherches amérindiennes au Québec* 31, no. 1 (2002): 17–33.

———. Personal correspondence. September 8, 2005.

Nash, Roderick. *Wilderness and the American Mind*. New Haven: Yale University Press, 2001.

Nilsen, Kim R. *History of Whitefield, New Hampshire, 1774–1974*. Town of Whitefield, New Hampshire, 1974.

Noble, Louis Legrand. *The Life and Works of Thomas Cole*. Edited by Elliot S. Vesell. Hensonville, New York: Black Dome Press, 1997.

Novak, Barbara. *Nature and Culture: American Landscape and Painting, 1825–1875*. New York: Oxford University Press, 1980.

Oelschlaeger, Max. *The Idea of Wilderness*. New Haven: Yale University Press, 1991.

Parkman, Francis. *A Half-Century of Conflict: France and England in North America*. Vols. 11 and 12, *The Works of Francis Parkman*. Boston: Little, Brown, 1897–1898.

Parry, Ellwood C., III. *The Art of Thomas Cole: Ambition and Imagination*. Newark: University of Delaware Press, 1988.

Pollard, John A. *John Greenleaf Whittier: Friend of Man*. Boston: Houghton Mifflin, 1949.

Powell, Earl A. *Thomas Cole*. New York: Abrams, 2000.

Preston, Richard Arthur. *Gorges of Plymouth Fort*. Toronto: University of Toronto Press, 1953.

Richter, Daniel I. *Facing East from Indian Country: A Native History of Early America*. Cambridge: Harvard University Press, 2001.

Robertson, Edwin B. *Building the Railroad Through Crawford Notch*. Westbrook, Maine, 1996.

Roth, Dennis M. *The Wilderness Movement and the National Forests, 1964–1980*. Washington, D.C.: U.S. Department of Agriculture, 1984.

Russell, Howard S. *Indian New England Before the Mayflower*. Hanover, New Hampshire: University Press of New England, 1980.

Salisbury, Neal. *Manitou and Providence: Indians, Europeans, and the Making of New England, 1500–1643*. New York: Oxford University Press, 1982.

Sargent, William. *A Year in the Notch: Exploring the Natural History of the White Mountains*. Hanover, New Hampshire: University Press of New England, 2001.

Schama, Simon. *Landscape and Memory*. New York: Vintage, 1995.

Schneider, Paul. *The Adirondacks: America's First Wilderness*. New York: Henry Holt, 1997.

Scott, Dennis. *The Enduring Wilderness*. Golden, Colorado: Fulcrum Publishing, 2004.

Sears, John F. *Sacred Places: American Tourist Attractions in the Nineteenth Century*. New York: Oxford University Press, 1989.

Sellars, Richard West. *Preserving Nature in the National Parks: A History*. New Haven: Yale University Press, 1997.

Simmons, William S. *Spirit of the New England Tribes: Indian History and Folklore, 1620– 1984*. Hanover, New Hampshire: University Press of New England, 1986.

Simo, Melanie L. *Forest and Garden: Traces of Wildness in a Modernizing Land, 1897–1949*. Charlottesville: University of Virginia Press, 2003.

Smith, Charles D. "Gentlemen, You Have My Scalp." *American Forestry*, February 1962, 16–19.

Steen, Harold K. *The U.S. Forest Service: A History*. Seattle: University of Washington Press, undated.

Stewart-Smith, David. "The Pennacook Indians and the New England Frontier, circa 1604–1733." PhD diss., The Union Institute, 1998.

Stier, Maggie, and Ron McAdow. *Into the Mountains*. Boston: Appalachian Mountain Club Books, 1995.

Sutter, Paul S. *Driven Wild: How the Fight Against Automobiles Launched the Modern Wilderness Movement*. Seattle: University of Washington Press, 2002.

Tolles, Bryant F., Jr. *The Grand Resort Hotels of the White Mountains: A Vanishing Architectural Legacy*. Boston: Godine, 1998.

Tuckerman, Frederick. "Early Visits to the White Mountains and Ascents of the Great Range." *Appalachia* 15, no. 2 (1921): 111–127.

Vogel, Charles O. "'Wanderings after the Wild and Beautiful': The Life and Career of Benjamin Champney." In *Beauty Caught and Kept: Benjamin Champney in the White Mountains*. Special issue, *Historical New Hampshire* 51, nos. 3–4 (1996): 71–89.

Wagenknecht, Edward. *John Greenleaf Whittier: A Portrait in Paradox*. New York: Oxford University Press, 1967.

Washburn, Charles G. *The Life of John W. Weeks*. Boston: Houghton Mifflin, 1928.

Waterman, Laura, and Guy Waterman. *Forest and Crag: A History of Hiking, Trail Blazing, and Adventure in the Northeast Mountains*. Boston: Appalachian Mountain Club Books, 2003.

———. "Reverends, Soldiers, Scientists: The Belknap-Cutler Ascent of Mount Washington, 1784." *Appalachia* 45, no. 1 (Summer 1984): 41–52.

———. *Wilderness Ethics*. Woodstock, Vermont: Countryman Press, 1993.

Welch, Sarah N. *History of Franconia, New Hampshire*. Littleton, New Hampshire: Courier Printing Company, 1972.

Wilson, Gregory C., ed. *Bethlehem, New Hampshire: A Bicentennial History*. Littleton, New Hampshire: Courier Printing Company, 1973.

Wilson, James. *The Earth Shall Weep*. New York: Atlantic Monthly Press, 1998.

Wiseman, Frederick Matthew. *The Voice of the Dawn: An Autohistory of the Abenaki Nation*. Hanover, New Hampshire: University Press of New England, 2001.

Zaslowsky, Dyan, and the Wilderness Society. *These American Lands: Parks, Wilderness, and the Public Lands*. New York: Henry Holt, 1986.

Index

MacKaye, Benton, 4, 148, 190, 197, 201, 213, 215–225, 217*il*, 230, 231, 262; as camp counselor, 218–219; childhood and education, 215–217; concept of wilderness/planning, 253; "elemental environments," 223; first hiking in the Whites, 216–218; Forest Service work, 219–220; founding of Wilderness Society, 220; *From Geography to Geotechnics* (1968), 224*il*; Midwest tour, 220; *The New Exploration,* 222–225; proposal and creation of the Appalachian Trail, 220–222; social thinking, 220, 221; studying forestry, 219; wilderness as regional planning, 222–225

Mahoosuc Range Trail, 205

Maine: border with New Hampshire, 24; patent for province of, 18, 19

Maine Wilderness Act of 1990, 259

manitou, 12

Maplewood (hotel), 144, 145

Maps: Appalachian Mountain Club making, 153; Belknap sketch of expedition route, 30*il*; Carrigain's map of New Hampshire, 34*il*, 52*il*, 54, 67; Franklin Leavitt's White Mountain map, 62*il*, 63, 141*il*, 142*il*

Marsh, Sylvester, 131–132, 138

Marshall, Robert (Bob), 4, 148, 197, 201, 213, 215, 225–231, 229*il*; death of, 231; defining wilderness, 226–227; federal government land purchases, 229–230; forestry career, 226; founding of Wilderness Society, 220; landmark article on wilderness, 226–227; *The People's Forests* (1933), 230; plant physiology degree, 226; types of recreational areas proposed by, 228–229; Wilderness Society, 225; work in the Rockies, 226; writing for Copeland Report, 228–229; youth, 225

Mason, John, 18, 19, 21

mast trade, 23, 24; end of, 39

Maury, Draper, 216, 217*il*

McArdle, Richard, 242, 245–246

McGrath, Robert L., 67, 74, 80–81, 111, 112, 121

Meine, Curt, 232

Merriam, John Campbell, 230

Merrill, Joshua, 39

Merrill, Mary, 37

Merrill, Stephen, 39

minerals, discovery and mining of, 41

Mitchell, Bob, 217

Monongahela National Forest, West Virginia, 242

Morse, George, 151

Morse, John, 44

Morton, Thomas, 15

Mount Chocorua: Cole's ascent of, 72; in Cole's paintings, 75, 76, 77*il*, 78*il*, 79–80, 84; in paintings, 111*il*, 112, 119

Mount Crawford House, 131

Mount Garfield, trail building on, 205

Mount Kearsarge, in Starr King's writing, 105–106

Mount Pleasant Hotel, 180

Mount Pleasant House, 144

Mount Tripyramid: AMC exploration of, 154–156; MacKaye hike in 1897, 218

Mount Washington: Alpine Club of Williamstown climb, 149–150; Belknap-Cutler expedition climb, 27–31; Cole paintings of, 72, 73*il*; creation of Crawford Path, 54; Fanny Whitman climb of, 157–158, 159; first travellers to visit, with Crawford family as guides, 53; first white man to climb, 22; Helen Emerson Anthony's journal of climb, 206–208; MacKaye hike in 1897, 217–218; naming of other peaks and, 54; in paintings, 72, 73*il*, 74–75, 84–85, 118*il*, 120*il*, 121

Mount Washington Carriage Road, 13

Mount Washington Hotel, 144–146

Mount Washington Hotel Company, 132

Mount Washington House, 61, 131

Mount Washington Railway, 138, 139*il*

Mount Wollaston, 15

Mountain View Hotel, 190*il*

Mountains, as symbols of wild nature in paintings, 125

Muir, John, 147

Nash, Roderick, 14–15

Nash, Timothy, 25

Nash and Sawyer's Location, 50

National Conference on Outdoor Recreation, 228

National Forest Reservation Commission, established by Weeks Act, 189

National Forest Wild Areas bill, 251

Pinkham Notch; hotels in area, 137; road through, 27
Pinkham Notch Visitor Center, 27
political structure, Abenaki, 12–13
Portsmouth, 19
potash, 40
Pourtales, L. F., 154
Pratt, Henry Cheever, 65, 71
Pray, James Sturgis, 216
predators, 236–37
preservation, hiking clubs and argument for, 154. *See also* conservation efforts; wilderness preservation
Presidential Range–Dry River, 25, 215, 252, 254
Price, Sir Uvedale, 109
primeval environment, idea of, 223
primitive camping, 208–209
primitive wilderness areas, idea of, 211, 212
privately held land, government purchase of, 197–198
Profile House, 135, 136*il*, 137, 145, 192
property rights, and deforestation issues, 181, 182, 183
Puritans: view of native Americans, 15; view of wilderness, 14, 15
"purity policy," 250, 252

railroads: and development of tourism, 129–130; and logging, 173
Randolph, N.H., 36, 44
RARE I, 250
RARE II, 253–254
recreation camp, idea of, 221
reforestation: first priority, in White Mountains, 200; government management of, 198
resources. *See* natural resources
road building/construction, 24, 26, 43; through the Notch, 51; within wilderness areas, 248
rock climbing, 206, 209–210
Roenke, Karl, 255
Rogers, Major Robert, 24–25
Romanticism, 4–5, 58, 262; and attitudes toward wilderness, 67; as distinct period of art, 108; and hiking, 153; Indian legends and, 82; influence of in 1800s, 87; shift away from, 96–97; in United States, 67–68

Roosevelt, Franklin D., 198, 229
Roosevelt, Theodore, 198
Rosebrook, Eleazer, 49, 50, 51, 132
Rosebrook, Hannah, 50
Rosebrook, Lucius M., 138
Rosebrook, Mary, 49
Roth, Dennis M., 243, 250, 251
rural environment, idea of, 223

sagamore, 12
Salisbury, Neal, 9
Sand County Almanac, A (1948), 232, 236, 237, 239
Sandwich Range, 215, 254–255, 257; expansion of wilderness, 260, 261
Sapleigh, Frank H., 120–21
Sargent, Charles Sprague, 174, 175, 182
sawmills, 39, 40*il*
Sawyer, Warren, 97
Saylor, John P., 243, 247
Sayward, Perceval, 214
Scott, Doug, 251
Second Great Awakening, 73
second homes, 241
selective harvesting, 200
settlement: early, 32–35; ecological impact of, 45–46; patterns of, 33–35; practical concerns of, 32, 33, 34
Shaler, Nathaniel Southgate, 216
shelters, 204*il*; in wilderness areas, 251, 255
Sidley, Ted, 254, 256
Sierra Club: criticism of RARE I, 250; disagreement with Wilderness Society, 252; and Eastern wilderness area, 252; New England Chapter of, 255, 256, 257
Sinclair (hotel), 144
skiing, 241
Society for the Protection of New Hampshire Forests (SPNHF), 177, 185, 242, 255, 258; lobbying efforts of, 191
Sonntag, William Lewis, and *Carter Dome from Carter Lake, New Hampshire* (1880), 124, 124*il*
Southern Appalachians, forest preserve creation in, 184
Spaulding, John Hubbard, 89–90
Spaulding, Samuel Fitch, 89
St. Francis, Quebec, 11, 24, 25
stagecoach lines, to hotels, 137
Stahl, Carl, 232